The field of computer vision and pattern recognition has a rich history of nearly 50 years. In the past decade, however, the field has experienced remarkable advances in scene understanding and image generation. This advancement is driven by three key factors: (a) the availability of large, diverse datasets, (b) the accessibility of cloud and personal computing, and (c) the open release of advanced neural network architectures and models. These breakthroughs have led to significant successes across numerous application domains, including intelligent transportation, augmented reality, healthcare, agriculture, oceanography, and more. The ACVPR book series aims to introduce, analyze, and synthesize recent and foundational research, offering valuable references to both beginners and expert practitioners. The series covers timely topics such as:

- Deep Learning for Vision
- Large-scale Foundational Models
- Generative Methods
- Multimodal Learning (vision, audio, language, action, etc.)
- Neural Fields for Vision
- 3D Computer Vision
- Computational Photography, Display and Illumination
- Video Understanding and Synthesis
- Virtual, Mixed and Augmented Reality
- Biological and Human Vision
- Physics-based Vision
- Vision for Graphics
- Ethics in Computer Vision
- Applications (Robotics, Agriculture, Health, Intelligent Transportation, Oceanography, Safety/Security, etc.)

This series includes monographs, introductory and advanced textbooks, and state-of-the-art collections. Furthermore, it supports Open Access publication mode.

Yulan Guo · Sheng Ao · Zhiheng Fu · Hao Liu ·
Qingyong Hu

Point Cloud Intelligence

Springer

Yulan Guo
School of Electronics and Communication Engineering
Sun Yat-sen University
Shenzhen, China

Zhiheng Fu
Department of Aeronautical and Aviation Engineering
The HongKong Polytechnic University
HongKong, China

Qingyong Hu
Independent Researcher
Beijing, China

Sheng Ao
School of Informatics
Xiamen University
Xiamen, China

Hao Liu
School of Geospatial Artificial Intelligence
East China Normal University
Shanghai, China

ISSN 2191-6586 ISSN 2191-6594 (electronic)
Advances in Computer Vision and Pattern Recognition
ISBN 978-981-95-0647-7 ISBN 978-981-95-0648-4 (eBook)
https://doi.org/10.1007/978-981-95-0648-4

This Springer imprint is published by the registered company Springer Nature Singapore Pte Ltd.
The registered company address is: 152 Beach Road, #21-01/04 Gateway East, Singapore 189721, Singapore

Preface

The proliferation of 3D sensing technologies, including LiDAR, depth cameras and structured light systems, has revolutionized the way machines harvest and interact with the physical world. As an efficient representation of 3D environments, point clouds have become the cornerstone of a wide range of applications such as autonomous driving, robotics, augmented reality, and remote sensing. However, effective processing of point clouds still faces numerous challenges due to their unstructured, sparse, and noisy characteristics.

Deep learning technology has powerful representation learning capabilities, which has greatly promoted the development of point cloud processing. However, there is currently a lack of academic resources that combine theoretical research with practical applications in this rapidly developing field. To this end, this book provides a systematic and in-depth exploration of existing methods in the field, aiming to provide assistance to researchers, engineers, and students in understanding point cloud processing with deep learning. The book is divided into four main parts, each addressing a key aspect of point cloud processing:

Session I—Fundamental Point Cloud Processing (Chaps. 2–3) lays the groundwork for deep learning-based point cloud analysis. It begins with a discussion on local feature learning (Chap. 2) and introduces SpinNet, a neural network designed for learning rotation-invariant local descriptors that facilitate robust surface matching across diverse datasets. The session continues with a focus on point cloud registration (Chap. 3), where a novel registration frameworkBUFFERis introduced to balance accuracy, efficiency, and generalization by integrating point-wise and patch-wise processing with geometric inlier generation.

Session II—3D Object Detection and Segmentation (Chaps. 4–5) delves into core perception tasks, including object detection and segmentation. The section begins with IA-SSD (Chap. 4), an instance-aware single-stage 3D object detector that employs task-oriented downsampling and centroid perception to achieve realtime performance. The next chapter (Chap. 5) introduces the Semantic Query Network (SQN), a weakly supervised segmentation method that achieves state-ofthe- art results while requiring only 0.1% labeled annotations.

Session III—Tracking in Dynamic Point Clouds (Chaps. 6–7) focuses on motion analysis in sequential point cloud data, a critical component of 3D vision in real-world applications. Chap. 6 presents DeepPCT, a CNN-based single-object tracker optimized for Intersection-over-Union (IoU) prediction, which significantly improves 3D localization accuracy and object tracking robustness. The following chapter (Chap. 7) introduces CenterTube, a unified framework for multi-object tracking via 4D tubelet detection, along with AnchorPoint, a transformer-based query design that enhances efficiency and detection robustness for real-time tracking.

Session IV—Shape Completion and Scene Understanding (Chaps. 8–9) addresses the challenge of reconstructing missing or occluded 3D data for real-world applications. Chapter 8 introduces two powerful frameworks, VAPCNet and AEDNet, which perform viewpoint-aware point cloud completion without requiring explicit viewpoint estimation, and adaptive point cloud sampling for point cloud completion, respectively. In Chap. 9, the discussion expands to semantic instance completion with WSSIC-Net, a weakly supervised approach that leverages unpaired synthetic data to enhance real-world 3D object detection and segmentation, making high-quality shape completion more accessible with limited supervision.

By elaborating on the latest research progress, this book provides a valuable resource for researchers and practitioners who are committed to exploring the application of deep learning in the field of point cloud processing.We hope that this work will not only enable more people to understand the field of point cloud processing, but also catalyze the emergence of a series of related research, thereby bringing more profound contributions to the entire academic and technical community.

Shenzhen, China — Yulan Guo
Xiamen, China — Sheng Ao
HongKong, China — Zhiheng Fu
Shanghai, China — Hao Liu
Beijing, China — Qingyong Hu
April 2025

Acknowledgements This research was supported in part by the National Natural Science Foundation of China (Grants U20A20185, 62372491, and 62501502) and the Guangdong Basic and Applied Basic Research Foundation (Grants 2022B1515020103 and 2023B1515120087). The authors gratefully acknowledge these funding agencies for their financial support.

Professor Yulan Guo wishes to extend his sincere gratitude to his research team members whose dedicated efforts in point cloud understanding over the past decade have been instrumental to this work. Their persistent commitment to scientific exploration and collaborative spirit have fundamentally shaped the trajectory of this research program.

Competing Interests The authors have no competing interests to declare that are relevant to the content of this manuscript.

Contents

Acronyms

3D	Three-Dimensional
3DCCN	3D Cylindrical Convolutional Network
AEDNet	Adaptive Embedding-Disentanglement Network
BEV	Bird's Eye View
CAD	Computer-Aided Design
CIoU	Center Intersection over Union
CNN	Convolutional Neural Network
DIoU	Distance Intersection over Union
DoF	Degrees of Freedom
EFCN	Equivariant Fully Convolutional Network
FCGF	Fully Convolutional Geometric Feature
FMR	Feature Matching Recall
FPS	Farthest Point Sampling
GAN	Generative Adversarial Network
GeM	Generalized-Mean pooling
GIoU	Generalized Intersection over Union
GNN	Graph Neural Networks
GPT	Generative Pre-training Transformer
GPU	Graphics Processing Unit
HL	Hausdorff Distance Loss
IA-SSD	Instance-aware Single-stage Detector
ICP	Iterative Closest Point
InfoNCE	Information Noise-Contrastive Estimation
IoU	Intersection over Union
JDT	Joint Detection and Tracking
KITTI	Karlsruhe Institute of Technology and Toyota Technological Institute Dataset
KPConv	Kernel Point Convolution
LiDAR	Light Detection and Ranging
LRF	Adaptive Embedding-Disentanglement Network
MLP	Multilayer Perceptron

MOT	Multiple Object Tracking
NLP	Natural Language Processing
NMS	Non-Maximum Suppression
RANSAC	RANdom SAmple Consensus
RRE	Relative Rotation Error
RS	Random Sampling
RTE	Relative Translation Error
SLAM	Simultaneous Localization and Mapping
SO	Special Orthogonal Group
SOT	Single Object Tracking
SQN	Semantic Query Network
SR	Success Rate
STD	Standard Deviation
SVD	Singular Value Decomposition
TBD	Tracking-by-Detection
VAE	Variational Autoencoder
VAPCNet	Viewpoint-Aware Point Cloud Completion Network
VFE	Voxel Feature Encoding
ViT	Vision Transformer
VN	Vector Neuron
WSSIC-Net	Weakly Supervised Semantic Instance Completion

Chapter 1
Introduction

1.1 Importance of Deep Learning for Point Clouds

With the rapid advancement of 3D acquisition technologies, 3D sensors are becoming increasingly available and affordable. This includes various types of 3D scanners, LiDAR systems, and RGB-D cameras, such as Kinect, RealSense, and Apple's depth cameras. The 3D data captured by these sensors provides rich geometric, shape, and scale information, offering a more comprehensive understanding of the surrounding environment when combined with 2D images. This enhanced understanding is crucial for machines, enabling applications across diverse fields such as autonomous driving, robotics, remote sensing, and medical treatment.

3D data can usually be represented in various formats, including depth images, point clouds, meshes, and volumetric grids. Among these, point clouds are particularly valuable because they preserve the original geometric information in 3D space without discretization, making them the preferred choice for many scene perception and understanding tasks. In recent decades, point cloud processing has evolved from relying on handcrafted algorithms to employing sophisticated deep learning techniques. Compared to the traditional heuristics for point cloud, deep learning has several advantages in the following aspects:

- **Feature descriptiveness**. Traditional methods rely on manually engineered features, which can be suboptimal and require expert knowledge. In contrast, deep learning models can automatically discover the relevant features directly from the point cloud data, which simplifies the process and improves the model's ability to capture complex patterns.
- **Robustness to noise.** Deep learning can be trained to handle noisy or incomplete data effectively, improving reliability and performance in real-world scenarios where data quality varies. However, traditional methods may be more sensitive to noise and missing data, often requiring additional preprocessing to clean or complete the data.

Y. Guo et al., *Point Cloud Intelligence*, Advances in Computer Vision and Pattern Recognition, https://doi.org/10.1007/978-981-95-0648-4_1

- **Model performance**. Unlike traditional pipelines that require separate stages for feature extraction, feature selection, and classification, deep learning allows for end-to-end training of point cloud classifiers. This streamlines the workflow and can lead to better performance as the entire pipeline is optimized jointly.
- **Method adaptability**. Traditional methods typically require significant re-engineering and customization for different tasks or environments, which can limit flexibility and adaptability. In contrast, deep learning models can be adapted to new tasks or environments through transfer learning, allowing them to generalize well across different datasets and applications.

In summary, the integration of deep learning into point cloud processing represents a significant leap forward, leveraging the advantages of 3D data while overcoming the limitations of traditional methods. This book systematically explores the intersection of these two rapidly evolving fields. By providing a comprehensive overview of deep learning techniques specifically tailored for point cloud processing, this book seeks to empower researchers, practitioners, and students to harness the full potential of 3D data in their work. Understanding these concepts is essential not only for academic advancement but also for driving innovation in industries reliant on spatial data.

1.2 Issues and Challenges of Deep Learning for Point Clouds

While humans can effortlessly interpret and analyze 3D objects and scenarios based on spatial and geometric cues, translating this understanding into computers remains a significant hurdle. The issue of deep learning for point clouds is how to automate these tasks, which are instinctive for humans but intricate for machines. Below, we briefly summarize a few of them.

- **Registration**. Registration involves aligning multiple point clouds into a unified coordinate system. This is critical for creating comprehensive 3D models from scans taken from different viewpoints. The challenges in registration include dealing with variability in sensor data, partial overlaps, and noise. Effective registration techniques allow for the accurate integration of spatial data, facilitating improved mapping and environmental understanding.
- **Detection**. Object detection in point clouds focuses on identifying and localizing specific objects within a 3D space. This task is essential for applications like autonomous driving, where recognizing pedestrians, vehicles, and obstacles is vital. The complexities of detection stem from the irregular structure of point clouds, varied object shapes, and the necessity for context-aware models. Advanced deep learning techniques enhance detection accuracy by leveraging unique features of 3D data.
- **Segmentation**. Segmentation is the process of partitioning a point cloud into meaningful segments, typically corresponding to different objects or areas within

a scene. This task is important for scene understanding and robotic perception. Challenges include handling complex geometries, noise, and overlapping objects. Deep learning models tailored for segmentation can effectively delineate boundaries and categorize various components of a scene, contributing to a more nuanced understanding of 3D environments.

- **Generation**. Point cloud generation refers to the creation of new point clouds or the completion of existing, partial point clouds. This task is significant for applications in virtual reality and 3D reconstruction. Key challenges include achieving high fidelity and realism in generated data, handling sparsity, and accommodating a variety of object forms. Generative models, such as GANs and VAEs, are employed to learn distributions that allow for plausible and continuous point cloud generation.

Implementing these representative analysis tasks requires solving a set of challenges, and each has been the subject of important research and contributions. One of the primary challenges stems from the intricacies involved in **data collection and annotation**. Point clouds are generated from various sensing technologies, such as LiDAR, RGB-D cameras, and stereo vision systems, each with unique strengths and weaknesses. Variability in sensor quality, resolution, and environmental conditions can lead to inconsistencies in the data, making it difficult to establish a uniform dataset suitable for training deep learning models. Additionally, point clouds are often noisy and may suffer from occlusions, resulting in incomplete data that complicates subsequent analysis. The annotation process itself adds another layer of complexity; accurately labeling point cloud data requires significant expertise and is time-consuming. Unlike 2D images, where labeling can be more straightforward, annotating 3D data necessitates a deeper understanding of spatial relationships and object boundaries. This scarcity of labeled datasets poses a critical barrier to developing robust models, as insufficient training data can lead to overfitting and poor generalization in real-world applications.

The next significant challenge lies in **feature representation** within point clouds. Extracting meaningful features from 3D data is inherently more complex than in 2D image processing due to the irregular and unordered nature of point clouds. Traditional convolutional neural networks (CNNs) excel in structured environments, but their architectures must be adapted to accommodate the unique characteristics of point clouds. This adaptation involves designing neural networks capable of learning both local and global features while maintaining spatial coherence, which is essential for effective analysis. Furthermore, achieving invariance to transformations—such as variations in orientation, scale, and position—adds another layer of difficulty. Developing robust architectures that can effectively capture the intricate geometric relationships inherent in 3D data is crucial for tasks such as registration, detection, and Segmentation. As researchers strive to create novel models that can accurately represent these features, they must also ensure that the learning process does not compromise performance, particularly in real-time applications.

Higher **computational complexity** is a significant challenge for large-scale point clouds. Point clouds typically consist of thousands to millions of points, resulting in high-dimensional data that demands substantial computational resources for effective processing. Training deep learning models on such data requires significant memory and processing power, often necessitating the use of specialized hardware, such as GPUs. This resource intensity can present a barrier to entry for many practitioners, particularly in fields where real-time analysis is critical, such as robotics and autonomous driving. Furthermore, achieving fast inference speeds while maintaining high accuracy poses additional challenges, as the balance between computational efficiency and model performance must be carefully managed. Researchers must develop optimized algorithms and architectures that can handle large datasets without sacrificing speed or accuracy, ensuring that deep learning techniques can be effectively applied in practical, real-world scenarios.

Finally, **generalization across domains** is a crucial challenge in the application of deep learning to point cloud processing. Models trained on specific datasets may struggle to perform well in new environments due to domain shifts that arise from variations in object shapes, densities, and sensor modalities. This lack of generalization can significantly limit the applicability of trained models in real-world scenarios, where conditions can vary widely from those encountered during training. To address this issue, researchers must develop strategies for domain adaptation and transfer learning that allow models to adjust to new data distributions without extensive retraining. Additionally, methods such as few-shot learning, which enable models to learn from limited examples, can help improve adaptability across diverse datasets. By focusing on enhancing the robustness and versatility of deep learning models, researchers can ensure that their techniques are capable of performing effectively in a wide range of practical applications, ultimately advancing the field of point cloud processing.

1.3 How to Read This Book

This book is structured into four sessions, each focusing on essential aspects of deep learning for point cloud processing, ranging from fundamental techniques to advanced applications and future prospects.

Session I—Fundamental Point Cloud Processing: This session lays the groundwork for point cloud analysis. Chapter 2 introduces SpinNet, a neural network designed for learning rotation-invariant local descriptors, facilitating robust surface matching across diverse datasets. Chapter 3 presents BUFFER, a registration framework that achieves a balance between accuracy, efficiency, and generalization by integrating point-wise and patch-wise processing with geometric inlier generation.

Session II—3D Object Detection and Segmentation: Focusing on key perception tasks, this session explores efficient detection and segmentation strategies. Chapter 4 introduces IA-SSD, an instance-aware single-stage detector that employs task-oriented downsampling and centroid perception for real-time performance. Chapter 5 discusses weakly supervised semantic segmentation with the Semantic

Query Network (SQN), which achieves competitive results using only 0.1% labeled annotations.

Session III—Tracking in Dynamic Point Clouds: This session addresses motion analysis in sequential point cloud data. Chapter 6 presents DeepPCT, a CNN-based single-object tracker that optimizes IoU prediction for robust 3D localization. Chapter 7 introduces CenterTube, a unified framework for multi-object tracking via 4D tubelet detection, along with AnchorPoint, a transformer-based query design that improves detection and tracking efficiency.

Session IV—Shape Completion and Scene Understanding: Focusing on reconstruction and semantic understanding, Chap. 8 introduces VAPCNet and AEDNet, which perform viewpoint-aware and adaptive point cloud completion without the need for explicit viewpoint estimation. Chapter 9 presents WSSIC-Net, a weakly supervised framework for semantic instance completion that leverages unpaired synthetic data and 3D object detection.

Each chapter provides in-depth theoretical insights, algorithmic innovations, and empirical validations, making this book a valuable resource for researchers and practitioners seeking to advance deep learning techniques for point cloud processing.

Chapter 2
Local Feature Learning for Point Clouds

Learning robust, distinctive, and generalizable 3D local features is crucial for point cloud registration and other geometric processing tasks. Conventional methods often depend on handcrafted descriptors susceptible to noise or deep learning models that fail to preserve rotation invariance, leading to unreliable surface matching. This chapter presents SpinNet, a lightweight yet powerful neural network designed to learn rotation-invariant local surface descriptors with high discriminability and generalization. The framework introduces a Spatial Point Transformer that maps the input surface onto a cylindrical representation, ensuring SO(2) rotation equivariance and enabling end-to-end learning. To extract rich geometric structures, a Neural Feature Extractor is employed, combining point-based operations with 3D cylindrical convolutions. Finally, an invariant projection layer generates rotation-agnostic descriptors for robust feature matching. Comprehensive evaluations on multiple datasets demonstrate that SpinNet surpasses existing approaches, exhibiting strong generalization across diverse environments and sensor modalities.

2.1 Introduction

Accurate matching of partial 3D surfaces is essential for numerous applications, including 3D reconstruction [59], place localization [13], object recognition [19], semantic segmentation [23], and pose estimation [36]. Among these tasks, point cloud registration stands out as a fundamental procedure that aligns multiple partially overlapping 3D scans into a unified coordinate system through point correspondence obtained from surface matching. Achieving this requires a compact surface descriptor capable of effectively capturing local geometric patterns shared between overlapping scans. Furthermore, the descriptors must maintain consistent performance across unseen datasets, as point clouds are often captured using different sensors under diverse conditions. However, this is particularly challenging due to several factors:

Y. Guo et al., *Point Cloud Intelligence*, Advances in Computer Vision and Pattern Recognition, https://doi.org/10.1007/978-981-95-0648-4_2

(1) variations in viewing angles between scans introduce rotation differences, (2) raw 3D scans are frequently incomplete, noisy, and exhibit varying point densities, and (3) significant domain gaps arise from datasets acquired with different sensor modalities.

Traditional methods, including Point Signature (PS) [7], 3D Shape Context (3DSC) [15], Intrinsic Shape Signatures (ISS) [60], Signature of Histograms of Orientations (SHOT) [49], and Rotational Projection Statistics (RoPS) [21], were developed to extract local surface descriptors through heuristic techniques. These approaches rely on calculating basic features such as faces [33], surface normals [46], and manually crafted statistical histograms [35]. While these methods perform well on clean, synthetic 3D point clouds, their adaptability to noisy, large-scale, real-world data is significantly limited [20].

Motivated by the advancements of deep learning in 2D vision, learning-based methods for 3D surface descriptors [12, 59] have gained considerable attention. These methods typically encode the local 3D region around a keypoint into a compact descriptor, while some process entire point cloud fragments in a single forward pass to generate dense feature representations. Generally, they can be categorized into patch-based and fragment-based approaches. By utilizing large-scale labeled 3D datasets [22, 59], these techniques surpass traditional handcrafted methods in capturing local geometric structures. Nevertheless, their generalization capability remains a challenge, particularly when applied to unseen 3D scans acquired from different sensor modalities.

The limitations stem from several factors. **First**, many methods, such as D3Feat [3] and FCGF [6], use kernel-based point convolution [47] or submanifold sparse convolution [18] to learn point-wise features. This results in rotation-variant local patterns, leading to significant performance drops when tested on datasets with varying rotation distributions. **Second**, although some recent patch-based methods [11, 17] achieve rotation invariance, they rely on handcrafted features, including point-pair relationships, point densities, or external local reference frames (LRFs) [54]. These handcrafted elements are inherently sensitive to noise, varying densities, and sensor-induced data distribution differences[53]. **Third**, fragment-based descriptors [3, 6] incorporate large receptive fields and extensive context, which exceed the representational capacity of the feature descriptors. This results in homogenized features for nearby points, reducing matching accuracy. Additionally, the convolutional blocks in fragment-based networks are less effective at capturing detailed local geometry, further limiting the framework's generalization capabilities.

In this chapter, we propose a novel neural architecture capable of extracting descriptive local features while maintaining strong generalization to unseen scenarios. The designed network adheres to three critical principles: (1) Rotation-Invariance. It ensures the extraction of consistent features from 3D scans regardless of rotational variations. (2) Descriptiveness. It effectively retains key local geometric patterns, even in the presence of noise, surface incompleteness, or varying point densities. (3) Without handcrafted features. The model is constructed entirely from point transformations and straightforward neural layers, leveraging a fully end-to-end optimization process. This approach results in a highly expressive and generalizable descriptor, suitable for handling the complexities of real-world 3D surface data.

Our proposed network, SpinNet, is composed of two primary modules: (1) a **Spatial Point Transformer**,[1] which maps the input 3D patch into a refined cylindrical coordinate space, ensuring SO(2) equivariance while preserving the geometric structure of the local surface; (2) a **Neural Feature Extractor**, which utilizes advanced point-based operations and convolutional neural layers to capture robust and generalizable local patterns. This module subsequently produces a rotation-invariant and compact feature descriptor using an invariant layer.

These two modules empower SpinNet to effectively learn robust and general local features, enabling highly accurate 3D point cloud registration. The network achieves state-of-the-art results on both the indoor 3DMatch [59] dataset and the outdoor KITTI [16] dataset, demonstrating exceptional generalization to unseen scenarios. Additionally, we extend the patch-based SpinNet into a convolutional block, which can be incorporated into hierarchical feature learning frameworks to develop fragment-based descriptors. Comprehensive comparative experiments are conducted to evaluate and analyze the two descriptor categories. The primary contributions of this work are summarized as follows:

- We introduce a novel neural feature learning framework for 3D surface matching, designed to be rotation-invariant, highly distinctive, and capable of exceptional generalization to unseen scenarios.
- By representing the transformed 3D surface as a cylindrical volume, we propose an effective 3D cylindrical convolution mechanism to capture rich and generalizable features.
- We perform extensive experiments and ablation studies, highlighting the exceptional generalization capability of our approach and offering a thorough discussion and analysis of generalization across various architectures.

2.2 Related Work

2.2.1 Handcrafted Descriptors

Traditional handcrafted descriptors can be broadly classified into two categories based on their reliance on an external canonical reference: 1) LRF-free methods and 2) LRF-based methods.

LRF-free methods: Stein and Medioni [46] introduced Splash, a local surface descriptor that leverages the positional and normal variations between a keypoint and its neighbors. This data is encoded as a set of 3D vectors and converted into curvatures and torsion angles. Johnson and Hebert [25] developed the spin

[1] Distinct from Transformers used in natural language processing.

image, where a 2D image is first established using the keypoint's normal as the reference axis, and neighboring points are then binned by rotating the 2D image around the reference axis. Frome et al. [15] partitioned the spherical support region into bins and generated a histogram by counting the points within each bin. Later, Rusu et al. [43] proposed the point feature histogram (PFH), which records normal deviations and distances between point pairs on the local surface. However, PFH was computationally expensive, prompting the introduction of a simplified point feature histogram (SPFH) [42], which characterizes individual points and combines them into an efficient fast point feature histogram (FPFH) using weighted summation.

LRF-based methods: Chua and Jarvis [7] introduced the point signature, which measures the projection distance from the edge contour of a local surface to the orthometric plane defined by the keypoint's normal. Mian et al. [33] developed a method that defines a local reference frame (LRF) for vertex pairs meeting specific geometric constraints, followed by constructing a 3D grid where the intersecting surface area in each cube is stored as a 3D tensor. Zhong [60] proposed an LRF based on covariance analysis of the local surface, creating a descriptor by projecting neighboring points onto a discrete spherical grid and aggregating them through weighted summation. Tombari et al. [49] utilized covariance analysis to establish a robust LRF and divided the local support region into spherical voxels. For each voxel, they computed a feature that captures the normal deviations between the keypoint and its neighbors, forming a histogram by concatenating all voxel features. Guo et al. [21] introduced the Rotational Projection Statistics (RoPS) descriptor by rotating the local surface onto three orthogonal planes defined by the LRF, generating 2D projections. They computed central moments and Shannon entropy for each projection and concatenated these statistics to construct the descriptor.

2.2.2 Learning-Based Descriptors

Based on the input data modalities utilized by neural networks, existing learning-based descriptors can be categorized into two main types: (1) patch-based approaches and (2) fragment-based approaches.

Patch-based Descriptors: A groundbreaking work in this domain is 3DMatch [59], which uses a 3D volumetric representation of local patches as input and employs 3D convolutional neural networks (CNNs) to learn geometric features. However, its performance is highly susceptible to rotation transformations. To address this limitation, subsequent studies have focused on developing rotation-invariant local surface descriptors. Deng et al. [12] introduced a method that computes a collection of point pair features (PPFs) for each local patch, concatenates these features, and processes them through multiple MLPs to derive a global descriptor. In a follow-up study, they proposed PPF-FoldNet [11], an unsupervised local descriptor that adopts FoldNet [56] as its backbone. Gojcic et al. [17] voxelized local patches into 3D representations, subsequently processed by a 3D CNN to generate descriptors.

Spezialetti et al. [45] transformed input patches into spherical signal representations, which were then input into Spherical CNNs [8] to learn unsupervised equivariant descriptors. Li et al. [31] implemented a trainable multi-view rendering approach across patches and fused multiple feature maps to generate final descriptors. Later, they introduced UPDesc [30], a weakly supervised descriptor that incorporates a differentiable voxelization module for gradient backpropagation to optimize support size, using PerfectMatch [17] to capture the encapsulated local surface information.

Fragment-based Descriptors: Choy et al. [6] introduced the Fully Convolutional Geometric Feature (FCGF) as the first dense feature descriptor designed specifically for point cloud registration, leveraging the 4D convolutional framework from [5]. Bai et al. [3] proposed D3Feat, a deep learning-based method that simultaneously learns dense 3D feature detectors and descriptors using KPConv [48] as its core network. More recently, Huang et al. [24] developed PREDATOR, which focuses on detecting overlapping regions between two unregistered fragments and learning both 3D detectors and descriptors within these regions. Despite their contributions, these methods remain sensitive to rigid transformations in Euclidean space.

To achieve SO(3) invariance for fragment-based descriptors, Wang et al. [51] proposed rotating the entire point cloud fragment within the SO(3) subgroup, specifically the icosahedral group, and processing them through the FCGF framework [6] to compute equivariant voxel features. These features were then compressed into a compact and invariant descriptor using multiple icosahedral group convolutional layers [14] followed by max-pooling. However, this approach struggles to generalize effectively to previously unseen scenarios.

2.3 General Surface Descriptor Learning: SpinNet

2.3.1 Problem Statement

Given two partially overlapped point clouds $\mathcal{P} = \{\boldsymbol{p}_i \in \mathbb{R}^3 | i = 1, \dots, N\}$ and $\mathcal{Q} = \{\boldsymbol{q}_j \in \mathbb{R}^3 | j = 1, \dots, M\}$, the goal of point cloud registration is to determine an optimal rigid transformation $\mathbf{T} = \{\mathbf{R}, \boldsymbol{t}\}$, along with the corresponding point pairs, that align the two fragments. This process ultimately aims to recover the complete scene. The point correspondences $(\boldsymbol{p}_i, \boldsymbol{q}_j)$ should satisfy the following condition:

$$\boldsymbol{q}_j = \mathbf{R}\boldsymbol{p}_i + \boldsymbol{t} + \epsilon_i, \tag{2.1}$$

where $\mathbf{R} \in SO(3)$ represents the rotational matrix, $\boldsymbol{t} \in \mathbb{R}^3$ is the translation vector, and ϵ_i is the residual error. In practice, simultaneously determining the correspondences and estimating the transformation is infeasible due to the non-convex nature of the problem [29]. However, if a subset of points $\mathcal{P}^c \subset \mathcal{P}$ and $\mathcal{Q}^c \subset \mathcal{Q}$ with one-to-one correspondences can be identified, the registration problem can be simplified to an L_2 norm minimization problem, expressed as:

$$\mathcal{L}(\mathcal{P}^c, \mathcal{Q}^c|\mathfrak{P}, \mathbf{R}, t) = \frac{1}{\mathcal{N}} \left\| \mathcal{Q}^c - \mathbf{R}\mathcal{P}^c\mathfrak{P} - t \right\|^2 \tag{2.2}$$

where $\mathcal{N}$ denotes the total number of successfully matched correspondences, and $\mathfrak{P} \in \mathbb{R}^{N \times N}$ is a permutation matrix. The entries of $\mathfrak{P}$ are defined such that $\mathfrak{P}_{u,v} = 1$ if the uth point in $\mathcal{P}^c$ corresponds to vth point in $\mathcal{Q}^c$, and $\mathfrak{P} = 0$ otherwise.

We introduce a novel surface feature learner, SpinNet, formulated as a mapping function $\mathcal{M}$. This mapping ensures that $\mathcal{M}(\boldsymbol{p}_i) = \mathcal{M}(\boldsymbol{q}_j)$ under any rigid transformations, including rotation and translation, provided that $\boldsymbol{p}_i$ and $\boldsymbol{q}_j$ form a valid correspondence. Specifically, SpinNet is composed of two key modules: a Spatial Point Transformer, which transforms the spatial structure of the input, and a Neural Feature Extractor, which learns discriminative and invariant features.

2.3.2 Spatial Point Transformer

This module aims to spatially transform input 3D surfaces into a cylindrical volume, addressing rotation variance while preserving essential local patterns. As illustrated in Fig. 2.1, it comprises five key components, which are elaborated on below.

Input Support Patch: For a specific point $\boldsymbol{p} \in \mathcal{P}$, we first extract a local patch by identifying all neighboring points within a defined support radius R, such that $\mathcal{P}^{\mathrm{n}} = \{\boldsymbol{p}_i : \left\| \boldsymbol{p}_i - \boldsymbol{p} \right\|^2 \leq R\}$. Since patches in different regions often have varying cardinalities, we randomly sample each patch to ensure a fixed cardinality of C, i.e., $|\mathcal{P}^{\mathrm{n}}| = C$, enabling efficient parallel computation. Next, we determine a reference axis $\boldsymbol{n_p}$ for each patch by performing eigendecomposition on the covariance matrix Σ:

$$\Sigma = \frac{1}{C} \sum_{\boldsymbol{p}_i \in \mathcal{P}^{\mathrm{n}}} (\boldsymbol{p}_i - \boldsymbol{p})(\boldsymbol{p}_i - \boldsymbol{p})^{\mathrm{T}} \tag{2.3}$$

The eigenvector associated with the smallest eigenvalue of Σ is chosen as the reference axis [32]. To address the inherent lack of an explicit reference orientation in eigenvectors, the axis $\boldsymbol{n_p}$ is reoriented towards the viewpoint, thereby resolving its sign ambiguity [1].

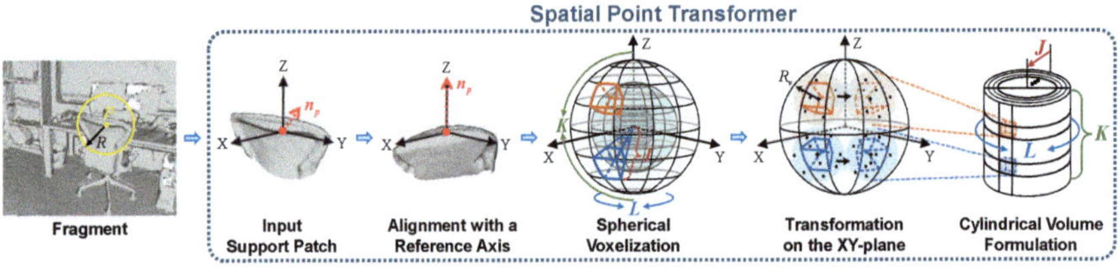

Fig. 2.1 The detailed components and processing steps of our Spatial Point Transformer (This figure is reproduced from [2])

Alignment with a Reference Axis: To achieve translation and rotation invariance for the local patch, we first normalize $\mathcal{P}^{\mathrm{n}}$ by translating it to the origin, i.e., $\widehat{\mathcal{P}}^{\mathrm{n}} = \mathcal{P}^{\mathrm{n}} - \boldsymbol{p}$. Subsequently, we align the reference axis $\boldsymbol{n}_p$ with the Z-axis using a rotation matrix $\mathbf{R}_z$. This transformation results in a neighboring point set $\widehat{\mathcal{P}}^{\mathrm{n}}_{\mathrm{r}} = \mathbf{R}_z\widehat{\mathcal{P}}^{\mathrm{n}}$. The normalization ensures translation invariance, while the alignment reduces the challenge of handling SO(3) rotation variance to achieving only SO(2) rotation invariance. As a result, the patch $\widehat{\mathcal{P}}^{\mathrm{n}}_{\mathrm{r}}$ is aligned with the Z-axis, leaving residual rotational freedom confined to the XY-plane. In scenarios where only SO(2) rotations are present, this alignment step can be omitted, as the Z-axis of each patch is already aligned. Compared to external local reference frames, which can suffer from ambiguity and instability, the reference axis $\boldsymbol{n}_p$ provides a more robust and reliable alignment under varying rotational conditions [37]. Unlike other methods [15, 25] that also employ reference axes, our approach avoids incorporating handcrafted features in subsequent steps, enhancing the descriptiveness and generalization capability of the resulting learned descriptor.

Spherical Voxelization: To address rotation variance on the XY-plane, we employ a spherical representation that is robust to rotation. Specifically, we model the patch $\widehat{\mathcal{P}}^{\mathrm{n}}_{\mathrm{r}}$ as a sphere and partition it into $J \times K \times L$ voxels, corresponding to the radial distance ρ, elevation angle ϕ, and azimuth angle θ. The center of each voxel is represented by $\boldsymbol{v}_{jkl}$, where $j \in \{1, ..., J\}$, $k \in \{1, ..., K\}$, and $l \in \{1, ..., L\}$. For each voxel, we identify the neighboring points around the center $\boldsymbol{v}_{jkl}$. To achieve this, we apply a radius query method, which retrieves the neighboring points $\mathcal{P}_{jkl} \subset \widehat{\mathcal{P}}^{\mathrm{n}}_{\mathrm{r}}$ within a fixed radius R_v, where $\mathcal{P}_{jkl} = \{\widehat{\boldsymbol{p}}_i : \left\|\widehat{\boldsymbol{p}}_i - \boldsymbol{v}_{jkl}\right\|^2 \leq R_v, \widehat{\boldsymbol{p}}_i \in \widehat{\mathcal{P}}^{\mathrm{n}}_{\mathrm{r}}\}$. To match the receptive field of each voxel to the support radius R, we define $R_v = \delta R/J$, with δ as a hyperparameter. Finally, we randomly sample and retain a fixed number of k_v points for each voxel to enable parallel computation. This spherical voxelization is crucial for the subsequent spatial point transformation.

Transformation on the XY-Plane: To ensure that each spherical voxel is rotation-invariant on the XY-plane, we rotate each voxel around the Z-axis so that its center $\boldsymbol{v}_{jkl}$ aligns with the YZ-plane. The corresponding rotation matrix $\mathbf{R}_{jkl}$ is defined as:

$$\mathbf{R}_{jkl} = \begin{bmatrix} \cos(\pi/2 - 2\pi l/L) & -\sin(\pi/2 - 2\pi l/L) & 0 \\ \sin(\pi/2 - 2\pi l/L) & \cos(\pi/2 - 2\pi l/L) & 0 \\ 0 & 0 & 1 \end{bmatrix} \quad (2.4)$$

This transformation removes an additional rotational degree of freedom for each voxel on the XY-plane while preserving the local geometric patterns of each voxel. In contrast to existing methods [45, 58], which typically rely on handcrafted features to achieve rotation invariance and often lose valuable local information, our straightforward approach ensures that these patterns are retained and can be effectively learned by the neural network layers.

Cylindrical Volume Formulation: To maintain larger spatial relationships among the transformed voxels, it is essential to capture the relative positions of all voxels within the framework. This necessitates the conversion of the spherical voxels into a cylindrical representation, which preserves the topological consistency across multiple voxels. By doing so, the rotation-invariance of individual voxels is retained, forming an SO(2) equivariant representation that is suitable for the following 3D cylindrical convolutional network. Specifically, after the spherical voxels are transformed, each voxel has associated neighboring points. These spherical voxels are then mapped into a cylindrical volume, represented as $\mathbf{C} \in \mathbb{R}^{J \times K \times L \times 3 \times k_v}$. The entire procedure is illustrated in Fig. 2.1.

In summary, for a given input surface patch, our Spatial Point Transformer first aligns the Z-axis with a reference axis and then actively transforms the spherical voxel patterns on the XY-plane. Additionally, it preserves the topological surface structures by converting them into a cylindrical volume. This module serves as an equivariant mapping for the 2D rotational group, while simultaneously retaining all surface patterns, ensuring effective feature learning for the subsequent Neural Feature Extractor.

Definition 2.1 Given a discrete 2D rotation group[2] $\mathcal{R} \subset \mathbf{SO}(2)$, where $\mathcal{R} = \{\boldsymbol{r}_i \in \mathbb{R}^{3\times 3}, i = 1, 2, ..., L\}$, the proposed Spatial Point Transformer[3] serves as an equivariant map for the 2D rotation group $\mathcal{R}$.

Proof For a local patch $\mathcal{P}^{\text{n}}$, the Spatial Point Transformer in our framework can be viewed as a mapping $\mathcal{M}_v$ from $\mathcal{P}^{\text{n}}$ to a cylindrical volume $\mathbf{C} : \mathbb{R}^{3\times|\mathcal{P}^{\text{n}}|} \rightarrow \mathbb{R}^{J \times K \times L \times 3 \times k_v}$. For a group action $\boldsymbol{ri}$ in $\mathcal{R}$, let $\widetilde{\mathcal{P}}^{\text{n}} = \boldsymbol{r}_i \circ \mathcal{P}^{\text{n}} = \boldsymbol{r}_i \mathcal{P}^{\text{n}}$, and the rotated local neighboring set is given by $\widetilde{\mathcal{P}}_{jk(l+i)} = \boldsymbol{r}_i \mathcal{P}_{jkl}$. Moreover, for the rotation matrix defined in Eq. 2.4, we have $\mathbf{R}_{jkl} = \mathbf{R}_{jk(l+i)} \boldsymbol{r}_i$. Therefore, the (j^{th}, k^{th}, l^{th}) element $\mathbf{c}_{jkl}$ of the cylindrical volume $\mathbf{C}$ satisfies:

$$
\begin{aligned}
\mathbf{c}_{jkl} &= \mathbf{R}_{jkl} \mathcal{P}_{jkl} = \mathbf{R}_{jk(l+i)} \boldsymbol{r}_i \mathcal{P}_{jkl} \\
&= \mathbf{R}_{jk(l+i)} \widetilde{\mathcal{P}}_{jk(l+i)} = \widetilde{\mathbf{c}}_{jk(l+i)},
\end{aligned} \tag{2.5}
$$

where $\widetilde{\mathbf{c}}_{jk(l+i)} \in \widetilde{\mathbf{C}}$, which is the cylindrical volume corresponding to $\widetilde{\mathcal{P}}^{\text{n}}$. Based on Eq. 2.5, we can infer that $\mathbf{c}_{jk(l-i)} = \widetilde{\mathbf{c}}_{jkl}$, hence the transformed cylindrical volume $\widetilde{\mathbf{C}}$ can be formulated as:

$$
\begin{aligned}
\widetilde{\mathbf{C}} =& \mathcal{M}_v(\boldsymbol{r}_i \circ \mathcal{P}^{\text{n}}) = \mathcal{M}_v(\widetilde{\mathcal{P}}^{\text{n}}) \\
&= [\widetilde{\mathbf{c}}_{111}, ..., \widetilde{\mathbf{c}}_{jkl}, ..., \widetilde{\mathbf{c}}_{JKL}] \\
&= [\mathbf{c}_{11(1-i)}, ..., \mathbf{c}_{jk(l-i)}, ..., \mathbf{c}_{JK(L-i)}],
\end{aligned} \tag{2.6}
$$

where $\mathbf{c}_{jkl} = \mathbf{c}_{jk(l+L)}$ if $l < 1$, due to the periodic property of the cylindrical volume on the XY plane. In the meantime, $\boldsymbol{r}_i \circ \mathcal{M}_v$ means rotating the cylindrical volume $\mathbf{C}$ around the Z-axis, that is:

---

[2] The minimum rotational unit depends on the partition size along the azimuth dimension, i.e., $\frac{2\pi}{L}$.

[3] The reference axis alignment is omitted here to ensure stricter equivariance.

$$\begin{aligned} \boldsymbol{r}_i \circ \mathcal{M}_v(\mathcal{P}^{\text{n}}) &= \boldsymbol{r}_i \circ [\mathbf{c}_{111}, ..., \mathbf{c}_{jkl}, ..., \mathbf{c}_{JKL}] \\ &= [\mathbf{c}_{11(1-i)}, ..., \mathbf{c}_{jk(l-i)}, ..., \mathbf{c}_{JK(L-i)}] \\ &= \mathcal{M}_v(\boldsymbol{r}_i \circ \mathcal{P}^{\text{n}}), \end{aligned} \tag{2.7}$$

which completes our proof that the Spatial Point Transformer $\mathcal{M}_v$ is an equivariant map for the rotational group $\mathcal{R}$. □

2.3.3 *Neural Feature Extractor*

This module is designed to extract general features from transformed points within each cylindrical voxel and generate a compact, rotation-invariant feature descriptor using neural layers. As depicted in Fig. 2.2, the Neural Feature Extractor consists of three primary components: a point-based layer, 3D cylindrical convolutional layers, and an invariant layer.

Point-based Layer: Once the cylindrical volume is obtained, it is crucial to explicitly encode the x-y-z coordinates of the points residing in each voxel. To accomplish this, we employ shared MLPs followed by a max-pooling function $\mathcal{A}(\cdot)$, which aggregates point-wise information to construct an initial signature for each voxel. Formally, the point-based layer is defined as:

$$\boldsymbol{f}_{jkl} = \mathcal{A}(\textbf{MLPs}(\mathbf{c}_{jkl})) \tag{2.8}$$

In this formulation, $\mathbf{c}_{jkl}$ denotes the (j^{th}, k^{th}, l^{th}) element within the cylindrical volume $\mathbf{C}$, while $\boldsymbol{f}_{jkl}$ represents the corresponding learned feature of dimensionality D. Importantly, the MLP weights are shared across all voxels to ensure consistency. As a result, we construct a set of 3D cylindrical feature maps $\mathbf{F} \in \mathbb{R}^{J\times K\times L\times D}$. Notably, the point-based layer not only captures intricate geometric patterns but also preserves SO(2) rotation equivariance.

Definition 2.2 For a discrete 2D rotation group $\mathcal{R} \subset \mathbf{SO}(2)$, defined as $\mathcal{R} = \{\boldsymbol{r}_i \in \mathbb{R}^{3\times 3}, i = 1, 2, ..., L\}$, the point-based layer serves as an equivariant mapping under the group $\mathcal{R}$.

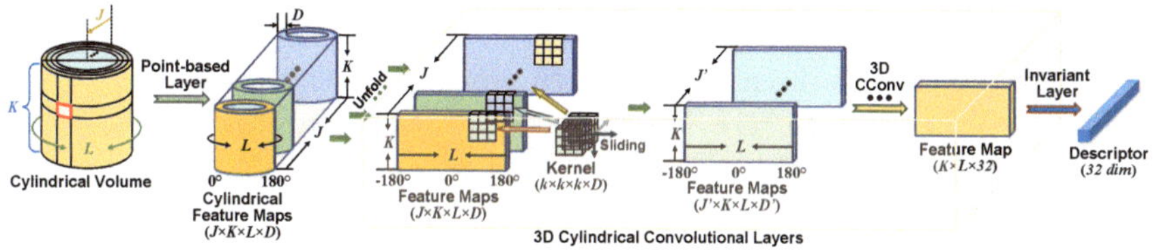

Fig. 2.2 Illustration of the proposed Neural Feature Extractor (This figure is reproduced from [2])

Proof Referring to Eq. 2.8, the point-based layer can be formulated as a mapping $\mathcal{M}_p$ from $\mathbf{C}$ to $\mathbf{F}: \mathbb{R}^{J\times K\times L\times 3\times k_v} \rightarrow \mathbb{R}^{J\times K\times L\times D}$. Given a group action $\boldsymbol{r}_i \in \mathcal{R}$, we derive:

$$\begin{aligned} \boldsymbol{r}_i \circ \mathcal{M}_p(\mathbf{C}) &= \boldsymbol{r}_i \circ [\boldsymbol{f}_{111}, ..., \boldsymbol{f}_{jkl}, ..., \boldsymbol{f}_{JKL}] \\ &= [\boldsymbol{f}_{11(1-i)}, ..., \boldsymbol{f}_{jk(l-i)}, ..., \boldsymbol{f}_{JK(L-i)}] \\ &= \mathcal{A}(\mathbf{MLPs}([\mathbf{c}_{11(1-i)}, ..., \mathbf{c}_{jk(l-i)}, ..., \mathbf{c}_{JK(L-i)}]) \\ &= \mathcal{A}(\mathbf{MLPs}(\boldsymbol{r}_i \circ [\mathbf{c}_{111}, ..., \mathbf{c}_{jkl}, ..., \mathbf{c}_{JKL}]) \\ &= \mathcal{M}_p(\boldsymbol{r}_i \circ \mathbf{C}), \end{aligned} \tag{2.9}$$

which confirms that the point-based layer $\mathcal{M}_p$ is an equivariant mapping with respect to the 2D rotation group $\mathcal{R}$, completing the proof. □

3D Cylindrical Convolutional Layer: The cylindrical feature maps derived from point-based layers only incorporate localized geometric details within each voxel. To extract more discriminative and comprehensive features, it is essential to encode broader spatial structures across multiple bins of the cylindrical feature maps while maintaining their equivariant characteristics. To achieve this, we introduce an efficient 3D cylindrical convolutional network (3DCCN). Specifically, for a bin situated at position (j, k, l) on the d'th cylindrical feature map in the sth layer, the 3DCCN operation is formulated as follows:

$$\boldsymbol{f}^{sd'}_{jkl} = \sum_{d=1}^{D}\sum_{r=1}^{R_s}\sum_{y=1}^{Y_s}\sum_{x=1}^{X_s} \omega^{sd'd}_{ryx} \boldsymbol{f}^{(s-1)d}_{(j+r)(k+y)(l+x)}, \tag{2.10}$$

where R_s, Y_s, and X_s denote the kernel size along the radial, height, and width dimensions, respectively. The learnable parameters are represented by $\omega^{sd'd}_{ryx}$.

The proposed 3DCCN introduces two significant differences compared to conventional convolutional operations. **First**, unlike standard 3D-CNNs that require explicit padding at the boundaries of feature maps, our 3DCCN accommodates the continuity of cylindrical feature maps across the 360° range, wrapping seamlessly from −180° to 180°. **Second,** unlike 3D manifold sparse convolutions [6] or kernel point convolutions [3], the continuous convolution over the cylindrical 360° volume ensures that the resulting feature maps maintain SO(2) equivariance. This property ultimately enables the framework to achieve rotation invariance.

Definition 2.3 Given a discrete 2D rotation group $\mathcal{R} \subset \mathbf{SO}(2)$, where $\mathcal{R} = \{\boldsymbol{r}_i \in \mathbb{R}^{3\times 3}, i = 1, 2, ..., L\}$, then 3D cylindrical convolution serves as an equivariant map for the 2D rotation group $\mathcal{R}$.

Proof The proposed 3D cylindrical convolution can be formulated as a set of convolutional filters Ψ on the cylindrical feature maps $\mathbf{F}$:

$$(\mathbf{F} * \Psi)(j,k,l) = \sum_{d=1}^{D}\sum_{\rho=1}^{J}\sum_{z=1}^{K}\sum_{\theta=1}^{L} f^{d}_{\rho z\theta}\psi^{d}_{(\rho-j)(z-k)(\theta-l)}, \tag{2.11}$$

where ρ, z, and θ denote radial distance, height, and azimuth angle, respectively.

Suppose a group action $\boldsymbol{r}_i$ in $\mathcal{R}$ operating on cylindrical feature maps $\mathbf{F}$, we have $(\boldsymbol{r}_i \circ \mathbf{F})(j,k,l) = \mathbf{F}(j,k,l-i)$. This indicates that the $\boldsymbol{r}_i$-transformed feature maps $\boldsymbol{r}_i \circ \mathbf{F}$ at position (j,k,l) correspond to the value at position $(j,k,l-i)$ in the original feature map $\mathbf{F}$. Leaving out the summation over feature maps for clarity, we have:

$$((\boldsymbol{r}_i \circ \mathbf{F}) * \Psi)(j,k,l) = \sum_{\rho=1}^{J}\sum_{z=1}^{K}\sum_{\theta=1+i}^{L+i} f_{\rho z(\theta-i)}\psi_{(\rho-j)(z-k)(\theta-l)}. \tag{2.12}$$

Using the substitution $\theta \rightarrow \theta + i$, then Eq. 2.12 can be transformed into:

$$\begin{aligned}((\boldsymbol{r}_i \circ \mathbf{F}) * \Psi)(j,k,l) &= \sum_{\rho=1}^{J}\sum_{z=1}^{K}\sum_{\theta=1}^{L} f_{\rho z\theta}\psi_{(\rho-j)(z-k)(\theta-(l-i))} \\ &= (\mathbf{F} * \Psi)(j,k,l-i) = (\boldsymbol{r}_i \circ (\mathbf{F} * \Psi))(j,k,l),\end{aligned} \tag{2.13}$$

which completes our proof that 3D cylindrical convolution is an equivariant map for the 2D rotation group $\mathcal{R}$. □

Invariant Layer: After stacking multiple 3D cylindrical convolutional layers, the resulting cylindrical feature map retains equivariance under SO(2) rotations. However, for surface matching tasks, a feature descriptor that is invariant to rotation is more desirable. Existing approaches [8, 10, 55] often apply max/mean pooling or compute a set of invariant attributes to transform the equivariant feature map into an invariant feature vector. These strategies, however, inevitably discard a significant portion of the information contained in the original feature map. To address this limitation, we introduce an invariant layer designed to efficiently aggregate the global contexts of the cylindrical feature map, producing a compact, expressive, and rotation-invariant feature descriptor.

For a cylindrical feature map $\mathbf{F}$ with D channels extracted from the final 3D cylindrical convolutional layer, we introduce a shared function $G_\Theta(\cdot)$ to compute attention scores for each pixel across all channels. This function consists of two 1×1 convolutional layers, where Θ denotes the learnable parameters. The final descriptor $\boldsymbol{d}$ is then derived through a channel-wise weighted summation, formulated as:

$$\boldsymbol{d} = \sum_{k=1}^{K}\sum_{l=1}^{L} \boldsymbol{f}_{kl} \odot G_\Theta(\boldsymbol{f}_{kl}). \tag{2.14}$$

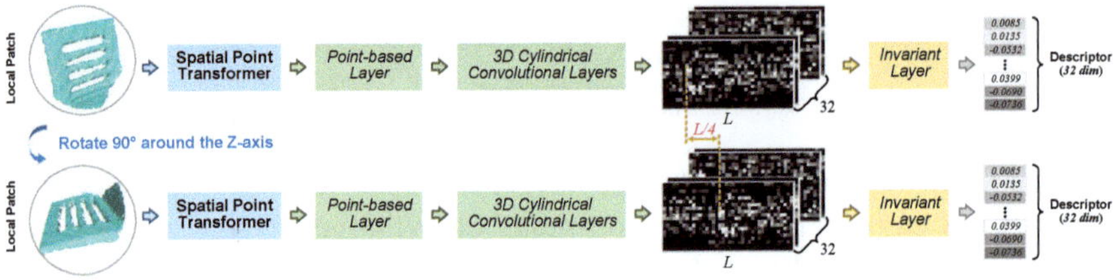

Fig. 2.3 Visualization of rotation equivariance and invariance (This figure is reproduced from [2])

Here, f_{kl} represents the feature at position (k, l) on the feature map $\mathbf{F}$, with D channels, and $\odot$ denotes the element-wise product. Given that the function $G\Theta(\cdot)$ and the summation operation are independent of the spatial distribution of the feature map, the resulting descriptor remains invariant to rotations.

The initial two neural layers effectively extract local geometric patterns and progressively integrate contextual information, ensuring that the generated cylindrical feature map remains SO(2) equivariant at each stage. The final invariant layer further refines global information, producing a rotation-invariant local surface descriptor.

Beyond the theoretical proof of rotation equivariance (see Lemmas 1, 2, and 3), we provide an intuitive visualization to illustrate the concepts of rotation equivariance and invariance. As depicted in Fig. 2.3, even when the input local patch undergoes a 90-degree rotation around the Z-axis, the resulting latent feature map–after passing through the key components (i.e., Spatial Point Transformer[4], point-based layer, and 3D cylindrical convolutional layers)–only exhibits a translation shift relative to the original feature map. Specifically, this shift is $\frac{L}{4}$, precisely corresponding to a 90-degree rotation of the cylindrical feature map around the Z-axis. Moreover, the final feature descriptors, after the invariant layer, remain identical. This provides further evidence that the proposed Spatial Point Transformer, point-based layer, and 3D cylindrical convolutional layers preserve SO(2) equivariance, while the learned feature descriptor is inherently rotation-invariant.

Detailed Architecture: We design a hierarchical learning framework that leverages the 3D cylindrical convolutional layer as its core operator, as shown in Fig. 2.4. To facilitate reproducibility, we provide a detailed specification of the kernel size, stride, and filter count in this figure. A series of cylindrical convolutional layers are stacked to progressively capture compact and informative local feature representations. It is important to highlight that the maximum number of channels in our cylindrical feature map is constrained to 256, which is substantially fewer than the 1024 channels employed in D3Feat [3]. This architectural decision results in a more efficient network that is less prone to overfitting.

End-to-End Implementation: The Spatial Point Transformer is seamlessly integrated with the Neural Feature Extractor to create the SpinNet framework. During

[4] For clarity, reference axis alignment is omitted.

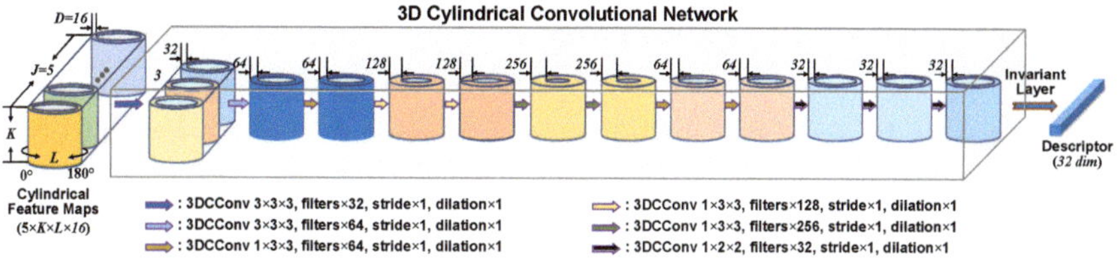

Fig. 2.4 Detailed architecture of our 3DCCN (This figure is reproduced from [2])

training, paired input patches are processed through a Siamese network with shared weights across its two branches, and we utilize the existing contrastive loss [3] for end-to-end optimization. Furthermore, the *hardest-in-batch* sampling strategy [34] is applied dynamically to enhance the distance between the positive patch and its closest negative counterpart. Given a batch $\mathcal{B} = (\mathcal{A}_i, \mathcal{P}_i)_{i=1...n}$ consisting of matching 3D local patches, where $(\mathcal{A}_i, \mathcal{P}_i)$ denotes a pair of positive patches, their corresponding descriptors $\mathcal{D} = (\boldsymbol{d}_{\mathcal{A}_i}, \boldsymbol{d}_{\mathcal{P}_i})_{i=1...n}$ are extracted in a single forward pass. The contrastive margin loss is then formulated as:

$$
\begin{aligned}
\mathcal{L} = \frac{1}{n}\sum_{i=1}^{n}(\max(0, \left\|\boldsymbol{d}_{\mathcal{A}_i} - \boldsymbol{d}_{\mathcal{P}_i}\right\| - M_p) \\
+ \max(0, M_n - \min(\left\|\boldsymbol{d}_{\mathcal{A}_i} - \boldsymbol{d}_{\mathcal{P}_j}\right\|)_{j=1...n, j\neq i})) \qquad (2.15)
\end{aligned}
$$

where M_p and M_n are the margins for positive and negative pairs, respectively.

Our SpinNet is implemented using PyTorch. The batch size is set to 250, with the positive margin M_p and negative margin M_n for the contrastive loss defined as 0.1 and 1.4, respectively. We utilize the Adam optimizer [28] with its default parameters for training the network. The initial learning rate is set to 10^{-3}, and it decays by a factor of 0.5 every 5 epochs. The model with the highest performance on the validation set is selected for testing. To ensure consistency and fairness, identical settings are maintained across all experiments. All experiments were conducted on a system equipped with an Intel Xeon CPU @2.30GHz and dual NVIDIA RTX2080Ti GPUs.

2.4 Experiments

We begin by presenting the dataset description and hyperparameter settings, followed by an evaluation of the proposed SpinNet on the indoor 3DMatch dataset [59] and the outdoor KITTI dataset [16]. We then assess the generalization capability of our approach across several unseen datasets [16, 40, 59] collected using different sensors. Finally, we conduct extensive ablation studies to further analyze the performance of our method.

2.4.1 Datasets and Preprocessing

3DMatch: This dataset [59] is an RGB-D reconstruction collection consisting of 62 real-world indoor scenes, derived from several existing datasets [9, 27, 44, 50, 52]. We adhered to the official protocol outlined in [3] to partition these scenes into training and test sets. Each scene comprises multiple partially overlapping fragments, with ground-truth transformations between these fragments available for evaluation purposes. Training samples were generated as described in [3, 59], considering only point cloud fragment pairs that exhibited more than 30% overlap. This resulted in 35,297 fragment pairs from 54 training scenes and 1,623 fragment pairs from 8 test scenes. For each fragment pair $\mathcal{P}$ and $\mathcal{Q}$, we randomly selected a fixed number of anchor points from the overlapping region of $\mathcal{P}$ and used the ground-truth transformation $\mathbf{T} = \{\mathbf{R}, \boldsymbol{t}\}$ to map these points to their corresponding locations in $\mathcal{Q}$. Specifically, 20 point pairs were randomly chosen from the overlapping region of each fragment pair. In total, 705,940 patch pairs were collected to form the training set.

KITTI: The KITTI odometry dataset [16] is a large-scale outdoor LiDAR point cloud collection obtained using a Velodyne-64 sensor. It includes 11 sequences of outdoor scans, primarily from urban settings such as streets, vehicles, and buildings. For consistency in comparison, we adopted the same dataset splits as in [3, 6]. Specifically, sequences 0 to 5 were designated for training, sequences 6 to 7 for validation, and sequences 8 to 10 for testing. From the LiDAR scans, we selected pairs of adjacent scans that were at least 10 meters apart to form point cloud fragments. This resulted in 1,358 fragment pairs for training, 180 pairs for validation, and 555 pairs for testing.

Due to inaccuracies in the ground-truth transformation $\mathbf{T} = \{\mathbf{R}, \boldsymbol{t}\}$ provided by the dataset authors, we followed the refinement approach in [3, 6] and applied the iterative closest point (ICP) algorithm [4] to adjust $\mathbf{T}$. During training, we randomly selected 600 point pairs from the overlapping region of each fragment pair, resulting in a total of 814,800 patch pairs. For the validation set, 200 point pairs were randomly sampled from the overlapping region of each fragment pair.

ETH: The ETH dataset [40] comprises sparse point clouds captured outdoors using a Hokuyo UTM-30LX laser scanner. It focuses on street-level scenes, including grass and trees, and consists of four scenes recorded across different seasons: Gazebo in Summer, Gazebo in Winter, Wood in Summer, and Wood in Autumn. The dataset provides 713 pairs of point cloud fragments with more than 30% overlap. Since the ETH dataset is solely used for testing, no preprocessing was applied to it.

2.4.2 Hyperparameter Settings

While point density and data distributions differ among datasets, most hyperparameters remain fixed, except for the support radius R, which adapts to density variations.

Table 2.1 Hyperparameter configuration of our SpinNet across different datasets

Dataset	J	K	L	R	C	δ	k_v
Training settings							
3DMatch [59]	5	20	40	0.3 m	2048	0.8	30
KITTI [16]	5	20	40	4.0 m	2048	0.8	30
Test settings							
3DMatch [59]	5	20	40	0.3 m	2048	0.8	30
KITTI [16]	5	20	40	4.0 m	2048	0.8	30
ETH [40]	5	20	40	1.0 m	2048	0.8	30

Table 2.1 outlines the specific configurations, where J, K, and L denote the divisions along the radial, elevation, and azimuth dimensions, respectively. The support radius is represented by R, while C specifies the cardinality of a local patch. The parameter δ defines the receptive field size, and k_v indicates the number of points allocated to each voxel. Notably, the same hyperparameter values are utilized for both training and testing within each dataset (as described in Sects. 2.4.3 and 2.4.4). This approach differs from the varying settings adopted in [39]. For cross-dataset generalization experiments (Sect. 2.4.5), the model trained on the source dataset is directly applied to the target dataset, with the support radius R modified during inference to accommodate differences in point density across datasets.

2.4.3 Evaluation on the Indoor 3DMatch Dataset

Consistent with [3], we adopt feature matching recall (FMR) and registration recall (RR) as the evaluation metrics to measure the performance of SpinNet.

Comparisons to the State-of-the-art Methods: We evaluate the feature matching recall (FMR) performance of SpinNet against several baseline methods, including PREDATOR [24], LMVD [31], D3Feat [3], FCGF [6], PerfectMatch [17], PPFNet [12], and PPF-FoldNet [11], on the 3DMatch dataset. For this comparison, the number of sampled keypoints n is set to 5,000, with a distance threshold τ_1 of 10 cm and an inlier ratio threshold τ_2 of 5%. Furthermore, to assess the methods' sensitivity to rotations, we adopted the approach in [3, 12] by generating a rotated 3DMatch benchmark through the application of random rotations from the SO(3) group to the dataset fragments. The rotation distribution in both the original and rotated 3DMatch datasets is depicted in Fig. 2.5a, where the ground-truth rotations of all paired fragments are converted into three Euler angles for visualization.

Table 2.2 demonstrates that the descriptor from SpinNet surpasses existing state-of-the-art methods, obtaining the highest average FMR score and the lowest standard deviation on both the original and rotated datasets. In Table 2.2, STD refers to the standard deviation, Feat. Dim. denotes the dimensionality of feature, and Rot. Aug.

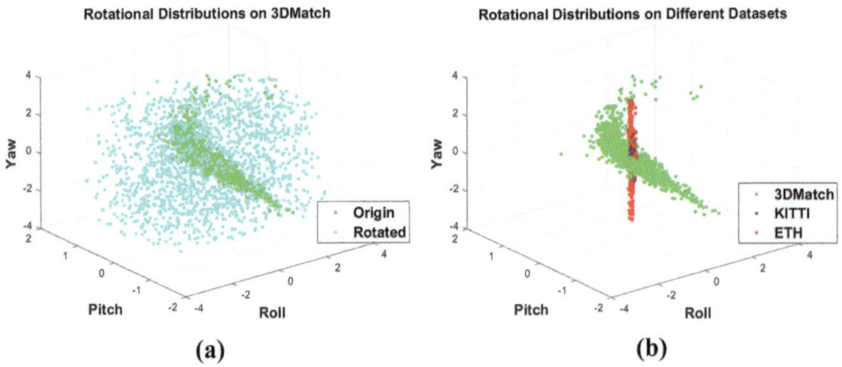

Fig. 2.5 The rotation distributions for various datasets (This figure is reproduced from [2])

Table 2.2 Quantitative results on the 3DMatch dataset

Methods	Origin		Rotated		Feat.	Rot.
	FMR (%)	STD	FMR (%)	STD	Dim.	Aug.
FPFH [42]	35.9	13.4	36.4	13.6	33	No
SHOT [49]	23.8	10.9	23.4	9.5	352	No
3DMatch [59]	59.6	8.8	1.1	–	512	No
CGF [26]	58.2	14.2	58.5	14.0	32	No
PPFNet [12]	62.3	10.8	0.3	–	64	No
PPF-FoldNet [11]	71.8	10.5	73.1	10.4	512	No
PerfectMatch [17]	94.7	2.7	94.9	2.5	32	No
FCGF [6]	97.4	–	–	–	32	Yes
D3Feat-rand [3]	95.3	2.7	95.2	3.2	32	Yes
D3Feat-pred [3]	95.8	2.9	95.5	3.5	32	Yes
DIP [38]	94.8	4.6	94.6	4.6	32	No
LMVD [31]	<u>97.5</u>	2.8	<u>96.9</u>	–	32	No
PREDATOR [24]	96.6	–	–	-	32	Yes
SpinNet (Ours)	**97.8**	**1.7**	**97.8**	**1.9**	**32**	**No**

indicates the application of rotation-based data augmentation. The symbol—signifies that the corresponding results are either unavailable or not applicable. Notably, the SpinNet descriptor is naturally rotation-invariant, eliminating the need for rotation-based augmentations as required by [3, 6].

Performance under Varying Numbers of Sampled Keypoints: We further evaluate the performance of SpinNet on the 3DMatch dataset by varying the number of sampled keypoints. As presented in Table 2.3, SpinNet consistently achieves the highest FMR scores, even as the number of sampled keypoints decreases from 5,000 to 500. The symbol ◇ denotes keypoints obtained through random sampling, while

Table 2.3 Quantitative results on the 3DMatch and 3DLoMatch datasets

# Keypoints Num.	3DMatch				3DLoMatch			
	5000	2500	1000	500	5000	2500	1000	500
	Feature matching recall (%)							
PerfectMatch$^\diamond$ [17]	95.0	94.3	92.9	90.1	63.6	61.7	53.6	45.2
FCGF$^\diamond$ [6]	97.4	97.3	97.0	96.7	76.6	75.4	74.2	71.7
D3Feat* [3]	95.6	95.4	94.5	94.1	67.3	66.7	67.0	66.7
PREDATOR* [24]	96.6	96.2	96.2	95.8	71.7	73.8	73.8	72.9
SpinNet$^\diamond$ (Ours)	<u>97.8</u>	<u>97.8</u>	<u>97.6</u>	<u>97.0</u>	<u>80.9</u>	<u>80.7</u>	<u>79.4</u>	<u>74.8</u>
SpinNet + [24]	**98.1**	**98.1**	**98.2**	**98.4**	**84.1**	**85.5**	**84.3**	**85.6**
	Registration recall (%)							
PerfectMatch$^\diamond$ [17]	78.4	76.2	71.4	67.6	33.0	29.0	23.3	17.0
FCGF$^\diamond$ [6]	85.1	84.7	83.3	81.6	40.1	41.7	38.2	35.4
D3Feat* [3]	81.6	84.5	83.4	82.4	37.2	42.7	46.9	43.8
PREDATOR* [24]	88.3	88.3	89.0	<u>88.4</u>	54.2	55.8	56.7	56.1
SpinNet$^\diamond$ (Ours)	<u>92.4</u>	<u>91.5</u>	<u>90.3</u>	87.5	<u>71.6</u>	<u>69.4</u>	<u>65.3</u>	<u>57.5</u>
SpinNet + [24]	**93.4**	**93.0**	**92.9**	**92.0**	**73.3**	**73.7**	**72.4**	**71.6**

$*$ indicates keypoints learned by neural networks. Moreover, SpinNet maintains the highest registration recall when the keypoint count is reduced from 5,000 to 1,000. Notably, despite relying on random keypoint selection for feature description, SpinNet surpasses methods that incorporate explicit keypoint detection modules, such as D3Feat [3] and PREDATOR [24].

In addition to experiments on the high-overlap 3DMatch dataset, we also assess SpinNet on the low-overlap 3DLoMatch [24] dataset. While both datasets share similar contexts, they differ in the distribution of overlaps. In the 3DMatch dataset, all fragment pairs have overlaps greater than 30%, while in the 3DLoMatch dataset, overlaps range from 10 to 30%. Notably, in low-overlap cases, human operators often face challenges in registering point clouds successfully, making the 3DLoMatch dataset particularly difficult. The experimental results, as shown in Table 2.3, indicate that all methods experience significant performance degradation in low-overlap scenarios. This is mainly due to most keypoints being located in non-overlapping regions, which complicates the establishment of correct correspondences. Despite these difficulties, SpinNet still achieves the highest FMR scores and registration recall, outperforming PREDATOR, which is specifically designed to address low-overlap registration challenges. Moreover, combining SpinNet with PREDATOR's detection module leads to a significant performance improvement, underscoring the effectiveness and scalability of the proposed SpinNet descriptor in both high- and low-overlap settings.

Performance under Different Error Thresholds: The robustness of SpinNet is further evaluated by varying the error thresholds, τ_1 and τ_2. As illustrated in Fig. 2.6,

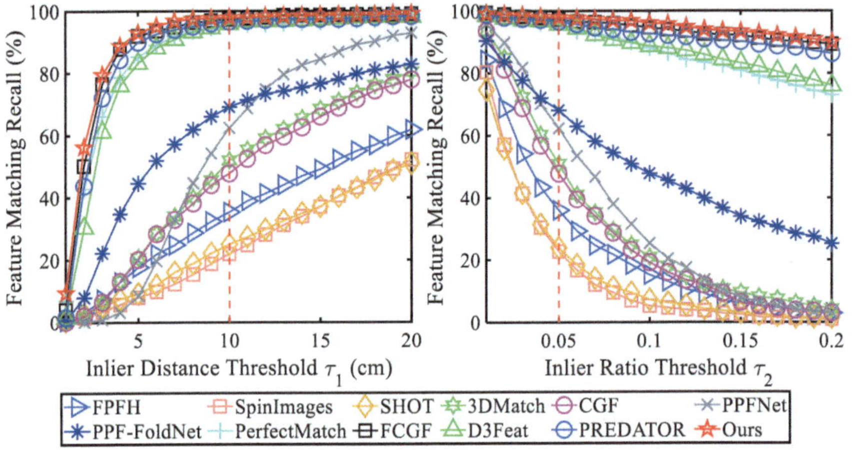

Fig. 2.6 The feature matching recall (FMR) on the 3DMatch dataset (This figure is reproduced from [2])

SpinNet consistently outperforms competing methods across all threshold settings. Under the stringent condition of $\tau_2 = 0.2$, SpinNet achieves a high FMR score of 90.0%, while FCGF and PREDATOR exhibit declines, with scores of 89.3% and 86.3%, respectively. These findings highlight the robustness of SpinNet, especially in demanding scenarios.

2.4.4 Evaluation on the Outdoor KITTI Dataset

Following the methodology outlined in [57], we assess the performance of various feature descriptors using relative translation error (RTE), relative rotation error (RRE), and success rate (SR). A registration is deemed successful if the RTE is below $\tau_t = 2$m and the RRE is under $\tau_r = 5°$, as defined in [57]. However, these thresholds are considered too lenient for practical outdoor scene reconstruction. To address this, we adopt stricter criteria in our experiments, setting $\tau_t = 0.3$m and $\tau_r = 1°$. Moreover, since the point clouds in the KITTI dataset are gravity-aligned, the alignment of local patches with a reference axis is omitted in our framework.

As shown in Table 2.4, SpinNet achieves the highest success rate under both relaxed and strict threshold conditions. Specifically, it attains a success rate of 99.82% with the lenient thresholds, meaning only one fragment pair out of 555 failed during testing. Although D3Feat-pred also performs well in terms of relative translation error (RTE) and relative rotation error (RRE), its success is largely due to its robust keypoint detection module. However, when D3Feat's keypoint detection is replaced by random sampling, its performance consistently lags behind that of SpinNet across all metrics. This highlights SpinNet can effectively learn descriptors using random

Table 2.4 Quantitative evaluation of various methods on the KITTI odometry dataset

Methods	RTE (cm)		RRE (°)		SR (%)
	AVG	STD	AVG	STD	
$\tau_t = 2.0$m && $\tau_r = 5°$					
3DFeat-Net [57]	25.9	26.2	0.57	0.46	95.97
FCGF [6]	18.5	2.27	0.38	0.16	99.10
DIP [38]	8.69	0.69	0.44	0.49	97.30
D3Feat-rand [3]	8.78	0.44	0.32	0.07	**99.82**
D3Feat-pred [3]	6.90	**0.30**	**0.24**	**0.06**	**99.82**
SpinNet (Ours)	**6.84**	0.37	0.32	0.07	**99.82**
$\tau_t = 0.3$m && $\tau_r = 1°$					
FCGF [6]	13.3	0.48	0.31	0.04	81.80
D3Feat-rand [3]	6.18	0.11	0.24	0.03	96.58
D3Feat-pred [3]	**5.46**	**0.11**	**0.22**	0.03	97.12
SpinNet (Ours)	5.55	**0.11**	0.24	**0.02**	**97.48**

sampling, while also indicating the potential for further improvement by integrating keypoint detection modules.

2.4.5 Generalization Across Unseen Datasets

In this section, we conduct comprehensive experiments to evaluate the generalization ability of SpinNet. By default, unless explicitly specified, the network is trained using one dataset and tested on an entirely different dataset that it has not encountered before.

Generalization from 3DMatch to ETH: To evaluate the generalization ability, we examine the transfer performance from the 3DMatch dataset to the ETH dataset. The 3DMatch dataset, primarily consisting of indoor scenes captured with an RGB-D sensor, contrasts with the ETH dataset, which contains outdoor street-level scenes acquired using static terrestrial scanners. As a result, the point cloud fragments in the ETH dataset have lower resolution and more complex geometric structures compared to those in 3DMatch. This significant domain gap poses a challenge for the generalization of feature description methods. Following the experimental setup in [3],

Table 2.5 Quantitative results on the ETH dataset

Methods	Gazebo		Wood		Avg.
	Summer	Winter	Autumn	Summer	
FPFH† [42]	38.6	14.2	14.8	20.8	22.1
SHOT† [49]	73.9	45.7	60.9	64.0	61.1
3DMatch [59]	22.8	8.3	13.9	22.4	16.9
CGF [26]	37.5	13.8	10.4	19.2	20.2
PerfectMatch [17]	<u>91.3</u>	84.1	67.8	72.8	79.0
FCGF [6]	22.8	10.0	14.8	16.8	16.1
DIP [38]	90.8	<u>88.6</u>	<u>96.5</u>	<u>95.2</u>	<u>92.8</u>
D3Feat-rand [3]	45.7	23.9	13.0	22.4	26.2
D3Feat-pred [3]	85.9	63.0	49.6	48.0	61.6
LMVD [31]	85.3	72.0	84.0	78.3	79.9
SpinNet (Ours)	**99.5**	**100**	**100**	**100**	**99.9**

all models are trained solely on the 3DMatch dataset and evaluated on the ETH dataset [40].

As presented in Table 2.5, all existing methods, including 3DMatch, CGF, FCGF, and D3Feat, experience a considerable drop in performance when directly applied to the unseen ETH dataset. Notably, the FMR scores of fragment-based descriptors, such as FCGF and D3Feat, decrease by up to 80% compared to their performance on the original 3DMatch dataset (see Table 2.2), falling even below that of handcrafted descriptors like SHOT. This poor generalization is likely due to the excessively large receptive field, as discussed in detail in Sect. 2.4.7. In contrast, the limited generalization ability of some patch-based descriptors (e.g., 3DMatch and CGF) can primarily be attributed to their sensitivity to rotations or reliance on handcrafted features, which are prone to noise.

In contrast, the descriptor produced by our SpinNet demonstrates strong generalization to the ETH dataset, achieving the highest FMR scores across all scenes and outperforming the second-best approach (i.e., DIP) by 7.1%. These results highlight the exceptional generalization capability of SpinNet to unseen datasets captured with different sensors. This robustness is primarily attributed to SpinNet's inherent design, which ensures rotation invariance and supports end-to-end optimization without relying on handcrafted features. Qualitative results, depicted in the first row of Fig. 2.7, further illustrate the effectiveness of our method, showing accurate registration between two partial point clouds of a tree.

Generalization from 3DMatch to KITTI: The generalization performance of various methods is further assessed by transferring from the 3DMatch dataset to the KITTI dataset. All models were trained exclusively on the indoor 3DMatch dataset, which consists of dense point clouds reconstructed from RGB-D images, and then tested on the outdoor KITTI dataset, primarily consisting of sparse LiDAR point clouds. The quantitative results, summarized in Table 2.6, show that FCGF and

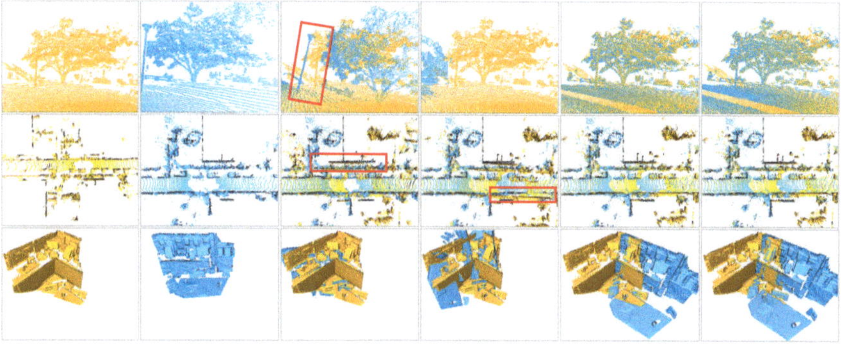

Fig. 2.7 Qualitative results of our method in the cross-dataset generalization experiment (This figure is reproduced from [2])

Table 2.6 Quantitative results on the KITTI dataset

Methods	RTE (cm)		RRE (°)		SR (%)
	AVG	STD	AVG	STD	
$\tau_t = 2.0$m && $\tau_r = 5°$					
FCGF [6]	20.8	2.59	0.99	0.74	92.25
D3Feat-rand [3]	<u>19.7</u>	3.20	<u>0.95</u>	0.70	92.07
D3Feat-pred [3]	21.5	<u>2.26</u>	<u>0.95</u>	<u>0.67</u>	<u>93.15</u>
SpinNet (Ours)	**9.74**	**0.48**	**0.50**	**0.17**	**99.28**
$\tau_t = 0.3$m && $\tau_r = 1°$					
FCGF [6]	15.5	0.43	0.51	0.06	57.11
D3Feat-rand [3]	14.8	0.44	0.49	<u>0.05</u>	60.00
D3Feat-pred [3]	<u>12.6</u>	<u>0.35</u>	<u>0.46</u>	0.06	<u>69.55</u>
SpinNet (Ours)	**7.00**	**0.16**	**0.33**	**0.04**	**94.59**

D3Feat exhibit limited generalization due to the significant differences between the two datasets. In contrast, SpinNet demonstrates superior performance, achieving a success rate of 99.28% under the relaxed thresholds of $\tau_t = 2.0$m and $\tau_r = 5°$. Notably, SpinNet outperforms the second-best method by a margin of 25% under the stricter thresholds of $\tau_t = 0.3$m and $\tau_r = 1°$. The qualitative results, shown in the second row of Fig. 2.7, highlight that the registration results of SpinNet are closely aligned with the ground truth, further emphasizing its strong generalization capability.

Table 2.7 Quantitative results of different methods on the indoor 3DMatch dataset

Methods	Origin		Rotated	
	FMR (%)	STD (%)	FMR (%)	STD (%)
FPFH† [42]	35.9	13.4	36.4	13.6
SHOT† [49]	23.8	10.9	23.4	9.5
FCGF [6]	32.5	7.4	1.0	1.0
D3Feat-rand [3]	60.7	7.7	17.2	4.6
D3Feat-pred [3]	62.7	8.1	17.8	3.2
SpinNet (Ours)	**92.7**	4.4	**92.6**	4.4

Generalization from KITTI to 3DMatch: The generalization capability of various methods is evaluated by transferring models trained on the KITTI dataset to the 3DMatch dataset. Specifically, all models are trained using outdoor scenes from the KITTI dataset and subsequently tested on indoor scenes from the 3DMatch dataset. As summarized in Table 2.7, both D3Feat and FCGF exhibit limited generalization performance, particularly when applied to the rotated 3DMatch dataset containing arbitrary SO(3) rotations. This performance degradation can be attributed to the substantial differences in rotation distributions between the KITTI and 3DMatch datasets. As illustrated in Fig. 2.5, the KITTI dataset is characterized by SO(2) rotations, while the original and rotated 3DMatch datasets include more diverse SO(3) rotations. The lack of rotation invariance in D3Feat and FCGF hinders their ability to adapt to these changes. Furthermore, the reliance of these methods on extensive rotation-based data augmentation significantly increases their parameter count, making them prone to overfitting the KITTI dataset. Consequently, these approaches fail to capture representative and generalizable local features applicable to new datasets. In contrast, SpinNet demonstrates a robust generalization capability, achieving an FMR score of 92.7% on the 3DMatch dataset. Qualitative results (as depicted in the third row of Fig. 2.7, where † represents a handcrafted descriptor) confirm that SpinNet successfully registers indoor scene point clouds, whereas both D3Feat and FCGF fail under the same conditions.

Generalization from KITTI to ETH: Finally, We assess the generalization performance from the KITTI to the ETH dataset. All models were exclusively trained on the outdoor KITTI dataset and then directly evaluated on the outdoor ETH dataset. As illustrated in Table 2.8, both FCGF and D3Feat demonstrate notable performance improvements compared to the previous cross-dataset generalization from 3DMatch to ETH. This improvement can be attributed to the smaller domain gap between the KITTI and ETH datasets, in contrast to the larger gap between 3DMatch and ETH. Specifically, both the KITTI and ETH datasets are characterized by SO(2) rotations (see Fig. 2.5b), which benefits methods like FCGF and D3Feat, known to be sensitive to rotation distributions. Despite this, our SpinNet still outperforms all methods across the four evaluation scenarios, achieving the highest FMR scores, even surpassing D3Feat-pred, which integrates a keypoint detection module.

Table 2.8 Quantitative results on the ETH dataset

Methods	Gazebo		Wood		Avg.
	Summer	Winter	Autumn	Summer	
FPFH† [42]	38.6	14.2	14.8	20.8	22.1
SHOT† [49]	73.9	45.7	60.9	64.0	61.1
FCGF [6]	29.3	21.1	34.8	46.4	32.9
D3Feat-rand [3]	86.4	78.2	82.6	87.2	83.6
D3Feat-pred [3]	95.1	97.6	98.3	99.2	97.5
SpinNet (Ours)	**100**	**97.9**	**100**	**100**	**99.5**

2.4.6 Ablation Studies

In this section, we conduct a series of comprehensive ablative experiments on the 3DMatch and ETH datasets to systematically evaluate the contribution of each component in our proposed SpinNet. Specifically, all ablated models were trained on the 3DMatch dataset and then tested on both the 3DMatch and ETH datasets.

SpinNet is composed of several essential components: the reference axis (RA), transformation, point-based layer (PL), 3D cylindrical convolutional network (3DCCN), and invariant layer (IL). To assess the significance of each component, we performed six distinct ablative experiments. The results demonstrate the individual contribution of each component to the overall performance of the model.

1. **Removing alignment with a reference axis**. The reference axis is initially introduced to align the input patch with the Z-axis, ensuring rotational invariance to SO(3) transformations. By omitting this step, the framework's invariance is limited to only SO(2) rotations, reducing its ability to handle more complex rotational variations.
2. **Removing the transformation on the XY plane**. The transformation on the XY plane is designed to address the rotational variance within this plane. In this experiment, we excluded the transformation and directly processed the untransformed spherical voxels, resulting in a cylindrical volume without the corrective effect of the transformation.
3. **Combination of (1) and (2)**. In this experiment, both the alignment with the reference axis and the transformation on the XY-plane were removed. Consequently, the network loses its rotational invariance, becoming more sensitive to rotational variations in the input data.
4. **Replacing the point-based layer with density**. Here, we replaced the point-based layer with a manual computation of the point density for each cylindrical voxel, using it as the feature signature (similar to the handcrafted 3DSC feature [15]).

Table 2.9 The FMR scores of all ablated models on the 3DMatch and ETH datasets

Inlier ratio	3DMatch				ETH	
	Origin		Rotated		Origin	Rotated
$\tau_2 =$	0.05	0.2	0.05	0.2	0.05	0.05
(1) W/o RA	96.1	86.9	80.2	37.9	97.5	27.5
(2) W/o Tran.	92.8	71.2	90.7	57.9	81.3	77.1
(3) W/o RA and Tran.	65.5	47.4	25.4	6.84	55.9	3.51
(4) Replacing PL	96.5	81.0	96.7	81.1	96.5	96.7
(5) Replacing 3DCCN	84.1	37.6	84.2	37.5	45.9	46.0
(6) Replacing IL	97.5	86.1	97.4	85.7	98.4	98.0
(7) **The full method**	**97.8**	**90.0**	**97.8**	**89.7**	**99.9**	**99.7**

This setup helps evaluate whether the features learned through our point-based layer offer greater generality and representational power compared to traditional handcrafted features, which are more limited.

5. **Replacing 3DCCN with MLPs.** The 3D cylindrical convolutional network (3DCCN) is designed to capture larger spatial patterns across multiple voxels while maintaining rotation equivariance. In this experiment, we replaced the 3DCCN layers with multi-layer perceptron (MLP) layers applied uniformly across all cylindrical voxels. It is important to note that MLPs lack the capacity to capture broader contextual information.
6. **Replacing the invariant layer with max-pooling**. The invariant layer is specifically built to efficiently aggregate data from a cylindrical feature map, producing a descriptor that is both discriminative and invariant to rotations. In this experiment, we substituted the invariant layer with a max-pooling operation. While max-pooling preserves the rotational invariance of the descriptor, it does not capture the same level of contextual information.

Analyses: Table 2.9 presents the outcomes of the various ablated networks evaluated on the 3DMatch dataset, along with their generalization capabilities on the ETH datasets. It can be found that:

1. When the reference axis alignment or spherical voxel transformation step is removed (Table 2.11-(1,2)), the ablated models struggle to match point clouds effectively on both the 3DMatch and ETH datasets, particularly with rotated point clouds. Specifically, removing both components (Table 2.11-(3)) results in significantly degraded descriptiveness and generalization performance. These findings highlight the critical role of the Spatial Point Transformer in enhancing the performance of our SpinNet.
2. When the advanced point-based neural layers are not employed to learn signatures for spherical voxels (as shown in Table 2.11-(4)), the ablated method achieves consistent results on the 3DMatch dataset using a simple handcrafted feature (i.e., point density). However, it fails to generalize to the unseen ETH dataset,

primarily due to the significant distribution gap between the two datasets. This clearly illustrates that learned local features are generally more robust and versatile than handcrafted features.

3. When the proposed 3DCCN is replaced with MLPs for learning underlying surface structures (as indicated in Table 2.11-(5)), the ablated model achieves substantially lower scores on both the 3DMatch and ETH datasets. This strongly indicates that our 3DCCN is essential for capturing local spatial patterns.
4. When the invariant layer is replaced with a simple max-pooling operator to aggregate the feature map information (Table 2.11-(6)), the performance of the ablated models shows a slight decline on both the 3DMatch and ETH datasets, while maintaining rotation invariance. The performance degradation is more pronounced under stricter thresholds (i.e., $\tau_2 = 0.2$). This highlights the importance of the invariant layer in enhancing the descriptiveness and generalization ability of the feature descriptor.

Justification of Neural Architecture Design: We further assess the performance of our SpinNet across various parameter configurations and architectural designs to justify the chosen parameters and neural architecture. Specifically, we conducted comprehensive ablative experiments focusing on several crucial hyperparameters in the Spatial Point Transformer, including the receptive field size δ for each voxel, the number of points k_v within each voxel, the support radius R of a local patch, the cardinality C of a local patch, and the number of divisions J, K, L along the radial, elevation, and azimuth axes, respectively.

Additionally, we explore various other factors that may influence the performance of SpinNet, such as feature dimensions, batch sizes, loss functions, rotation-based augmentation methods, and keypoint sampling strategies. It is important to note that the keypoint sampling scheme is solely used during inference, while the other configurations are applied exclusively during the training phase.

The quantitative results for all ablated models are presented in Table 2.10. Initially, we observe that variations in the parameters J, K, L, δ, and k_v have a minimal effect on performance when both the training and test data originate from the same dataset. Specifically, the difference in FMR scores across different settings is less than 0.3% on the 3DMatch dataset, indicating that SpinNet demonstrates robustness to these hyperparameters.

We then examine the ablative results of the support radius R and cardinality C of local patches, as presented in Nos. 9 to 12 of Table 2.10. The following observations can be made: (1) As the support radius R decreases, the performance of SpinNet declines, primarily due to the limited distinctive information captured by local patches with a smaller support radius, which fails to adequately represent the underlying local surface. (2) Increasing the support radius R does not always lead to better performance, as a larger support radius can introduce occlusion and clutter, which negatively affect the distinctiveness of the features, as discussed in Sect. 2.4.7. (3) The cardinality C of a local patch has a negligible impact on SpinNet.

The ablative results regarding feature dimensionality and batch size are provided in Nos. 13 to 15 of Table 2.10. The following insights can be drawn: (1) A low feature

Table 2.10 Quantitative results obtained by our SpinNet under different configurations across three benchmark datasets

No.	J	K	L	δ	k_v	R	C	Feat. Dim.	Batch Size	Loss Function	Rot. Aug.	Keypoint Sampling	3DMatch FMR (%)	3DMatch STD	ETH FMR (%)	ETH STD	KITTI SR (%)
1	**3**	20	40	0.8	30	0.3 m	2048	32	250	Contrast	No	Random	97.8	1.90	95.2	1.64	99.28
2	**7**	20	40	0.8	30	0.3 m	2048	32	250	Contrast	No	Random	97.7	1.83	99.1	1.11	99.28
3	5	**15**	**30**	0.8	30	0.3 m	2048	32	250	Contrast	No	Random	98.0	1.87	98.4	0.72	98.56
4	5	**25**	**50**	0.8	30	0.3 m	2048	32	250	Contrast	No	Random	97.8	1.80	97.1	0.69	98.74
5	5	20	40	**0.6**	30	0.3 m	2048	32	250	Contrast	No	Random	97.9	1.81	99.7	0.47	98.92
6	5	20	40	**1.0**	30	0.3 m	2048	32	250	Contrast	No	Random	97.8	1.74	98.9	1.33	99.10
7	5	20	40	0.8	**20**	0.3 m	2048	32	250	Contrast	No	Random	97.7	1.85	99.3	0.61	98.20
8	5	20	40	0.8	**40**	0.3 m	2048	32	250	Contrast	No	Random	97.8	1.78	99.5	0.67	98.56
9	5	20	40	0.8	30	**0.2 m**	2048	32	250	Contrast	No	Random	96.3	2.89	98.4	1.60	98.02
10	5	20	40	0.8	30	**0.4 m**	2048	32	250	Contrast	No	Random	97.8	2.08	99.6	0.71	98.92
11	5	20	40	0.8	30	0.3 m	**1024**	32	250	Contrast	No	Random	97.8	1.89	99.9	0.24	98.74
12	5	20	40	0.8	30	0.3 m	**3072**	32	250	Contrast	No	Random	97.8	1.82	98.9	0.60	98.56
13	5	20	40	0.8	30	0.3 m	2048	**16**	250	Contrast	No	Random	96.8	2.12	79.3	5.31	96.76
14	5	20	40	0.8	30	0.3 m	2048	**64**	250	Contrast	No	Random	98.2	2.09	99.7	0.47	98.56
15	5	20	40	0.8	30	0.3 m	2048	32	**100**	Contrast	No	Random	97.5	1.96	98.6	1.49	99.10
16	5	20	40	0.8	30	0.3 m	2048	32	250	**Hardest**	No	Random	97.6	1.99	98.4	0.84	98.38
17	5	20	40	0.8	30	0.3 m	2048	32	250	Contrast	**Yes**	Random	97.8	1.65	99.5	0.67	99.28
18	5	20	40	0.8	30	0.3 m	2048	32	250	Contrast	No	[3]	98.1	1.77	100	0.00	99.82
Ours	5	20	40	0.8	30	0.3 m	2048	32	250	Contrast	No	Random	97.8	1.74	99.9	0.24	99.28

dimensionality hampers the descriptiveness and generalization ability of the model, as it fails to capture the rich information required for accurate feature representation. (2) Using a small batch size results in a slight degradation in performance, likely due to the *hardest-in-batch* sampling strategy employed during training [34], which requires a sufficiently large batch to include a diverse set of challenging negative samples.

Lastly, the ablative results concerning the loss function, rotation-based augmentation, and keypoint sampling are summarized in Nos. 16 to 18 of Table 2.10. The following key observations can be drawn from these experiments: (1) Replacing the contrastive loss with the hardest-contrastive loss [6] results in a slight decline in FMR scores across all three datasets. (2) Rotation-based augmentation has no effect on SpinNet's performance, as the model is inherently invariant to SO(3) transformations. (3) Employing 3D keypoint detectors improves both the descriptor's discriminability and generalization, as the D3Feat sampling strategy [3] effectively captures the geometric characteristics of the local surface during keypoint selection.

2.4.7 Discussion

Finally, we conduct a detailed comparison and analysis of the patch-based and fragment-based approaches, as the descriptors generated by patch-based methods have demonstrated superior generalization performance compared to those produced by fragment-based methods. However, the underlying factors contributing to this performance disparity remain unclear. To address this, we perform a series of extensive experiments based on the SpinNet architecture to investigate several potential factors that may influence the observed differences in generalization performance.

Fragment-based or Patch-based Framework? What Factors Influence Generalization Ability? To investigate these questions, we propose a fragment-based variant of SpinNet by incorporating the patch-based SpinNet as a self-contained convolutional module, referred to as SSN, within a hierarchical structure comprising multiple sampling layers. As illustrated in Fig. 2.8, where C denotes the number of points within the support radius R, and N represents the number of points in a point cloud fragment. To manage memory consumption efficiently, key hyperparameters in the fragment-based SpinNet are adaptively set to $J = 3$, $K = 6$, and $L = 9$. Additionally, the four core components of the fragment-based SpinNet–the reference axis, spherical voxelization, 3D cylindrical convolutional network (3DCCN), and invariant layer–are streamlined to enhance computational efficiency while maintaining performance. Extensive experiments on the 3DMatch and ETH datasets were conducted to analyze the factors affecting generalization ability, with the results detailed in Table 2.11. All networks were trained on the 3DMatch dataset and subsequently evaluated on the 3DMatch and ETH datasets without fine-tuning. The inference time is reported in milliseconds per feature. The network configurations are defined as follows: *SpinNet*(C_{in}, C_{out}, R) represents our SpinNet model, which takes C_{in} input features, applies convolution within a patch of support radius R, and produces

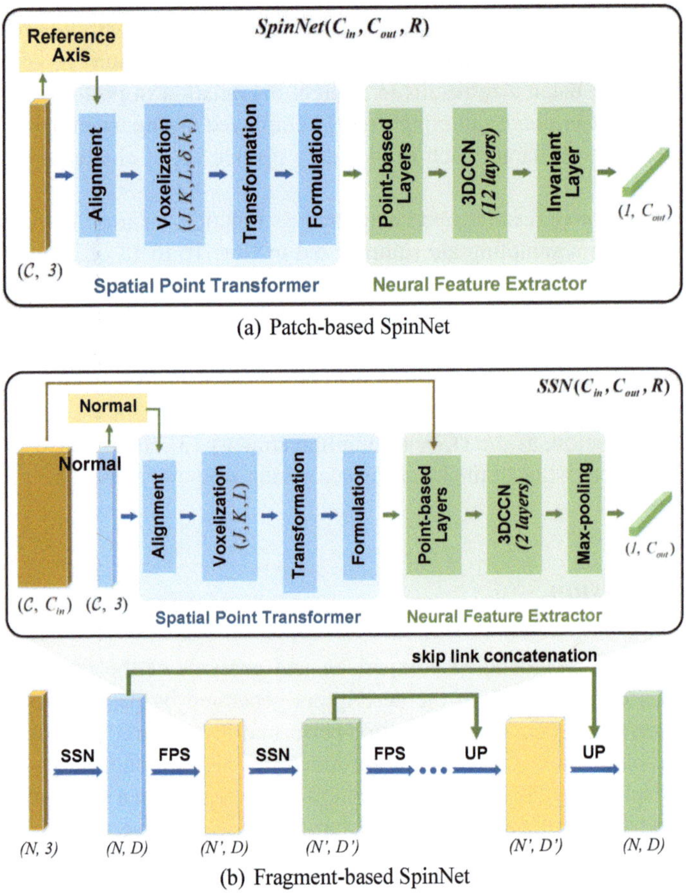

Fig. 2.8 The architectures of our patch-based SpinNet and fragment-based SpinNet (This figure is reproduced from [2])

C_{out} output features. $SSN(C_{in}, C_{out}, R)$ denotes a simplified variant of $SpinNet(C_{in}, C_{out}, R)$. *FPS* refers to farthest point sampling [41]. $UP(C_{in}, C_{out})$ indicates nearest-neighbor upsampling followed by shared MLPs, which transform C_{in} input features into C_{out} output features.

1. **Architecture**. As observed in Nos. 1 and 11 of Table 2.11, the fragment-based architecture exhibits weaker learning capacity compared to the patch-based approach. Despite employing the same hyperparameters, the fragment-based SpinNet lags behind its patch-based counterpart by 4.2 and 21.3% in FMR scores on the 3DMatch and ETH datasets, respectively. Additionally, architectural constraints necessitate different hyperparameter settings, further influencing performance. Due to the high computational and memory demands, the fragment-based SpinNet restricts J, K, and L to 3, 6, 3, whereas the patch-based version allows

for values 5, 20, 40, leading to an FMR improvement of approximately 1.7 and 26% on the 3DMatch and ETH datasets, respectively (as reported in Nos. 11 and 13).

2. **Receptive Field**. The generalization ability of descriptors is negatively affected by an overly large receptive field or support radius. When the support radius is increased from 0.3 to 1.2, both patch-based and fragment-based networks exhibit a substantial performance decline (as shown in Nos. 1 and 2, Nos. 11 and 12). Several factors may contribute to this degradation: (1) A larger receptive field introduces more occlusions and background clutter, diminishing the uniqueness of the descriptors. (2) Capturing fine-grained structural information over an extensive local region is challenging due to the network's limited expressiveness. (3) An excessive support radius reduces the discriminability between different local surfaces, impairing feature matching accuracy. The detailed network architecture is outlined in Table 2.11, as referenced by the bottom index. In the first and third rows, the learned descriptors in 3D space are visualized using PCA, where the first three principal components are encoded as RGB colors, illustrating results on the ETH and 3DMatch datasets, respectively. The second and fourth rows depict the distance errors between the estimated corresponding points (matched by the source point cloud in feature space) and the ground-truth correspondences on the ETH and 3DMatch datasets, respectively. As shown in Nos. 1 and 2 in Fig. 2.9, expanding the support radius results in smoother feature distributions, which, while enhancing descriptor uniformity, ultimately weakens distinctiveness and matching precision.
3. **Sampling Layers**. The choice of sampling and upsampling strategies significantly impacts the generalization of fragment-based descriptors. From Nos. 1 and 3 of Table 2.11, it is evident that connecting *SSN* directly to *FPS* and *UP* enhances descriptor distinctiveness but compromises generalization. A similar pattern is observed in Nos. 2 and 4. This behavior can be attributed to the upsampling layer *UP*, which, within a hierarchical framework, introduces additional learnable parameters and enlarges the receptive field. As a consequence, the model becomes more prone to overfitting on the 3DMatch dataset, leading to reduced generalization performance.
4. **Network Depth**. Increasing the depth of the fragment-based network tends to hinder its generalization capability. As highlighted in Nos. 1, 5, 9, and 10 of Table 2.11, the performance of descriptors on the unseen ETH dataset deteriorates as network depth increases. This decline is primarily attributed to the additional trainable parameters and enlarged receptive fields introduced by deeper networks, which exacerbate overfitting and degrade generalization ability.

In summary, fragment-based descriptors exhibit superior computational efficiency, being nearly two orders of magnitude faster than patch-based methods, but they generally have poorer generalization performance compared to patch-based descriptors. Here, we identify and investigate several factors that may influence generalization performance. It is worth further exploring strategies to enhance the generalization capabilities of the fragment-based architecture.

Table 2.11 The quantitative results of both patch-based and fragment-based SpinNet

No.	Category	Network configuration	J	K	L	FMR(%)		Time
						3DMatch	ETH	(ms)
1	Fragment-based	$SSN(3, 32, 0.3)$	3	6	3	91.9	52.6	0.035
2	Fragment-based	$SSN(3, 32, 1.2)$	3	6	3	82.1	16.9	0.034
3	Fragment-based	$SSN(3, 32, 0.3) \rightarrow FPS \rightarrow UP(64, 32)$	3	6	3	92.3	43.0	0.037
4	Fragment-based	$SSN(3, 32, 1.2) \rightarrow FPS \rightarrow UP(64, 32)$	3	6	3	86.7	12.5	0.036
5	Fragment-based	$SSN(3, 32, 0.3) \rightarrow FPS \rightarrow SSN(32, 64, 0.3) \rightarrow UP(96, 32)$	3	6	3	96.5	38.3	0.044
6	Fragment-based	$SSN(3, 32, 1.2) \rightarrow FPS \rightarrow SSN(32, 64, 1.2) \rightarrow UP(96, 32)$	3	6	3	85.6	7.38	0.044
7	Fragment-based	$SSN(3, 32, 0.3) \rightarrow FPS \rightarrow SSN(32, 64, 0.3) \rightarrow FPS \rightarrow UP(128, 64) \rightarrow UP(96, 32)$	3	6	3	95.4	35.1	0.046
8	Fragment-based	$SSN(3, 32, 1.2) \rightarrow FPS \rightarrow SSN(32, 64, 1.2) \rightarrow FPS \rightarrow UP(128, 64) \rightarrow UP(96, 32)$	3	6	3	85.6	6.67	0.045
9	Fragment-based	$SSN(3, 32, 0.3) \rightarrow FPS \rightarrow SSN(32, 64, 0.3) \rightarrow FPS \rightarrow SSN(64, 128, 0.6) \rightarrow UP(192, 64) \rightarrow UP(96, 32)$	3	6	3	95.2	5.59	0.049
10	Fragment-based	$SSN(3, 32, 0.3) \rightarrow FPS \rightarrow SSN(32, 64, 0.3) \rightarrow FPS \rightarrow SSN(64, 128, 0.6) \rightarrow FPS \rightarrow SSN(128, 256, 1.2) \rightarrow UP(384, 128) \rightarrow UP(192, 64) \rightarrow UP(96, 32)$	3	6	3	94.1	3.95	0.051
11	Patch-based	$SpinNet(3, 32, 0.3)$	3	6	3	96.1	73.9	0.953
12	Patch-based	$SpinNet(3, 32, 1.2)$	3	6	3	91.2	44.2	0.964
13	Patch-based	$SpinNet(3, 32, 0.3)$	5	20	40	97.8	99.9	1.540
14	Patch-based	$SpinNet(3, 32, 1.2)$	5	20	40	95.8	92.3	1.553

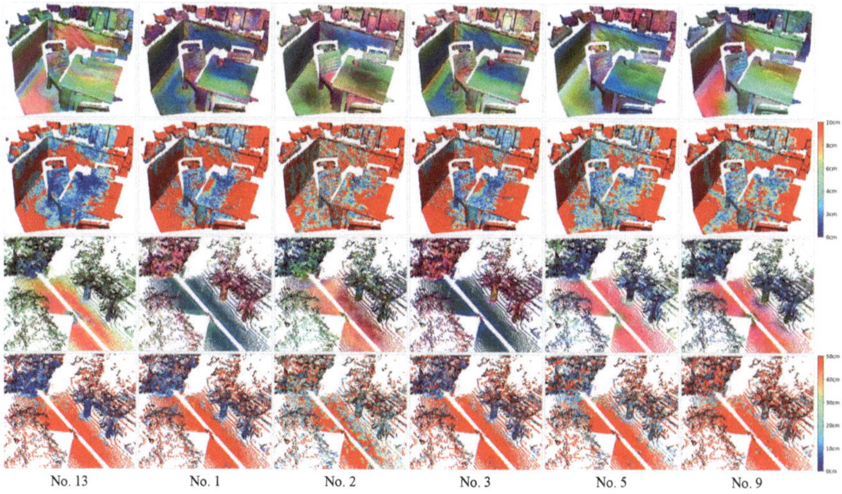

Fig. 2.9 The qualitative results of the proposed patch-based and fragment-based SpinNet models (This figure is reproduced from [2])

2.5 Conclusion and Future Work

In this chapter, we present a novel neural architecture for learning compact representations of intricate local 3D surfaces. Unlike conventional learning-based descriptors that either exhibit sensitivity to rotational transformations or rely on handcrafted features, our approach introduces a Spatial Point Transformer that refines the input local surface into an SO(2)-equivariant representation. To further enhance feature extraction, we design a Neural Feature Extractor that captures both spatial and contextual information from the transformed representation, ultimately producing a rotation-invariant descriptor through end-to-end optimization. Extensive experiments demonstrate that our method not only achieves superior descriptiveness but also exhibits strong generalization to unseen scenarios, surpassing existing approaches.

Future work could explore several promising directions building upon the achievements presented in this thesis. Firstly, extending the proposed representation learning approach to broader application scenarios, such as large-scale urban environments or complex natural landscapes, would greatly enhance its practical value. Furthermore, developing more efficient and scalable algorithms to facilitate real-time processing and analysis of massive point cloud data could bridge the gap between theoretical research and industry requirements. Lastly, integrating our descriptor framework into diverse downstream tasks beyond registration, including semantic segmentation, object recognition, and 3D scene understanding, could broaden its applicability.

References

1. Ao S, Guo Y, Tian J, Tian Y, Li D (2020) A repeatable and robust local reference frame for 3d surface matching. PR
2. Ao S, Hu Q, Yang B, Markham A, Guo Y (2021) SpinNet: learning a general surface descriptor for 3d point cloud registration. In: CVPR
3. Bai X, Luo Z, Zhou L, Fu H, Quan L, Tai CL (2020) D3Feat: joint learning of dense detection and description of 3d local features. In: CVPR
4. Besl PJ, McKay ND (1992) Method for registration of 3-D shapes. In: Sensor fusion IV: control paradigms and data structures
5. Choy C, Gwak J, Savarese S (2019) 4D Spatio-Temporal convnets: Minkowski convolutional neural networks. In: CVPR
6. Choy C, Park J, Koltun V (2019) Fully convolutional geometric features. In: ICCV
7. Chua CS, Jarvis R (1997) Point signatures: a new representation for 3d object recognition. IJCV
8. Cohen TS, Geiger M, Koehler J, Welling M (2018) Spherical CNNs. In: ICLR
9. Dai A, Nießner M, Zollhöfer M, Izadi S, Theobalt C (2017) BundleFusion: real-time globally consistent 3d reconstruction using on-the-fly surface reintegration. TOG
10. Defferrard M, Milani M, Gusset F, Perraudin N (2020) DeepSphere: a graph-based spherical CNN. In: ICLR
11. Deng H, Birdal T, Ilic S (2018) PPF-FoldNet: unsupervised learning of rotation invariant 3d local descriptors. In: ECCV
12. Deng, H., Birdal, T., Ilic, S.: PPFNet: Global Context Aware Local Features for Robust 3D Point Matching. In: CVPR (2018)
13. Du J, Wang R, Cremers D (2020) DH3D: deep hierarchical 3D descriptors for robust large-scale 6DoF relocalization. In: ECCV
14. Esteves C, Xu Y, Allen-Blanchette C, Daniilidis K (2019) Equivariant multi-view networks. In: ICCV
15. Frome A, Huber D, Kolluri R, Bülow T, Malik J (2004) Recognizing objects in range data using regional point descriptors. In: ECCV
16. Geiger A, Lenz P, Urtasun R (2012) Are we ready for autonomous driving? CVPR, The KITTI Vision Benchmark Suite. In
17. Gojcic Z, Zhou C, Wegner JD, Wieser A (2019) The perfect match: 3D point cloud matching with smoothed densities. In: CVPR
18. Graham B, Engelcke M, Van Der Maaten L (2018) 3D semantic segmentation with submanifold sparse convolutional networks. In: CVPR
19. Guo Y, Bennamoun M, Sohel F, Lu M, Wan J (2014) 3D object recognition in cluttered scenes with local surface features: a survey. IEEE TPAMI
20. Guo Y, Bennamoun M, Sohel F, Lu M, Wan J, Kwok NM (2016) A comprehensive performance evaluation of 3D local feature descriptors. IJCV
21. Guo Y, Sohel F, Bennamoun M, Lu M, Wan J (2013) Rotational projection statistics for 3D local surface description and object recognition. IJCV
22. Hu Q, Yang B, Khalid S, Xiao W, Trigoni N, Markham A (2022) SensatUrban: learning semantics from urban-scale photogrammetric point clouds. IJCV
23. Hu Q, Yang B, Xie L, Rosa S, Guo Y, Wang Z, Trigoni N, Markham A (2021) Learning semantic segmentation of large-scale point clouds with random sampling. IEEE TPAMI
24. Huang S, Gojcic Z, Usvyatsov M, Wieser A, Schindler K (2021) PREDATOR: registration of 3D point clouds with low overlap. In: CVPR
25. Johnson AE, Hebert M (1999) Using spin images for efficient object recognition in cluttered 3D scenes. IEEE TPAMI
26. Khoury M, Zhou QY, Koltun V (2017) Learning compact geometric features. In: ICCV
27. Kim VG, Chaudhuri S, Guibas L, Funkhouser T (2014) Shape2pose: human-centric shape analysis. TOG

28. Kingma DP, Ba J (2015) Adam: a method for stochastic optimization. In: ICLR
29. Li H, Hartley R (2007) The 3D-3D registration problem revisited. In: ICCV
30. Li L, Fu H, Ovsjanikov M (2022) UPDesc: unsupervised point descriptor learning for robust registration. IEEE TVCG
31. Li L, Zhu S, Fu H, Tan P, Tai CL (2020) End-to-End learning local multi-view descriptors for 3D point clouds. In: CVPR
32. Mian A, Bennamoun M, Owens R (2010) On the repeatability and quality of keypoints for local feature-based 3D object retrieval from cluttered scenes. IJCV
33. Mian AS, Bennamoun M, Owens R (2006) Three-Dimensional model-based object recognition and segmentation in cluttered scenes. IEEE TPAMI
34. Mishchuk A, Mishkin D, Radenovic F, Matas J (2017) Working hard to know your neighbor's margins: local descriptor learning loss. In: NeurIPS
35. Novatnack J, Nishino K (2008) Scale-Dependent/Invariant local 3D shape descriptors for fully automatic registration of multiple sets of range images. In: ECCV
36. Papazov C, Haddadin S, Parusel S, Krieger K, Burschka D (2012) Rigid 3D geometry matching for grasping of known objects in cluttered scenes. IJRR
37. Petrelli A, Di Stefano L (2011) On the repeatability of the local reference frame for partial shape matching. In: ICCV
38. Poiesi F, Boscaini D (2021) Distinctive 3D local deep descriptors. In: ICPR
39. Poiesi F, Boscaini D (2022) Generalisable and distinctive 3D local deep descriptors for point cloud registration. IEEE TPAMI
40. Pomerleau F, Liu M, Colas F, Siegwart R (2012) Challenging data sets for point cloud registration algorithms. IJRR
41. Qi CR, Yi L, Su H, Guibas LJ (2017) PointNet++: deep hierarchical feature learning on point sets in a metric space. In: NeurIPS
42. Rusu RB, Blodow N, Beetz M (2009) Fast point feature histograms (FPFH) for 3D registration. In: ICRA
43. Rusu RB, Blodow N, Marton ZC, Beetz M (2008) Aligning point cloud views using persistent feature histograms. In: IROS
44. Shotton J, Glocker B, Zach C, Izadi S, Criminisi A, Fitzgibbon A (2013) Scene coordinate regression forests for camera relocalization in RGB-D images. In: CVPR
45. Spezialetti R, Salti S, Stefano LD (2019) Learning an effective equivariant 3D descriptor without supervision. In: ICCV
46. Stein F, Medioni G et al (1992) Structural indexing: efficient 3D object recognition. IEEE TPAMI
47. Thomas H, Qi CR, Deschaud JE, Marcotegui B, Goulette F, Guibas LJ (2019) Kpconv: flexible and deformable convolution for point clouds. In: ICCV
48. Thomas H, Qi CR, Deschaud JE, Marcotegui B, Goulette F, Guibas LJ (2019) KPConv: flexible and deformable convolution for point clouds. In: CVPR
49. Tombari F, Salti S, Di Stefano L (2010) Unique signatures of histograms for local surface description. In: ECCV
50. Valentin J, Dai A, Nießner M, Kohli P, Torr P, Izadi S, Keskin C (2016) Learning to navigate the energy landscape. In: 3DV
51. Wang H, Liu Y, Dong Z, Wang W, Yang B (2021) You only hypothesize once: point cloud registration with rotation-equivariant descriptors. arXiv:2109.00182
52. Xiao J, Owens A, Torralba A (2013) Sun3d: a database of big spaces reconstructed using SfM and object labels. In: ICCV
53. Yang J, Xian K, Wang P, Zhang Y (2019) A performance evaluation of correspondence grouping methods for 3D rigid data matching. IEEE TPAMI
54. Yang J, Xiao Y, Cao Z (2018) Toward the repeatability and robustness of the local reference frame for 3D shape matching: an evaluation. IEEE TIP
55. Yang Q, Li C, Dai W, Zou J, Qi GJ, Xiong H (2020) Rotation equivariant graph convolutional network for spherical image classification. In: CVPR

56. Yang Y, Feng C, Shen Y, Tian D (2018) FoldingNet: point cloud auto-encoder via deep grid deformation. In: CVPR (2018)
57. Yew ZJ, Lee GH (2018) 3DFeat-Net: weakly supervised local 3D features for point cloud registration. In: ECCV
58. You Y, Lou Y, Liu Q, Tai YW, Ma L, Lu C, Wang W (2020) Pointwise rotation-invariant network with adaptive sampling and 3D spherical voxel convolution. In: AAAI
59. Zeng A, Song S, Nießner M, Fisher M, Xiao J, Funkhouser T (2017) 3DMatch: learning local geometric descriptors from RGB-D reconstructions. In: CVPR
60. Zhong Y (2009) Intrinsic shape signatures: a shape descriptor for 3D object recognition. In: ICCVW

Chapter 3
Registration of Point Clouds

A robust point cloud registration framework should simultaneously exhibit high accuracy, computational efficiency, and strong generalizability. Achieving a balanced optimization of these three aspects remains a significant challenge, as existing methods often compromise one or more of these requirements. In this study, we introduce BUFFER, a novel registration approach designed to **b**alance acc**u**racy, e**ff**iciency, and gen**er**alizability. Our strategy leverages the strengths of both point-wise and patch-wise processing techniques while systematically addressing their inherent limitations. Unlike straightforward combinations of existing approaches, each module within our framework is meticulously designed to address specific challenges. Specifically, we propose a Point-wise Learner to enhance computational efficiency through keypoint prediction and to improve feature representation by estimating point orientations. This is complemented by a Patch-wise Embedder that employs a lightweight local feature extractor to generate efficient and generalized patch descriptors. Furthermore, we introduce an Inliers Generator, which integrates simple neural layers with general geometric features to identify reliable inlier correspondences. Comprehensive evaluations on real-world datasets demonstrate that BUFFER achieves an optimal trade-off between accuracy, efficiency, and generalization. Notably, our method attains state-of-the-art success rates on unseen datasets and outperforms competitive baselines by being nearly 30 times faster while maintaining superior performance.

3.1 Introduction

Point cloud registration is fundamental to applications such as LiDAR SLAM [24, 26], 3D reconstruction [45], and robotic navigation [23, 37]. An effective registration framework must not only ensure precise and efficient geometric alignment but also

Y. Guo et al., *Point Cloud Intelligence*, Advances in Computer Vision and Pattern Recognition, https://doi.org/10.1007/978-981-95-0648-4_3

demonstrate robust generalizability to unseen environments captured by various sensors. Nevertheless, achieving an optimal balance between accuracy, efficiency, and generalization remains a significant challenge, largely due to variations in data quality (e.g., noise characteristics, non-uniform point density, diverse viewing angles, and domain discrepancies across different sensors).

Existing registration methods can generally be divided into two categories: correspondences-based approaches [31, 64, 67] and correspondences-free approaches [4, 61, 62]. Correspondences-based methods, which rely on establishing reliable correspondences, often achieve superior registration performance, particularly in large-scale scenarios, compared to their correspondences-free counterparts. However, despite their advantages, these methods face significant limitations in real-world large-scale applications, as they often suffer from insufficient accuracy, low computational efficiency, or poor generalizability.

The limitations of current correspondence-based registration methods can be summarized in two primary aspects. **First**, the absence of a unified, efficient, and general framework for feature learning. Patch-wise methods [22, 67] often utilize complex networks combined with intricate steps to encode fine-grained geometric details of local 3D patches. These methods excel in generalization due to their reliance on localized features, which are inherently robust to occlusion and highly discriminative. However, this comes at the cost of computational efficiency. On the other hand, point-wise methods [6, 27] attempt to enhance efficiency by employing hierarchical architectures [52] to iteratively downsample raw point clouds. While these architectures capture global contextual information, they often fail to preserve local geometric details, leading to homogenized point-wise features that are difficult to match accurately, especially in unseen scenarios [1]. **Second**, there is a lack of efficient and general mechanisms for correspondence search. Many correspondence-based frameworks [1, 53] rely on RANSAC [19] or coarse-to-fine matching strategies [65] to identify reliable correspondences. The efficiency of RANSAC, however, is highly dependent on the proportion of inliers, making it computationally expensive when inlier rates are low. Moreover, coarse-to-fine strategies often struggle to generalize across unseen domains due to their reliance on global context matching.

A few recent studies have explored alternative approaches, such as employing unsupervised domain adaptation techniques [25] or simplifying network architectures [1], to strike a better balance between generalization and efficiency. However, these methods come with trade-offs: domain adaptation techniques typically require additional target datasets for training, while simplified architectures often compromise the representation capacity of the learned models. In general, efficiency and generalization appear to be at odds, as current methods are inherently designed to excel in one area, failing to achieve complementary advantages across both dimensions.

In this chapter, we present BUFFER, a novel registration framework that achieves a harmonious balance between efficiency and generalization by integrating point-wise and patch-wise techniques. Additionally, an efficient and general correspondence search mechanism is proposed to enhance the inlier rate during registration. BUFFER comprises three primary components: a *Point-wise Learner*, a *Patch-wise Embedder*, and an *Inliers Generator*. Initially, the input point clouds are processed by the *Point-wise Learner*, which employs an innovative equivariant fully convolutional architecture to predict point-wise saliencies and orientations. This design reduces computational overhead while improving the representational power of the features. Using the identified keypoints and predicted orientations, the *Patch-wise Embedder* leverages a lightweight patch-based feature learner, Mini-SpinNet [1], to extract efficient and general local features along with cylindrical feature maps. These local features are matched to establish an initial set of correspondences alongside their associated cylindrical feature maps. Subsequently, the general cylindrical feature maps are input into the *Inliers Generator*, which utilizes a lightweight 3D cylindrical convolutional network [1] to estimate a rigid transformation for each correspondence. This process identifies a set of reliable correspondences by optimizing the transformation. Finally, RANSAC [19] refines the transformation, achieving an accurate registration result.

Achieving a satisfactory balance among accuracy, efficiency, and generalizability is far from straightforward when simply merging existing methods. For instance, while the point-wise method PREDATOR [27] struggles to generalize to unseen scenarios, the patch-wise method SpinNet [1] suffers from excessive computational costs. A direct combination of these two approaches results in a framework that is neither efficient nor generalizable. In contrast, the components of BUFFER are meticulously designed to address specific challenges, making it possible to achieve a more optimal balance. The main contributions of this chapter are summarized as follows:

- We introduce a novel point cloud registration framework that seamlessly integrates the strengths of point-wise and patch-wise paradigms, effectively achieving a superior balance among accuracy, efficiency, and generalizability.
- We present an equivariant fully convolutional architecture designed to predict point-wise orientations and saliencies.
- We propose a novel correspondence search strategy aimed at improving the inlier ratio of initial correspondences.

3.2 Related Work

3.2.1 Correspondences-Based Registration

As the name suggests, correspondence-based registration involves first extracting point cloud features, then establishing explicit point correspondences between two scans through feature matching, and finally estimating the rigid transformation. From a feature perspective, existing correspondence-based registration methods can generally be classified into two categories: patch-wise and point-wise approaches.

Patch-wise Methods: This class of techniques employs a weight-sharing network to depict local 3D patches centered on keypoints, thereby producing sparse representations for each segment. The initial work in learned descriptors is 3DMatch, which transforms the input local 3D patch into a voxel format and subsequently applies multiple neural layers to derive deep features. Subsequent studies [15, 22, 38, 43] have incrementally enhanced the descriptiveness of features. Recently, a few works have focused on investigating the generalization capacity of descriptors. Ao et al. introduced a versatile feature descriptor SpinNet [1, 3] by incorporating an ingenious cylindrical representation and a robust neural architecture. A concurrent work, Gedi [49], integrates the quaternion network [54] with PointNet++ [52], attaining commendable generalization ability. Despite the high registration accuracy and strong generalization achieved by patch-wise methods, they are exceedingly time-consuming.

Point-wise Methods: This group of methods processes the entire point cloud in a single forward pass using a hierarchical architecture, resulting in dense descriptions for each fragment. Utilizing Minkowski convolutional neural networks [10] as the backbone network, FCGF [11] was the pioneering work to learn dense feature descriptors for point cloud registration. Subsequently, D3Feat [6], as a representative learning framework, was proposed to predict point-wise 3D keypoints and descriptors. Following this paradigm, several point-wise methods [16, 27] were developed to jointly learn keypoints and feature descriptors. Recently, Yu et al. [65] introduced a coarse-to-fine registration framework, which initially constructs coarse correspondences through superpoint matching and subsequently generates fine correspondences by performing point-wise matching within plausible regions. Notably, this method lacks an explicit detection component. Building on this, Qin et al. [53] incorporated the Geometric Transformer to learn more representative features for robust superpoint matching by encoding intra- and inter-point-cloud geometric patterns. In summary, due to the advantages of the hierarchical architecture, point-wise methods are generally much faster than patch-wise methods, although their drawback is the lower generalization capacity to unseen scenarios.

In addition to efforts at the feature level, several methods have focused on improving registration performance from the correspondence level. RANSAC [19], a classic method, presents the most commonly used hypothesis-verification pipeline for robustly pruning outliers. Recently, deep learning techniques have dominated the field of 3D outlier rejection. A number of works [9, 46] have formulated outlier rejection as an inlier/outlier classification problem, leveraging neural networks to predict the inlier probability of each correspondence. Additionally, several methods [5, 32] have combined traditional techniques such as geometric consistency [8] and Hough voting [56] with deep learning architectures to achieve better outlier removal. However, these methods primarily utilize input point coordinates, neglecting the characteristics underlying local geometry. Our BUFFER considers both global information (spatial coordinates) and local embeddings (cylindrical features), significantly improving the inlier rate.

3.2.2 *Correspondences-Free Registration*

Correspondence-free registration involves directly estimating the rigid transformation between two point cloud fragments, typically implemented via an end-to-end differentiable network. Existing correspondence-free registration methods are generally categorized into two types based on their network architecture: soft correspondences-based and direct regression-based.

Soft Correspondence Based Methods: Despite not relying on explicit correspondences, these methods [20, 39, 40, 60, 63] typically employ soft correspondences between features, followed by a differentiable Singular Value Decomposition (SVD) [47] to estimate the rigid transformation. To obtain accurate soft correspondences, many registration networks integrate well-established techniques, such as Graph Neural Networks (GNN) [18, 44] and Transformers [7, 36], to learn more distinctive features. Although promising results have been reported, these methods still face significant challenges in generalizing to unseen scenarios, particularly those captured by different sensors.

Direct Regression Based Methods: Intuitively, these methods strive to directly regress the rigid transformation without relying on any hard or soft correspondences. PointNetLK [4] is the pioneering effort in direct regression methods, which initially extracts a global feature for each scan using PointNet [51] and subsequently employs a differentiable Lucas-Kanade algorithm [41] to minimize the feature distance, ultimately iteratively aligning the two point clouds. Inspired by this approach, subsequent methods [28, 35, 66] generally adhere to the embedding-regression pipeline, with the primary distinctions residing in the selection of the regression algorithm. These methods are highly efficient since they do not necessitate point-to-point correspondences. However, most of them are primarily suited for object-level registration and struggle to generalize to large-scale scenes.

In summary, current methods demonstrate commendable performance in terms of registration accuracy but have yet to achieve a balance between efficiency and generalization. In this chapter, we address this issue by adeptly combining patch-wise and point-wise networks and devising a novel 3D registration framework. Within this framework, the point-wise component primarily serves to enhance efficiency and facilitate the patch-wise module in extracting generalizable features.

3.3 Efficient Point Cloud Registration: BUFFER

3.3.1 *Preliminaries*

Problem Statement: Consider two partially overlapping point clouds, $\mathcal{P} = \{\boldsymbol{p}_i \in \mathbb{R}^3 \mid i = 1, \ldots, N\}$ and $\mathcal{Q} = \boldsymbol{q}_j \in \mathbb{R}^3 \mid j = 1, \ldots, M$. The aim of point cloud registration is to determine an optimal rigid transformation $\mathbf{T} = \mathbf{R} \in \mathrm{SO}(3), \boldsymbol{t} \in \mathbb{R}^3$

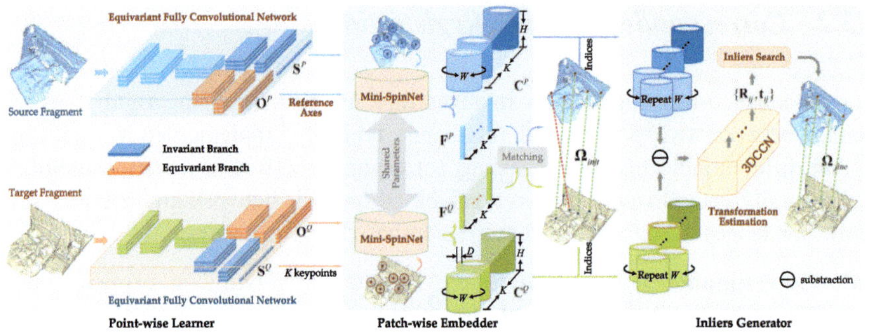

Fig. 3.1 The overall framework of the proposed BUFFER (This figure is reproduced from [2])

that aligns $\mathcal{P}$ with $\mathcal{Q}$. As described in [33], if one-to-one ground-truth correspondences exist between the subsets $\mathcal{P}_c \subset \mathcal{P}$ and $\mathcal{Q}_c \subset \mathcal{Q}$, the registration problem can be reformulated as a minimization problem:

$$\mathcal{L}(\mathcal{P}_c, \mathcal{Q}_c|\mathbf{P}, \mathbf{R}, \boldsymbol{t}) = \frac{1}{N_c} \|\mathcal{Q}_c - \mathbf{R}\mathcal{P}_c\mathbf{P} - \boldsymbol{t}\|^2 . \tag{3.1}$$

In this formulation, N_c denotes the number of accurately matched correspondences, and $\mathbf{P} \in \mathbb{R}^{N_c \times N_c}$ represents the corresponding permutation matrix.

To extract the point subsets $\mathcal{P}_c$ and $\mathcal{Q}_c$, we introduce a novel registration framework, BUFFER, which is composed of three key components: a Point-wise Learner, a Patch-wise Embedder, and an Inliers Generator. The overall pipeline is depicted in Fig. 3.1.

Equivariance: For a specified function $f : X \to Y$ and an associated group G, the function f is deemed equivariant with respect to a group action $g \in G$ if,

$$f(g \circ x) = g \circ f(x), \quad x \in X. \tag{3.2}$$

Vector Neuron: Since our Point-wise Learner incorporates an SO(3)-equivariant operation, namely Vector Neuron (VN) [14], we provide a brief overview of VN to ensure the chapter remains self-contained.

The fundamental principle of VN is to extend a scalar $z \in \mathbb{R}$ into a vector $\boldsymbol{v} \in \mathbb{R}^3$ to ensure SO(3) equivariance. Given a point cloud $\mathcal{P}$, Vector Neuron initially transforms the raw representation $\mathcal{P} \in \mathbb{R}^{N\times3}$ into a set of vector representations $\mathbf{V} \in \mathbb{R}^{N\times C\times3}$, where the simplest scenario is $C = 1$. Next, a linear mapping $f_{lin}(;\mathbf{W})$ is applied to $\mathbf{V}$ to adjust the number of latent channels: $f_{lin}(\mathbf{V};\mathbf{W}) = \mathbf{W}\mathbf{V} \in \mathbb{R}^{N\times C'\times3}$, where $\mathbf{W}$ is the weight matrix $\mathbb{R}^{C'\times C}$. It can be shown that this mapping remains equivariant under any SO(3) rotation $\mathbf{R}$: $f_{lin}(\boldsymbol{r} \circ \mathbf{V};\mathbf{W}) = \mathbf{W}\mathbf{V}\boldsymbol{r}^{\mathrm{T}} = \boldsymbol{r} \circ f_{lin}(\mathbf{V};\mathbf{W})$, where $\boldsymbol{r}$ represents a group action in $\mathbf{R}$.

Furthermore, VN redefines the nonlinear layer $f_{ReLU}(\cdot)$, pooling layer $f_p(\cdot)$, and normalization layer $f_n(\cdot)$. For a comprehensive explanation, we refer readers to [14]. Under this formulation, Eq. 3.4 in the main chapter can be expressed as

$$\boldsymbol{v}_i^{l+1} = \mathbf{VN}(\boldsymbol{v}_j^l; \mathbf{W}) = f_p(f_{ReLU}(f_n(f_{lin}(\boldsymbol{v}_j^l; \mathbf{W})))). \tag{3.3}$$

3.3.2 Point-Wise Learner

The Point-wise Learner aims to identify rotation-invariant keypoints and estimate rotation-equivariant orientations, thereby enhancing both the efficiency and accuracy of registration. As illustrated in Fig. 3.1, it is composed of two main components.

Equivariant Fully Convolutional Network: To extract robust keypoints and point orientations, the initial step involves constructing a backbone network capable of learning dense, rotation-equivariant features. However, existing approaches such as [13, 14] often suffer from excessive spatial and computational complexity or depend on global point coordinates, making them susceptible to translational variations.

In this chapter, we introduce an Equivariant Fully Convolutional Network (EFCN), which is both computationally efficient and inherently invariant to translations. To achieve rotational equivariance and translational invariance, we leverage the following three geometric attributes of the point cloud $\mathcal{P}$:
(1) *relative coordinate*: $\boldsymbol{p}_{ji} = \boldsymbol{p}_j - \boldsymbol{p}_i$,
(2) *neighborhood center*: $\boldsymbol{c}_i = \frac{1}{|N_i|}\sum_{\boldsymbol{p}_j \in N_i} \boldsymbol{p}_{ji}$,
(3) *initial orientation*: $\boldsymbol{n}_i$ is the eigenvector corresponding to the smallest eigenvalue of $\Sigma = \frac{1}{|N_i|}\sum_{\boldsymbol{p}_j \in N_i} \boldsymbol{p}_{ji}^{\mathrm{T}} \boldsymbol{p}_{ji}$.
Here, N_i denotes the set of neighboring points of $\boldsymbol{p}_i$ within a support radius R. Based on this definition, the equivariant convolution operation at point $\boldsymbol{p}_i$ in the l-th layer can be expressed as

$$\boldsymbol{v}_i^{l+1} = \mathbf{VN}(\boldsymbol{v}_j^l; \mathbf{W}), \forall \boldsymbol{p}_j \in N_i, \tag{3.4}$$

where $\boldsymbol{v}_j^0 = [\boldsymbol{p}_{ji}; \boldsymbol{n}_j; \boldsymbol{n}_j \times \boldsymbol{p}_{ji}; \boldsymbol{c}_i]^{\mathrm{T}}$, $\mathbf{W}$ represents a weight matrix, and **VN** refers to the equivariant mapping introduced in [14]. Given that $\boldsymbol{v}_j^0$ remains equivariant under SO(3) rotations and invariant to translations, the entire convolutional network naturally inherits these equivariance and invariance properties.

Definition 3.1 The linear combination of rotation-equivariant mappings preserves rotational equivariance.

Proof Given two rotation-equivariant mappings $\mathcal{M}_1 : X \to Y$ and $\mathcal{M}_2 : X \to H$, along with a group action $\boldsymbol{r}$ in SO(3), the following holds:

$$
\begin{aligned}
\boldsymbol{r} \circ \mathcal{M}_3(x) &= \boldsymbol{r} \circ \big(A\mathcal{M}_1(x) + B\mathcal{M}_2(x)\big) \\
&= A\big(\boldsymbol{r} \circ \mathcal{M}_1(x)\big) + B\big(\boldsymbol{r} \circ \mathcal{M}_2(x)\big) \\
&= A\mathcal{M}_1(\boldsymbol{r} \circ x) + B\mathcal{M}_2(\boldsymbol{r} \circ x) \\
&= \mathcal{M}_3(\boldsymbol{r} \circ x), \quad x \in X,
\end{aligned}
\tag{3.5}
$$

where A and B are linear coefficients. According to Eq. 3.5, it follows that the linear combination of $\mathcal{M}_1$ and $\mathcal{M}_2$ retains rotational equivariance. □

Definition 3.2 The vector representation $\boldsymbol{v}_j^0 = [\boldsymbol{p}_{ji}; \boldsymbol{n}_j; \boldsymbol{n}_j \times \boldsymbol{p}_{ji}; \boldsymbol{c}_i]^{\mathrm{T}}$ exhibits equivariance to the rotation group SO(3) while maintaining invariance to translations.

Proof According to the geometric relationships among points, $\boldsymbol{p}_{ji}$ is naturally equivariant to SO(3) and invariant to translations. Since $\boldsymbol{c}_i$ is derived as a linear combination of $\boldsymbol{p}_{ji}$, it follows from Lemma 1 that $\boldsymbol{c}_i$ inherits these properties.

Given a covariance matrix $\Sigma = \frac{1}{|N_i|}\sum_{\boldsymbol{p}_j \in N_i} \boldsymbol{p}_{ji}^{\mathrm{T}}\boldsymbol{p}_{ji}$, its decomposition via Singular Value Decomposition (SVD) yields $\Sigma = \mathbf{U}\Lambda\mathbf{U}^{\mathrm{T}}$, where Λ is a 3×3 diagonal matrix of singular values, and $\mathbf{U}$ consists of the corresponding 3×3 eigenvectors. For clarity in proof, we define Σ as a mapping $\mathcal{M}_c : \mathbb{R}^{1\times 3} \rightarrow \mathbb{R}^{3\times 3}$. Given a group action $\boldsymbol{r}$ in SO(3), we obtain

$$
\begin{aligned}
\mathcal{M}_c(\boldsymbol{r} \circ \boldsymbol{p}_i) &= \frac{1}{|N_i|}\sum_{\boldsymbol{p}_j \in N_i} (\boldsymbol{r} \circ \boldsymbol{p}_{ji})^{\mathrm{T}}(\boldsymbol{r} \circ \boldsymbol{p}_{ji}) \\
&= \frac{1}{|N_i|}\sum_{\boldsymbol{p}_j \in N_i} (\boldsymbol{p}_{ji}\boldsymbol{r}^{\mathrm{T}})^{\mathrm{T}}(\boldsymbol{p}_{ji}\boldsymbol{r}^{\mathrm{T}}) \\
&= \frac{1}{|N_i|}\sum_{\boldsymbol{p}_j \in N_i} \boldsymbol{r}\boldsymbol{p}_{ji}^{\mathrm{T}}\boldsymbol{p}_{ji}\boldsymbol{r}^{\mathrm{T}} \\
&= \boldsymbol{r}\Sigma\boldsymbol{r}^{\mathrm{T}} = \boldsymbol{r}\mathbf{U}\Lambda\mathbf{U}^{\mathrm{T}}\boldsymbol{r}^{\mathrm{T}}.
\end{aligned}
\tag{3.6}
$$

From the above equation, it is evident that the eigenvector $\boldsymbol{n}_i$ undergoes the same rotation as $\boldsymbol{p}_i$, confirming that $\boldsymbol{n}_i$ remains equivariant to rotations and invariant to translations. Since each component of $\boldsymbol{v}_j^0$ possesses equivariance to SO(3) and translation invariance, it follows that $\boldsymbol{v}_j^0$ as a whole shares these properties. □

Equivariant and Invariant Branches: The subsequent step involves predicting rotation-invariant keypoints and rotation-equivariant orientations. To achieve this, the equivariant features extracted from the final convolutional layer are processed through two distinct decoder branches, generating dense orientations $\mathbf{O}^P$ and saliencies $\mathbf{S}^P$, as depicted in Fig. 3.1. An identical operation is performed on the point cloud Q.

Leveraging the equivariance property preserved across layers, the resulting orientations $\mathbf{O}^P \in \mathbb{R}^{N\times 1\times 3}$ inherently maintain equivariance to SO(3) rotations. In the invariant branch, we apply the same invariant transformation proposed in [14] to

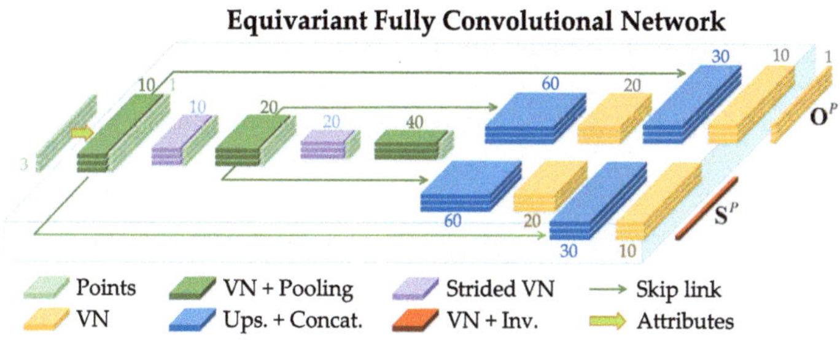

Fig. 3.2 The detailed architecture of the proposed EFCN (This figure is reproduced from [2])

derive an invariant signal $\mathbf{I}^P \in \mathbb{R}^{N \times C \times 3}$. By flattening $\mathbf{I}^P$ and passing it through three MLP layers followed by a Softplus activation function, we obtain the final point-wise saliencies $\mathbf{S}^P \in \mathbb{R}^{N \times 1}$. The K points with the highest saliencies are then selected as keypoints.

Our EFCN is constructed based on the hierarchical framework of KPConv [55]. To facilitate reproducibility, we present the detailed network architecture of EFCN in Fig. 3.2. Here, "Ups. + Concat." represents the nearest upsampling followed by a concatenation, the term "Attributes" refers to extracting three geometric properties for each neighboring point to form $\boldsymbol{v}_j^0 \in \mathbb{R}^{4 \times 3}$. By stacking multiple VN layers, a sequence of equivariant features is progressively learned, ultimately producing the rotation-invariant saliencies $\mathbf{S}^P$ and the rotation-equivariant orientations $\mathbf{O}^P$. Notably, the entire network employs a minimal number of channels and straightforward processing steps for feature extraction, making EFCN both lightweight and computationally efficient.

Additionally, the EFCN is primarily composed of multiple VN layers, sampling/upsampling operations, and feature concatenation. Since the VN layer inherently serves as an equivariant mapping under the rotation group SO(3), and neither sampling/upsampling nor concatenation disrupts the rotational equivariance of features, the entire EFCN remains equivariant to SO(3) transformations.

Compared to existing equivariant networks [17, 29], our EFCN demonstrates higher efficiency and is well-suited for scene-level tasks. Although the hierarchical sampling/upsampling process may introduce minor quantitative errors, the underlying mathematical formulation provides a strong inductive bias, facilitating the network's ability to learn equivariant representations. The same EFCN structure is applied to the point cloud $\boldsymbol{Q}$.

In conclusion, leveraging our EFCN, the Point-wise Learner predicts dense saliencies to extract keypoints that are more likely to be correctly matched, thereby enhancing registration efficiency. Simultaneously, it learns robust point orientations, which further aids the Patch-wise Embedder in extracting highly descriptive features.

Definition 3.3 Given a set of equivariant vector representations $\mathbf{V} \in \mathbb{R}^{N \times C \times 3}$, a corresponding list of reference frames $\mathbf{F} \in \mathbb{R}^{N \times 3 \times 3}$ is computed through multiple VN layers, which define an equivariant mapping $\mathcal{M} : \mathbb{R}^{N\times C\times 3} \rightarrow \mathbb{R}^{N\times 3\times 3}$. The signal $\mathbf{I} = \mathbf{V}\mathbf{F}^{\mathrm{T}} = \mathbf{V}\mathcal{M}(\mathbf{V})^{\mathrm{T}} \in \mathbb{R}^{N\times C\times 3}$ is invariant to arbitrary SO(3) rotations.

Proof Suppose a group action $\boldsymbol{r} \in$ SO(3) operates on **V**, we derive

$$\begin{aligned} \mathbf{I}' &= (\boldsymbol{r} \circ \mathbf{V})\big(\mathcal{M}(\boldsymbol{r} \circ \mathbf{V})\big)^{\mathrm{T}} \\ &= (\mathbf{V}\boldsymbol{r}^{\mathrm{T}})\big(\mathcal{M}(\mathbf{V}\boldsymbol{r}^{\mathrm{T}})\big)^{\mathrm{T}} \\ &= \mathbf{V}\boldsymbol{r}^{\mathrm{T}}\boldsymbol{r}\mathcal{M}(\mathbf{V})^{\mathrm{T}} \\ &= \mathbf{V}\mathbf{F}^{\mathrm{T}} = \mathbf{I}. \end{aligned} \tag{3.7}$$

It is evident that the derived signal **I** remains invariant under arbitrary SO(3) transformations. □

3.3.3 *Patch-Wise Embedder*

This module is designed to extract efficient and generalizable features for the selected keypoints. It comprises two essential components, which are elaborated on below.

Mini-SpinNet: We employ a local feature learner, i.e., SpinNet [1], to extract generalizable features. However, the original SpinNet is computationally expensive and memory-intensive. To mitigate these issues, we propose a lightweight variant, termed Mini-SpinNet, designed to extract compact local patch features efficiently. The detailed architecture of Mini-SpinNet is illustrated in Fig. 3.3, while Table 3.1 outlines the key differences between SpinNet and Mini-SpinNet. Here, N_p denotes the number of sampled points within a local patch, while J, K, and L represent the number of divisions along the radial, elevation, and azimuth dimensions, respectively. Additionally, δ and k_v correspond to the receptive field size and the number of points within each voxel, respectively. The "Time" metric indicates the computational cost required to extract each feature. Notably, Mini-SpinNet encodes the input patch into a 32-dimensional feature descriptor. By optimizing hyperparameters

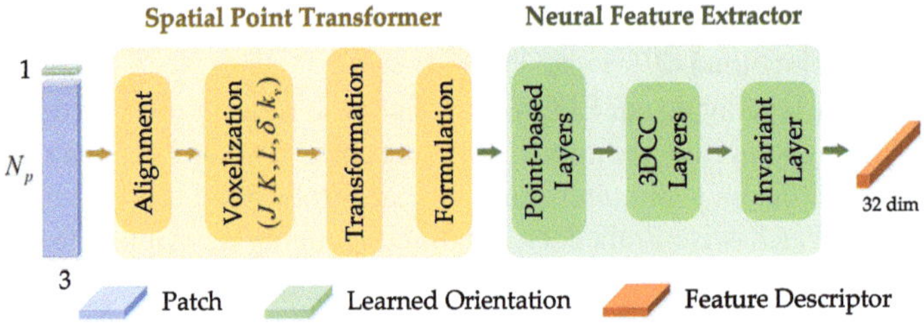

Fig. 3.3 The detailed architecture of the Mini-SpinNet (This figure is reproduced from [2])

Table 3.1 The architecture discrepancies between SpinNet and Mini-SpinNet

Method	Voxelization						3D cylinderical convolutional layers [kernel size, number of filters]	Time (ms)
	N_p	J	K	L	δ	k_v		
SpinNet	2048	5	20	40	0.8	30	$[3 \times 3 \times 3, 32] \rightarrow [3 \times 3 \times 3, 64] \rightarrow [1 \times 3 \times 3, 64] \rightarrow [1 \times 3 \times 3, 128] \rightarrow [1 \times 3 \times 3, 128] \rightarrow [1 \times 3 \times 3, 256] \rightarrow [1 \times 3 \times 3, 256] \rightarrow [1 \times 2 \times 2, 32] \rightarrow [1 \times 2 \times 2, 32] \rightarrow [1 \times 2 \times 2, 32]$	0.75
Mini-S	512	3	7	20	0.8	10	$[3 \times 3 \times 3, 64] \rightarrow [1 \times 3 \times 3, 64] \rightarrow [1 \times 3 \times 3, 128] \rightarrow [1 \times 3 \times 3, 128] \rightarrow [1 \times 3 \times 3, 64] \rightarrow [1 \times 3 \times 3, 64] \rightarrow [1 \times 3 \times 3, 32] \rightarrow [1 \times 3 \times 3, 32]$	0.09

in voxelization and simplifying the 3DCC layers, Mini-SpinNet achieves nearly a $9\times$ speedup compared to the original SpinNet.

Reference Axes: While achieving significant improvements in efficiency, we acknowledge that this lightweight structure inevitably compromises feature discriminability. To mitigate this, we leverage the learned orientations as reference axes—these orientations are more repeatable and robust compared to the handcrafted Z-axes used in the original SpinNet (as demonstrated in Sect. 3.4.4)—allowing for the extraction of more distinctive features.

Ultimately, we obtain a set of general local features $\mathbf{F}^P$ and cylindrical feature maps $\mathbf{C}^P$. By performing feature matching between $\mathbf{F}^P$ and $\mathbf{F}^Q$, we establish a series of initial correspondences Ω_{init}, as illustrated in Fig. 3.1. Overall, our Patch-wise Embedder is not only inherently lightweight and efficient but also capable of learning highly distinctive and generalizable local features for robust feature matching.

3.3.4 *Inlier Generator*

This module aims to refine the initial correspondences by identifying inliers, ultimately improving the overall registration accuracy. As depicted in Fig. 3.1, it consists of two essential components, elaborated as follows.

Transformation Estimation: Here, we approach the inlier search problem from a novel feature-based perspective. Given a set of initial point correspondences Ω_{init}, we extract two cylindrical feature maps $\mathbf{C}_i^P$ and $\mathbf{C}_j^Q \in \mathbb{R}^{H \times W \times D}$ for each correspondence pair $\{\boldsymbol{p}_i, \boldsymbol{q}_j\} \in \Omega_{init}$, where H, W, and D denote the height, width, and feature dimensionality of the cylindrical feature map, respectively. As discussed in

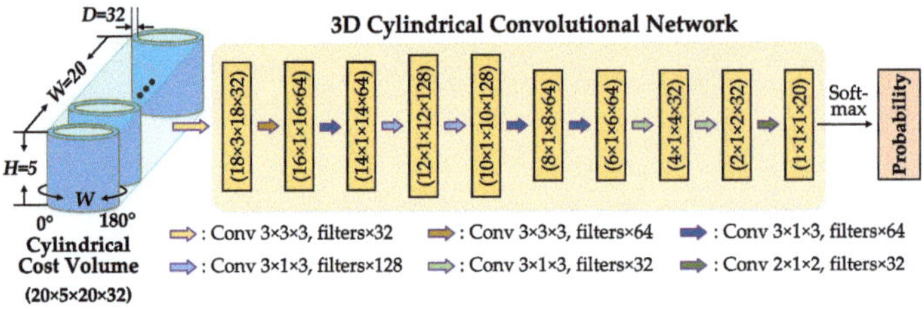

Fig. 3.4 The detailed architecture of the 3DCCN (This figure is reproduced from [2])

Sect. 3.3.3, the local patch centered at keypoint $\boldsymbol{p}_i$ is pre-aligned using a learned orientation with a rotation matrix $\mathbf{R}_i^P$. Consequently, the only remaining transformation between $\mathbf{C}_i^P$ and $\mathbf{C}_j^Q$ is an SO(2) rotation $\mathbf{R}_{ij}^c$. Leveraging this property, our goal is to estimate the SO(2) rotation between the two cylindrical feature maps, thereby recovering the rigid transformation between the corresponding local patches.

Inspired by disparity regression in stereo matching [30], we first construct a 4D matching cost volume $\mathbf{V} \in \mathbb{R}^{H\times W\times W\times D}$ by computing the difference between two cylindrical feature maps across different width values. Notably, the cost volume remains continuous over a full 360° rotation in the cylindrical space. To preserve this property, we employ a lightweight 3D cylindrical convolutional network (3DCCN) [1] for cost aggregation, represented as $C : \mathbb{R}^{H\times W\times W\times D} \rightarrow \mathbb{R}^W$. The detailed architecture of 3DCCN is provided in Fig. 3.4. Unlike the 3DCC layers in Mini-SpinNet, the convolutions in 3DCCN are not required to maintain SO(2) equivariance. This is because the SO(2) rotation estimation has already been reformulated into a permutation problem through the construction of the cylindrical cost volume. Consequently, in our Inliers Generator, the 3DCCN effectively simplifies to a standard 3D convolutional network (3DCNN).

Followed by a softmax operation $\sigma(\cdot)$, the probability distribution over possible offsets is obtained. The predicted offset d is then computed using a soft-argmax operation:

$$d = \sum_{i=1}^{W} i \times \sigma_i(C(\mathbf{V})). \tag{3.8}$$

Accordingly, the SO(2) rotation between two cylindrical feature maps $\mathbf{C}_i^P$, $\mathbf{C}_j^Q$ can be derived by

$$\mathbf{R}_{ij}^c = \begin{bmatrix} \cos(2\pi d/W) & -\sin(2\pi d/W) & 0 \\ \sin(2\pi d/W) & \cos(2\pi d/W) & 0 \\ 0 & 0 & 1 \end{bmatrix}. \tag{3.9}$$

Further, a rotation matrix $\mathbf{R}_{ij} = (\mathbf{R}_j^q)^{\mathrm{T}}\mathbf{R}_{ij}^c\mathbf{R}_i^p$ and a translation vector $\boldsymbol{t}_{ij} = \boldsymbol{q}_j - \boldsymbol{p}_i\mathbf{R}_{ij}^{\mathrm{T}}$ are computed for each correspondence pair $\{\boldsymbol{p}_i, \boldsymbol{q}_j\}$ to facilitate inlier search.

Inlier Search: Since inlier correspondences exhibit similar estimated transformations, identifying them among putative correspondences becomes straightforward.

Specifically, we first determine the best transformation $\hat{\mathbf{T}} = \{\hat{\mathbf{R}}, \hat{\boldsymbol{t}}\}$ by maximizing the number of correspondences that satisfy each transformation.

$$\{\hat{\mathbf{R}}, \hat{\boldsymbol{t}}\} = \underset{\mathbf{R}_{ij}, \boldsymbol{t}_{ij}}{\arg\max} \sum_{\{\boldsymbol{p}, \boldsymbol{q}\} \in \Omega_{init}} \mathbb{1}(\| \boldsymbol{p}\mathbf{R}_{ij}^{\mathrm{T}} + \boldsymbol{t}_{ij} - \boldsymbol{q} \| < \tau), \tag{3.10}$$

where $\mathbb{1}$ is the indicator function, $\|\cdot\|$ denotes the Euclidean distance, and τ denotes an inlier distance threshold. The inlier correspondences are then obtained as follows:

$$\Omega_{fine} = \left\{ \{\boldsymbol{p}_i, \boldsymbol{q}_j\} | \left\| \hat{\mathbf{R}}\boldsymbol{p}_i + \hat{\boldsymbol{t}} - \boldsymbol{q}_j \right\| < \tau \right\}. \tag{3.11}$$

Overall, our Inliers Generator initially utilizes lightweight neural layers and cylindrical features to derive a coarse rigid transformation for each correspondence pair. Subsequently, it identifies reliable correspondences by evaluating the transformation consistency among inliers. Unlike traditional methods that operate directly at the correspondence level, our approach eliminates outliers at the feature level. Therefore, the proposed Inliers Generator is complementary to existing outlier rejection techniques [5, 9, 46] and can be seamlessly integrated with them to further refine the estimated rigid transformation.

3.3.5 Training and Inference

Loss Functions: We optimize the entire model using a loss function $\mathcal{L}$ consisting of four components: $\mathcal{L} = \mathcal{L}_o + \mathcal{L}_f + \mathcal{L}_k + \mathcal{L}_g$. Given a set of ground-truth correspondences $\Omega^* = \{\boldsymbol{p}_i, \boldsymbol{q}_i\}_{i=1...N_c}$ and the ground-truth transformation $\mathbf{T} = \{\mathbf{R}, \boldsymbol{t}\}$, the Point-wise Learner provides the corresponding orientations $\{\boldsymbol{o}_i^p, \boldsymbol{o}_i^q\}$. Inspired by the probabilistic Chamfer loss introduced in [34], we formulate a probabilistic cosine loss $\mathcal{L}_o$ to supervise the learning of orientations:

$$\mathcal{L}_o = \frac{1}{N_c} \sum_{i=1}^{N_c} \left(\ln \epsilon_i + \frac{e_i}{\epsilon_i} \right), \quad e_i = 1 - \cos(\boldsymbol{o}_i^p \mathbf{R}^{\mathrm{T}}, \boldsymbol{o}_i^q). \tag{3.12}$$

Here, N_c denotes the number of ground-truth matched correspondences, and ϵ_i represents a learnable parameter. For feature learning, we adopt the contrastive loss $\mathcal{L}_f$ following D3Feat [6], while keypoint detection is supervised using the detection loss $\mathcal{L}_k$. To train the proposed Inliers Generator, we first determine the ground-truth offset d^* between two cylindrical feature maps and then utilize the L1 loss to supervise transformation estimation:

$$\mathcal{L}_g = \frac{1}{N_c} \sum_{i=1}^{N_c} | \left\| d_i - d_i^* \right\|_1 . \tag{3.13}$$

Hypothesis Generation: The RANSAC [19] algorithm demonstrates high efficiency when applied to correspondences Ω_{fine} that exhibit a significant inlier rate. Within the overall registration pipeline, the computational cost of RANSAC is negligible. As a result, we utilize RANSAC on the point correspondences Ω_{fine} to derive a precise rigid transformation.

3.4 Experiments

This section begins with an evaluation of our BUFFER's registration performance when both the training and testing sets originate from the same domains. Subsequently, a series of extensive experiments are conducted on previously unseen domains to assess the model's generalization capabilities. Finally, we present a set of ablation studies.

3.4.1 *Datasets and Settings*

Datasets: In accordance with [1], we select four datasets: the indoor 3DMatch [67] and 3DLoMatch [27] datasets, along with the outdoor KITTI [21] and ETH [50] datasets, to assess the registration performance of all methods. The primary distinctions between these datasets are illustrated in Table 3.2.

1. **3DMatch dataset**. This dataset comprises a set of RGB-D frames, consisting of 62 real-world indoor scenes. We adhere to the official protocol in [67] for training and testing splits. All fragment pairs in the 3DMatch dataset have overlapping regions exceeding 30%. A total of 35,297 fragment pairs are used for training, while 1,623 fragment pairs are designated for testing.
2. **3DLoMatch dataset**. The 3DLoMatch dataset serves as a more challenging counterpart to the 3DMatch test set. Unlike the 3DMatch test set, which features overlaps of over 30%, the 3DLoMatch dataset consists of fragment pairs with overlaps ranging from 10% to 30%, with a total of 1,781 fragment pairs selected for testing.
3. **KITTI dataset**. This dataset contains 11 sequences of outdoor scans collected using Velodyne-64 3D LiDAR scanners. We follow the same dataset splits and

Table 3.2 Datasets used in the evaluation

Dataset	Acquisition	#Training	#Test	Type	Quality	Scale	Scenario
3DMatch [67]	RGBD camera	35,297	1,623	Real	Dense	Indoor	Room
3DLoMatch [27]	RGBD camera	–	1,781	Real	Dense	Indoor	Room
KITTI [21]	Velodyne-64 LiDAR	1,358	555	Real	Sparse	Outdoor	Urban
ETH [50]	Hokuyo UTM-30LX Laser	–	713	Real	Sparse	Outdoor	Street

preprocessing procedures as described in [11]. Each pair of point cloud fragments is separated by a minimum distance of 10 meters. The dataset includes 1,358 fragment pairs for training, 180 fragment pairs for validation, and 555 fragment pairs for testing.
4. **ETH dataset**. This outdoor street-level dataset was captured using a Hokuyo UTM-30LX laser scanner. It includes four scenes from different seasons, with 713 point cloud fragments featuring overlaps greater than 30% used for testing.

For both the 3DMatch and 3DLoMatch datasets, we employ the Registration Recall (RR) [67] as our evaluation metric. The Registration Recall (RR) is defined as

$$\mathrm{RR} = \frac{1}{H}\sum_{h=1}^{H} \mathbb{1}\left(\sqrt{\frac{1}{N_c}\sum_{(\boldsymbol{p}_i,\boldsymbol{q}_i)\in\boldsymbol{\Omega}^*} \|\hat{\mathbf{R}}\boldsymbol{p}_i+\hat{\boldsymbol{t}}-\boldsymbol{q}_i\|^2} < \tau_r\right), \tag{3.14}$$

where H represents the total number of fragment pairs, $\boldsymbol{\Omega}^* = \{\boldsymbol{p}_i, \boldsymbol{q}_i\}_{i=1...N_c}$ denotes the set of ground-truth point correspondences between $\mathcal{P}$ and $\mathcal{Q}$, and $\hat{\mathbf{T}} = \{\hat{\mathbf{R}}, \hat{\boldsymbol{t}}\}$ is the estimated rigid transformation. The threshold τ_r for the Mean Squared Error (MSE) is set to 0.2 m.

For both the KITTI and ETH datasets, we use Relative Translational Error (RTE), Relative Rotation Error (RRE), and Success rate as evaluation metrics [42]. The RRE is defined as

$$\mathrm{RRE} = \arccos\left(\frac{\mathrm{trace}(\hat{\mathbf{R}}^T\mathbf{R}) - 1}{2}\right)\frac{180}{\pi}, \tag{3.15}$$

Similarly, the RTE is given by

$$\mathrm{RTE} = \left\|\hat{\boldsymbol{t}} - \boldsymbol{t}\right\|. \tag{3.16}$$

Here, $\hat{\mathbf{T}} = \{\hat{\mathbf{R}}, \hat{\boldsymbol{t}}\}$ and $\mathbf{T} = \{\mathbf{R}, \boldsymbol{t}\}$ represent the estimated and ground-truth transformations, respectively. Finally, the Success rate (SR) is computed as

$$\mathrm{SR} = \frac{1}{H}\sum_{h=1}^{H} \mathbb{1}\left(\mathrm{RRE} < \tau_1 \text{ and } \mathrm{RTE} < \tau_2\right). \tag{3.17}$$

For the KITTI dataset, we set $\tau_1 = 1°$ and $\tau_2 = 0.3$ m. For the ETH dataset, τ_1 and τ_2 are set to 2° and 0.3 m, respectively.

Implementation Details: Our BUFFER is implemented using PyTorch. To ensure a fair comparison, we utilize the code and pre-trained models provided by the authors for conducting experiments. All methods are implemented with PyTorch and run on a machine equipped with an Intel Xeon CPU @2.30GHz and an NVIDIA RTX 3090 GPU. Since the PyTorch implementation of D3Feat is not available for the KITTI dataset, we exclude its runtime from the related experiments. For methods such as FCGF, D3Feat, Predator, YOHO, Gedi, and SpinNet, we observe improved registration performance when more keypoints are used. To strike a balance between efficiency and generalization, we follow the guidelines in [1, 6] and select 5000 keypoints for feature matching, employing RANSAC with a maximum of 50,000 iterations to estimate the transformation matrices.

- **Training**. To accelerate convergence, we first pre-train each module and then fine-tune the entire network. Random rotation augmentation is applied to the target point cloud, and matched correspondences are computed using the ground-truth transformation for training. For the Point-wise Learner, we adopt the same hyper-parameters (e.g., voxel size and convolutional radius) as those used in [6]. For the Patch-wise Embedder, the support radius is set as in [1]. The Adam optimizer with default parameters is employed for network training. The initial learning rate is set to 0.001, and we train each module for 10 epochs, reducing the learning rate by half every 2 epochs.
- **Inference**. On the ETH dataset, we use a voxel size of 0.08 m and sample a maximum of 30,000 points from the raw scan. To select keypoints, we first apply a sigmoid function to the predicted point saliencies, keeping those with scores ≥ 0.5. From the remaining points, 1500 keypoints are randomly selected. For datasets with gravity-aligned point clouds, we follow [1] and skip the alignment to a canonical orientation in the Patch-wise Embedder. To search for inlier correspondences, we correlate the inlier distance threshold τ with keypoints $\boldsymbol{p}_i$, where $\tau = \|\boldsymbol{p}_i\| \pi / W$. During the hypothesis generation phase, we apply RANSAC with a maximum of 50,000 iterations, using the default parameters.

3.4.2 Evaluation on Datasets of Same Domains

Results on Indoor 3DMatch Datasets: We evaluate the proposed BUFFER against state-of-the-art methods in terms of registration recall and computational efficiency on both the 3DMatch and 3DLoMatch datasets. As presented in Table 3.3, BUFFER achieves the highest registration recall and exhibits exceptional computational efficiency on the 3DMatch dataset. Thanks to the use of efficient submanifold sparse convolution, FCGF is the fastest method. However, its registration recall is notably the lowest among all methods, being nearly 8% lower than that of BUFFER. On the low-overlap 3DLoMatch dataset, BUFFER delivers comparable performance to the state-of-the-art methods. Notably, BUFFER is the most lightweight method, achieving speeds approximately 35 times faster than the vanilla SpinNet.

Results on Outdoor KITTI Datasets: We compare the proposed BUFFER with strong baseline methods on the KITTI dataset, as summarized in Table 3.4. It is clear that BUFFER outperforms all other methods, achieving the highest success rate while remaining the most lightweight and efficient model. Although FCGF is faster than BUFFER, its registration success rate is significantly lower, by 15.86%. Additionally, it is observed that all methods require more time to register point clouds on the KITTI dataset compared to the 3DMatch dataset. This difference in time consumption is attributed to the larger scale and higher number of sampling points in the outdoor KITTI dataset.

Table 3.3 Results on the 3DMatch and 3DLoMatch datasets

Method	3DMatch		3DLoMatch		#Param
	RR(%)↑	Time(s)↓	RR(%)↑	Time(s)↓	(M)↓
FCGF [11]	85.1	**0.16**	40.1	**0.16**	8.76
D3Feat [6]	81.6	0.40	37.2	0.40	24.30
Predator [27]	90.5	0.54	62.5	0.54	7.43
YOHO [58]	90.8	3.31	65.2	3.30	12.38
Gedi [49]	85.3	6.65	48.7	6.65	3.11
SpinNet [1]	92.4	7.12	71.6	7.11	<u>1.41</u>
GeoTrans [53]	92.5	0.23	**74.0**	0.23	9.83
RoReg [59]	**93.2**	2.67	71.2	2.64	12.71
Ours	<u>92.9</u>	<u>0.20</u>	<u>71.8</u>	<u>0.20</u>	**0.92**

Table 3.4 Results on the KITTI odometry dataset

Method	RTE	RRE	Success	Time	#Param
	(cm)↓	(°)↓	(%)↑	(s)↓	(M)↓
FCGF [11]	13.3	0.31	81.80	**0.18**	8.76
D3Feat [6]	5.55	<u>0.23</u>	97.12	–	14.08
Predator [27]	**5.17**	0.25	96.94	0.69	22.77
SpinNet [1]	5.55	0.24	<u>97.48</u>	14.57	<u>1.41</u>
GeoTrans [53]	7.02	<u>0.23</u>	96.76	0.31	25.50
Ours	<u>5.37</u>	**0.22**	**97.66**	<u>0.30</u>	**0.92**

3.4.3 Generalizing to Unseen Domains

To assess the generalizability of the proposed BUFFER across unseen domains, we perform three sets of experiments based on the framework outlined in [1]: generalization from indoor to outdoor, from outdoor to indoor, and from outdoor to outdoor. In each experiment group, all methods are trained on one dataset and then tested directly on other unseen datasets.

From Indoor 3DMatch to Outdoor ETH and KITTI: The results of generalizing from 3DMatch to ETH and from 3DMatch to KITTI are presented in Table 3.5 and Table 3.6, respectively. Here, ⋄ represents point-wise methods while † denotes patch-wise methods. It is evident that all point-wise methods show low success rates when applied to unseen datasets. This limitation arises mainly because these methods rely on hierarchical network architectures to learn feature descriptors, which hampers generalization [1]. In contrast, patch-wise methods demonstrate excellent generalization capabilities but suffer from significantly higher computational costs, often being an order of magnitude slower than point-wise methods. Our BUFFER, however, effectively combines both approaches, achieving the highest success rate across

Table 3.5 Results of generalization from 3DMatch to ETH

Method	RTE	RRE	Success	Time	#Param
	(cm)↓	(°)↓	(%)↑	(s)↓	(M)↓
FCGF$^\diamond$ [11]	9.98	0.94	61.43	**0.17**	8.76
D3Feat$^\diamond$ [6]	5.54	**0.65**	74.47	0.26	24.30
Predator$^\diamond$ [27]	7.82	0.89	69.00	0.37	7.43
YOHO$^\diamond$ [58]	7.79	1.07	66.90	3.13	12.38
GeoTrans$^\diamond$ [53]	7.97	**0.65**	90.18	0.27	9.83
RoReg$^\diamond$ [59]	7.24	0.99	74.33	2.56	12.71
Gedi† [49]	4.80	0.75	99.24	6.65	3.11
SpinNet† [1]	**3.88**	**0.65**	97.62	7.12	1.41
Ours	5.22	**0.65**	**99.30**	0.26	**0.92**

Table 3.6 Results of generalization from 3DMatch to KITTI

Method	RTE	RRE	Success	Time	#Param
	(cm)↓	(°)↓	(%)↑	(s)↓	(M)↓
FCGF [11]	14.4	0.49	62.52	**0.15**	8.76
D3Feat [6]	12.6	0.46	69.55	-	24.3
Predator [27]	16.5	1.38	46.13	0.48	7.43
GeoTrans [53]	10.2	0.37	88.47	0.29	9.83
Gedi [49]	**5.99**	**0.28**	95.68	6.31	3.11
SpinNet [1]	7.00	0.33	94.59	14.6	1.41
Ours	8.58	0.30	**95.86**	0.28	**0.92**

unseen domains while being far more efficient than patch-wise methods. Although BUFFER slightly lags behind SpinNet in terms of RTE and RRE, this is primarily due to SpinNet utilizing a larger number of sampling points.

From Outdoor KITTI to Indoor 3DMatch: As shown in Table 3.7, point-wise methods such as FCGF, D3Feat, Predator, and GeoTrans perform poorly when generalized to the 3DMatch dataset due to the significant domain gap. Notably, our method outperforms SpinNet by 3.6% in registration recall on the 3DMatch dataset, and the gap widens to 11.7% on the 3DLoMatch dataset. This difference is mainly attributed to SpinNet's ability to generate point correspondences with a lower inlier rate on the low-overlap 3DLoMatch dataset. In contrast, our Inliers Generator significantly boosts the inlier rate, enhancing the registration performance of the entire framework. Remarkably, BUFFER achieves the highest registration recall of 91.2% when generalized directly to the unseen 3DMatch dataset, even surpassing strong baselines such as Predator and YOHO. This highlights the strong generalization capability of BUFFER and its potential for practical applications.

Table 3.7 Results of generalization from KITTI to 3DMatch

Method	3DMatch		3DLoMatch		#Param
	RR(%)↑	Time(s)↓	RR(%)↑	Time(s)↓	(M)↓
FCGF [11]	19.7	**0.16**	2.26	**0.16**	8.76
D3Feat [6]	53.6	–	11.6	–	14.08
Predator [27]	23.2	0.30	3.31	0.30	22.77
GeoTrans [53]	54.4	0.27	13.8	0.27	25.50
SpinNet [1]	87.6	7.12	52.8	7.12	1.41
Ours	**91.2**	0.24	**64.5**	0.24	**0.92**

Table 3.8 Results of generalization from KITTI to ETH

Method	RTE	RRE	Success	Time	#Param
	(cm)↓	(°)↓	(%)↑	(s)↓	(M)↓
FCGF [11]	6.13	0.80	39.55	**0.17**	8.76
D3Feat [6]	4.04	0.60	98.18	–	14.08
Predator [27]	7.88	0.87	71.95	0.38	22.77
GeoTrans [53]	8.01	0.89	93.55	0.27	25.50
SpinNet [1]	**3.63**	0.62	99.44	7.10	1.41
Ours	3.85	**0.57**	**99.86**	0.26	**0.92**

From Outdoor KITTI to Outdoor ETH: The results of generalizing from KITTI to ETH are shown in Table 3.8. Compared to the generalization from 3DMatch to ETH, point-wise methods such as GeoTrans and D3Feat show significant performance improvements in this setting. This can be attributed to the fact that both the KITTI and ETH datasets contain primarily SO(2) rotations, with a smaller domain gap between them. While this experimental setup favors point-wise methods, which are more sensitive to rotations and domain shifts, our BUFFER still achieves the best success rate, demonstrating its robustness and versatility across different domains.

Comprehensive Performance: To provide a clear comparison of the registration performance across different methods, we visualize the results in a "radar chart", as shown in Fig. 3.5. It is evident that BUFFER stands out as the most comprehensive registration method, excelling in accuracy, efficiency, and generalization. The qualitative results for generalization across unseen domains are presented in Fig. 3.6. It is observed that GeoTrans and SpinNet often struggle to align 3D scans, especially in indoor scenarios with many planes or featureless regions like floors and walls. Geometrically symmetric objects, such as indoor desks or outdoor buildings, also contribute to registration failures in GeoTrans and SpinNet. Additionally, the scenes and data distributions in the 3DMatch dataset differ substantially from those in the KITTI dataset. Despite these challenging conditions, BUFFER consistently outperforms other methods, demonstrating its robustness and superior registration capabilities.

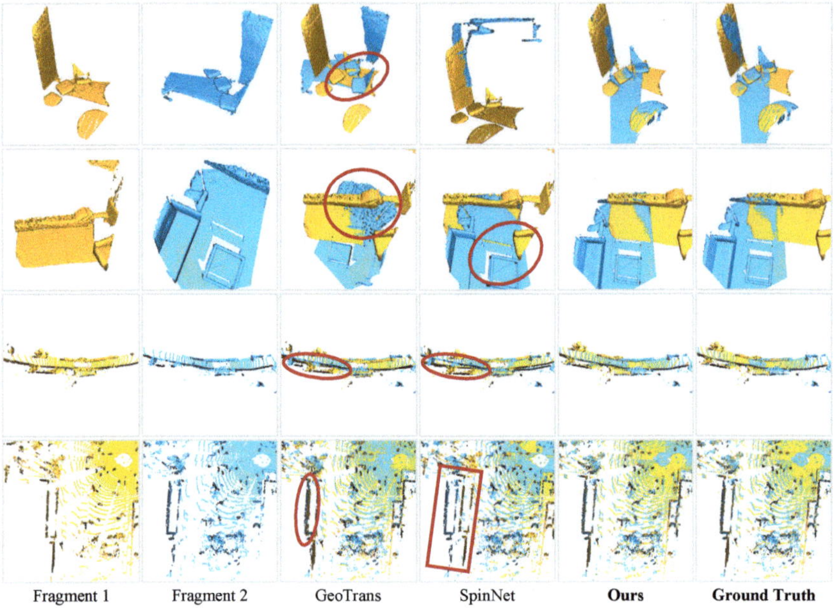

Fig. 3.5 Comparison of the registration accuracy, generalization ability, efficiency, and lightweight of different methods (This figure is reproduced from [2])

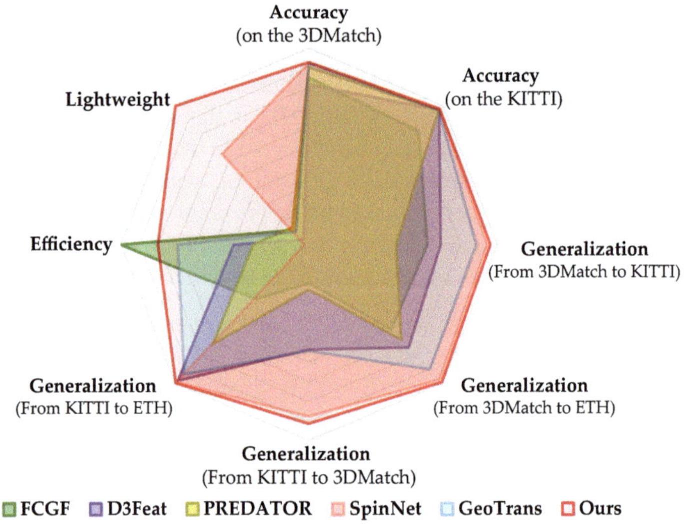

Fig. 3.6 Qualitative results of generalization from outdoor KITTI to indoor 3DMatch and indoor 3DMatch to outdoor KITTI, respectively (This figure is reproduced from [2])

3.4.4 Ablation Studies

To evaluate the effectiveness of the proposed Equivariant Fully Convolutional Network, we perform a series of ablative experiments on the 3DMatch dataset. Subsequently, we conduct comprehensive ablation studies to systematically assess the contribution of each component in our BUFFER framework.

Ablation of Learned Orientation: To assess the impact of various settings on the repeatability of orientation, we conduct three ablation studies as follows:
(1) Replacing the learned orientation with handcrafted methods. In this case, the orientations are computed using traditional handcrafted methods, including normal [12], SHOT [57], FLARE [48], and SpinNet [3].
(2) Replacing the proposed equivariant convolution with KPConv [55]. Here, the model becomes invariant to translations but is no longer equivariant to rotations.
(3) Replacing the proposed equivariant convolution with vector neuron (VN) [14]. In this setting, the model is equivariant to rotations but not invariant to translations.

Figure 3.7 presents the quantitative results of orientation errors for all ablated models on the 3DMatch dataset, where the errors denote the deviation angles of estimated orientations between the ground-truth point pairs. The following observations can be made: (1) Our method outperforms handcrafted techniques in terms of repeatability and robustness for real-world point clouds. This is because the proposed EFCN can learn robust deep equivariant features, whereas handcrafted methods rely solely on low-level geometry. 2) If the neural network is not equivariant to rotations or invariant to translations, it is hopeless to estimate repeatable and robust orientations. This is reasonable because the network can only memorize orientations brutely, which undoubtedly fails for new data. We can also find that the proposed EFCN is significant for equivariant feature learning and orientation estimation, and has great potential to be extended to more tasks.

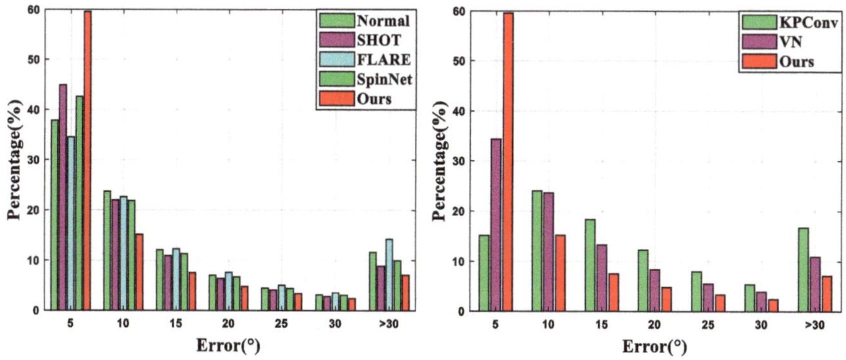

(a) Comparisons with handcrafted methods (b) Comparisons with learned methods

Fig. 3.7 Histogram of the orientation repeatability on the 3DMatch dataset (This figure is reproduced from [2])

Table 3.9 Quantitative results of combining point-wise detector with the patch-wise descriptor

Method	3DMatch		Generalized to ETH	
	RR(%)↑	Time(s)↓	Success(%)↑	Time(s)↓
SpinNet	92.4	7.12	97.62	7.12
USIP [34]+SpinNet	85.4	0.90	77.42	0.78
D3Feat+SpinNet	91.6	2.28	90.18	2.40
PREDATOR+SpinNet	**93.0**	2.56	93.69	2.51
Ours	92.9	**0.20**	**99.30**	**0.26**

Additionally, we combine a patch-wise descriptor with three point-wise detectors and conduct a series of comparative experiments to test the accuracy, efficiency, and generalizability of these methods. The quantitative results are shown in Table 3.9. It is found that the combination of detector and descriptor can achieve encouraging registration accuracy with fewer keypoints. This is primarily because the detected keypoints are more likely to be correctly matched. However, the simple combinations between detector and descriptor still suffer from low efficiency and inferior generalizability, which are difficult to meet practical requirements.

Ablation on Outlier Rejection: As discussed in the main chapter, our BUFFER framework is compatible with existing outlier rejection techniques and can be integrated with them to accurately estimate the rigid transformation. To explore the impact of different outlier rejection modules on BUFFER, we perform two sets of experiments. The quantitative results are presented in Table 3.10. We observe that the traditional RANSAC method achieves better accuracy and efficiency compared to the learned method, PointDSC. This suggests that RANSAC is particularly effective when the point correspondences have a high inlier rate. However, when applied to unseen domains, PointDSC marginally outperforms RANSAC. This indicates that while RANSAC is highly effective in many cases, there is potential for further improvement in BUFFER when combined with a more advanced outlier rejection technique.

Ablation of BUFFER Framework: The BUFFER framework integrates three critical components: learned orientation (LO), predicted keypoint (PK), and inliers generator (IG). To assess the contribution of each module, we conduct six ablation studies to evaluate the effectiveness of each component. Specifically, all ablated models are trained on the 3DMatch dataset and subsequently tested on the 3DMatch, 3DLoMatch, and ETH datasets.

Table 3.10 Quantitative results of our BUFFER with different outlier rejection methods

Method	3DMatch		Generalized to ETH	
	RR(%)↑	Time(s)↓	Success(%)↑	Time(s)↓
With RANSAC [19]	**92.9**	**0.20**	99.30	**0.26**
With PointDSC [5]	92.2	0.23	**99.58**	0.30

Table 3.11 presents the quantitative results of all ablated networks. The observations are as follows: (1) The baseline (Mini-SpinNet [1]), which does not include any of the proposed components, achieves the lowest registration recall on both the indoor 3DMatch and 3DLoMatch datasets, along with the worst generalization performance on the outdoor ETH dataset. (2) Utilizing either the learned orientation (LO) or predicted keypoint (PK) (Nos. 2 and 3) enhances both registration accuracy and generalization capability. When both LO and PK are incorporated (No. 4), the model significantly outperforms the baseline, achieving a 2.9% improvement in recall on the 3DLoMatch dataset and a 5.19% higher success rate on the ETH dataset. This demonstrates that the Point-wise Learner not only improves registration accuracy but also contributes to the model's generalization ability. (3) Even when only

Table 3.11 The quantitative results of all ablated models

No.	LO	PK	IG	3DMatch	3DLoMatch	Generalized to ETH
				RR(%)↑	RR(%)↑	Success(%)↑
1	✗	✗	✗	89.9	66.4	90.74
2	✓	✗	✗	90.1	67.8	93.69
3	✗	✓	✗	90.6	68.9	94.95
4	✓	✓	✗	90.9	69.3	95.93
5	✗	✗	✓	90.9	70.7	97.05
6	✓	✓	✓	**92.9**	**71.8**	**98.88**

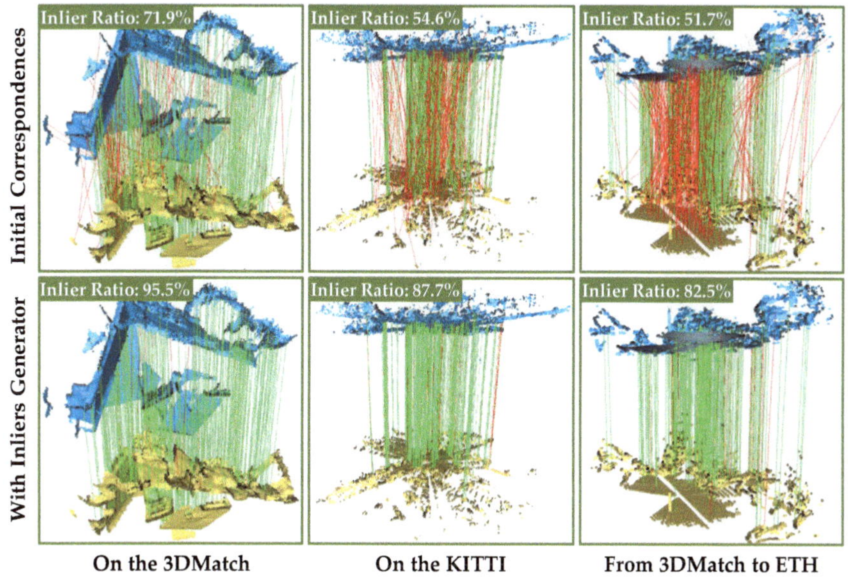

Fig. 3.8 Qualitative results of the ablated model (This figure is reproduced from [2])

the inliers generator (IG) is used (No. 5), the registration performance is notably improved. This is because the IG effectively removes many outliers from the initial correspondences (as shown in the qualitative results in Fig. 3.8), which simplifies the pose estimation during the hypothesis generation stage.

3.5 Conclusion and Future Work

In this chapter, we introduced BUFFER, a novel deep learning framework for point cloud registration. BUFFER combines an efficient feature learning architecture with a robust correspondence search mechanism. Extensive experiments demonstrate that our method strikes the best balance between accuracy, efficiency, and generalization, outperforming state-of-the-art methods by a substantial margin. Future research could focus on further enhancing the BUFFER framework by incorporating advanced overlap estimation techniques. Additionally, exploring improved outlier rejection methods could further increase the robustness of the registration process. Finally, extending the framework to handle dynamic point cloud data could lead to more versatile applications in fields such as robotics, autonomous navigation, and environmental monitoring.

References

1. Ao S, Guo Y, Hu Q, Yang B, Markham A, Chen Z (2022) You only train once: learning general and distinctive 3D local descriptors. IEEE TPAMI
2. Ao S, Hu Q, Wang H, Xu K, Guo Y (2023) BUFFER: balancing accuracy, efficiency, and generalizability in point cloud registration. In: CVPR, pp 1255–1264 (2023)
3. Ao S, Hu Q, Yang B, Markham A, Guo Y (2021) SpinNet: learning a general surface descriptor for 3D point cloud registration. In: CVPR
4. Aoki Y, Goforth H, Srivatsan RA, Lucey S (2019) PointNetLK: robust and efficient point clou registration using PointNet. In: CVPR
5. Bai X, Luo Z, Zhou L, Chen H, Li L, Hu Z, Fu H, Tai CL (2021) PointDSC: robust point cloud registration using deep spatial consistency. In: CVPR
6. Bai X, Luo Z, Zhou L, Fu H, Quan L, Tai CL (2020) D3Feat: joint learning of dense detection and description of 3d local features. In: CVPR
7. Cao AQ, Puy G, Boulch A, Marlet R (2021) PCAM: product of cross-attention matrices for rigid registration of point clouds. In: ICCV
8. Chen H, Bhanu B (2007) 3D free-form object recognition in range images using local surface patches. PRL (2007)
9. Choy C, Dong W, Koltun V (2020) Deep global registration. In: CVPR
10. Choy C, Gwak J, Savarese S (2019) 4D Spatio-Temporal convnets: minkowski convolutional neural networks. In: CVPR
11. Choy C, Park J, Koltun V (2019) Fully convolutional geometric features. In: ICCV (2019)
12. Chua CS, Jarvis R (1997) Point signatures: a new representation for 3d object recognition. IJCV
13. Cohen TS, Geiger M, Koehler J, Welling M (2018) Spherical CNNs. In: ICLR

14. Deng C, Litany O, Duan Y, Poulenard A, Tagliasacchi A, Guibas LJ (2021) Vector neurons: a general framework for SO(3)-equivariant networks. In: CVPR (2021)
15. Deng H, Birdal T, Ilic S (2018) PPFNet: global context aware local features for robust 3d point matching. In: CVPR
16. Du J, Wang R, Cremers D (2020) DH3D: deep hierarchical 3d descriptors for robust large-scale 6DoF relocalization. In: ECCV
17. Esteves C, Xu Y, Allen-Blanchette C, Daniilidis K (2019) Equivariant multi-view networks. In: ICCV
18. Fischer K, Simon M, Olsner F, Milz S, Gross HM, Mader P (2021) StickyPillars: robust and efficient feature matching on point clouds using graph neural networks. In: CVPR
19. Fischler MA, Bolles RC (1981) Random sample consensus: a paradigm for model fitting with applications to image analysis and automated cartography. COMMUN ACM
20. Fu K, Liu S, Luo X, Wang M (2021) Robust point cloud registration framework based on deep graph matching. In: CVPR
21. Geiger A, Lenz P, Urtasun R (2012) Are we ready for autonomous driving? In: The KITTI Vision Benchmark Suite, CVPR
22. Gojcic Z, Zhou C, Wegner JD, Wieser A (2019) The perfect match: 3d point cloud matching with smoothed densities. In: CVPR
23. Guo Y, Bennamoun M, Sohel F, Lu M, Wan J (2014) 3D object recognition in cluttered scenes with local surface features: a Survey. IEEE TPAMI
24. Guo Y, Wang H, Hu Q, Liu H, Liu L, Bennamoun M (2020) Deep learning for 3d point clouds: a survey. IEEE TPAMI
25. Horache S, Deschaud JE, Goulette F (2021) 3D point cloud registration with multi-scale architecture and self-supervised fine-tuning. In: 3DV
26. Hu Q, Yang B, Xie L, Rosa S, Guo Y, Wang Z, Trigoni N, Markham A (2020) RandLA-Net: efficient semantic segmentation of large-scale point clouds. In: CVPR
27. Huang S, Gojcic Z, Usvyatsov M, Wieser A, Schindler K (2021) PREDATOR: registration of 3d point clouds with low overlap. In: CVPR
28. Huang X, Mei G, Zhang J (2020) Feature-metric registration: a fast semi-supervised approach for robust point cloud registration without correspondences. In: CVPR
29. Jing B, Eismann S, Suriana P, Townshend RJ, Dror R (2020) Learning from protein structure with geometric vector perceptrons. ICLR
30. Kendall A, Martirosyan H, Dasgupta S, Henry P, Kennedy R, Bachrach A, Bry A (2017) End-to-end learning of geometry and context for deep stereo regression. In: ICCV
31. Khoury M, Zhou QY, Koltun V (2017) Learning compact geometric features. In: ICCV (2017)
32. Lee J, Kim S, Cho M, Park J (2021) Deep Hough Voting for Robust Global Registration. In: ICCV
33. Li H, Hartley R (2007) The 3D-3D registration problem revisited. In: ICCV
34. Li J, Lee GH (2019) USIP: unsupervised stable interest point detection from 3d point clouds. In: ICCV
35. Li X, Pontes JK, Lucey S (2021) PointNetLK revisited. In: CVPR
36. Li Y, Harada T (2022) Lepard: learning partial point cloud matching in rigid and deformable scenes. In: CVPR
37. Liu MY, Tuzel O, Veeraraghavan A, Taguchi Y, Marks TK, Chellappa R (2012) Fast object localization and pose estimation in heavy clutter for robotic bin picking. IJRR
38. Lu F, Chen G, Liu Y, Qu Z, Knoll A (2020) RSKDD-Net: random sample-based keypoint detector and descriptor. In: NeurIPS
39. Lu F, Chen G, Liu Y, Zhang L, Qu S, Liu S, Gu R (2021) HRegNet: a hierarchical network for large-scale outdoor LiDAR point cloud registration. In: ICCV
40. Lu W, Wan G, Zhou Y, Fu X, Yuan P, Song S (2019) DeepVCP: an end-to-end deep neural network for point cloud registration. In: ICCV
41. Lucas BD, Kanade T et al (1981) An iterative image registration technique with an application to stereo vision. In: DARPA Image Understanding Workshop

42. Ma Y, Guo Y, Zhao J, Lu M, Zhang J, Wan J (2016) Fast and accurate registration of structured point clouds with small overlaps. In: CVPRW
43. Marcon M, Spezialetti R, Salti S, Stefano LD (2021) Unsupervised learning of local equivariant descriptors for point clouds. IEEE TPAMI (2021)
44. Min T, Song C, Kim E, Shim I (2021) Distinctiveness oriented positional equilibrium for point cloud registration. In: ICCV
45. Musialski P, Wonka P, Aliaga DG, Wimmer M, Van Gool L, Purgathofer W (2013) A survey of urban reconstruction. CGF
46. Pais GD, Ramalingam S, Govindu VM, Nascimento JC, Chellappa R, Miraldo P.: 3DRegNet: a deep neural network for 3d point registration. In: CVPR (2020)
47. Paszke A, Gross S, Chintala S, Chanan G, Yang E, DeVito Z, Lin Z, Desmaison A, Antiga L, Lerer A (2017) Automatic differentiation in pytorch. In: NeurIPS
48. Petrelli A, Di Stefano L (2011) On the repeatability of the local reference frame for partial shape matching. In: ICCV
49. Poiesi F, Boscaini D (2022) Learning general and distinctive 3d local deep descriptors for point cloud registration. IEEE TPAMI
50. Pomerleau F, Liu M, Colas F, Siegwart R (2012) Challenging data sets for point cloud registration algorithms. IJRR
51. Qi CR, Su H, Mo K, Guibas LJ (2017) Deep learning on point sets for 3d classification and segmentation. In: CVPR
52. Qi CR, Yi L, Su H, Guibas LJ (2017) PointNet++: deep hierarchical feature learning on point sets in a metric space. In: NeurIPS
53. Qin Z, Yu H, Wang C, Guo Y, Peng Y, Xu K (2022) Geometric transformer for fast and robust point cloud registration. In: CVPR
54. Sarode V, Li X, Goforth H, Aoki Y, Srivatsan RA, Lucey S, Choset H (2019) PCRNet: point cloud registration network using pointnet encoding. arXiv:1908.07906
55. Thomas H, Qi CR, Deschaud JE, Marcotegui B, Goulette F, Guibas LJ (2019) Kpconv: flexible and deformable convolution for point clouds. In: ICCV
56. Tombari F, Di Stefano L (2010) Object recognition in 3d scenes with occlusions and clutter by hough voting. In: PSIVT
57. Tombari F, Salti S, Di Stefano L (2010) Unique signatures of histograms for local surface description. In: ECCV
58. Wang H, Liu Y, Dong Z, Wang W, Yang B (2022) You only hypothesize once: point cloud registration with rotation-equivariant descriptors. In: ACM MM
59. Wang H, Liu Y, Hu Q, Wang B, Chen J, Dong Z, Guo Y, Wang W, Yang B (2023) RoReg: pairwise point cloud registration with oriented descriptors and local rotations. TPAMI
60. Wang Y, Solomon JM (2019) Deep closest point: learning representations for point cloud registration. In: ICCV
61. Xu H, Liu S, Wang G, Liu G, Zeng B (2021) OMNet: learning overlapping mask for partial-to-partial point cloud registration. In: ICCV
62. Xu H, Ye N, Liu S, Liu G, Zeng B (2022) FINet: dual branches feature interaction for partial-to-partial point cloud registration. In: AAAI
63. Yew ZJ, Lee GH (2020) RPM-Net: robust point matching using learned features. In: CVPR
64. Yew ZJ, Lee GH (2022) REGTR: end-to-end point cloud correspondences with transformers. In: CVPR (2022)
65. Yu H, Li F, Saleh M, Busam B, Ilic S (2021) CoFiNet: reliable coarse-to-fine correspondences for robust point cloud registration. In: NeurIPS
66. Yuan W, Eckart B, Kim K, Jampani V, Fox D, Kautz J (2020) DeepGMR: learning latent gaussian mixture models for registration. In: ECCV
67. Zeng A, Song S, Nießner M, Fisher M, Xiao J, Funkhouser T (2017) 3DMatch: learning local geometric descriptors from RGB-D reconstructions. In: CVPR

Chapter 4
3D Object Detection in Point Clouds

The detection of objects in 3D LiDAR point clouds presents unique challenges in computer vision, particularly when balancing computational efficiency with detection accuracy. This chapter introduces an innovative approach to this challenge through IA-SSD, a highly efficient single-stage point-based 3D detector. At its core, IA-SSD addresses a fundamental observation in point cloud processing: not all points carry equal importance for object detection. The method introduces two learnable, task-oriented, instance-aware downsampling strategies that specifically target and preserve foreground points belonging to objects of interest. This selective approach is complemented by a contextual centroid perception module that enhances the precision of instance center estimation. Built on an encoder-only architecture, IA-SSD achieves remarkable efficiency while maintaining competitive detection performance. Experimental results across multiple large-scale detection benchmarks demonstrate the method's effectiveness, achieving processing speeds exceeding 80 frames per second on the KITTI dataset using a single RTX2080Ti GPU, while maintaining low memory requirements.

4.1 Introduction

Three-dimensional object detection represents a cornerstone challenge in computer vision, with applications ranging from autonomous driving to robotic navigation [9]. Among various 3D data representations, point clouds have emerged as a particularly promising format due to their ability to capture spatial information directly and efficiently. However, detecting objects in LiDAR point clouds presents unique challenges that extend beyond traditional computer vision problems. The task requires predicting 3D bounding boxes with seven degrees of freedom—encompassing 3D location, size, orientation, and class labels—while contending with complex geometric structures and non-uniform point density distributions. The evolution of point cloud processing approaches has followed several distinct paths. Early methods focused

Y. Guo et al., *Point Cloud Intelligence*, Advances in Computer Vision and Pattern Recognition, https://doi.org/10.1007/978-981-95-0648-4_4

on converting raw point clouds into more manageable formats, either through projection onto 2D images [1, 16, 17, 38, 39, 46, 57] or transformation into 3D voxel grids [45, 58]. While these approaches enabled the adaptation of established 2D detection frameworks to 3D scenarios, they introduced inherent limitations through quantization errors and information loss during the conversion process. An alternative approach emerged with point-based methods that operate directly on raw point clouds [11, 12, 14, 35, 37, 44, 48]. These methods leverage point-wise feature learning and symmetric aggregation functions, building upon foundational work like PointNet [28, 29]. While this direct approach preserves spatial information more faithfully, it often struggles with computational efficiency and memory requirements. This chapter introduces IA-SSD, a novel framework that addresses the core inefficiencies in existing point-based detection systems. Our analysis reveals that current sampling strategies often discard critical foreground points before the final bounding box regression step, fundamentally limiting detection performance, especially for smaller objects like pedestrians. We propose that the key to improving efficiency lies in recognizing that not all points carry equal weight in object detection tasks—specifically, foreground points demand priority attention. To implement this insight, we develop a task-oriented, instance-aware downsampling framework that explicitly preserves foreground points while reducing computational overhead. The framework incorporates two specialized sampling strategies—class-aware and centroid-aware sampling—complemented by a contextual instance centroid perception module that leverages surrounding context for improved center point regression. Built on a bottom-up single-stage architecture, as shown in Fig. 4.1, IA-SSD achieves remarkable efficiency, processing up to 100 frames simultaneously with speeds of 83 FPS on a single RTX 2080Ti GPU while maintaining high detection accuracy on the KITTI benchmark [7]. The key contributions presented in this chapter include

- A novel approach to point cloud sampling that recognizes and addresses the sampling inefficiencies in existing point-based detectors through two learning-based instance-aware downsampling strategies.
- Development of an efficient point-based 3D detector capable of processing multiple object classes simultaneously, supported by comprehensive analysis of memory usage and inference speed.
- Extensive experimental validation across multiple large-scale datasets, demonstrating both superior efficiency and detection accuracy.

4.2 Related Works

The field of 3D object detection has evolved along several parallel paths, each offering distinct advantages and facing unique challenges. This section examines three main approaches that have shaped the field: voxel-based methods, point-based methods, and hybrid point-voxel techniques. Understanding these approaches provides essential context for the development of more efficient detection systems.

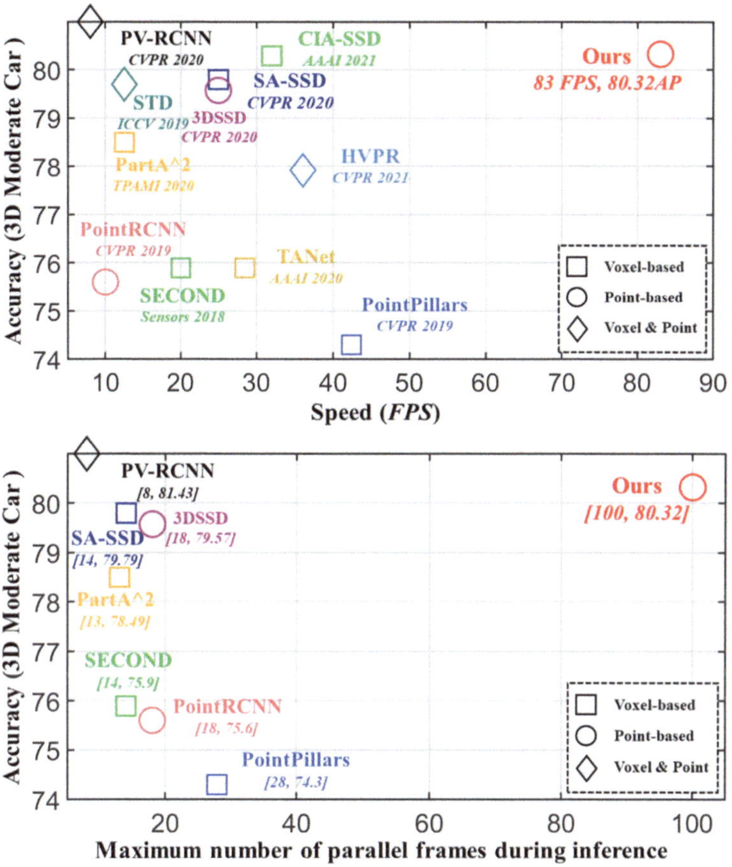

Fig. 4.1 Performance analysis of detection methods on the KITTI benchmark (This figure is reproduced from [53])

4.2.1 Voxel-Based Detection Methods

Voxel-based detection represents one of the earliest approaches to processing 3D point clouds, addressing the inherent challenge of unstructured data by converting point clouds into regular voxel grids. This transformation enables the application of conventional convolutional neural architectures, providing a bridge between 2D and 3D detection paradigms. Early implementations, such as the work by Wang et al. [42], employed dense voxelization followed by convolutional neural networks to identify geometric patterns. However, this approach faced significant computational challenges, as processing requirements increased cubically with input resolution. A breakthrough came with SECOND [45], which introduced 3D submanifold sparse convolution [8] to significantly reduce computational overhead by focusing only on non-empty voxels. PointPillars [17] further simplified this approach by reducing voxelization to the planar dimension, creating pillar-like structures. Contemporary voxel-based detectors typically follow either single-stage [6, 10, 50, 51, 54, 55] or two-stage [3, 33–36, 49] architectures. Single-stage detectors prioritize efficiency but often struggle with detection accuracy, particularly for small objects with sparse point representation. Recent works have addressed this limitation through various innovations: SA-SSD [10] incorporates auxiliary networks to leverage structural information, HVNet [50] implements attentive multi-scale feature aggregation, and CIA-SSD [55] focuses on spatial-semantic feature extraction. Two-stage detectors generally achieve superior detection performance at the cost of increased computational demands. Notable examples include Part-A^2 [36], which employs part-aware and aggregation modules to analyze intra-object part locations, and advanced implementations of PV-RCNN [4] that incorporate fully convolutional networks for simultaneous raw point cloud processing and refinement. While voxel-based methods have demonstrated impressive efficiency and detection capabilities, they face an inherent trade-off between resolution and information loss. Efforts to mitigate structural distortion often require complex architectural additions [19, 22, 24, 25, 32], which can significantly impact detection efficiency. Moreover, determining optimal voxel resolution remains challenging, particularly when dealing with objects of varying scales and geometric complexity.

4.2.2 Point-Based Detection Methods

Point-based detection methods take a fundamentally different approach by operating directly on raw point clouds [27, 35, 48]. These methods typically employ PointNet [28] and its variants [20, 29, 30, 41, 43] to process unordered point sets through point-wise feature learning and symmetric aggregation functions. The development of point-based methods has seen several significant innovations. PointRCNN [35] introduced a two-stage framework that first generates object proposals from segmented foreground points before refining 3D bounding boxes using semantic features and local spatial information. VoteNet [27] pioneered a single-stage approach based on deep Hough voting for instance centroid prediction. 3DSSD [48] advanced the field with a fusion sampling strategy that combines feature-based and Euclidean-space farthest point sampling. PointGNN [37] demonstrated the potential of graph neural networks in 3D object detection. While point-based methods offer the advantage of preserving complete spatial information without preprocessing artifacts, they often struggle with computational efficiency and feature learning capacity. These limitations have motivated the development of hybrid approaches that combine the strengths of both point and voxel-based methods.

4.2.3 Hybrid Point-Voxel Methods

Hybrid point-voxel methods have emerged as an attempt to balance the advantages and limitations of both point-based and voxel-based approaches. These methods aim to preserve the geometric fidelity of point-based processing while leveraging the computational efficiency of voxel representations [2, 15, 33, 34, 49]. PV-RCNN [33] and its subsequent iterations [34] exemplify this hybrid approach by combining voxel-based feature extraction with point-wise feature refinement. HVPR [26] introduces an efficient memory module for point-based feature augmentation, offering an effective balance between accuracy and computational efficiency. BANet [31] employs lightweight region aggregation through local neighborhood graph construction to enhance boundary prediction accuracy. Each detection paradigm offers distinct advantages while facing specific challenges. Voxel-based methods excel in efficiency but struggle with information loss, point-based methods preserve geometric detail but face computational challenges, and hybrid approaches attempt to balance these trade-offs. Our work builds upon these foundations while introducing novel solutions to address their limitations, particularly in the context of efficient point-based detection.

Our proposed IA-SSD builds upon these foundations while introducing two key innovations: instance-aware sampling strategy and contextual centroid perception. These additions address fundamental limitations in existing point-based approaches, enabling both higher accuracy and improved efficiency, as detailed in subsequent sections.

4.3 Efficient 3D Object Detection: IA-SSD

Unlike dense prediction tasks such as 3D semantic segmentation, which require point-wise outputs, 3D object detection inherently focuses on small but critical foreground instances (e.g., cars, pedestrians). This fundamental difference suggests an opportunity for optimization. Current point-based detectors typically employ general-purpose downsampling methods like random sampling [13] or farthest point sampling [29, 48], which reduce computational costs but often discard crucial foreground points indiscriminately.

Furthermore, existing approaches frequently require separate models for different object categories, each with carefully tuned parameters to account for variations in object size and geometry. This limitation creates practical deployment challenges in real-world applications. Our research addresses a fundamental question: *Can we develop a single, efficient point-based model capable of detecting multiple object classes in a single pass?*

To address this challenge, we present IA-SSD, an efficient single-stage detector that introduces two key innovations: instance-aware downsampling and contextual centroid perception. As illustrated in Fig. 4.2, our architecture adopts a lightweight

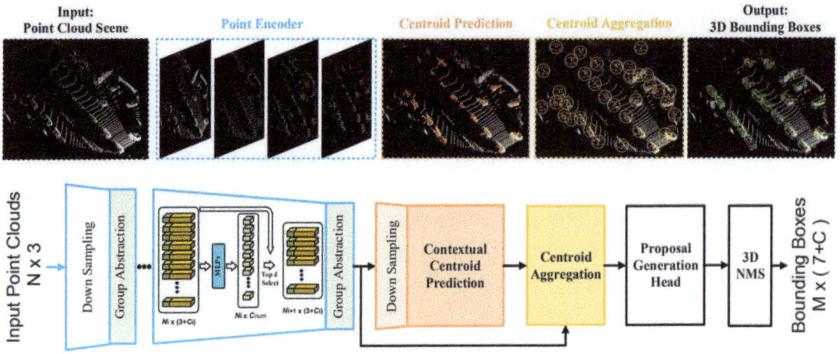

Fig. 4.2 Illustration of the proposed IA-SSD (This figure is reproduced from [53])

encoder-only design inspired by [48]. The system processes raw LiDAR point clouds through several stages: (1) initial feature extraction from input points; (2) progressive dimensionality reduction using instance-aware downsampling while preserving informative foreground points; (3) proposal generation and bounding box regression using contextual centroid perception.

4.3.1 *Instance-Aware Downsampling Strategy*

Processing large-scale point clouds efficiently requires strategic downsampling to reduce memory and computational demands. However, aggressive downsampling risks losing critical information about objects of interest. This creates a fundamental tension between computational efficiency and detection accuracy.

To better understand this trade-off, we conducted an empirical study comparing different sampling approaches using a standard PointNet++ [29] architecture with four encoding layers. We evaluated three common sampling methods: (1) Random point sampling [13]; (2) Farthest Point Sampling based on Euclidean distance (D-FPS) [29]; (3) Feature-based Farthest Point Sampling (Feat-FPS) [48].

We measured Instance Recall (the proportion of instances retained after sampling) at each layer. Our analysis revealed two key findings: 1. Random sampling leads to significant loss of foreground points 2. While D-FPS and Feat-FPS better preserve instances initially, they still lose critical foreground points in later layers. This loss of foreground points particularly impacts the detection of smaller objects like pedestrians and cyclists, where every point carries significant information. To address this limitation, we develop two task-oriented sampling approaches that leverage semantic information during training: Class-aware Sampling and Centroid-aware Sampling.

4.3.1.1 Class-Aware Sampling

This approach incorporates semantic understanding into the sampling process. We add specialized branches with two MLP layers to predict point-wise semantic categories, supervised using one-hot labels derived from bounding box annotations. The loss function is defined as:

$$\mathcal{L}_{cls\text{-}aware} = -\sum_{c=1}^{C}(s_i log(\hat{s_i}) + (1 - s_i)log(1 - \hat{s_i})) \tag{4.1}$$

where C represents the number of categories, s_i denotes one-hot labels, and $\hat{s_i}$ represents predicted logits. During inference, we retain the top k points with highest foreground scores.

4.3.1.2 Centroid-Aware Sampling

This strategy incorporates geometric relationships by considering points' positions relative to object centers. We compute a soft mask score for each point:

$$Mask_i = \sqrt[3]{\frac{min(f^*, b^*)}{max(f^*, b^*)} \times \frac{min(l^*, r^*)}{max(l^*, r^*)} \times \frac{min(u^*, d^*)}{max(u^*, d^*)}} \tag{4.2}$$

where $f^*, b^*, l^*, r^*, u^*, d^*$ represent distances to the six faces of the bounding box. Points closer to object centers receive higher scores (maximum 1), while surface points score 0. This geometric information is incorporated into training through a weighted cross-entropy loss:

$$\mathcal{L}_{ctr\text{-}aware} = -\sum_{c=1}^{C}(Mask_i \cdot s_i log(\hat{s_i}) + (1 - s_i)log(1 - \hat{s_i})). \tag{4.3}$$

During inference, we simply retain the top k highest-scoring points after downsampling.

4.3.2 Contextual Instance Centroid Perception

Drawing inspiration from contextual learning in 2D vision [5, 47], we develop a novel approach for predicting instance centers that leverages surrounding contextual information. The system predicts offset vectors $\Delta\hat{c}_{ij}$ to instance centers while incorporating uncertainty minimization:

$$\mathcal{L}_{cent} = \frac{1}{|\mathcal{F}_+|}\frac{1}{|\mathcal{S}_+|}\sum_i\sum_j(|\Delta\hat{c_{ij}} - \Delta c_{ij}| + |\hat{c_{ij}} - \overline{c_i}|) \cdot \mathbf{I}_{\mathcal{S}}(p_{ij})$$
$$where \ \ \overline{c_i} = \frac{1}{|\mathcal{S}_+|}\sum_j \hat{c_{ij}}, \quad \mathbf{I}_{\mathcal{S}} : \mathcal{P} \rightarrow \{0, 1\} \tag{4.4}$$

where Δc_{ij} represents ground-truth offsets, $\mathbf{I}_{\mathcal{S}}$ determines point eligibility for center estimation, and $|S_+|$ counts points used for prediction. Unlike previous approaches that only consider points within bounding boxes [27, 48], we exploit broader contextual information by expanding the search region around objects.

The system processes predicted centers through three stages: (1) Centroid-based Instance Aggregation: using PointNet++ to learn instance representations in local coordinate systems; (2) Feature Aggregation: combining point features through shared MLPs and symmetric functions; (3) Proposal Generation: predicting final bounding boxes with location, scale, and orientation parameters.

4.3.3 End-to-End Learning

IA-SSD employs end-to-end training with a multi-task loss function:

$$L_{total} = L_{sample} + L_{cent} + L_{cls} + L_{box}. \tag{4.5}$$

The box generation component includes several specialized losses:

$$L_{box} = L_{loc} + L_{size} + L_{angle\text{-}bin} + L_{angle\text{-}res} + L_{corner}. \tag{4.6}$$

4.3.4 Implementation Details

Our implementation builds on a lightweight encoder-only architecture using Set Abstraction (SA) layers [29] for feature extraction. We employ multi-scale grouping with progressively larger radius groups ([0.2, 0.8], [0.8, 1.6], [1.6, 4.8]) to capture local geometric features effectively. The first two encoding layers use D-FPS, followed by instance-aware downsampling in later layers. The system processes 256 representative points through contextual centroid prediction (using three MLP layers: 256→256→3) before final classification and regression.

Table 4.1 Quantitative detection performance achieved by different methods on the KITTI *test* set

	Method	Reference	Type	3D Car (IoU =0.7)			3D Ped. (IoU = 0.5)			3D Cyc. (IoU = 0.5)			Speed
				Easy	Mod.	Hard	Easy	Mod.	Hard	Easy	Mod.	Hard	
Voxel-based	VoxelNet [58]	CVPR 2018	1-stage	77.47	65.11	57.73	39.48	33.69	31.5	61.22	48.36	44.37	4.5
	SECOND [45]	Sensors 2018	1-stage	84.65	75.96	68.71	45.31	35.52	33.14	75.83	60.82	53.67	20
	PointPillars [17]	CVPR 2019	1-stage	82.58	74.31	68.99	51.45	41.92	38.89	77.10	58.65	51.92	42.4
	3D IoU Loss [56]	3DV 2019	1-stage	86.16	76.50	71.39	–	-	–	–	–	–	12.5
	Associate-3Ddet [6]	CVPR 2020	1-stage	85.99	77.40	70.53	–	–	–	–	–	–	20
	SA-SSD [10]	CVPR 2020	1-stage	88.75	79.79	74.16	–	–	–	–	–	–	25
	CIA-SSD [55]	AAAI 2021	1-stage	89.59	80.28	72.87	–	–	–	–	–	–	32
	TANet [21]	AAAI 2020	2-stage	84.39	75.94	68.82	53.72	<u>44.34</u>	40.49	75.70	59.44	52.53	28.5
	Part-A^2 [36]	TPAMI 2020	2-stage	87.81	78.49	73.51	53.10	43.35	40.06	79.17	63.52	56.93	12.5
Point-Voxel	Fast Point R-CNN [2]	ICCV 2019	2-stage	85.29	77.40	70.24	–	–	–	–	–	–	16.7
	STD [49]	ICCV 2019	2-stage	87.95	79.71	75.09	53.29	42.47	38.35	78.69	61.59	55.30	12.5
	PV-RCNN [33]	CVPR 2020	2-stage	<u>90.25</u>	<u>81.43</u>	<u>76.82</u>	52.17	43.29	40.29	78.60	63.71	<u>57.65</u>	12.5
	VIC-Net [15]	ICRA 2021	1-stage	88.25	80.61	75.83	43.82	37.18	35.35	78.29	63.65	57.27	17
	HVPR [26]	CVPR 2021	1-stage	86.38	77.92	73.04	53.47	43.96	<u>40.64</u>	–	–	–	36.1
Point-based	PointRCNN [35]	CVPR 2019	2-stage	86.96	75.64	70.70	47.98	39.37	36.01	74.96	58.82	52.53	10
	3D IoU-Net [18]	Arxiv 2020	2-stage	87.96	79.03	72.78	–	–	–	–	–	–	10
	Point-GNN [37]	CVPR 2020	1-stage	88.33	79.47	72.29	51.92	43.77	40.14	78.60	63.48	57.08	1.6
	3DSSD [48]	CVPR 2020	1-stage	88.36	79.57	74.55	<u>54.64</u>	44.27	40.23	<u>82.48</u>	64.10	56.90	25
	3DSSD†(Reproduced)	CVPR 2020	1-stage	87.73	78.58	72.01	35.03	27.76	26.08	66.69	59.00	55.62	23
	3DSSD‡(OpenPCDet)	CVPR 2020	1-stage	87.91	79.55	74.71	3.63	3.18	2.57	27.08	21.38	19.68	28
	IA-SSD (single-class)	–	**1-stage**	**88.87**	**80.32**	**75.10**	**49.01**	**41.20**	**38.03**	**80.78**	<u>**66.01**</u>	<u>**58.12**</u>	<u>**85**</u>
	IA-SSD (multi-class)	–	**1-stage**	**88.34**	**80.13**	**75.04**	**46.51**	**39.03**	**35.60**	**78.35**	**61.94**	**55.70**	<u>**83**</u>

Table 4.2 Quantitative comparison of different approaches on the *validation* split of the KITTI dataset

	Method	References	Type	Car Mod (IoU = 0.7)	Ped. Mod (IoU = 0.5)	Cyc. Mod (IoU = 0.5)
Voxel-based	VoxelNet [58]	CVPR 2018	1-stage	65.46	53.42	47.65
	SECOND [45]	Sensors 2018	1-stage	76.48	–	–
	PointPillars [17]	CVPR 2019	1-stage	77.98	–	–
	TANet [21]	AAAI 2020	1-stage	77.85	63.45	64.95
	Associate-3Ddet [6]	CVPR 2020	1-stage	79.17	–	–
	SA-SSD [10]	CVPR 2020	1-stage	79.91	–	–
	CIA-SSD [55]	AAAI 2021	1-stage	79.81	–	–
	Part-A^2 [36]	TPAMI 2020	2-stage	79.47	<u>63.84</u>	<u>73.07</u>
Point-voxel	Fast Point R-CNN [2]	ICCV 2019	2-stage	79.00	–	–
	STD [49]	ICCV 2019	2-stage	79.8	–	–
	PV-RCNN [33]	CVPR 2020	2-stage	<u>83.90</u>	–	–
	VIC-Net [15]	ICRA 2021	1-stage	79.25	–	–
Point-based	PointRCNN [35]	CVPR 2019	2-stage	78.63	–	–
	3D IoU-Net [18]	Arxiv 2020	2-stage	79.26	–	–
	PointGNN [37]	CVPR 2020	1-stage	78.34	–	–
	3DSSD [48]	CVPR 2020	1-stage	79.45	–	–
	IA-SSD (Ours)	**–**	**1-stage**	**79.57**	**58.91**	**71.24**

4.4 Experiments

4.4.1 Evaluation on KITTI Dataset

In the KITTI benchmark, objects belonging to *car*, *pedestrian*, and *cyclist* are classified into three subsets ("Easy", "Moderate", and "Hard") based on the levels of difficulty. The results on "Moderate" are usually adopted as the main indicator for final ranking. We report the results achieved by different methods (voxel-based, point-based, and point-voxel-based methods) on the test set of the KITTI dataset in Table 4.1. Note that, since [48] does not provide reproducible implementation or pre-trained models for *pedestrian* and *cyclist*, we provide the results reported in their paper, the best-reproduced results, and the results achieved by OpenPCDet[1] implementation for a fair comparison.

Analysis: It can be seen that (1) the proposed IA-SSD achieves the best *cyclist* detection performance, even outperforming several strong point-voxel based and voxel based detectors [33, 36]. This is mainly because the proposed instance aware sampling can effectively preserve foreground points, enabling accurate detection of small objects. (2) Our IA-SSD also achieves the best *car* detection performance compared with other point-based detectors, outperforming PointRCNN [35] by (1.91%, 4.68%, 4.4%), and the SOTA method 3DSSD [48] by (0.51%, 0.75%, 0.55%) mAP. (3) Despite the competitive detection performance, the proposed IA-SSD also shows

[1] https://github.com/open-mmlab/OpenPCDet.

Table 4.3 Quantitative detection performance achieved by different methods on the Waymo [40] *validation* set

Method	Type	Vehicle (LEVEL 1)		Vehicle (LEVEL 2)		Ped. (LEVEL 1)		Ped. (LEVEL 2)		Cyc. (LEVEL 1)		Cyc. (LEVEL 2)	
		mAP	mAPH	mAP	mAPH	mAP	mAPH	mAP	mAPH	mAP	mAPH	mAP	mAPH
PointPillars [17]	Voxel-based	60.67	59.79	52.78	52.01	43.49	23.51	37.32	20.17	35.94	28.34	34.60	27.29
SECOND [45]	Voxel-based	68.03	67.44	59.57	59.04	61.14	50.33	53.00	43.56	54.66	53.31	52.67	51.37
Part-A^2 [36]	Voxel-based	71.82	71.29	64.33	63.82	63.15	54.96	54.24	47.11	65.23	63.92	62.61	61.35
PV-RCNN [33]	Point-Voxel	74.06	73.38	64.99	64.38	62.66	52.68	53.80	45.14	63.32	61.71	60.72	59.18
IA-SSD (Ours)	Point-based	**70.53**	**69.67**	**61.55**	**60.80**	**69.38**	**58.47**	**60.30**	**50.73**	**67.67**	**65.30**	**64.98**	**62.71**

Table 4.4 Quantitative detection performance on the ONCE [23] *validation* set

Method	Type	Vehicle				Pedestrian				Cyclist				mAP
		Overall	0–30 m	30–50 m	>50 m	Overall	0–30 m	30–50 m	>50 m	Overall	0–30 m	30–50 m	>50 m	
PointPillars [17]	Voxel-based	68.57	80.86	62.07	47.04	17.63	19.74	15.15	10.23	46.81	58.33	40.32	25.86	44.34
SECOND [45]	Voxel-based	71.19	84.04	63.02	47.25	26.44	29.33	24.05	18.05	58.04	69.96	52.43	34.61	51.89
CenterPoints [52]	Voxel-based	66.79	80.10	59.55	43.39	49.90	56.24	42.61	26.27	63.45	74.28	57.94	41.48	60.05
PV-RCNN [33]	Point-Voxel	77.77	89.39	72.55	58.64	23.50	25.61	22.84	17.27	59.37	71.66	52.58	36.17	53.55
PointRCNN [35]	Point-based	52.09	74.45	40.89	16.81	4.28	6.17	2.40	0.91	29.84	46.03	20.94	5.46	28.74
IA-SSD (Ours)	Point-based	**70.30**	**83.01**	**62.84**	**47.01**	**39.82**	**47.45**	**32.75**	**18.99**	**62.17**	**73.78**	**56.31**	**39.53**	**57.43**

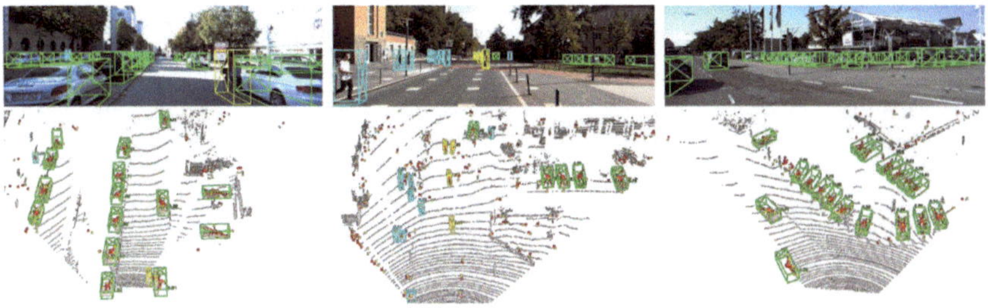

Fig. 4.3 Qualitative results achieved on the KITTI *test* set (This figure is reproduced from [53])

superior efficiency. It can detect with a speed of 85 FPS on a single NVIDIA RTX 2080Ti with Intel I9-10900X CPU@3.7GHz. 4) Thanks to the instance-aware sampling strategy and the contextual centroid perception module, our framework can be trained on multiple classes together (*i.e.*, training a single model for detecting multi-class objects), rather than training separate models for different objects [48]. In particular, the performance is still comparable with other state-of-the-art approaches. This allows our model much more efficient and flexible during inference. Finally, we also show the qualitative results achieved by our IA-SSD in Fig. 4.3. We can clearly see that the proposed IA-SSD is capable of detecting small and far-away instances such as *pedestrian* and *cyclist*.

Apart from the detection results on the *test* split, we also report the performance comparison on the *validation* set of the KITTI dataset in Table 4.2. We can see our IA-SSD achieved the best performance for all three classes among all point-based detectors. In particular, our IA-SSD is single-stage, lightweight, and efficient, requiring only a single model for detecting multi-class objects.

4.4.2 Evaluation on Waymo Dataset

We further evaluate the performance of our IA-SSD on the Waymo [40] dataset. This dataset is composed of nearly 160k 360-degree LiDAR samples in the *training* set and 40k in the *validation* set with panoramic annotated objects. For a fair comparison, we adapt our framework on the Waymo Dataset by only changing the number of input points from 16384 to 65536, and increasing the sampling scale up to fourfold in each sampling layer, while remaining the rest unchanged. Additionally, all baselines are implemented based on the OpenPCDet codebase for a rigorous comparison. As shown in Table 4.3, our IA-SSD achieves significantly better detection performance on *pedestrian* and *cyclist* compared with other strong baselines, showing that the proposed instance-aware sampling can indeed improve the perception capacity of small objects. We also noticed that our IA-SSD shows slightly inferior detection performance on *vehicle* compared with other voxel-based methods. This may be caused by the relatively complicated distribution of the 3D size of such instances. We will leave this issue for future exploration.

Table 4.5 Efficiency comparison of different methods on the KITTI *validation* set

Method	Mem. (MB)	Paral.	Speed$^{\perp}$	Speed$^{\top}$	Input scale
PointPillars [17]	354	28	48	58	2~9k
SECOND [45]	710	14	30	40	11~17k
TANet [21]	3000	3	20	28	<12k
3DSSD [48]	502	19	11	28	16384
PointRCNN [35]	560	18	10	14	16384
Part-A^2 [36]	702	13	12	19	11~17k
PV-RCNN [33]	1223	8	8	10	11~17k
IA-SSD (Ours)	**102**	**100**	**23/48**†	**83**	16384

4.4.3 Evaluation on ONCE Dataset

To further verify the generalization of IA-SSD on more complex and realistic situations, we also evaluate the performance of our IA-SSD on the latest ONCE Dataset [23]. Specifically, we feed 60k points into the IA-SSD similar to the setting on the Waymo Dataset, and train 80 epochs for a fair comparison. As shown in Table 4.4, our method yields the competitive performance among all baselines. This again verifies the superiority of the proposed component and the efficiency of our method applied on the large-scale complicated LiDAR scenarios.

4.4.4 Efficiency of IA-SSD

Next, we evaluate the computational and memory efficiency of the proposed IA-SSD. In light of the performance variations on different hardware configurations, we re-implemented several representative approaches and report the memory and speed on the same platform for a fair comparison. Note that we report the memory consumption by feeding the same input point cloud with 16384 points following the OpenPCDet configuration. For speed evaluation, different models are inferred with batch point clouds with the full utilization of the same hardware. In Table 4.5, "Mem." and "Paral." denote the GPU memory footprint per frame during inference and the maximum number of batches that can be parallelized on one RTX2080Ti (11GB). "Speed$^{\perp}$", "Speed$^{\top}$" is inference speed when processing one frame or full-loaded GPU memory, † means dividing the scene into four parallel parts to speed up the first sampling layer. For a fair comparison, we also report each input scale of voxels/points according to their official setting. As shown in Table 4.5, the proposed IA-SSD has the lowest GPU memory consumption (up to 100 frames in parallel) with the highest inference speed (83 FPS) compared with existing benchmark approaches.

Table 4.6 Ablation study of IA-SSD on different sampling strategies

	D-FPS	Feat-FPS	Cls-aware	Ctr-aware	Car Mod (IoU = 0.7)	Ped. Mod (IoU = 0.5)	Cyc. Mod (IoU = 0.5)
(1)	✓	–	–	–	78.12	50.46	65.19
(2)	✓	✓	–	–	79.00	54.31	71.08
(3)	✓	–	✓	–	79.19	58.81	70.15
(4)	✓	–	✓	✓	79.54	58.49	71.33
(5)	✓	–	–	✓	**79.57**	**58.91**	**71.24**

4.4.5 Ablation Studies

In the following ablation studies, we train our IA-SSD with multi-class objects in a single model, and all experiments are conducted on the KITTI validation set.

Ablation on Downsampling Strategies: To further verify the effectiveness of the proposed instance-aware sampling, we replace it with the D-FPS and Feat-FPS. As shown in Table 4.6, the proposed instance-aware sampling achieves the best detection performance in all three categories, especially the small objects such as *pedestrian* and *cyclist*. This shows that the proposed sampling strategy can effectively preserve the foreground information during down-sampling process, thereby achieving better detection performance. We also find that centroid-aware sampling (row 5) performs better on *pedestrian* and *car*, but slightly inferior in detecting *cyclist* compared with mixed sampling (row 4), primarily because this sampling strategy focuses on the instance center, hence tends to ignore the distal geometric details of objects such as *cyclist* with large aspect ratios.

Ablation on Contextual Centroid Perception: We further validate the effectiveness of the proposed contextual centroid perception module. Here, by replacing this module with the vanilla center-assign[2] or original-assign used in [27], the detection performance show a clear decrease. Table 4.7 shows that the inclusion of contextual points can indeed improve the detection performance, especially for small objects, since the representative points lying in the ground-truth bounding boxes are actually quite limited. We also notice that both the extend-factor (2× size for each bounding box) and extend-length (+1.0 m for each bounding box) have their own advantage in specific categories, showing that different contextual information may have a varying impact on different objects.

[2] https://github.com/qiqihaer/3DSSD-pytorch-openPCDet.

Table 4.7 Ablation study of IA-SSD framework with different centroid perception strategies

	Centroid perception type	Car Mod (IoU = 0.7)	Ped. Mod (IoU = 0.5)	Cyc. Mod (IoU = 0.5)
(1)	Centers-assign	79.27	24.90	37.12
(2)	Origin-assign	79.18	55.62	69.37
(3)	Extend-factor assign	79.37	58.36	68.16
(4)	Extend-length assign	**79.57**	**58.91**	**71.24**

4.5 Conclusion

In this chapter, we propose an efficient solution termed IA-SSD for point-based 3D object detection in LiDAR point clouds. Considering the task of object detection inherently focuses on the foreground information, we propose an instance-aware learning-based downsampling method to automatically select the sparse yet important instance points. Additionally, a dedicated contextual centroid perception module is proposed to fully exploit the geometrical structure around the bounding boxes. Extensive experiments conducted on three detection benchmarks demonstrated the superior efficiency and accuracy of the proposed IA-SSD.

Limitations: Although the proposed IA-SSD can achieve remarkable efficiency in object detection of large-scale LiDAR point clouds, it also has limitations. e.g., the instance-aware sampling relies on the semantic prediction of each point, which is susceptible to class imbalance distribution. For future work, we will further explore advanced techniques to alleviate the imbalanced issue.

References

1. Ali W, Abdelkarim S, Zidan M, Zahran M, El Sallab A (2018) Yolo3D: end-to-end real-time 3D oriented object bounding box detection from lidar point cloud. In: ECCVW
2. Chen Y, Liu S, Shen X, Jia J (2019) Fast point R-CNN. In: ICCV, pp 9775–9784
3. Deng J, Shi S, Li P, Zhou W, Zhang Y, Li H (2021) Voxel R-CNN: towards high performance voxel-based 3D object detection. In: AAAI
4. Deng J, Shi S, Li P, Zhou W, Zhang Y, Li H (2021) Voxel R-CNN: towards high performance voxel-based 3D object detection. In: AAAI
5. Divvala SK, Hoiem D, Hays JH, Efros AA, Hebert M (2009) An empirical study of context in object detection. In: CVPR, pp 1271–1278
6. Du L, Ye X, Tan X, Feng J, Xu Z, Ding E, Wen S (2020) Associate-3Ddet: perceptual-to-conceptual association for 3D point cloud object detection. In: CVPR, pp 13329–13338
7. Geiger A, Lenz P, Urtasun R (2012) Are we ready for autonomous driving? the KITTI vision benchmark suite. In: CVPR, pp 3354–3361
8. Graham B, van der Maaten L (2017) Submanifold sparse convolutional networks (2017). arXiv:1706.01307

9. Guo Y, Wang H, Hu Q, Liu H, Liu L, Bennamoun M (2020) Deep learning for 3D point clouds: a survey. IEEE TPAMI
10. He C, Zeng H, Huang J, Hua XS, Zhang L (2020) Structure aware single-stage 3D object detection from point cloud. In: CVPR, pp 11873–11882
11. Hu Q, Yang B, Fang G, Guo Y, Leonardis A, Trigoni N, Markham A (2021) SQN: weakly-supervised semantic segmentation of large-scale 3D point clouds with 1000x fewer labels. arXiv:2104.04891
12. Hu Q, Yang B, Khalid S, Xiao W, Trigoni N, Markham A (2022) Sensaturban: learning semantics from urban-scale photogrammetric point clouds. Int J Comput Vis 1–28
13. Hu Q, Yang B, Xie L, Rosa S, Guo Y, Wang Z, Trigoni N, Markham A (2020) Randla-net: efficient semantic segmentation of large-scale point clouds. In: CVPR, pp 11108–11117
14. Hu Q, Yang B, Xie L, Rosa S, Guo Y, Wang Z, Trigoni N, Markham A (2021) Learning semantic segmentation of large-scale point clouds with random sampling. IEEE Trans Pattern Anal Mach Intell (2021)
15. Jiang T, Song N, Liu H, Yin R, Gong Y, Yao J (2021) Vic-net: voxelization information compensation network for pointcloud 3D object detection. In: ICRA
16. Ku J, Mozifian M, Lee J, Harakeh A, Waslander SL (2018) Joint 3D proposal generation and object detection from view aggregation. In: IROS, pp 1–8
17. Lang AH, Vora S, Caesar H, Zhou L, Yang J, Beijbom O (2019) Pointpillars: fast encoders for object detection from point clouds. In: CVPR, pp 12697–12705
18. Li J, Luo S, Zhu Z, Dai H, Krylov AS, Ding Y, Shao L (2020) 3D IoU-Net: IoU guided 3D object detector for point clouds. arXiv:2004.04962
19. Li Z, Wang F, Wang N (2021) Lidar R-CNN: an efficient and universal 3d object detector. In: CVPR, pp 7546–7555
20. Liu Y, Fan B, Xiang S, Pan C (2019) Relation-shape convolutional neural network for point cloud analysis. In: CVPR, pp 8895–8904
21. Liu Z, Zhao X, Huang T, Hu R, Zhou Y, Bai X (2020) Tanet: robust 3D object detection from point clouds with triple attention. In: AAAI, pp 11677–11684
22. Mao J, Niu M, Bai H, Liang X, Xu H, Xu C (2021) Pyramid R-CNN: towards better performance and adaptability for 3d object detection. In: ICCV, pp 2723–2732
23. Mao J, Niu M, Jiang C, Liang X, Li Y, Ye C, Zhang W, Li Z, Yu J, Xu C et al (2021) One million scenes for autonomous driving: once dataset
24. Mao J, Xue Y, Niu M, Bai H, Feng J, Liang X, Xu H, Xu C (2021) Voxel transformer for 3D object detection. In: ICCV, pp 3164–3173
25. Miao Z, Chen J, Pan H, Zhang R, Liu K, Hao P, Zhu J, Wang Y, Zhan X (2021) PVGNet: a bottom-up one-stage 3D object detector with integrated multi-level features. In: CVPR, pp 3279–3288
26. Noh J, Lee S, Ham B (2021) HVPR: hybrid voxel-point representation for single-stage 3D object detection. In: CVPR
27. Qi CR, Litany O, He K, Guibas LJ (2019) Deep hough voting for 3D object detection in point clouds. In: ICCV, pp 9277–9286
28. Qi CR, Su H, Mo K, Guibas LJ (2017) PointNet: deep learning on point sets for 3D classification and segmentation. In: CVPR, pp 652–660
29. Qi CR, Yi L, Su H, Guibas LJ (2017) PointNet++: deep hierarchical feature learning on point sets in a metric space. In: NeurIPS, pp 5099–5108
30. Qian R, Garg D, Wang Y, You Y, Belongie S, Hariharan B, Campbell M, Weinberger KQ, Chao WL (2020) End-to-end pseudo-lidar for image-based 3D object detection. In: CVPR, pp 5881–5890
31. Qian R, Lai X, Li X (2021) Boundary-aware 3D object detection from point clouds. arXiv:2104.10330
32. Sheng H, Cai S, Liu Y, Deng B, Huang J, Hua XS, Zhao MJ (2021) Improving 3D object detection with channel-wise transformer. In: ICCV, pp 2743–2752
33. Shi S, Guo C, Jiang L, Wang Z, Shi J, Wang X, Li H (2020) PV-RCNN: point-voxel feature set abstraction for 3D object detection. In: CVPR, pp 10529–10538

34. Shi S, Jiang L, Deng J, Wang Z, Guo C, Shi J, Wang X, Li H (2021) PV-RCNN++: point-voxel feature set abstraction with local vector representation for 3D object detection (2021). arXiv:2102.00463
35. Shi S, Wang X, Li H (2019) PointRCNN: 3D object proposal generation and detection from point cloud. In: CVPR, pp 770–779
36. Shi S, Wang Z, Shi J, Wang X, Li H (2020) From points to parts: 3D object detection from point cloud with part-aware and part-aggregation network. IEEE TPAMI
37. Shi W, Rajkumar R (2020) Point-GNN: graph neural network for 3D object detection in a point cloud. In: CVPR, pp 1711–1719
38. Simon M, Amende K, Kraus A, Honer J, Samann T, Kaulbersch H, Milz S, Michael Gross H (2019) Complexer-YOLO: real-time 3D object detection and tracking on semantic point clouds. In: CVPR Workshops
39. Simony M, Milzy S, Amendey K, Gross HM (2018) Complex-YOLO: an Euler-region-proposal for real-time 3D object detection on point clouds. In: ECCVW
40. Sun P, Kretzschmar H, Dotiwalla X, Chouard A, Patnaik V, Tsui P, Guo J, Zhou Y, Chai Y, Caine B et al (2020) Scalability in perception for autonomous driving: Waymo open dataset. In: CVPR, pp 2446–2454
41. Thakur S, Peethambaran J (2020) Dynamic edge weights in graph neural networks for 3D object detection. arXiv:2009.08253
42. Wang DZ, Posner I (2015) Voting for voting in online point cloud object detection. In: Robotics: science and systems, pp 10–15607
43. Wang Y, Sun Y, Liu Z, Sarma SE, Bronstein MM, Solomon JM (2019) Dynamic graph CNN for learning on point clouds. In: TOG, pp 1–12
44. Wei Y, Liu H, Xie T, Ke Q, Guo Y (2022) Spatial-temporal transformer for 3D point cloud sequences. In: WACV, pp 1171–1180
45. Yan Y, Mao Y, Li B (2018) Second: sparsely embedded convolutional detection. Sensors 3337
46. Yang B, Luo W, Urtasun R (2018) PIXOR: real-time 3D object detection from point clouds. In: CVPR, pp 7652–7660
47. Yang M, Wu Y, Hua G (2008) Context-aware visual tracking. IEEE TPAMI 1195–1209
48. Yang Z, Sun Y, Liu S, Jia J (2020) 3DSSD: point-based 3D single stage object detector. In: CVPR, pp 11040–11048
49. Yang Z, Sun Y, Liu S, Shen X, Jia J (2019) STD: sparse-to-dense 3D object detector for point cloud. In: ICCV, pp 1951–1960
50. Ye M, Xu S, Cao T (2020) Hvnet: hybrid voxel network for lidar based 3D object detection. In: CVPR, pp 1631–1640 (2020)
51. Yi H, Shi S, Ding M, Sun J, Xu K, Zhou H, Wang Z, Li S, Wang G (2020) SegVoxelNet: exploring semantic context and depth-aware features for 3D vehicle detection from point cloud. In: ICRA, pp 2274–2280
52. Yin T, Zhou X, Krahenbuhl P (2021) Center-based 3D object detection and tracking. In: CVPR, pp 11784–11793
53. Zhang Y, Hu Q, Xu G, Ma Y, Wan J, Guo Y (2022) Not all points are equal: learning highly efficient point-based detectors for 3D LiDAR point clouds. In: CVPR, pp 18953–18962
54. Zhao N, Chua TS, Lee GH (2020) SESS: self-ensembling semi-supervised 3D object detection. In: CVPR, pp 11079–11087
55. Zheng W, Tang W, Chen S, Jiang L, Fu CW (2021) CIA-SSD: confident IoU-aware single-stage object detector from point cloud. In: AAAI
56. Zhou D, Fang J, Song X, Guan C, Yin J, Dai Y, Yang R (2019) IoU loss for 2D/3D object detection. In: 3DV, pp 85–94
57. Zhou Y, Sun P, Zhang Y, Anguelov D, Gao J, Ouyang T, Guo J, Ngiam J, Vasudevan V (2020) End-to-end multi-view fusion for 3D object detection in lidar point clouds. In: CoRL, pp 923–932
58. Zhou Y, Tuzel O (2018) VoxelNet: end-to-end learning for point cloud based 3D object detection. In: CVPR, pp 4490–4499

Chapter 5
Semantic Segmentation of Point Clouds

Labeling point clouds completely is extremely time-consuming and expensive. As larger point cloud datasets with billions of points become increasingly common, we wonder whether full annotation is truly necessary. Our results show that models designed under the assumption of complete supervision only suffer a slight degradation when using 1% random point annotations. However, below this threshold, *e.g.*, at 0.1% annotations, segmentation accuracy becomes unacceptably low. We observe that since point clouds are samples of the 3D world, the point distribution in a local neighborhood is relatively uniform and exhibits strong semantic consistency. Motivated by this, we propose a new weak supervision method that implicitly reinforces very sparse supervision signals. Extensive experiments demonstrate that the proposed Semantic Query Network (SQN) delivers promising performance on seven large-scale open datasets under weak supervision, while requiring only 0.1% randomly annotated points for training, thereby significantly reducing both annotation cost and effort. The code is available at https://github.com/QingyongHu/SQN.

5.1 Introduction

Learning precise semantics of large-scale point clouds is crucial for intelligent machines to truly understand complex 3D scenes in the real world. This capability is a key enabler for autonomous vehicles, augmented reality devices, *etc.*, to rapidly interpret their surroundings for better navigation and planning.

With the availability of extensive labeled 3D data for fully supervised learning, the task of 3D semantic segmentation has advanced significantly over the past four years. Following the seminal works PointNet [39] and SparseConv [15], a series of sophisticated neural architectures [10, 11, 23, 31, 34, 40, 56, 87] have been proposed, greatly improving both the accuracy and efficiency of semantic estimation on raw point clouds. The performance of these fully supervised methods can be further enhanced

Y. Guo et al., *Point Cloud Intelligence*, Advances in Computer Vision and Pattern Recognition, https://doi.org/10.1007/978-981-95-0648-4_5

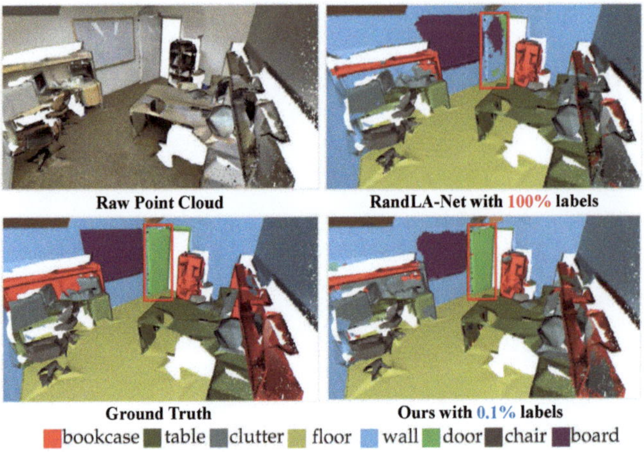

Fig. 5.1 Qualitative results of RandLA-Net [23] and our SQN on the S3DIS dataset (This figure is reproduced from [21])

using self-supervised pretraining as shown in recent studies [7, 32, 55, 60, 73, 80]. However, these methods depend heavily on densely annotated per-point labels to train deep neural networks. Fully annotating 3D point clouds is extremely costly due to their unordered, unstructured, and non-uniform nature (e.g., over 1700 person-hours to annotate a typical dataset [3] and about 22.3 minutes for a single indoor scene (5 m×5 m×2 m) [13]). In very large-scale scenarios e.g., an entire city, manually labeling every point is simply infeasible.

Inspired by the success of weakly-supervised learning techniques in 2D images, several recent works have begun addressing 3D semantic segmentation with fewer point labels. These methods generally fall into five categories: (1) using 2D image labels for training as in [61, 86]; (2) utilizing fewer 3D labels with approaches such as gradient approximation/supervision propagation/perturbation consistency [63, 67, 75, 79]; (3) generating pseudo 3D labels from limited indirect annotations [51, 66]; (4) employing superpoint annotations obtained through over-segmentation [9, 33, 51]; and (5) applying contrastive pretraining followed by fine-tuning with fewer 3D labels [20, 73, 81]. Although these approaches yield encouraging results on multiple datasets, several limitations remain unresolved.

Firstly, current methods often use customized strategies to annotate varying amounts of data (e.g., 10%/5%/1% of raw points or superpoints) for training, making it unclear what fraction of raw points should be labeled. **Secondly**, to fully exploit the sparse annotations, existing weak labeling pipelines typically involve multiple stages—including careful data augmentation, self-pretraining, fine-tuning, and/or post-processing such as dense CRF [26]—which complicates parameter tuning and hinders practical deployment compared to a standard end-to-end training scheme. **Thirdly**, these techniques often overlook or insufficiently leverage the strong local semantic homogeneity among neighboring points in large-scale point clouds, causing the limited yet valuable annotations to be underused.

Motivated by these issues, we introduce a new paradigm for weakly-supervised semantic segmentation on large-scale point clouds that addresses these shortcomings. In particular, we first explore weak supervision schemes based purely on existing fully supervised methods, and then propose an effective approach to learn accurate semantics with extremely limited point annotations.

In our investigation of weak supervision schemes, we consider two key questions: (1) *whether, and how, existing fully supervised methods deteriorate when trained with varying amounts of annotated data, and* (2) *at what point does the weakly-supervised regime actually begin as the number of labels decreases?* By exploring these questions, we aim to understand the limits of current fully supervised methods, allowing us to leverage mature architectures for this challenging task rather than simply applying off-the-shelf 2D image techniques [52]. Surprisingly, we find that the accuracy of existing fully supervised baselines drops only slightly when only 1% of points are randomly labeled. However, once the annotation falls to e.g., 0.1%, performance degrades rapidly.

Based on this insight, we propose a novel yet simple **S**emantic **Q**uery **N**etwork, named **SQN**, designed for semantic segmentation with as few as 0.1% labeled points for training. Our SQN first encodes the entire raw point cloud into hierarchical latent representations using an existing feature extractor, and then accepts an arbitrary 3D point as input to query a subset of latent representations from a local neighborhood. The queried representations are condensed into a compact vector and processed through a series of multilayer perceptrons (MLPs) to predict the final semantic label. Essentially, SQN explicitly leverages the semantic similarity among nearby 3D points, allowing extremely sparse training signals to propagate over a larger spatial area, thereby achieving superior performance under weak supervision.

Overall, this chapter bridges the gap between highly successful fully supervised methods and emerging weakly-supervised schemes, aiming to reduce the time and labor costs of point cloud annotation. Unlike existing weak supervision methods, our SQN requires no self-supervised pretraining, hand-crafted constraints, or complex post-processing steps, yet it achieves performance close to fully supervised approaches using only 0.1% training labels on multiple large-scale open datasets. Remarkably, for comparable accuracy, our empirical evaluation indicates that labeling costs (in terms of time) can be reduced by up to 98%. Figure 5.1 illustrates the qualitative results of our method. Our main contributions are

- We propose a new weakly-supervised method that leverages a point neighborhood query to fully utilize the sparse training signals.
- We observe that existing fully-supervised methods degrade slowly until 1% sparse point annotation, demonstrating that full, dense labeling is redundant and not necessary.
- We demonstrate a significant improvement over baselines in our benchmark, and surpass the state-of-the-art weak-supervision methods by large margins.

5.2 Related Works

5.2.1 Learning with Full Supervision

End-to-End Full Supervision: With the availability of densely annotated point cloud datasets [2, 3, 17, 22, 43, 49, 58], deep learning methods have achieved remarkable progress in 3D semantic segmentation in recent years. Most existing approaches adhere to a standard end-to-end training scheme and can be broadly classified into three groups based on the representation of 3D point clouds [16]: **(1) Voxel-based methods**. These methods [10, 15, 36, 76] typically convert irregular 3D point clouds into regular cubes [11, 54], cylinders [87], or spheres [30]. **(2) 2D Projection-based methods**. In this approach, unstructured 3D points are projected into 2D images via multi-view [6, 27], bird's-eye view [1], or spherical projections [12, 37, 68, 69, 74], and mature 2D architectures [19, 35] are then used for semantic learning. **(3) Point-based methods**. These techniques [23, 31, 39, 40, 56, 71, 84] operate directly on raw point clouds using shared MLPs. Hybrid approaches, such as the point-voxel representation [34, 42, 50] or 2D-3D representations [24, 77], are also explored.
Self-supervised Pretraining + Full Fine-tuning: Inspired by the success of self-supervised representation learning in 2D images [7, 18], several recent studies [8, 25, 32, 44, 55, 60, 73, 80] have applied contrastive techniques to 3D semantic segmentation. These methods typically pretrain networks on additional 3D datasets to learn initial per-point representations via self-supervised contrastive losses, before fine-tuning on target datasets with full labels. This approach substantially improves overall accuracy.

Although these methods have achieved impressive results on current datasets, they rely on extensive labeled data, which is both costly and impractical in many real-world applications. In contrast, our work aims to learn semantic information from only a small fraction of annotations, making it a more cost-effective and practical solution.

5.2.2 Unsupervised Learning

Saudar and Sievers [44] learn point semantics by reconstructing the correct voxel position for each 3D point after randomly shuffling the point cloud. Sun et al. propose Canonical Capsules [48] to decompose point clouds into object parts and elements through self-canonicalization and auto-encoding. Although these methods show promise, they are limited to simple objects and struggle with complex, large-scale point clouds.

5.2.3 Learning with Weak Supervision

Limited Indirect Annotations: Instead of using point-level semantic labels, some approaches rely on sub-cloud or segmentation-level labels. Wei et al. [66] first train a classifier with sub-cloud labels and then generate point-level pseudo labels using class activation mapping techniques [85]. Tao et al. [51] propose a grouping network to learn both semantic and instance segmentation of 3D point clouds using segmentation-level labels obtained from over-segmentation preprocessing. Ren et al. [41] introduce a multi-task learning framework that simultaneously tackles semantic segmentation and 3D object detection using scene-level tags.

Limited Point Annotations: With only a small fraction of points accurately labeled, Xu and Lee [75] develop a weakly-supervised point cloud segmentation method that approximates gradients and incorporates hand-crafted spatial and color smoothness constraints. Zhang et al. [79] add a perturbation branch to enforce predictive consistency for weakly-supervised learning on 3D point clouds. Shi et al. [46] further explore label-efficient learning by introducing an active learning strategy based on superpoints. Additionally, self-supervised pretraining methods [20, 32, 45, 73, 80, 81] can be adapted to fine-tune networks with limited annotations. Our SQN is specifically designed for scenarios with limited point annotations, and we believe it offers significant potential in practical applications. It requires no pretraining, post-processing, or active labeling strategies, yet achieves performance on par with or even superior to fully supervised methods using only 0.1% randomly annotated points for training.

Ensuring Fair Comparison with supervoxel -Based Methods [33, 72] **on ScanNet**: To promote fair and reproducible comparisons, it is important to highlight that certain published works claim state-of-the-art.

- **Misuse of ScanNet-provided segments as supervoxels**. 1T1C [33] employs the segments provided by the ScanNet dataset as the supervoxel partition.[1] This approach assumes that the labels of points within each supervoxel after over-segmentation are pure and consistent. While this assumption may hold for ScanNet, as its labeling process is based on the provided segments, its applicability to other datasets is questionable. In instances where labels within each supervoxel are not pure and consistent, propagating the label to the entire voxel could introduce errors, thereby affecting the network's training (as possibly evidenced by the decreased performance in the S3DIS dataset).
- **Ambiguous labeling ratios**. 1T1C calculates its labeling ratio by dividing the number of clicks by the total number of raw points, resulting in a remarkably low labeling ratio (e.g., 0.02%).[2] A more equitable method, as employed in prior works [75, 78, 81], is to use the total number of labeled points (i.e., to maintain consistency) divided by the total number of points. Given that semantic annotations within each supervoxel are clean and consistent, one click per supervoxel equates to

[1] https://github.com/liuzhengzhe/One-Thing-One-Click/issues/13.

[2] https://github.com/liuzhengzhe/One-Thing-One-Click/issues/8.

labeling all points within that supervoxel. Consequently, the supervoxel semantic labels used by 1T1C are effectively dense in ScanNet, and significantly exceed 0.02%. Detailed analysis and discussions between us and the creators of ScanNet can be found at this Link.

Therefore, our method cannot be directly compared with these methods on ScanNet. We recommend that future research in this area addresses these issues to ensure more accurate and fair comparisons between different approaches.

5.3 Exploring Weak Supervision

As weakly-supervised 3D semantic segmentation is still in its infancy, there is no consensus about what the sensible formulations of weak training signals are, and what approach should be used to sparsely annotate a dataset such that a direct comparison is possible. We first explore the issue, then we investigate how existing fully supervised techniques perform under a weak labeling regime.

Weak Annotation Strategy: The fundamental objective of weakly-supervised segmentation is to obtain accurate estimations with as low annotation cost as possible, in terms of labeller time. However, it is non-trivial to compare the cost of different annotation methods in practice. Existing annotation options include (1) randomly annotating sparse point labels [75, 78, 79], (2) actively annotating sparse point labels [20, 46] or region-wise labels [70], (3) annotating seg-level labels or superpoint labels [9, 33, 51], and 4) annotating sub-cloud labels [66]. For the purpose of fair reproducibility, we opt for the random point annotation strategy, considering the practical simplicity of building such an annotation tool.

Annotation Tool: To verify the feasibility of random sparse annotations in practice, we develop a user-friendly labeling pipeline based on the off-the-shelf CloudCompare[3] software. Specifically, we first import raw 3D point clouds to the software and randomly downsample them to 10%/1%/0.1% of the total points for sparse annotation. Considering the sparsity of the remaining points, we explicitly enlarge the size of selected points and take the original full point clouds as a reference. As illustrated in the left part of Fig. 5.2, we then use the standard labeling mode such as polygonal edition for point-wise annotating.

Annotation Cost: With the developed annotation tool, it takes less than 2 minutes to annotate 0.1% of points of a standard room in the S3DIS dataset. For comparison, it requires more than 20 minutes to fully annotate all points for the same room. Note that, the sparse annotation scheme is particularly suitable for large-scale 3D point clouds with billions of points. It only takes about 18 h to annotate 0.1% of the urban-scale SensatUrban dataset [22], while annotating all points requires more than 600 person-hours.

[3] https://www.cloudcompare.org/.

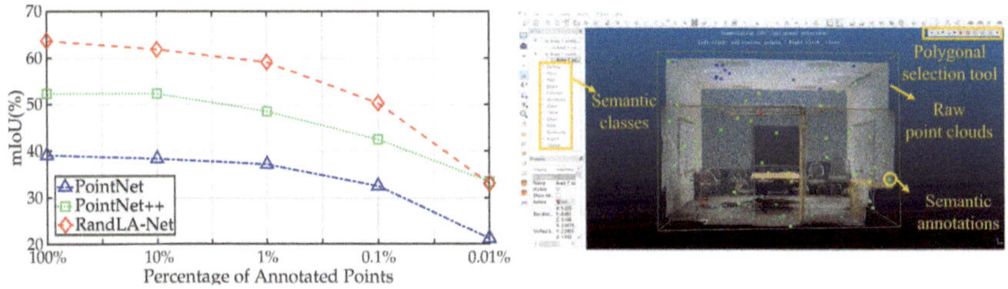

Fig. 5.2 The mIoU scores of all models (This figure is reproduced from [21])

Experimental Settings: We choose the well-known S3DIS dataset [2] as the testbed. The Areas 1, 2, 3, 4, and 6 are selected as the training point clouds, while the Area 5 is fully annotated for testing only. With the random sparse annotation strategy, we set up the following four groups of weak signals for training. Specifically, we only annotate the randomly selected 10%/1%/0.1%/0.01% of the 3D points in each room in all training areas.

Using Fully-supervised Methods as Baselines: We select the seminal works PointNet/PointNet++ [39, 40] and the recent large-scale point cloud-friendly RandLA-Net [23] as baselines. These methods are end-to-end trained on the four groups of weakly annotated data without using any additional modules. During training, only the labeled points are used to compute the loss for backpropagation. In total, 12 models (3 models/group $\times$ 4 groups) are trained for evaluation on the full Area 5.

Results and Findings: Figure 5.2 shows the mIoU scores of all models for segmenting the total 13 classes. The results under full supervision (100% annotations for all training data) are included for comparison. It can be seen that:

- The performance of all baselines only decreases marginally (less than 4%) even though the proportion of point annotations drops significantly from 100 to 1%. This clearly shows that the dense annotations are actually unnecessary to obtain a comparable and favorable segmentation accuracy under the simple random annotation strategy.
- The performance of all baselines drops significantly once the annotated points are lower than 0.1%. This critical point indicates that keeping a certain amount of training signals is also essential for weak supervision.

Above all, we may conclude that for segmenting large-scale point clouds which are usually dominated by major classes and have numerous repeatable local patterns, it is desirable to develop weakly-supervised methods which have an excellent trade-off between annotation costs and estimation accuracy. With this motivation, we propose SQN which achieves close to fully-supervised accuracy using only 0.1% labels for training.

5.4 Label Efficient Semantic Segmentation: SQN

5.4.1 Overview

Given point clouds with sparse annotations, the primary challenge in weakly-supervised learning is how to fully leverage the limited yet valuable training signals to update the network parameters, thereby enabling the learning of more geometrically meaningful local patterns. To address this, we design a simple SQN composed of two major components: (1) a point local feature extractor to capture diverse visual patterns, and (2) a flexible point feature query network to gather as many pertinent semantic features as possible for weakly-supervised training. As illustrated in Fig. 5.3, our two sub-networks are represented as stacked blocks.

5.4.2 Point Local Feature Extractor

This module is designed to extract local features for every point. As discussed in Sect. 5.2.1, many robust backbone networks can extract per-point features. Typically, these networks employ multiple encoding layers along with downsampling operations to capture hierarchical local features. In this work, we adopt the encoder from RandLA-Net [23] due to its efficiency on large-scale point clouds. Note that SQN is not limited to a specific backbone network.

As shown in the top block of Fig. 5.3, the encoder consists of four Local Feature Aggregation (LFA) layers, each followed by a Random Sampling (RS) operation. Details can be found in RandLA-Net [23]. Given an input point cloud $\mathcal{P}$ with N points, four levels of hierarchical point features are extracted after each encoding

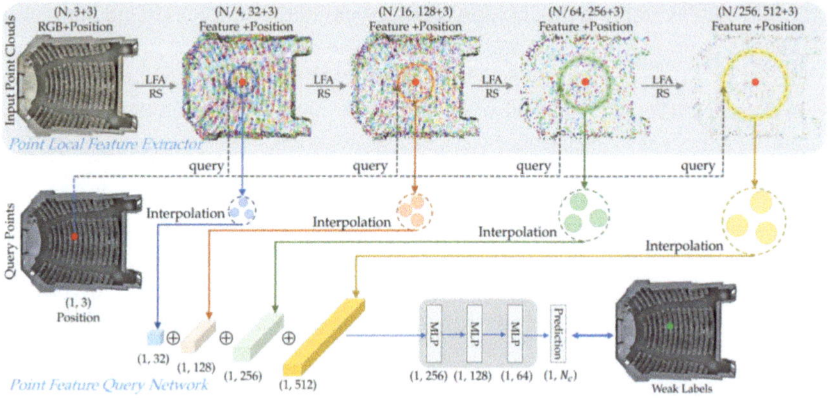

Fig. 5.3 The pipeline of our SQN at the training stage with weak supervision (This figure is reproduced from [21])

layer, namely: (1) $\frac{N}{4} \times 32$, (2) $\frac{N}{16} \times 128$, (3) $\frac{N}{64} \times 256$, and (4) $\frac{N}{256} \times 512$. To support the subsequent query network, the corresponding point coordinates xyz are preserved for each hierarchical feature vector.

5.4.3 Point Feature Query Network

Leveraging the extracted point features, this query network is designed to accumulate as many relevant features as possible using the available sparse signals. As illustrated in the bottom block of Fig. 5.3, the network takes a specific 3D query point as input and retrieves a set of learned point features pertinent to that point. The underlying assumption is that the query point shares similar semantic information with the collected features, allowing the training signals from the query point to be shared and back-propagated to these neighboring points. The network comprises three main steps: (1) Searching for Spatial Neighboring Point Features, (2) Interpolating Query Point Features, and (3) Inferring Query Point Semantics.

Searching Spatial Neighboring Point Features: Given a 3D query point p with its coordinates xyz, this module searches for the nearest K points in each of the four hierarchical encoded features using the point-wise Euclidean distance. For example, at the first level of extracted features, the K most relevant points are selected, yielding the raw features $\{\boldsymbol{F}_p^1, \ldots, \boldsymbol{F}_p^K\}$.

Interpolating Query Point Features: At each feature level, the K queried vectors are aggregated into a compact representation for the query point p. For simplicity, we employ a trilinear interpolation method to compute a feature vector for p, based on the Euclidean distances between p and the K neighboring points. The four hierarchical feature vectors are then concatenated to form a comprehensive representation of all relevant point features from the 3D point cloud.

Inferring Query Point Semantics: After obtaining a distinctive and representative feature vector for the query point p, the vector is passed through a series of MLPs to directly infer the semantic category of p.

Overall, by querying neighboring point features in parallel for a sparse set of annotated points, valuable training signals can be effectively back-propagated across a wider spatial region. During testing, all 3D points are processed by the two sub-networks for semantic estimation. In essence, our simple query mechanism enables the network to infer the semantic category of points from a significantly larger receptive field.

5.4.4 Implementation Details

The hyperparameter K is set to 3 for the semantic query in our framework and is **kept consistent across all experiments**. Our SQN follows the dataset preprocessing used in RandLA-Net [23] and is trained end-to-end with 0.1% randomly annotated points. All experiments are carried out on a PC with an Intel Core™ i9-10900X CPU and an NVIDIA RTX Titan GPU. Note that the proposed SQN framework supports flexible use of different backbone networks, such as the voxel-based MinkowskiNet [11].

5.5 Experiments

5.5.1 Comparison with SOTA Approaches

We first evaluate the performance of our SQN on three commonly-used benchmarks including S3DIS [2], ScanNet [13], and Semantic3D [17]. Following [23], we use the Overall Accuracy (OA) and mean Intersection-over-Union (mIoU) as the main evaluation metrics.

Evaluation on S3DIS: Following [75], we report the results on Area 5 in Table 5.1. Note that, our SQN is compared with three groups of approaches: (1) Fully-supervised methods including SPGraph [29], KPConv [56] and RandLA-Net with 100% training labels; (2) weakly-supervised approaches that learn from limited superpoint annotations including 1T1C [33] and SSPC-Net [9]; (3) Weakly-supervised methods [28, 52, 75] that learn from limited annotations. We also list the proportion of annotations used for training.

Considering different backbones and different labeling ratios are used by existing methods, we focus on the comparison of our SQN and the baseline RandLA-Net under the same weakly-supervised settings. It can be seen that our SQN outperforms RandLA-Net by nearly 9% under the same 0.1% random sparse annotations. In particular, our SQN is also comparable to the fully-supervised RandLA-Net [23]. Figure 5.4 shows qualitative comparisons of RandLA-Net and our SQN.

Evaluation on ScanNet: We report the quantitative results achieved by different approaches on the hidden test set in Table 5.2 . It can be seen that our SQN achieves higher mIoU scores with only 0.1% training labels, compared with MPRM [66] which is trained with sub-cloud labels, and Zhang et al. [78] and PSD [79] trained with 1% annotations. Considering that the actual training settings in the ScanNet Data-Efficient benchmark cannot be verified, hence we do not provide the comparison in this benchmark.

Evaluation on Semantic3D: Table 5.3 compares our SQN with a number of fully-supervised methods. It can be seen that our SQN trained with 0.1% labels achieves competitive performance with fully-supervised baselines on both *Semantic8* and *Reduced8* subsets. This clearly demonstrates the effectiveness of our semantic query framework, which takes full advantage of the limited annotations. Additionally, we also train our SQN with only 0.01% randomly annotated points, considering the

Table 5.1 Quantitative results of different methods on the *Area-5* of S3DIS dataset

	Methods	**mIoU(%)**	Ceiling	Floor	Wall	Beam	Column	Window	Door	Table	Chair	Sofa	Bookcase	Board	Clutter
Full supervision	PointNet [39]	41.1	88.8	97.3	69.8	0.1	3.9	46.3	10.8	58.9	52.6	5.9	40.3	26.4	33.2
	PointCNN [31]	57.3	92.3	98.2	79.4	0.0	17.6	22.8	62.1	74.4	80.6	31.7	66.7	62.1	56.7
	SPGraph [29]	58.0	89.4	96.9	78.1	0.0	42.8	48.9	61.6	84.7	75.4	69.8	52.6	2.1	52.2
	SPH3D [30]	59.5	93.3	97.1	81.1	0.0	33.2	45.8	43.8	79.7	86.9	33.2	71.5	54.1	53.7
	PointWeb [83]	60.3	92.0	98.5	79.4	0.0	21.1	59.7	34.8	76.3	88.3	46.9	69.3	64.9	52.5
	RandLA-Net [23]	63.0	92.4	96.7	80.6	0.0	18.3	61.3	43.3	77.2	85.2	71.5	71.0	69.2	52.3
	KPConv rigid [56]	65.4	92.6	97.3	81.4	0.0	16.5	54.5	69.5	80.2	90.1	66.4	74.6	63.7	58.1
Limited superpoint labels	1T1C (0.02%) [33]	50.1	–	–	–	–	–	–	–	–	–	–	–	–	–
	SSPC-Net (0.01%) [9]	51.5	–	–	–	–	–	–	–	–	–	–	–	–	–
Limited point-wise labels	Π Model (10%) [28]	46.3	91.8	97.1	73.8	0.0	5.1	42.0	19.6	67.2	66.7	47.9	19.1	30.6	41.3
	MT (10%) [52]	47.9	92.2	96.8	74.1	0.0	10.4	46.2	17.7	70.7	67.0	50.2	24.4	30.7	42.2
	Xu (10%) [75]	48.0	90.9	97.3	74.8	0.0	8.4	49.3	27.3	71.7	69.0	53.2	16.5	23.3	42.8
	Zhang et al. (1%) [78]	61.8	91.5	96.9	80.6	0.0	18.2	58.1	47.2	75.8	85.7	65.2	68.9	65.0	50.2
	PSD (1%) [79]	63.5	92.3	97.7	80.7	0.0	27.8	56.2	62.5	78.7	84.1	63.1	70.4	58.9	53.2
	Π Model (0.2%) [28]	44.3	89.1	97.0	71.5	0.0	3.6	43.2	27.4	63.1	62.1	43.7	14.7	24.0	36.7
	MT (0.2%) [52]	44.4	88.9	96.8	70.1	0.1	3.0	44.3	28.8	63.7	63.6	47.7	15.5	23.0	35.8
	Xu (0.2%) [75]	44.5	90.1	97.1	71.9	0.0	1.9	47.2	29.3	64.0	62.9	42.2	15.9	18.9	37.5
	RandLA-Net (0.1%)	52.9	89.9	95.9	75.3	0.0	7.5	52.4	26.5	62.2	74.5	49.1	60.2	49.3	45.1
	Ours (0.1%)	**61.4**	**91.7**	95.6	**78.7**	0.0	**24.2**	**55.9**	**63.1**	**70.5**	**83.1**	**60.7**	**67.8**	**56.1**	**50.6**

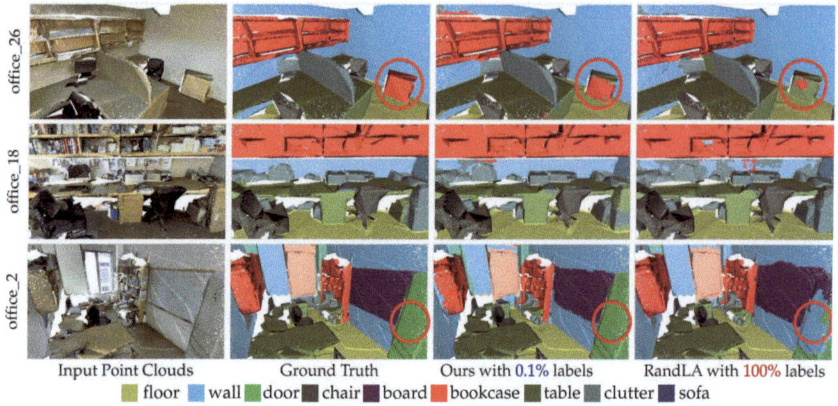

Fig. 5.4 Qualitative results achieved by our SQN and the fully-supervised RandLA-Net [23] on the *Area-5* of the S3DIS dataset (This figure is reproduced from [21])

Table 5.2 Quantitative results on ScanNet (online test set)

Settings	Methods	mIoU(%)
Full sup.	PointNet++ [40]	33.9
	SPLATNet [47]	39.3
	TangentConv [53]	43.8
	PointCNN [31]	45.8
	PointConv [71]	55.6
	SPH3D-GCN [30]	61.0
	KPConv [56]	68.4
	RandLA-Net [23]	64.5
Weak sup.	MPRM* [66]	41.1
	Zhang et al. (1%) [78]	51.1
	PSD (1%) [79]	54.7
	Ours (0.1%)	**56.9**

extremely large amount of 3D points scanned. We can see that our SQN trained with 0.01% labels also achieves satisfactory accuracy, though there is space to be improved in the future.

5.5.2 Evaluation on Large-Scale 3D Benchmarks

To validate the versatility of our SQN, we further evaluate our SQN on four point cloud datasets with different density and quality, including SensatUrban [22],

Table 5.3 Quantitative results on Semantic3D [17]

	Methods	*Semantic8*		*Reduced8*	
		OA(%)	**mIoU(%)**	OA(%)	**mIoU(%)**
Full sup.	SnapNet [6]	91.0	67.4	88.6	59.1
	PointNet++ [40]	85.7	63.1	–	–
	ShellNet [82]	–	–	93.2	69.3
	GACNet [62]	–	–	91.9	70.8
	RGNet [57]	90.6	72.0	94.5	74.7
	SPG [29]	92.9	76.2	94.0	73.2
	KPConv [56]	–	–	92.9	74.6
	ConvPoint [5]	93.4	76.5	–	–
	WreathProdNet [64]	94.6	77.1	–	–
	RandLA-Net [23]	95.0	75.8	94.8	77.4
Weak sup.	Zhang et al. (1%) [78]	–	–	–	72.6
	PSD (1%) [79]	–	–	–	75.8
	Ours (0.1%)	**94.8**	**72.3**	**93.7**	**74.7**
	Ours (0.01%)	91.9	58.8	90.3	65.6

Table 5.4 Quantitative results of different approaches on the DALES [58], SensatUrban [22], Toronto3D [49] and SemanticKITTI [3]

Settings	Methods	DALES [58]		SensatUrban [22]			Toronto3D [49]		SemanticKITTI [3]
		OA(%)	mIoU (%)	OA(%)	mAcc (%)	mIoU (%)	OA(%)	mIoU (%)	mIoU(%)
Full supervision	PointNet [39]	–	–	80.8	30.3	23.7	–	–	14.6
	PointNet++ [40]	95.7	68.3	84.3	40.0	32.9	84.9	41.8	20.1
	PointCNN [31]	97.2	58.4	–	–	–	–	–	–
	TangentConv [53]	–	–	77.0	43.7	33.3	–	–	40.9
	ShellNet [82]	96.4	57.4	–	–	-	–	–	–
	DGCNN [65]	–	–	–	–	–	94.2	61.8	–
	SPG [29]	95.5	60.6	85.3	44.4	37.3	–	–	17.4
	SparseConv [15]	–	–	88.7	63.3	42.7	–	–	–
	KPConv [56]	97.8	81.1	93.2	63.8	57.6	95.4	69.1	58.1
	ConvPoint [4]	97.2	67.4	–	–	–	–	–	–
	RandLA-Net [23]	97.1	80.0	89.8	69.6	52.7	92.9	77.7	53.9
Weak supervision	**Ours (0.1%)**	97.0	72.0	**91.0**	**70.9**	**54.0**	96.7	**77.7**	50.8
	Ours (0.01%)	95.9	60.4	85.6	49.4	37.2	94.2	68.2	39.1

Toronto3D [49], DALES [58], and SemanticKITTI [3]. Note that, all existing weakly-supervised approaches are only evaluated on the dataset with dense point clouds, and there are no results reported on these datasets. Therefore, we only compare our approach with existing fully-supervised methods in this section.

As shown in Table 5.4, the performance of our SQN is on par with the fully-supervised counterpart RandLA-Net on several datasets, whilst the model is only supplied with 0.1% labels for training. In particular, our SQN trained with 0.1% labels even outperforms the fully supervised RandLA-Net on the SensatUrban dataset. This shows the great potential of our method, especially for extremely large-scale point clouds with billions of points, where the manual annotation is unrealistic and impractical.

5.5.3 Ablation Studies

To evaluate the effectiveness of each module in our framework, we conduct the following ablation studies. All ablated networks are trained on Areas 1, 2, 3, 4, and 6 with 0.1% labels, and tested on the Area 5 of the S3DIS dataset.

Variants of Semantic Queries: The hierarchical point feature query mechanism is the major component of our SQN. To evaluate this component, we perform semantic query at different encoding layers. In particular, we train four additional models, each of which has a different combination of queried neighboring point features.

From Table 5.5 we can see that the segmentation performance drops significantly if we only collect the relevant point features at a single layer (e.g., the first or the last layer), while querying at the last layer can achieve much better results than in the first layer. This is because the points in the last encoding layer are quite sparse but representative, aggregating a large number of neighboring points. Additionally, querying at different encoding layers and combining them is likely to achieve better segmentation results, mainly because it integrates different spatial levels of semantic content and considers more neighboring points.

Varying Number of Queried Neighbors: Intuitively, querying a larger neighborhood is more likely to achieve better results. However, an overly large neighborhood may include points with very different semantics, diminishing overall performance. To investigate the impact of the number of neighboring points used in our semantic query, we conduct experiments by varying the number of neighboring points from 1 to 25. As shown in Fig. 5.5, the overall performance with differing numbers of neighboring points does not change significantly, showing that our simple query mechanism is robust to the size of the neighboring patch. Instead, the mixture of different feature levels plays a more important role as demonstrated in Table 5.5.

Varying annotated points: To verify the sensitivity of our SQN to different randomly annotated points, we train our models five times with exactly the same architectures, i.e., the only change is that different subsets of randomly selected 0.1% of points are labeled. The experimental results are reported in Table 5.6. It can be seen that there are slight, but not significant, differences between different runs. This indicates that the proposed SQN is robust to the choice of randomly annotated points. We also notice that the major performance change lies in minor categories such as *door*, *sofa*, and *board*, showing that the underrepresented classes are more sensitive to weak annotation.

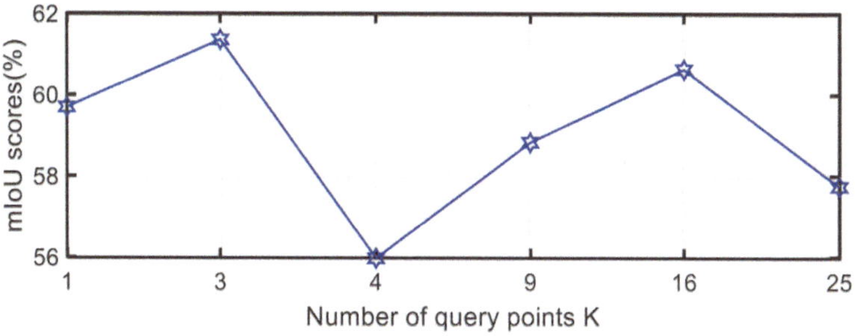

Fig. 5.5 The results of our SQN with different numbers of query points on the *Area-5* of the S3DIS dataset (This figure is reproduced from [21])

Table 5.5 Ablations of different levels of semantic query

Model	1st	2nd	3rd	4st	OA(%)	mIoU(%)
A	✓				48.66	22.89
B				✓	75.54	46.02
C	✓	✓			70.76	38.18
D	✓	✓	✓		82.37	54.21
E	✓	✓	✓	✓	**86.15**	**61.41**

Table 5.6 Sensitivity analysis of the proposed SQN on S3DIS dataset

	OA(%)	mIoU(%)
Trial1	86.15	61.41
Trial2	85.63	59.24
Trial3	86.39	60.93
Trial4	86.32	59.40
Trial5	**86.40**	**61.56**
Mean	86.25	60.42
STD	0.32	0.93

Varying proportion of annotated points: We further examine the performance of SQN with differing amounts of annotated points. As shown in Table 5.7, the proposed SQN can achieve satisfactory segmentation performance when there are only 0.1% labels available, but the performance drops significantly when there are only 0.01% labeled points available, primarily because the supervision signal is too sparse and limited in this case. It is also interesting to see that our framework achieves slightly better mIoU performance when using 10% labels compared with full supervision. In particular, the performance on minority categories such as *column/window/door* has improved by 2–5%. This implies that: (1) In a sense, the supervision signal is sufficient in this case; (2) Another way to address the critical issue of imbalanced class

Table 5.7 Quantitative results achieved by our SQN on *Area-5* of S3DIS under different amounts of labeled points

Settings	Methods	mIoU(%)	*Ceil.*	*Floor*	*Wall*	*Beam*	*Col.*	*Win.*	*Door*	*Chair*	*Table*	*Book.*	*Sofa*	*Board*	*Clutter*
100%	SQN	63.73	92.76	96.92	**81.84**	0.00	25.93	50.53	65.88	79.52	85.31	55.66	**72.51**	65.78	55.85
10%	SQN	**64.67**	**93.04**	**97.45**	81.55	0.00	**28.01**	55.77	68.68	**80.11**	**87.67**	55.25	72.31	63.91	**57.02**
1%	SQN	63.65	92.03	96.41	81.32	0.00	21.42	53.71	**73.17**	77.80	85.95	56.72	69.91	**66.57**	52.49
0.1%	SQN	61.41	91.72	95.63	78.71	0.00	24.23	**55.89**	63.14	70.50	83.13	**60.67**	67.82	56.14	50.63
0.01%	SQN	45.30	89.16	93.49	71.28	0.00	4.14	34.67	41.02	54.88	66.85	25.68	55.37	12.80	39.57

Table 5.8 Quantitative results achieved by different methods on the region-wise labeled S3DIS dataset

	SPVCNN [50]	MinkowskiUnet [11]	SQN (Ours)
Random	49.61	46.15	**60.19**
Softmax Confidence [59]	51.05	45.45	**57.24**
Softmax Margin [59]	50.80	44.33	**57.94**
Softmax Entropy [59]	50.35	49.99	**57.98**
MC Dropout [14]	50.39	49.94	**58.30**
ReDAL [70]	50.89	47.88	**54.24**

distribution may be to use a portion of training data (i.e., weak supervision). This is an interesting direction for further research, and we leave it for future exploration.

Extension to Region-wise Annotated Data: Beyond evaluating our method on randomly point-wise annotated datasets, we also extend our SQN on the region-wise sparsely labeled S3DIS dataset. Following [70], point clouds are firstly grouped into regions by unsupervised over-segmentation methods [38], and then a sparse number of regions are manually annotated through various active learning strategies [14, 59, 70]. As shown in Table 5.8, our SQN can consistently achieve better results than vanilla SPVCNN [50] and MinkowskiNet [11] under the same supervision signal (10 iterations of active selection), regardless of the active learning strategy used. This is likely because the SparseConv based methods [11, 50] usually have larger models and more trainable parameters compared with our point-based lightweight SQN, thus naturally exhibiting a stronger demand and dependence for more supervision signals. On the other hand, this result further validates the effectiveness and superiority of our SQN under weak supervision.

5.6 Conclusion

In this chapter, we propose SQN, a conceptually simple and elegant framework to learn the semantics of large-scale point clouds, with as few as 0.1% supplied labels for training. We first point out the redundancy of dense 3D annotations through extensive experiments, and then propose an effective semantic query framework based on the assumption of semantic similarity of neighboring points in 3D space. The proposed SQN simply follows the concept of wider label propagation, but shows great potential for weakly-supervised semantic segmentation of large-scale point clouds. It would be interesting to extend this method for weakly-supervised instance segmentation, panoptic segmentation, and interactive annotation based on active learning.

References

1. Aksoy EE, Baci S, Cavdar S (2019) Salsanet: Fast road and vehicle segmentation in LiDAR point clouds for autonomous driving. In: IV, pp 926–932
2. Armeni I, Sax S, Zamir AR, Savarese S (2017) Joint 2D-3D-semantic data for indoor scene understanding. In: ICCV
3. Behley J, Garbade M, Milioto A, Quenzel J, Behnke S, Stachniss C, Gall J (2019) SemanticKITTI: a dataset for semantic scene understanding of LiDAR sequences. In: ICCV, pp 9297–9307
4. Boulch A (2019) Generalizing discrete convolutions for unstructured point clouds. In: 3DOR, pp 71–78
5. Boulch A, Puy G, Marlet R (2020) Fkaconv: feature-kernel alignment for point cloud convolution. In: ACCV
6. Boulch A, Saux BL, Audebert N (2017) Unstructured point cloud semantic labeling using deep segmentation networks. In: 3DOR, pp 17–24
7. Chen T, Kornblith S, Norouzi M, Hinton G (2020) A simple framework for contrastive learning of visual representations. In: ICML, pp 1597–1607
8. Chen Y, Liu J, Ni B, Wang H, Yang J, Liu N, Li T, Tian Q (2021) Shape self-correction for unsupervised point cloud understanding. In: ICCV
9. Cheng M, Hui L, Xie J, Yang J (2021) Sspc-net: Semi-supervised semantic 3d point cloud segmentation network. arXiv:2104.07861
10. Cheng R, Razani R, Taghavi E, Li E, Liu B (2021) 2-S3Net: Attentive feature fusion with adaptive feature selection for sparse semantic segmentation network. arXiv:2102.04530
11. Choy C, Gwak J, Savarese S (2019) 4D spatio-temporal convnets: Minkowski convolutional neural networks. In: CVPR, pp 3075–3084
12. Cortinhal T, Tzelepis G, Aksoy EE (2020) SalsaNext: Fast semantic segmentation of LiDAR point clouds for autonomous driving. In: ISVC
13. Dai A, Chang AX, Savva M, Halber M, Funkhouser T, Nießner M (2017) ScanNet: richly-annotated 3D reconstructions of indoor scenes. In: CVPR, pp 5828–5839
14. Gal Y, Ghahramani Z (2016) Dropout as a bayesian approximation: representing model uncertainty in deep learning. In: ICML
15. Graham B, Engelcke M, van der Maaten L (2018) 3D semantic segmentation with submanifold sparse convolutional networks. In: CVPR
16. Guo Y, Wang H, Hu Q, Liu H, Liu L, Bennamoun M (2020) Deep learning for 3D point clouds: a survey. IEEE TPAMI
17. Hackel T, Savinov N, Ladicky L, Wegner JD, Schindler K, Pollefeys M (2017) Semantic3D.Net: a new large-scale point cloud classification benchmark. ISPRS
18. He K, Fan H, Wu Y, Xie S, Girshick R (2020) Momentum contrast for unsupervised visual representation learning. In: CVPR, pp 9729–9738
19. He K, Zhang X, Ren S, Sun J (2016) Deep residual learning for image recognition. In: CVPR
20. Hou J, Graham B, Nießner M, Xie S (2021) Exploring data-efficient 3D scene understanding with contrastive scene contexts. In: CVPR

21. Hu Q, Yang B, Fang G, Guo Y, Leonardis A, Trigoni N, Markham A (2022) SQN: weakly-supervised semantic segmentation of large-scale 3d point clouds. In: ECCV. Springer, pp 600–619
22. Hu Q, Yang B, Khalid S, Xiao W, Trigoni N, Markham A (2021) Towards semantic segmentation of urban-scale 3D point clouds: a dataset, benchmarks and challenges. In: CVPR
23. Hu Q, Yang B, Xie L, Rosa S, Guo Y, Wang Z, Trigoni N, Markham A (2020) RandLA-Net: efficient semantic segmentation of large-scale point clouds. In: CVPR
24. Jaritz M, Gu J, Su H (2019) Multi-view pointnet for 3D scene understanding. In: ICCVW, pp 0–0
25. Jiang L, Shi S, Tian Z, Lai X, Liu S, Fu CW, Jia J (2021) Guided point contrastive learning for semi-supervised point cloud semantic segmentation. In: ICCV
26. Krähenbühl P, Koltun V (2011) Efficient inference in fully connected CRFs with gaussian edge potentials. In: NeurIPS, pp 109–117
27. Kundu A, Yin X, Fathi A, Ross D, Brewington B, Funkhouser T, Pantofaru C (2020) Virtual multi-view fusion for 3D semantic segmentation. In: ECCV, pp 518–535
28. Laine S, Aila T (2017) Temporal ensembling for semi-supervised learning. In: ICLR
29. Landrieu L, Simonovsky M (2018) Large-scale point cloud semantic segmentation with superpoint graphs. In: CVPR, pp 4558–4567
30. Lei H, Akhtar N, Mian A (2020) Spherical kernel for efficient graph convolution on 3D point clouds. IEEE TPAMI
31. Li Y, Bu R, Sun M, Wu W, Di X, Chen B (2018) PointCNN: convolution on X-transformed points. In: NeurIPS
32. Liu Y, Yi L, Zhang S, Fan Q, Funkhouser T, Dong H (2020) P4contrast: contrastive learning with pairs of point-pixel pairs for rgb-d scene understanding. arXiv:2012.13089
33. Liu Z, Qi X, Fu CW (2021) One thing one click: a self-training approach for weakly supervised 3d semantic segmentation. In: CVPR, pp 1726–1736
34. Liu Z, Tang H, Lin Y, Han S (2019) Point-voxel CNN for efficient 3D deep learning. In: NeurIPS
35. Long J, Shelhamer E, Darrell T (2015) Fully convolutional networks for semantic segmentation. In: CVPR, pp 3431–3440
36. Meng HY, Gao L, Lai YK, Manocha D (2019) VV-Net: Voxel VAE net with group convolutions for point cloud segmentation. In: ICCV
37. Milioto A, Vizzo I, Behley J, Stachniss C (2019) Rangenet++: fast and accurate LiDAR semantic segmentation. In: IROS, pp 4213–4220
38. Papon J, Abramov A, Schoeler M, Worgotter F (2013) Voxel cloud connectivity segmentation-supervoxels for point clouds. In: CVPR
39. Qi CR, Su H, Mo K, Guibas LJ (2017) PointNet: Deep learning on point sets for 3D classification and segmentation. In: CVPR, pp 652–660
40. Qi CR, Yi L, Su H, Guibas LJ (2017) PointNet++: deep hierarchical feature learning on point sets in a metric space. In: NeurIPS
41. Ren Z, Misra I, Schwing AG, Girdhar R (2021) 3d spatial recognition without spatially labeled 3d. In: Proceedings of the IEEE/CVF conference on computer vision and pattern recognition, pp 13204–13213
42. Rethage D, Wald J, Sturm J, Navab N, Tombari F (2018) Fully-convolutional point networks for large-scale point clouds. In: ECCV
43. Roynard X, Deschaud JE, Goulette F (2018) Paris-Lille-3D: a large and high-quality ground-truth urban point cloud dataset for automatic segmentation and classification. IJRR 37(6):545–557
44. Sauder J, Sievers B (2019) Self-supervised deep learning on point clouds by reconstructing space. In: NeurIPS, pp 12962–12972
45. Sharma C, Kaul M (2020) Self-supervised few-shot learning on point clouds. In: NeurIPS
46. Shi X, Xu X, Chen K, Cai L, Foo CS, Jia K (2021) Label-efficient point cloud semantic segmentation: an active learning approach. arXiv:2101.06931

47. Su H, Jampani V, Sun D, Maji S, Kalogerakis E, Yang MH, Kautz J (2018) SPLATNet: sparse lattice networks for point cloud processing. In: CVPR, pp 2530–2539
48. Sun W, Tagliasacchi A, Deng B, Sabour S, Yazdani S, Hinton G, Yi KM (2020) Canonical capsules: Unsupervised capsules in canonical pose. arXiv:2012.04718
49. Tan W, Qin N, Ma L, Li Y, Du J, Cai G, Yang K, Li J (2020) Toronto-3D: a large-scale mobile LiDAR dataset for semantic segmentation of urban roadways. In: CVPRW, pp 202–203
50. Tang H, Liu Z, Zhao S, Lin Y, Lin J, Wang H, Han S (2020) Searching efficient 3D architectures with sparse point-voxel convolution. In: ECCV, pp 685–702
51. Tao A, Duan Y, Wei Y, Lu J, Zhou J (2020) Seggroup: Seg-level supervision for 3D instance and semantic segmentation. arXiv:2012.10217
52. Tarvainen A, Valpola H (2017) Mean teachers are better role models: weight-averaged consistency targets improve semi-supervised deep learning results. In: NeurIPS, pp 1195–1204
53. Tatarchenko M, Park J, Koltun V, Zhou QY (2018) Tangent convolutions for dense prediction in 3D. In: CVPR, pp 3887–3896
54. Tchapmi L, Choy C, Armeni I, Gwak J, Savarese S (2017) Segcloud: semantic segmentation of 3D point clouds. In: 3DV, pp 537–547
55. Thabet A, Alwassel H, Ghanem B (2020) Self-supervised learning of local features in 3D point clouds. In: CVPRW, pp 938–939
56. Thomas H, Qi CR, Deschaud JE, Marcotegui B, Goulette F, Guibas LJ (2019) KPConv: flexible and deformable convolution for point clouds. In: ICCV, pp 6411–6420
57. Truong G, Gilani SZ, Islam SMS, Suter D (2019) Fast point cloud registration using semantic segmentation. In: DICTA, pp 1–8
58. Varney N, Asari VK, Graehling Q (2020) DALES: a large-scale aerial LiDAR data set for semantic segmentation. In: CVPRW, pp 186–187
59. Wang D, Shang Y (2014) A new active labeling method for deep learning. In: IJCNN. IEEE, pp 112–119
60. Wang H, Liu Q, Yue X, Lasenby J, Kusner MJ (2020) Pre-training by completing point clouds. arXiv:2010.01089
61. Wang H, Rong X, Yang L, Wang S, Tian Y (2019) Towards weakly supervised semantic segmentation in 3D graph-structured point clouds of wild scenes. In: BMVC, p 284
62. Wang L, Huang Y, Hou Y, Zhang S, Shan J (2019) Graph attention convolution for point cloud semantic segmentation. In: CVPR
63. Wang P, Yao W (2021) A new weakly supervised approach for ALS point cloud semantic segmentation. arXiv:2110.01462
64. Wang R, Albooyeh M, Ravanbakhsh S (2020) Equivariant maps for hierarchical structures. arXiv:2006.03627
65. Wang Y, Sun Y, Liu Z, Sarma SE, Bronstein MM, Solomon JM (2019) Dynamic graph CNN for learning on point clouds. ACM TOG 38(5):1–12
66. Wei J, Lin G, Yap KH, Hung TY, Xie L (2020) Multi-path region mining for weakly supervised 3D semantic segmentation on point clouds. In: CVPR, pp 4384–4393
67. Wei J, Lin G, Yap KH, Liu F, Hung TY (2021) Dense supervision propagation for weakly supervised semantic segmentation on 3d point clouds. arXiv:2107.11267
68. Wu B, Wan A, Yue X, Keutzer K (2018) SqueezeSeg: Convolutional neural nets with recurrent CRF for real-time road-object segmentation from 3D LiDAR point cloud. In: ICRA, pp 1887–1893
69. Wu B, Zhou X, Zhao S, Yue X, Keutzer K (2019) SqueezeSegV2: Improved model structure and unsupervised domain adaptation for road-object segmentation from a LiDAR point cloud. In: ICRA, pp 4376–4382
70. Wu TH, Liu YC, Huang YK, Lee HY, Su HT, Huang PC, Hsu WH (2021) Redal: region-based and diversity-aware active learning for point cloud semantic segmentation. In: ICCV, pp 15510–15519
71. Wu W, Qi Z, Fuxin L (2018) PointConv: deep convolutional networks on 3D point clouds. In: CVPR, pp 9621–9630

72. Wu Y, Yan Z, Cai S, Li G, Yu Y, Han X, Cui S (2022) Pointmatch: a consistency training framework for weakly supervisedsemantic segmentation of 3d point clouds. arXiv:2202.10705
73. Xie S, Gu J, Guo D, Qi CR, Guibas L, Litany O (2020) PointContrast: unsupervised pre-training for 3D point cloud understanding. In: ECCV, pp 574–591
74. Xu C, Wu B, Wang Z, Zhan W, Vajda P, Keutzer K, Tomizuka M (2020) SqueezeSegV3: spatially-adaptive convolution for efficient point-cloud segmentation. In: ECCV, pp 1–19
75. Xu X, Lee GH (2020) Weakly supervised semantic point cloud segmentation: towards 10x fewer labels. In: CVPR, pp 13706–13715
76. Yan X, Gao J, Li J, Zhang R, Li Z, Huang R, Cui S (2020) Sparse single sweep lidar point cloud segmentation via learning contextual shape priors from scene completion. In: AAAI
77. Zhang F, Fang J, Wah B, Torr P (2020) Deep fusionnet for point cloud semantic segmentation. In: ECCV, vol 2, p 6
78. Zhang Y, Li Z, Xie Y, Qu Y, Li C, Mei T (2021) Weakly supervised semantic segmentation for large-scale point cloud. In: AAAI
79. Zhang Y, Qu Y, Xie Y, Li Z, Zheng S, Li C (2021) Perturbed self-distillation: weakly supervised large-scale point cloud semantic segmentation. In: ICCV, pp 15520–15528
80. Zhang Z, Girdhar R, Joulin A, Misra I (2021) Self-supervised pretraining of 3D features on any point-cloud. arXiv:2101.02691
81. Zhang Z, Girdhar R, Joulin A, Misra I (2021) Self-supervised pretraining of 3d features on any point-cloud. In: ICCV
82. Zhang Z, Hua BS, Yeung SK (2019) ShellNet: efficient point cloud convolutional neural networks using concentric shells statistics. In: ICCV, pp 1607–1616
83. Zhao H, Jiang L, Fu CW, Jia J (2019) PointWeb: enhancing local neighborhood features for point cloud processing. In: CVPR
84. Zhao H, Jiang L, Jia J, Torr P, Koltun V (2020) Point Transformer. arXiv:2012.09164
85. Zhou B, Khosla A, Lapedriza A, Oliva A, Torralba A (2016) Learning deep features for discriminative localization. In: CVPR, pp 2921–2929
86. Zhu X, Chen J, Zeng X, Liang J, Li C, Liu S, Behpour S, Xu M (2021) Weakly supervised 3d semantic segmentation using cross-image consensus and inter-voxel affinity relations. In: ICCV
87. Zhu X, Zhou H, Wang T, Hong F, Ma Y, Li W, Li H, Lin D (2021) Cylindrical and asymmetrical 3D convolution networks for LiDAR segmentation. In: CVPR

Chapter 6
Single Object Tracking in Point Cloud Sequences

Tracking a single object in dynamic point cloud sequences is a crucial task for various intelligent systems. In this chapter, we propose *DeepPCT*, a deep neural network designed for precise and robust object tracking in sequential point clouds. Unlike conventional methods that rely on bounding box classification and regression for localization, our framework directly optimizes Intersection-over-Union (IoU) prediction to improve 3D localization accuracy. To overcome the limitations of the standard IoU metric, we introduce a central distance normalized IoU, which effectively reduces ambiguity in object localization. In addition, we explore the benefits of incorporating a re-detection module to improve tracking robustness, as failures often arise from error accumulation and significant variations. Extensive experiments on the KITTI benchmark show that our tracker attains strong performance, with a 3D Precision of 63.7% and a 3D Success of 45.0%. Furthermore, our method demonstrates robust performance in challenging scenarios with severe illumination changes and occlusions, even outperforming existing 2D state-of-the-art trackers.

6.1 Introduction

Tracking an object of interest in 3D point cloud sequences is a fundamental research topic with numerous applications, including robot navigation, motion planning, and precision measurement [10, 34, 40]. This task is particularly demanding due to several factors. First, different from regular 2D image sequences, raw point clouds captured by 3D sensors are inherently *sparse*, *irregular*, and *unordered*, with no accompanying appearance information (e.g., RGB). This lack of structural and visual cues makes it exceptionally challenging to establish a reliable tracking model at the start of a sequence. Second, the search space and degrees of freedom (DoF) for objects in a 3D sequence are significantly larger than their 2D counterparts, posing greater challenges for efficient and precise 3D object localization. Third, the incomplete

Y. Guo et al., *Point Cloud Intelligence*, Advances in Computer Vision and Pattern Recognition, https://doi.org/10.1007/978-981-95-0648-4_6

geometry and uneven point distribution within point clouds often lead to tracking drift, which can escalate into irreversible tracking failures.

Early approaches for 3D single object tracking (SOT) [23, 44] address the task by projecting unstructured point clouds onto the bird's eye view (BEV) and then applying region proposal networks (RPN) on the resulting 2D representations. However, these methods fail to fully exploit the rich geometric details in 3D point clouds and suffer from significant information loss due to the 3D-to-2D projection process. Recently, a few methods [9] have attempted to directly track objects in raw point clouds. These methods formulate the problem of point cloud tracking as a regression problem for optimal candidate bounding boxes, which constrains their localization accuracy by limiting the number of candidate boxes. This limitation heavily hampers overall tracking performance. Furthermore, most existing methods [9, 23, 44] are designed for short-term tracking and lack mechanisms such as error correction or re-detection modules. Consequently, they are highly susceptible to drift, leading to irreversible tracking failures during long-term tracking.

In this chapter, we focus on long-term tracking in sequential point clouds for autonomous driving scenarios. We present a deep neural network architecture called *DeepPCT*, which performs tracking directly on dynamic point clouds without relying on projection techniques or two-stage box regression. Instead of using classification confidence scores to assess candidate proposals, our method estimates the Intersection-over-Union (IoU) between each candidate and the target object to measure localization confidence. To address the limitations of standard IoU, especially in cases where the predicted and ground truth boxes do not overlap, we introduce a central distance normalized IoU (CIoU) to reduce ambiguity in such situations. In addition, we examine the role of a re-detection module in enhancing the robustness of 3D SOT. Comprehensive experiments on the KITTI [8] benchmark demonstrate that DeepPCT achieves strong and consistent performance across diverse tracking scenarios. The main contributions of this work are summarized as follows:

- We introduce an efficient yet straightforward solution to conduct 3D single object tracking in point cloud sequences. Unlike traditional methods that rely on projection or two-stage box regression, our method achieves accurate object localization in a fully end-to-end manner.
- We investigate how the re-detection module impacts overall 3D tracking performance and observe that a straightforward re-detection-based strategy for 3D SOT surpasses several 2D tracking methods in the wild environments.
- Extensive experiments on the KITTI [8] benchmark highlight the substantial performance gains achieved by our tracker. Furthermore, our approach exhibits impressive robustness on the wild environments with severe illumination changes and occlusions.

6.2 Related Work

In this section, we briefly review prior work related to single object tracking (SOT), multiple object tracking (MOT), 3D object detection, and IoU-based evaluation metrics commonly used in object detection and tracking tasks. For a more detailed and comprehensive review, readers can refer to [11, 41].

6.2.1 *Single Object Tracking*

Single object tracking aims to estimate an object's trajectory across frames based solely on its initial location in the first frame. This task is commonly addressed using a tracking-by-detection paradigm, where an appearance model is learned from limited observations to distinguish the target from the surrounding background. According to the input data modality, existing approaches can be classified into two groups: image-based 2D SOT and point cloud-based 3D SOT.

2D SOT: Early methods primarily rely on correlation filter-based approaches [2, 12]. In contrast, recent advancements are largely driven by convolutional neural networks (CNNs), particularly those utilizing Siamese architectures [15]. SiamFC [1] is a groundbreaking work, which introduces a fully convolutional Siamese network to learn robust representations and employs a simple cross-correlation operation to locate the target object. Li et al. [20] extended SiamFC by integrating a region proposal network (RPN) for better aspect ratio estimation, achieving top-tier results in the VOT2018 [16] challenge. ATOM [5] further advanced this direction by incorporating target-specific features into the search branch to enable IoU prediction. Subsequent works have introduced various enhancements to Siamese-based tracking systems, including distraction handling [49], triple loss optimization [6], semantic integration [35], and improved feature learning techniques [19, 46], all of which contribute to improved robustness and tracking accuracy.

Tracking failure caused by the accumulation of errors over time is a persistent challenge in object tracking. To address this issue, several methods [21, 24, 33] have been proposed to incorporate re-detection mechanisms to recover lost targets. Ma et al. [24] developed a robust online module based on random ferns to re-detect objects during tracking. Liu et al. [21] introduced an instance-specific proposal generator to identify candidate regions for re-localizing the target. Voigtlaend et al. [33] proposed Siam R-CNN, a tracking-by-detection framework that jointly models both the target and surrounding distractors, thus achieving effective re-detection following long-term occlusions.

3D SOT: Thanks to the rich geometric cues inherent in 3D point cloud data, 3D object tracking holds the potential to address several challenges encountered in 2D SOT, such as sensitivity to lighting conditions and object scale variation. Inspired by the success of Siamese networks in 2D tracking, Giancola et al. [9] pioneered the adaptation of Siamese tracking frameworks to the 3D domain. Zarzar et al. [44] extended this approach by employing an RPN network to generate object candidates on BEV representations, followed by refinement via a 3D Siamese network [9]. Fang et al. [7] introduced a 3D variant of SiamRPN [20] tailored for raw point cloud sequences. Zhou et al. [48] incorporated Transformer-based architectures to model spatial relationships among points, while Qi et al. [27] developed P2B, an end-to-end framework that uses Hough voting to infer candidate target centers in 3D space and subsequently clusters neighboring points to generate final 3D proposals.

In this chapter, we introduce a tracking by re-detection approach for 3D SOT. While our method adopts the general structure of Siamese networks, it differs from P2B [27] in two significant ways. First, unlike P2B, which employs a regression-based paradigm that can be computationally intensive, our method utilizes a more efficient classification-based paradigm. Second, our design explicitly considers the challenges of long-term tracking, whereas P2B is designed for short-term tracking scenarios.

6.2.2 IoU Metric for Object Detection and Tracking

IoU is extensively adopted as both an evaluation criterion and loss function in object detection [4, 14, 47] and tracking [5]. Despite its widespread use, IoU suffers from a notable drawback: when a predicted 3D box does not intersect with the ground-truth box, its IoU score becomes zero, preventing differentiation among non-overlapping candidates. To alleviate this limitation, Rezatofighi et al. [28] introduced Generalized IoU (GIoU), which accounts for the area not covered between two boxes. Subsequently, Zheng et al. [47] proposed Distance IoU, which incorporates additional geometric attributes such as aspect ratio and overlap extent. Chen et al. [4] presented Pixels-IoU (PIoU), which further integrates orientation information. In this chapter, we aim to resolve the ambiguity of IoU by integrating the normalized distance between the center points of boxes into the IoU formulation.

6.3 Robust 3D Single Object Tracking with Re-Detection: DeepPCT

In this section, we begin by outlining our DeepPCT pipeline (Sect. 6.3.1). Then, we provide a detailed introduction of the key stages in the DeepPCT tracker (Sect. 6.3.2), including the feature learning, IoU prediction, and re-detection stages. Next, we evaluate the pros and cons of existing IoU metrics (Sect. 6.3.3) before introducing our proposed Center-IoU (Sect. 6.3.4). Finally, we provide a thorough explanation of the training (Sect. 6.3.5) and inference (Sect. 6.3.6) stages.

6.3.1 Overview

Given a sequential LiDAR point cloud stream and the initial target state (i.e., center position and spatial dimension) in the first frame, 3D SOT aims to estimate the target's trajectory and its state variation in each subsequent frame. To achieve this, a 3D bounding box must be predicted in each frame to accurately localize the object.

As illustrated in Fig. 6.1, our DeepPCT framework consists of three main stages: (1) feature learning, (2) IoU prediction, and (3) re-detection. Inspired by the well-established Siamese architectures [1, 9, 19, 33, 35], the framework utilizes a dual-branch design with shared backbone networks to process point cloud inputs. The IoU prediction module estimates the IoU or CIoU between each candidate box and its corresponding ground-truth. To further refine localization, a pre-trained 3D detector is employed as the re-detection module.

Although Siamese networks are widely applied to single object tracking, our DeepPCT differs from SC3D [9] in two key respects. First, instead of directly computing cosine similarity between the template and search branch features as in SC3D, we encode the similarity into a modulation vector that generates target-specific features for CIoU prediction. Second, to improve robustness in long-term tracking within sequential point clouds, we incorporate a re-detection module into our architecture.

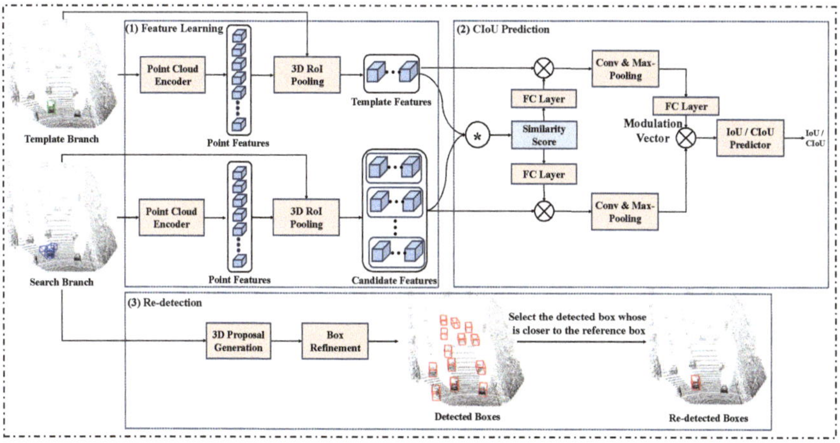

Fig. 6.1 The overall pipeline of the proposed DeepPCT (This figure is reproduced from [22])

6.3.2 Methodology

Bounding Box Representation: Following [13, 31, 43], the 3D bounding box is parameterized using seven parameters $(x, y, z, l, w, h, \theta)$. The triplet (x, y, z) specifies the box's center coordinates, while (l, w, h) describes its length, width, and height, respectively. The heading angle is represented by θ.

Feature Learning Stage: This stage aims to extract informative and discriminative feature embeddings for both the ground-truth bounding box and the candidate proposals. Given the input point clouds from the template branch Z and the search branch X, we begin by applying the preprocessing strategy from [31], where each point cloud resampled, either up-sampling or down-sampling, to a fixed size of 16,384 points before feeding it into the network. Subsequently, we employ PointNet++ [26] with multi-scale grouping as our backbone to generate point-wise features $f_Z \in \mathbb{R}^{N\times 128}$ for the template branch and $f_X \in \mathbb{R}^{N\times 128}$ for the search branch, where N is the number of points in each processed point cloud.

Following [5], our network's motion model (i.e., proposal generation) produces a set of 3D object proposals by perturbing the previously predicted bounding box with Gaussian noise. For each proposal, we apply 3D ROI pooling [31] to gather the features within its valid region, generating a fixed-size feature map of dimensions $n \times 128$. Furthermore, to incorporate additional contextual information, we expand the original proposal b_i using a factor α to form a new box $b_i^e = (x_i, y_i, z_i, l_i * (1 + \alpha), w_i * (1 + \alpha), h_i * (1 + \alpha), \theta_i)$.

IoU Prediction Stage: The per-proposal feature maps from the template and search branches, denoted as $\varphi(Z) \in \mathbb{R}^{1\times n\times 128}$ and $\varphi(X) \in \mathbb{R}^{m\times n\times 128}$ respectively (where m represents the number of candidate proposals), are input to the IoU prediction module. The proposal-wise correlation scores S are computed by treating $[\varphi(Z)]$ as a convolutional kernel for $[\varphi(X)]$:

$$S = [\varphi(X)] \star [\varphi(Z)], \tag{6.1}$$

where $\star$ represents the convolution operation. We then pass $S \in \mathbb{R}^{m\times 128}$ through a fully connected (FC) layer to obtain scaling factors that adaptively recalibrate features in both branches. Next, the refined template features are compressed into a coefficient vector and fused into the search branch via channel-wise multiplication to create a target-specific representation for IoU estimation. This representation is processed by three subsequent FC layers to predict the IoU. However, in cases where proposals do not overlap with the ground truth, the IoU metric becomes ineffective in expressing the similarity between candidate boxes and the ground-truth. To resolve this issue, we propose our Center-IoU (CIoU) metric, which is detailed in Sect. 6.3.4.

Re-detection Stage: Tracking failures frequently occur in long-term settings, especially when dealing with irregular 3D point cloud sequences. To mitigate such issues, we incorporate a re-detection mechanism to correct accumulated errors and enhance overall tracking robustness. Specifically, we adopt PointRCNN [31], an off-the-shelf 3D object detector, as our re-detection module. Once activated, the module re-initializes the tracking process using the detection results. The CIoU value serves as a confidence score for each frame, and whenever it falls below a predefined threshold, the re-detection module is triggered. Among the detection candidates, we select the bounding box closest to the current reference box for re-initialization.

Loss. We optimize the DeepPCT model by minimizing the absolute error between the predicted CIoU values and their corresponding ground-truth values:

$$L = \frac{1}{m} \sum_{i \in [0,m)} |CIoU_{gt}^{i} - CIoU_{\text{pred}}^{i}| \tag{6.2}$$

where m is the number of proposals. In addition, $CIoU_{gt}^{i}$ and $CIoU_{\text{pred}}^{i}$ represent the ground-truth and predicted CIoU values for the i-th candidate box, respectively.

6.3.3 *The Quest for an IoU Metric*

Although existing IoU-based metrics have been extensively adopted in 2D vision tasks, there remains a lack of established standard tailored to 3D point cloud tracking. To this end, we provide a comparative analysis of several representative IoU variants, highlighting their respective advantages and limitations:

- **Generalized Intersection over Union (GIoU).** GIoU extends the traditional IoU to handle cases where two boxes do not overlap. For two boxes A and B, it first finds the smallest bounding region C that contains both. It then calculates the ratio of the area of $C \backslash (A \cup B)$ to the area of C, i.e., $\frac{|C \backslash (A \cup B)|}{|C|}$. The GIoU is given by $GIoU = IoU - \frac{|C \backslash (A \cup B)|}{|C|}$.
- **Distance Intersection over Union (DIoU).** DIoU introduces additional geometric factors such as center distance and aspect ratio into the IoU calculation. Formally, $DIoU = IoU - R(A, B)$, where $R(A, B) = \rho(A, B) + \alpha v$. Here, $\rho(A, B)$ is a distance-based penalty term, α is a positive trade-off coefficient, v measures aspect ratio consistency.
- **Center Intersection over Union (CIoU).** CIoU considers both overlap (SOT metric (1) and center location error (SOT metric (2) simultaneously. The CIoU loss is defined as $L_{CIoU} = 1 - IoU + D_{\text{normalized}}$, with details of CIoU provided in Sect. 6.3.4. Larger CIoU values represent greater overlap between the predicted box and ground truth, alongside a reduced center distance error, which ultimately reflects better tracking accuracy.

In summary, while GIoU, DIoU, and CIoU all aim to reduce the ambiguity of standard IoU in the presence of non-overlapping predictions, GIoU and DIoU are primarily designed for detection tasks and do not fully reflect the temporal and localization dynamics critical in tracking. In contrast, our proposed CIoU formulation explicitly incorporates tracking-specific considerations, making it more suitable for 3D point cloud tracking scenarios.

6.3.4 Center-IoU

When two 3D bounding boxes do not overlap, the IoU is zero regardless of how far apart their centers are. This makes it difficult to distinguish between nearby and distant non-overlapping boxes. To overcome this limitation, we propose Center-IoU (CIoU), which incorporates a normalized center distance term to better reflect similarity in such cases. Formally, given a candidate box B_p and the ground-truth box B_{gt}, we define the normalized center distance as

$$D_{\text{normalized}} = \frac{d(c^p, c^{gt})}{D}, \tag{6.3}$$

where c^p and c^{gt} are the center coordinates of B_p and B_{gt}, respectively. $d(\cdot)$ represents the Euclidean distance, and D is the diagonal length of the minimal enclosing 3D box that contains both B_p and B_{gt}. Our CIoU is calculated as

$$CIoU = IoU - D_{\text{normalized}}. \tag{6.4}$$

Our CIoU satisfies

- CIoU is a lower bound of IoU, i.e., $CIoU \leq IoU$.
- For any two 3D boxes $A, B \in \mathbb{R}^7$, we have $-1 < CIoU(A, B) \leq 1$. In particular, $CIoU = 1$ only when the two boxes are perfectly overlapped, and it approaches -1 as the distance between their centers grows unbounded.

In summary, CIoU maintains IoU's essential properties while resolving ambiguity in non-overlapping cases. Therefore, we employ CIoU as a direct substitute for IoU to maximize our network's tracking performance.

6.3.5 Training

We begin by pre-training the re-detection network, PointRCNN, on the KITTI [8] tracking dataset. The resulting weights are then used to initialize both the template and search branches in our feature learning stage. Subsequently, we fine-tune DeepPCT by minimizing Eq. 6.2.

During training, two distinct point clouds from a sequence are randomly selected and fed into the template and search branches, respectively. We constrain the maximum temporal gap between these point clouds to 30 frames. Candidate boxes are generated by injecting Gaussian noise into the ground-truth box of the search frame.

6.3.6 Testing

As our focus lies in online 3D single object tracking, the predicted tracklet is generated in a frame-by-frame manner. The first frame is treated as the template, from which object features are extracted and encoded into a modulation vector. This vector is then applied to the search branch through channel-wise multiplication to produce a target-specific representation. Subsequently, CIoU scores are computed for all candidate proposals, and the one with the highest score is selected as the predicted target for the current frame.

If the CIoU score of the top candidate falls below a predefined confidence threshold, the re-detection mechanism is activated. In such cases, tracking is re-initialized by choosing the detection result that is spatially closest to the previously predicted bounding box.

6.4 Experiments

In this section, we extensively evaluate DeepPCT on the KITTI and nuScene-mini datasets. We first provide a brief introduction of the datasets and implementation details in Sect. 6.4.1, followed by an overview of the evaluation metrics in Sect. 6.4.2. Sections 6.4.3 and 6.4.5 then present our experimental findings.

6.4.1 Experimental Settings

Dataset: Following the protocol in [9], we evaluate our method on the KITTI tracking dataset [8] and adopt the same data split: sequences 00–16 for training, sequence 17 for validation, and sequences 18–20 for testing. To accommodate 3D single object tracking, we generate continuous tracklets for each car instance. We also evaluate the performance on the nuScenes dataset [3], a recently introduced large-scale benchmark for 3D detection and tracking. During both training and testing, we only utilize key frames and discard any tracklet whose first bounding box contains no points.

Implementation Details: Our model is optimized using Adam with a weight decay of 5e-4. Training begins with an initial learning rate of 1e-3, which is gradually reduced through exponential decay. We train for 50 epochs with a batch size of 32. Each input sample produces 24 3D proposals, and each proposal pools 128 points for processing.

6.4.2 Evaluation Metrics

To comprehensively evaluate the performance of our DeepPCT, we extend widely adopted precision and success plots from 2D SOT [39] to the 3D domain. These plots serve as a complementary evaluation to the metrics proposed in [9]. The specific definitions are detailed below.

3D Precision Plot: To evaluate tracking accuracy more robustly, we revisit the center location error (CLE) metric proposed in [9], which only considers center location errors within a fixed range of 0 to 2 m. While effective for vehicles, this metric is sensitive to object size, making it less suitable for other object categories such as pedestrians or cyclists. To address this limitation, we propose a normalized version of CLE, computed between the predicted box B_p and the ground-truth box B_{gt} as defined in Eq. 6.3. Building upon this, we introduce the 3D precision plot, which depicts the percentage of frames whose normalized CLE values are below various thresholds (e.g., from 0 to 0.5). This formulation improves robustness, as normalized CLE becomes uninformative when the tracker fully drifts away from the target, and thresholds offer a more interpretable assessment.

3D Success Plot: In addition to center localization, we also evaluate the overlap (3D IoU) between two bounding boxes, defined as $\frac{|B_p \cap B_{gt}|}{|B_p \cup B_{gt}|}$. Similarly, we propose the 3D success plot, which reports the fraction of frames whose overlap exceeds various thresholds (e.g., from 0 to 1).

Unlike the original metrics in [9], these newly introduced metrics are normalized and thus can be generalized to objects of any size. For quantitative analysis, we use the area under the curve (AUC) of both the precision and success plots as the final metrics of 3D tracking performance. To ensure a fair and thorough comparison, we report results using both our new metrics and the original metrics in [9] in subsequent experiments.

6.4.3 Experiments on the KITTI Dataset

The KITTI benchmark [8] is a widely used dataset for autonomous driving. Following [9], we transform the KITTI-MOT training set for 3D SOT by constructing separate tracklets for each individual car instance within every scene.

Overall Performance: We compare our proposed DeepPCT with two representative 3D point cloud tracking methods: SC3D [9] and P2B [27]. Following the evaluation protocol in [9], we design three experimental settings that differ in the strategy used to generate candidate boxes for each frame: (1) from the ground-truth box of the current frame, (2) from the ground-truth box of the previous frame, and (3) from the predicted box in the previous frame. Notice that setting (3) aligns with common 2D tracking practices [16, 39] and is closer to practical use. During the first two experimental setting, the re-detection module remains inactive.

Table 6.1 Performance comparison between DeepPCT and existing 3D tracking methods on Group (1) and Group (2)

Method	Group	Our metrics		Metrics in [9]	
		3D Prec.	3D Succ.	Prec.	Succ.
SC3D [9]	(1)	86.1	76.9	81.4	76.9
	(2)	73.2	59.3	65.0	59.3
P2B [27]	(1)	92.4	**80.0**	90.3	**80.0**
	(2)	**84.9**	**67.3**	**81.2**	**67.3**
DeepPCT (Ours)	(1)	**94.1**	78.6	**92.7**	78.6
	(2)	82.2	65.1	76.2	65.1

Table 6.2 Performance comparison between DeepPCT and existing 3D tracking methods on Group (3)

Method	Group	Our metrics		Metrics in [9]	
		3D Prec.	3D Succ.	Prec.	Succ.
SC3D [9]	(3)	37.2	25.4	32.6	25.4
DeepPCT (Ours)	(3)	45.3	35.7	41.5	35.7
SC3D [9] with re-detector	(3)	54.8	38.7	51.4	38.7
DeepPCT with re-detector	(3)	**63.7**	45.0	**57.7**	45.0

As shown in Table 6.1, DeepPCT achieves performance on par with P2B and significantly outperforms SC3D [9] across all three experimental settings. Notably, our method improves 3D precision by more than 8% and 3D success by over 1.7% in the first two settings. Furthermore, when the ground-truth box is no longer provided during tracking (i.e., group (3)), 3D precision and success rates increase from 54.8/38.7 to 63.7/45.0, as shown in Table 6.2. These results demonstrate highlight the robustness and effectiveness of DeepPCT in handling complex point cloud scenarios, showing its strong potential for deployment in practical applications.

Comparison with 3D Object Detectors: To further validate the effectiveness of DeepPCT, we compare it with two representative 3D object detectors, AVOD [17] and PointRCNN [31], given the limited number of dedicated 3D tracking methods currently available.

For fair comparison, we adopt the online association strategy introduced in [9], which links detections across frames by selecting the bounding box with the shortest distance to the previous result. Table 6.3 presents the quantitative results. It can be seen that DeepPCT achieves performance comparable to that of PointRCNN, while surpassing AVOD by 7.9% in 3D precision and 1.8% in 3D success. Furthermore, we observe that false negatives from 3D detectors can severely limit tracking, as one misalignment often leads to complete failure in subsequent frames.

Table 6.3 Performance comparison between DeepPCT and the modified 3D detection methods on the KITTI dataset

Method	Our metrics		Metrics in [9]	
	3D Prec.	3D Succ.	Prec.	Succ.
AVOD [17]	55.8	43.2	53.7	43.2
PointRCNN [31]	59.1	**45.6**	57.4	**45.6**
DeepPCT (Ours)	**63.7**	45.0	**57.7**	45.0

Table 6.4 Quantitative results achieved by DeepPCT and 2D tracking methods on the KITTI dataset

Method	2D Prec. [39]	2D Succ. [39]
SiamFC [1]	40.9	32.5
SiamRPN [20]	46.1	37.3
DaSiamRPN [49]	45.1	36.8
UpdateNet [45]	56.7	44.2
ItMDNet [25]	60.3	49.6
DeepPCT (Ours)	**61.1**	**52.3**

Fig. 6.2 Qualitative comparison among our DeepPCT and three 2D baseline trackers (This figure is reproduced from [22])

Comparison with 2D Trackers: Table 6.4 presents a comparison between DeepPCT and five recent 2D tracking methods, including four short-term trackers (e.g., SiamFC [1], SiamRPN [20], DaSiamRPN [49], and UpdateNet [45]) and a long-term 2D tracker, ItMDNet [25]. The pre-trained models for these 2D baselines are provided by their authors and were trained on the ILSVRC2015 dataset [29]. For consistency and fairness, we project our 3D bounding boxes onto the image plane and evaluate the results using the metrics proposed in [39].

As shown in Table 6.4, DeepPCT surpasses all competing 2D trackers by margins of 0.8–20.2% in 2D Precision and 2.7–19.8% in 2D Success. This highlights that well-known 2D trackers may fail in complex real-world settings (e.g., illumination changes, partial occlusions, or scale variations), as shown in Fig. 6.2. In contrast, 3D point cloud tracking is inherently less sensitive to such factors, making it an appealing alternative for robust object tracking in wild environments.

Comparison with 3D MOT Trackers: Table 6.5 presents a comparison of DeepPCT with two multi-object 3D trackers, AB3DMOT [36] and GNN3DMOT [37]. Both MOT methods rely on a frame-wise 3D detector to generate bounding boxes,

Table 6.5 Performance comparison between DeepPCT and 3D MOT methods on the KITTI dataset

Method	Our metrics		Metrics in [9]	
	3D Prec.	3D Succ.	Prec.	Succ.
AB3DMOT [36]	62.9	**45.6**	57.1	**45.6**
GNN3DMOT [37]	61.7	44.3	56.5	44.3
DeepPCT (Ours)	**63.7**	45.0	**57.7**	45.0

Fig. 6.3 Qualitative results of our DeepPCT on the *Seq_96* of the KITTI dataset (This figure is reproduced from [22])

followed by a combination of Kalman filtering and the Hungarian algorithm for object association. As shown in Table 6.5, DeepPCT achieves performance on par with AB3DMOT and surpasses GNN3DMOT by 2.0% in 3D Precision and 0.7% in 3D Success.

Runtime: We measure runtime by averaging the processing time of all test frames. On a single NVIDIA TITAN GPU, DeepPCT operates at 22.7 FPS, with the time breakdown as follows: 6.7 ms for point cloud processing, 12.3 ms for network forward pass, and 25.1 ms for re-detection. In comparison, SC3D [9], under its default configuration, runs at 6.8 FPS on the same hardware setup.

Qualitative Results: Figure 6.3 provides visualization results of our DeepPCT on several sequences. Notice that the visualizations on 2D images are provided just for better observation. We can observe that DeepPCT remains robust in cases with partial occlusions and low-resolution conditions. For instance, it successfully tracks a texture-less black car, which is challenging even for human observers and often problematic for 2D trackers.

6.4.4 Experiments on the NuScenes Dataset

We compare DeepPCT against P2B [27] on the nuScenes dataset, as shown in Table 6.6. Notice that our model is trained on the *train_track* subset of the nuScenes training set and evaluated on the validation set of the mini-version. We can observe, although tracking performance declines slightly due to the increased complexity of the scenes, DeepPCT achieves 27.5% in 3D Precision and 25.4% in 3D Success, surpassing P2B [27] by 1.5 and 1.7% on the respective metrics.

6.4.5 Ablation Studies

In this section, we conduct comprehensive ablation studies to verify the contribution of different architectural components and hyperparameter choices within the DeepPCT model.

How much does formulating IoU as objective help? In this experiment, we replace the IoU prediction objective with a simpler alternative that directly classifies the candidate bounding boxes based on confidence scores. Table 6.7 shows the results of both this variant and our CIoU-based approach. Notably, DeepPCT with CIoU improves 3D Precision and 3D Success by 3.0 and 3.9%, respectively. These results demonstrate that directly regressing localization quality is more effective than merely predicting classification confidence.

Comparison of CIoU, IoU, and DIoU: To further validate the effectiveness of the proposed CIoU, we train three separate models using IoU, DIoU [47], and CIoU as the optimization objectives, respectively. The quantitative results are presented in Table 6.7. As shown, the CIoU-based variant consistently outperforms the other two in terms of both 3D Precision and 3D Success. These improvements can be attributed to CIoU's ability to simultaneously capture two essential aspects of tracking, i.e., normalized center distance and overlap, thus mitigating the ambiguity inherent in standard IoU.

Impact of Re-detection: We next examine how crucial re-detection is by comparing DeepPCT with and without this module. As shown in Table 6.7, the re-detection module provides a substantial 18% improvement in 3D Precision and reduces tracking failures caused by accumulated errors, highlighting its necessity for 3D SOT.

Table 6.6 Performance comparison between DeepPCT and P2B on the mini-version of the nuScenes dataset

Method	Category	3D Prec.	3D Succ.
P2B† [27]	Car	26.0	23.7
DeepPCT (Ours)	Car	**27.5**	**25.4**

Table 6.7 Ablation study on the CIoU prediction module and the re-detection module of our framework on the KITTI dataset

	Our metrics		Metrics in [9]	
	3D Prec.	3D Succ.	Prec.	Succ.
Classifier	60.7	41.1	54.8	41.1
IoU predictor	61.2	43.1	55.3	43.1
DIoU [47] predictor	63.1	44.0	56.9	44.0
CIoU predictor	**63.7**	**45.0**	**57.7**	**45.0**
Without re-detection	45.3	35.7	41.5	35.7
With re-detection	**63.7**	**45.0**	**57.7**	**45.0**

Table 6.8 Ablation study on the backbone network on the KITTI dataset

Backbone	Our metrics		Metrics in [9]	
	3D Prec.	3D Succ.	Prec.	Succ.
PointConv [38]	61.5	43.7	56.4	43.7
KPConv [32]	**64.6**	**45.8**	**58.1**	**45.8**
PointNet++ [26]	63.7	45.0	57.7	45.0

Backbone Networks: Table 6.8 presents the influence of different backbone architectures on tracking performance. Among the evaluated options, DeepPCT equipped with KPConv [32] achieves the highest scores, with 64.6% in 3D Precision and 45.8% in 3D Success. It outperforms its PointNet++ [26] variant by 0.9% in 3D Precision and 0.8% in 3D Success. Nevertheless, considering the efficiency of the algorithm, we adopt PointNet++ as our default backbone. It is worth noting that our 3D SOT framework is compatible with various point cloud backbones.

Object Re-detectors: As discussed in Sect. 6.3.2, we utilize a pre-trained 3D object detector to re-initialize the tracker when drift occurs. To examine how different detectors affect our tracker, we compare performance using PointRCNN [31], PointPillars [18], 3DSSD [42], and PV-RCNN [30] in Table 6.9. Among these, PV-RCNN provides a slight improvement over PointRCNN, with gains of 1.0% in 3D Precision and 0.7% in 3D Success. Considering the trade-off between accuracy and computational cost, we adopt PointRCNN as our default re-detection module due to its favorable balance and seamless integration with the DeepPCT pipeline.

Number of 3D Object Proposals: In Table 6.10, we evaluate how varying the number of 3D candidate proposals influences tracking performance. As the number of proposals increases from 8 to 32, our framework achieves its best results when using 24 proposals. However, further increasing this number leads to additional memory consumption and computational overhead. To strike a balance between performance and efficiency, we fix the number of proposals to 24 in our final DeepPCT configuration.

Table 6.9 Ablation study on the object detector on the KITTI dataset

	Our metrics		Metrics in [9]	
	3D Prec.	3D Succ.	Prec.	Succ.
PointPillars [18]	62.7	44.8	57.2	44.8
3DSSD [42]	63.0	44.1	57.3	44.1
PV-RCNN [30]	**64.7**	**45.7**	**59.1**	**45.7**
PointRCNN [31]	63.7	45.0	57.7	45.0

Table 6.10 Tracking results achieved by our DeepPCT with different numbers of 3D object proposals on the KITTI dataset

# Proposals	Our metrics		Metrics in [9]	
	3D Prec.	3D Succ.	Prec.	Succ.
8	59.9	41.4	53.8	41.4
16	60.4	42.8	54.8	42.8
24	**63.7**	**45.0**	**57.7**	**45.0**
32	61.1	43.3	55.4	43.3

Table 6.11 Tracking results achieved by our DeepPCT with different context factors α of 3D ROI pooling on the KITTI dataset

Context factor α	Our metrics		Metrics in [9]	
	3D Prec.	3D Succ.	Prec.	Succ.
0	61.1	43.4	55.3	43.4
0.05	61.3	43.4	55.4	40.4
0.10	**63.7**	**45.0**	**57.7**	**45.0**
0.15	61.2	43.0	55.4	43.0
0.20	61.1	42.6	55.2	42.6
0.25	61.0	42.0	55.0	42.0
0.30	60.9	41.5	54.9	41.5

Context-Aware Point Cloud Pooling: As described in Sect. 6.3.2, we enlarge each candidate box by a scaling factor α to incorporate additional contextual points for improved IoU prediction. Table 6.11 reports the tracking results under different values of α. The highest precision and success scores are achieved when $\alpha = 0.1$. indicating that moderate contextual information effectively enhances feature similarity and IoU estimation, particularly in long-term tracking scenarios. However, setting α too large leads to a performance decline, likely due to the inclusion of irrelevant foreground points from nearby distractors within the pooled region.

Number of Pooled Points per Proposal: As detailed in Sect. 6.3.2, we use 3D ROI pooling operation to extract proposal-wise feature and then resize the extracted features into a fixed-size feature map. Table 6.12 presents the quantitative results of

Table 6.12 Tracking results of DeepPCT with different numbers of pooled points of 3D ROI pooling on the KITTI dataset

# Pooled points	Our metrics		Metrics in [9]	
	3D Prec.	3D Succ.	Prec.	Succ.
128	**63.7**	**45.0**	**57.7**	**45.0**
256	63.0	44.2	57.1	44.2
384	63.5	44.9	57.7	44.9
512	63.4	44.5	57.3	44.5

Table 6.13 Ablation study on the generalization of CIoU

Method	CIoU	3D Prec.	3D Succ.
P2B [27]		46.4	37.1
	✓	**47.7**	**38.0**

DeepPCT under varying numbers of pooled points. The results indicate that tracking accuracy remains relatively stable across different settings, which can be attributed to the use of max-pooling for aggregating point-wise features prior to modulation (as shown in Fig. 6.1).

Generalization of CIoU: To evaluate the generalizability of the proposed CIoU metric, we integrate it into the P2B tracker [27] by replacing the original probability-based scoring mechanism with CIoU. The performance comparison, reported in Table 6.13, shows that this substitution leads to notable improvements–raising 3D Precision from 46.4 to 47.7% and 3D Success from 37.1 to 38.0%. These results suggest that CIoU is a broadly applicable metric that can enhance performance beyond our own DeepPCT framework.

Car, Cyclist and Pedestrian Tracking: Table 6.14 presents DeepPCT's tracking results for cars (large), cyclists (medium), and pedestrians (small) on the KITTI dataset. We can observe that our CIoU metric enhances tracking performance for objects of various sizes. Notice that it brings significant improvements for medium and large objects. The main reason is that for smaller objects (e.g., pedestrians), once

Table 6.14 Car, cyclist and pedestrian tracking results of our method using IoU/CIoU on the KITTI dataset

	IoU type	Car	Cyclist	Pedestrian
Precision	IoU	61.2	46.2	51.3
	CIoU	**63.7**	**48.1**	**52.6**
Success	IoU	43.1	33.8	36.1
	CIoU	**45.0**	**35.2**	**37.0**

the predicted and ground-truth boxes no longer overlap, the CIoU value quickly converges to -1 (i.e., the center distance rapidly approaches the diagonal of the smallest enclosing box), making it more difficult to optimize.

6.5 Conclusion and Future Work

In this chapter, we comprehensively study the problem of 3D single object tracking in sequential point clouds. We introduce a two-branch Siamese network to learn similarity between per-proposal features and propose a center IoU metric to address the ambiguity of standard IoU when bounding boxes do not overlap. Furthermore, we incorporate a re-detection module based on an off-the-shelf 3D object detector to further enhance robustness of long-term tracking. Extensive experiments on the KITTI and nuScene datasets demonstrate that our tracker achieves state-of-the-art results, offering over a 25% improvement in both Precision and Success metrics. Meanwhile, the proposed tracker demonstrates strong adaptability to wild environments with severe illumination variations and scale changes.

Despite the growing interest in 3D single object tracking, there are still several open challenges that warrant further investigation. One major challenge lies in effectively modeling long-range temporal dependencies. Most existing methods rely on frame-by-frame matching, which may be insufficient for maintaining temporal coherence over extended sequences. Another significant challenge is the lack of robustness in sparse or occluded environments. Incorporating complementary modalities such as RGB images may help improve tracking accuracy, especially when the point cloud data is incomplete or noisy.

References

1. Bertinetto L, Valmadre J, Henriques JF, Vedaldi A, Torr PH (2016) Fully-convolutional siamese networks for object tracking. In: Proceedings of the European conference on computer vision (ECCV), pp 850–865
2. Bolme DS, Beveridge JR, Draper BA, Lui YM (2010) Visual object tracking using adaptive correlation filters. In: Proceedings of the IEEE conference on computer vision and pattern recognition (CVPR), pp 2544–2550
3. Caesar H, Bankiti V, Lang AH, Vora S, Liong VE, Xu Q, Krishnan A, Pan Y, Baldan G, Beijbom O (2020) nuscenes: a multimodal dataset for autonomous driving. In: Proceedings of the IEEE conference on computer vision and pattern recognition (CVPR), pp 11621–11631
4. Chen Z, Chen K, Lin W, See J, Yu H, Ke Y, Yang C (2020) PIoU loss: towards accurate oriented object detection in complex environments. In: Proceedings of the European conference on computer vision (ECCV), pp 195–211. Springer
5. Danelljan M, Bhat G, Khan FS, Felsberg M (2019) ATOM: accurate tracking by overlap maximization. In: Proceedings of the IEEE conference on computer vision and pattern recognition (CVPR), pp 4660–4669
6. Dong X, Shen J (2018) Triplet loss in siamese network for object tracking. In: Proceedings of the European conference on computer vision (ECCV), pp 459–474

7. Fang Z, Zhou S, Cui Y, Scherer S (2020) 3D-SiamRPN: an end-to-end learning method for real-time 3D single object tracking using raw point cloud. IEEE Sens J
8. Geiger A, Lenz P, Urtasun R (2012) Are we ready for autonomous driving. In: Proceedings of the IEEE conference on computer vision and pattern recognition (CVPR), pp 3354–3361
9. Giancola S, Zarzar J, Ghanem B (2019) Leveraging shape completion for 3D siamese tracking. In: Proceedings of the IEEE conference on computer vision and pattern recognition (CVPR), pp 1359–1368
10. Guo Y, Choi M, Li K, Boussaid F, Bennamoun M (2022) Soft exemplar highlighting for cross-view image-based geo-localization. IEEE Trans Image Process 31:2094–2105
11. Guo Y, Wang H, Hu Q, Liu H, Liu L, Bennamoun M (2020) Deep learning for 3D point clouds: a survey. IEEE Trans Pattern Anal Mach Intell (TPAMI)
12. Henriques JF, Caseiro R, Martins P, Batista J (2014) High-speed tracking with kernelized correlation filters. IEEE Trans Pattern Anal Mach Intell (TPAMI) 37(3):583–596
13. Jesus Z, Silvio G, Bernard G (2019) PointRGCN: graph convolution networks for 3D vehicles detection refinement. arXiv preprint arXiv:1911.12236
14. Jiang B, Luo R, Mao J, Xiao T, Jiang Y (2018) Acquisition of localization confidence for accurate object detection. In: Proceedings of the European conference on computer vision (ECCV), pp 784–799
15. Koch G, Zemel R, Salakhutdinov R (2015) Siamese neural networks for one-shot image recognition. In: Proceedings of the international conference on machine learning (ICML)
16. Kristan M, Leonardis A, Matas J, Felsberg M, Pflugfelder R, Cehovin Zajc L, Vojir T, Bhat G, Lukezic A, Eldesokey A, et al (2018) The sixth visual object tracking vot2018 challenge results. In: Proceedings of the European conference on computer vision (ECCV), pp 0
17. Ku J, Mozifian M, Lee J, Harakeh A, Waslander SL (2018) Joint 3D proposal generation and object detection from view aggregation. In: Proceedings of the IEEE/RSJ international conference on intelligent robots and systems (IROS)
18. Lang AH, Vora S, Caesar H, Zhou L, Yang J, Beijbom O (2019) Pointpillars: fast encoders for object detection from point clouds. In: Proceedings of the IEEE conference on computer vision and pattern recognition (CVPR), pp 12697–12705
19. Li B, Wu W, Wang Q, Zhang F, Xing J, Yan J (2019) SiamRPN++: evolution of siamese visual tracking with very deep networks. In: Proceedings of the IEEE conference on computer vision and pattern recognition (CVPR), pp 4282–4291
20. Li B, Yan J, Wu W, Zhu Z, Hu X (2018) High performance visual tracking with siamese region proposal network. In: Proceedings of the IEEE conference on computer vision and pattern recognition (CVPR), pp 8971–8980
21. Liu H, Hu Q, Li B, Guo Y (2019) Robust long-term tracking via instance specific proposals. IEEE Trans Instrum Meas (TIM)
22. Liu H, Hu Q, Ma Y, Xie K, Guo Y (2022) Deeppct: single object tracking in dynamic point cloud sequences. IEEE Trans Instrum Meas (TIM) 72:1–12
23. Luo W, Yang B, Urtasun R (2018) Fast and furious: real time end-to-end 3d detection, tracking and motion forecasting with a single convolutional net. In: Proceedings of the IEEE conference on computer vision and pattern recognition (CVPR), pp 3569–3577
24. Ma C, Yang X, Zhang C, Yang MH (2015) Long-term correlation tracking. In: Proceedings of the IEEE conference on computer vision and pattern recognition (CVPR), pp 5388–5396
25. Nam H, Han B (2016) Learning multi-domain convolutional neural networks for visual tracking. In: Proceedings of the IEEE conference on computer vision and pattern recognition (CVPR), pp 4293–4302
26. Qi CR, Yi, L, Su H, Guibas LJ (2017) PointNet++: deep hierarchical feature learning on point sets in a metric space. In: Proceedings of advances in neural information processing systems (NeurIPS), pp 5099–5108
27. Qi H, Feng C, Cao Z, Zhao F, Xiao Y (2020) P2B: point-to-box network for 3D object tracking in point clouds. In: Proceedings of the IEEE conference on computer vision and pattern recognition (CVPR), pp 6329–6338

28. Rezatofighi H, Tsoi N, Gwak J, Sadeghian A, Reid I, Savarese S (2019) Generalized intersection over union: a metric and a loss for bounding box regression. In: Proceedings of the IEEE conference on computer vision and pattern recognition (CVPR), pp 658–666
29. Russakovsky O, Deng J, Su H, Krause J, Satheesh S, Ma S, Huang Z, Karpathy A, Khosla A, Bernstein M et al (2015) Imagenet large scale visual recognition challenge. Int J Comput Vis (IJCV) 115(3):211–252
30. Shi S, Guo C, Jiang L, Wang Z, Shi J, Wang X, Li H (2020) Pv-rcnn: point-voxel feature set abstraction for 3d object detection. In: Proceedings of the IEEE conference on computer vision and pattern recognition (CVPR), pp 10529–10538
31. Shi S, Wang X, Li H (2019) Pointrcnn: 3D object proposal generation and detection from point cloud. In: Proceedings of the IEEE conference on computer vision and pattern recognition (CVPR), pp 770–779
32. Thomas H, Qi CR, Deschaud JE, Marcotegui B, Goulette F, Guibas LJ (2019) Kpconv: flexible and deformable convolution for point clouds. In: Proceedings of the IEEE international conference on computer vision (ICCV), pp 6411–6420
33. Voigtlaender P, Luiten J, Torr PH, Leibe B (2020) Siam R-CNN: visual tracking by re-detection. In: Proceedings of the IEEE conference on computer vision and pattern recognition (CVPR), pp 6578–6588
34. Wang H, Chen Z, Cai Y, Chen L, Li Y, Sotelo MA, Li Z (2022) Voxel-rcnn-complex: an effective 3-d point cloud object detector for complex traffic conditions. IEEE Trans Instrum Meas 71:1–12
35. Wang Q, Zhang L, Bertinetto L, Hu W, Torr PH (2019) Fast online object tracking and segmentation: A unifying approach. In: Proceedings of the IEEE conference on computer vision and pattern recognition (CVPR), pp 1328–1338
36. Weng X, Wang J, Held D, Kitani K (2020) Ab3dmot: a baseline for 3d multi-object tracking and new evaluation metrics. In: Proceedings of the European conference on computer vision workshop (ECCVW)
37. Weng X, Wang Y, Man Y, Kitani KM (2020) Gnn3dmot: graph neural network for 3d multi-object tracking with 2d-3d multi-feature learning. In: Proceedings of the IEEE conference on computer vision and pattern recognition (CVPR), pp 6499–6508
38. Wu W, Qi Z, Fuxin L (2019) Pointconv: deep convolutional networks on 3d point clouds. In: Proceedings of the IEEE conference on computer vision and pattern recognition (CVPR), pp 9621–9630
39. Wu Y, Lim J, Yang MH (2015) Object tracking benchmark. IEEE Trans Pattern Anal Mach Intell (TPAMI) 37(9):1834–1848
40. Xu X, Zhang L, Yang J, Cao C, Tan Z, Luo M (2021) Object detection based on fusion of sparse point cloud and image information. IEEE Trans Instrum Meas 70:1–12
41. Xu Z, Rong Z, Wu Y (2021) A survey: which features are required for dynamic visual simultaneous localization and mapping? Vis Comput Ind Biomed Art 4(1):1–16
42. Yang Z, Sun Y, Liu S, Jia J (2020) 3DSSD: point-based 3D single stage object detector. In: Proceedings of the IEEE conference on computer vision and pattern recognition (CVPR), pp 11040–11048
43. Yang Z, Sun Y, Liu S, Shen X, Jia J (2019) STD: sparse-to-dense 3D object detector for point cloud. In: Proceedings of the IEEE international conference on computer vision (ICCV), pp 1951–1960
44. Zarzar J, Giancola S, Ghanem B (2019) Efficient tracking proposals using 2D-3D siamese networks on lidar. arXiv preprint arXiv:1903.10168
45. Zhang L, Gonzalez-Garcia A, Weijer JVD, Danelljan M, Khan FS (2019) Learning the model update for siamese trackers. In: Proceedings of the IEEE international conference on computer vision (ICCV), pp 4010–4019
46. Zhang Z, Peng H (2019) Deeper and wider siamese networks for real-time visual tracking. In: Proceedings of the IEEE conference on computer vision and pattern recognition (CVPR), pp 4591–4600

47. Zheng Z, Wang P, Liu W, Li J, Ye R, Ren D (2020) Distance-iou loss: faster and better learning for bounding box regression. In: Proceedings of the AAAI conference on artificial intelligence (AAAI), pp 12993–13000
48. Zhou C, Luo Z, Luo Y, Liu T, Pan L, Cai Z, Zhao H, Lu S (2022) PTTR: relational 3D point cloud object tracking with transformer. In: Proceedings of the IEEE conference on computer vision and pattern recognition (CVPR)
49. Zhu Z, Wang Q, Li B, Wu W, Yan J, Hu W (2018) Distractor-aware siamese networks for visual object tracking. In: Proceedings of the European conference on computer vision (ECCV), pp 101–117

Chapter 7
Multiple Object Tracking in Point Cloud Sequences

Multiple object tracking in point cloud sequences aims to detect objects of interest in each frame and associate them across time to construct coherent trajectories for each individual object. Existing methods typically adopt a tracking-by-detection framework, where tracking is performed based on object boxes generated by a pre-trained detector. However, this two-stage paradigm often leads to suboptimal performance, as it decomposes the problem into two separate stages: object detection and temporal association, rather than optimizing tracking in a unified or end-to-end manner. This chapter presents two novel joint detection and tracking methods: Sect. 7.3 introduces a 4D object tubelet representation that encodes the spatio-temporal locations of objects, and formulates the tracking problem as a tubelet detection task. Section 7.4 proposes a point-based tracking framework, which achieves end-to-end object tracking by introducing a tracking head on top of a point-based detection model. Extensive experiments on several public datasets demonstrate that both methods achieve promising performance while maintaining satisfactory efficiency.

7.1 Introduction

With the rapid development of commercial grade 3D sensors, such as the Velodyne LiDAR scanner, acquiring massive 3D point clouds is becoming increasingly convenient for various intelligent systems, such as multimedia, autonomous driving, and robotics [29, 30, 36, 37]. However, the majority of existing methods focus on the processing of static point clouds, largely ignoring the fact that point clouds collected by sensors are usually dynamic and sequential. To this end, we seek to delve deeper into the processing of dynamic point cloud stream, with a particular focus on multi-object tracking (MOT) within sequential point clouds.

3D MOT aims to predict the spatio-temporal locations of objects of interest and identify their semantic categories. Intuitively, the task of 3D MOT is highly chal-

Y. Guo et al., *Point Cloud Intelligence*, Advances in Computer Vision and Pattern Recognition, https://doi.org/10.1007/978-981-95-0648-4_7

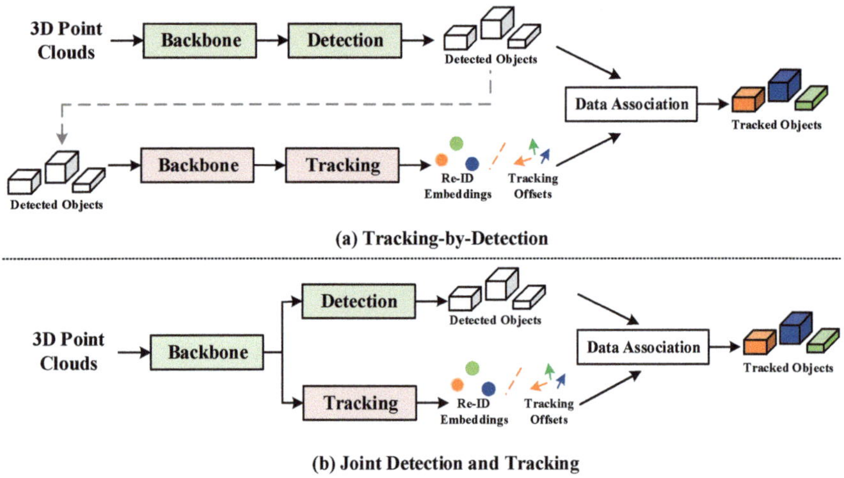

Fig. 7.1 Tracking-by-detection versus joint detection and tracking (This figure is reproduced from [30])

lenging. First, 3D MOT typically involves multiple interrelated subtasks such as object detection and data association. Second, 3D point cloud sequences are usually unordered, irregular and sparse in the spatial dimension, and unaligned in the temporal dimension (i.e., the correspondence between adjacent point cloud frames is unknown).

Previous MOT methods can be roughly grouped into two categories: tracking-by-detection (TBD) and joint detection and tracking (JDT), as shown in Fig. 7.1. TBD first detects objects and then tracks them, while JDT conducts both detection and tracking in a single forward pass. Current mainstream methods [9, 24, 66, 67, 70] for 3D MOT adopt a TBD framework. As a two-step approach, this framework fully decomposes the MOT task into two independent sub-tasks: object detection and object association. Consequently, these methods first apply a trained detector to detect objects in a 3D space, followed by another association network or algorithm to associate them. Although straightforward and effective, their drawbacks are also clear: (1) This step-wise design makes the tracker excessively reliant on the object detection results from the first step. Therefore, the tracking performance is positively correlated with and even dominated by the detector performance. (2) Due to the existence of frame-level detectors in the TBD framework, they cannot leverage spatio-temporal information in the sequence and benefit from end-to-end training. Thus, it may lead to sub-optimal tracking results, especially in cases of severe object occlusions.

In this chapter, we present two JDT methods for 3D MOT. First, we propose **CenterTube**, which introduces a 4D object tubelet representation to better model the spatio-temporal locations of objects within video sequences. Based on this representation, we develop a tubelet-based framework that performs 3D multi-object

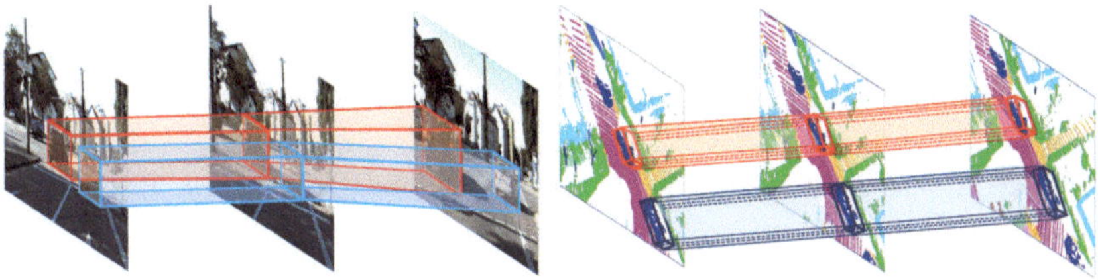

(a) 3D Tubelet. (b) 4D Tubelet.

Fig. 7.2 Example of (a) a 3D Tubelet and (b) a 4D Tubelet (This figure is reproduced from [30])

tracking by directly detecting and associating 4D tubelets in dynamic point cloud sequences (see Sect. 7.3). Second, we propose **AnchorPoint**, which represents each object with its corresponding anchor point and extend the point-based detection model to 3D MOT by introducing a dedicated tracking head (see Sect. 7.4).

CenterTube: Nowadays, a handful of works have started to develop a simple end-to-end network architecture that uses a spatio-temporal tubelet representation (i.e., a sequence of bounding boxes over time) in various video tasks such as action recognition [17, 20] and video object detection [21, 22]. In this way, the spatio-temporal location and inter-frame correlation of the object are well encoded in an object tubelet, as shown in Fig. 7.2. However, 4D object tubelet representation for dynamic point clouds has yet to be investigated. Notice that this 4D represents 1D temporal and 3D spatial dimensions. Therefore, it is natural to raise a question: *can we extend the concept of object tubelets to sequential point clouds and propose an end-to-end network for 3D MOT?*

Motivated by this, we propose a novel 4D tubelet representation to better model the spatio-temporal locations of objects within video segments. Different from the original tubelet whose dimension is too large to be regressed, our tubelet is simplified by the linear motion assumption and is therefore determined by a start box and an end box. The remaining boxes can be approximated by applying linear spline interpolation between the start box and the end box. On this basis, we develop a tubelet-based JDT network named **CenterTube** to achieve 3D MOT by detecting and associating 4D object tubelets across overlapping video segments. Our model is trained in an end-to-end manner, and performs detection and tracking simultaneously in a single forward pass. Inspired by center-based detector, we treat each object tubelet as a trajectory of moving center points since object size remains consistent within point cloud sequence. Consequently, we formulate the object tubelet detection task into three parallel subtasks: center point detection and box size regression for the end box, as well as offset prediction from the start box's center point to the end box's center point. Specifically, we divide the input point cloud sequence into multiple overlapping segments, using one segment as input each time. We then use a 3D encoder to extract features for each frame of the input video segment. The learned 3D features are compressed along the height dimension to obtain bird's eye view (BEV) features, which are fed into three parallel branches to jointly detect object tubelets. These three branches are the center branch for center point detection, the regression branch for box size regression, and the offset branch for offset prediction, respectively. Finally, based on the fact that only one target can exist at the same location in the outdoor scene, we propose a Tubelet BEV Intersection-of-Union (IoU) to link the produced tubelets and thus form final object trajectories.

AnchorPoint: Reviewing 2D object detectors [32, 45], the concept of anchors is widely used, providing interpretable physical meanings as they are closely tied to specific positions. Similarly, the point-based detector *PointRCNN* [52] leverages foreground points as anchors to generate object proposals. Motivated by this, we propose a 3D MOT framework built upon point-based detection model. Since each anchor point is responsible for its nearby object (i.e., each object is represented by its corresponding anchor point), 3D MOT can be achieved by tracking these anchor points across frames. To this end, we design a lightweight tracking head on the top of detection model to predict instance movements by aggregating the feature similarities of anchor points between consecutive frames.

The main contribution of this chapter can be summarized as follows:

- We propose a simplified 4D object tubelet representation and a tubelet-based JDT framework for 3D MOT. Compared with the TBD framework, our method exploits spatio-temporal information to enhance the tracker's robustness in cases of object occlusion and gets rid of excessive reliance on frame-level detectors.
- We propose a Tubelet BEV-IoU to match object tubelets across video segments to produce the entire tracks. Compared with traditional metrics, our method can provide more robust object association.
- We propose a novel anchor point-based query design to extend the Transformer architecture to 3D object detection. Furthermore, we propose an instance-aware downsampling strategy to retain informative foreground points as anchor points.
- We propose a joint detection and tracking-based 3D MOT model, which introduces a lightweight tracking head on the top of pre-trained detection model to achieve comparable performance to existing state-of-the-art 3D trackers.
- We conduct a group of experiments on the KITTI [14], nuScenes [5] and Waymo Open [59] datasets to verify the effectiveness of our framework. Experimental results show that our JDT framework achieves competitive performance against existing state-of-the-art methods.

7.2 Related Work

7.2.1 2D Multi-object Tracking

Existing 2D multi-object tracking (MOT) approaches can generally be categorized into (1) target prior-based methods and (2) target prior-free methods.

Target prior-based trackers: These methods focus on tracking objects belonging to specific pre-defined categories. Tracking-by-detection [4, 68] is the most widely used paradigm for these methods. It first uses a class-aware detector to identify objects of interest and subsequently tracks and associates detected objects across frames. SORT [4] predicts object displacements between frames using a Kalman filter and performs object association through an IoU-based bipartite matching. DeepSORT [68] is a subsequent extension of SORT [4], which incorporates object appearance features to reduce ID switches. Shen et al. [48] developed a strategy that refines tracking by iteratively generating alternative target hypotheses. Recent approaches [13, 43, 55, 70, 76, 82, 86] aim to unify detection and tracking into a single framework. D&T [13] computes correlation feature maps between adjacent frames and uses RoI pooling to predict instance-level movements. Shen et al. [47] proposed a tracklet-based submodular optimization framework to refine trajectories through selective tracklet association. TubeTK [42] introduces a 2D Btube representation with 15 of freedom to encode object spatio-temporal locations. However, this method relies on a complex non-maximum suppression (NMS) process to filter redundant predictions. Inspired by the Transformer architecture [60], several methods [39, 58, 78] utilize object queries for tracking. These approaches treat object features from previous frames as track queries, which are updated using current frame features to predict object locations. MOTR [78] transfers and updates track queries frame-by-frame to perform iterative tracking predictions.

Target prior-free trackers: These methods are not constrained to pre-defined target categories [1] and can be considered as an extension of single-object tracking (SOT). Zhu et al. [88] proposed a class-agnostic detector to identify generic objects of interest and used a tracking network to track and associate detected objects. On this basis, Liu et al. [28] introduced a graphic model that combines appearance and motion cues to handle occlusion and appearance changes. While promising, target prior-free methods are still at an early stage and require further investigation.

Our CenterTube and AnchorPoint-MOT are target prior-based trackers that adhere to the joint detection and tracking paradigm. Different from previous methods, our CenterTube directly predicts spatio-temporal locations of objects across consecutive frames without additional NMS operation, while AnchorPoint-MOT extends point-based detectors to 3D multi-object tracking by adding an extra head to predict the inter-frame displacement of objects.

7.2.2 3D Multi-object Tracking

3D multi-object tracking (MOT) can be considered as a downstream task of 3D object detection, which requires assigning an ID value that is consistent across frames to each detected object. Similar to MOT in images, there are two paradigms for 3D MOT: tracking-by-detection (TBD) and joint detection and tracking (JDT).

Most of existing methods [23, 50, 66, 67] follow the TBD framework, which first performs detection followed by tracking. AB3DMOT [66] is a pioneering work in this direction, which employs a combination of 3D Kalman filter and Hungarian algorithm to track objects produced by the first-stage detector. FlowMOT [79] utilizes a scene flow network to estimate motion information for each point, and then extracts instance motions based on predicted 3D boxes for association. Chiu et al. [9] used Mahalanobis distance instead of 3D IoU to enhance the robustness of data association stage. Subsequently, they [8] introduced deep feature distance as a supplement to the Mahalanobis distance. Yang et al. [73] proposed a quality network to estimate the quality scores of existing association clues, and then used the predicted scores to synthesize a robust association metric. ByteTrack [83] introduces a hierarchical data association strategy, where high-confidence detection boxes are first matched with trajectories, followed by associating low-confidence detection boxes with unmatched trajectories. This strategy mines true objects with low detection scores, effectively alleviating the problem of fragmented trajectories. EagerMOT [24] integrates object instances detected from both 2D images and 3D point clouds for tracking. Wang et al. [61] proposed an occlusion head that selects optimal object appearance features and designed a confidence score-based motion module to mitigate the impact of false positive detections.

In contrast, JDT performs detection and tracking (i.e., predicting instance movements) simultaneously in a unified network. The pioneering work PC-TCNN [69] is inspired by two-stage detector, which generates several 4D tubelet proposals in overlapping video segments and then extracts proposal-wise features to refine these tubelets. These refined tubelets are matched to form final object trajectories. CenterTube [30] introduces a Simplified 4D object tubelet representation and decomposes the 4D tubelet detection task into three sub-tasks: center detection, size regression, and orientation prediction. These three sub-tasks are achieved by three parallel anchor-free heads. Compared with PC-TCNN, CenterTube is more efficient and does not require non-maximum suppression (NMS) operations to remove redundant tubelets.

7.2.3 Vision Transformer for Object Detection and Tracking

Transformer [60], first introduced by Vaswani et al., has demonstrated state-of-the-art performance in numerous NLP tasks. Inspired by this success, several efforts [6, 12, 57, 64, 89] have been made to adapt Transformer architectures for vision tasks, particularly object detection and tracking. As a groundbreaking work, DETR [6] employs a set of learned object queries to model relationships between objects and their surrounding image context. Inspired by deformable convolutions, Deformable DETR [89] enhances DETR by introducing spatially sparse sampling, significantly accelerating convergence while retaining detection accuracy. Anchor DETR [64] introduce a concept of anchor-based object query, which embeds location priors into the Transformer to improve interpretability and optimization.

Recently, Transformers on 3D object detection and tracking have gradually become thriving. Sheng et al. [49] introduced a channel-wise Transformer to model long-range interactions among points, enabling more effective feature aggregation in point cloud data. Guan et al. [15] leveraged the Transformer architecture to integrate multi-scale features from diverse point cloud representations, such as raw point clouds, voxels, and BEV. Mao et al. [38] proposed a Transformer-based voxel backbone tailored for voxel-based detectors, demonstrating its potential in capturing both local and global voxel-level interactions. In this work, we encode the downsampled foreground points into object queries and then use the Transformer decoder to regress 3D oriented boxes from object queries.

7.3 Multiple 3D Object Tracking with 4D Tubelets: CenterTube

In this section, we propose *CenterTube*, a unified framework for joint detection and tracking in point cloud sequences. Our method reformulates multi-object trajectory prediction as a 4D tubelet detection task. The 4D tubelet detection task is further decompose into three distinct sub-tasks: center prediction, size regression and movement estimation, which are implemented by center branch, regression branch and movement branch of CenterTube respectively. Furthermore, we propose a tubelet-based BEV-IoU metric to associate detected tubelets across overlapping segments to form the final object trajectories. Comprehensive evaluations on the KITTI-MOT and nuScenes datasets show that our framework delivers competitive results even if no ready-made detection results are adopted.

7.3.1 Methodology

7.3.1.1 Overview

We propose a tubelet-based joint detection and tracking framework, called CenterTube, which performs 3D MOT by detecting and associating 4D object tubelets across overlapping video segments. Compared with the TBD framework, our model leverages spatio-temporal information to enhance the tracker's robustness in cases of object occlusion and gets rid of the restrictions from frame-level detectors.

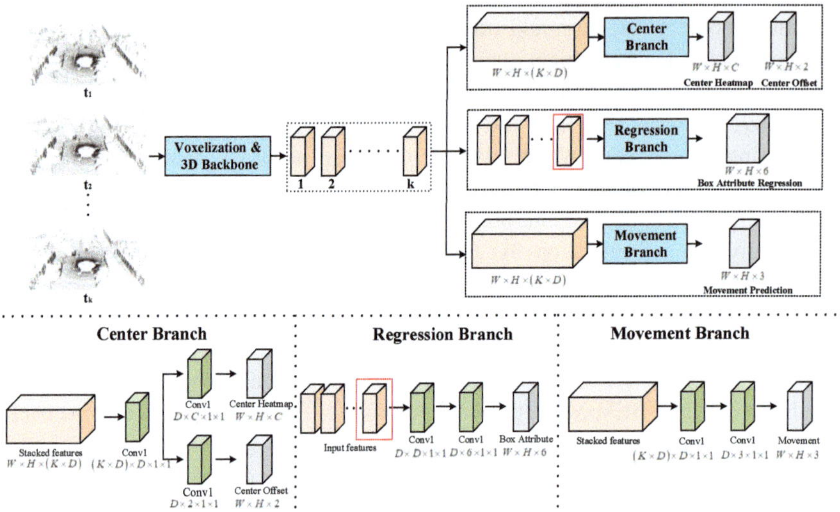

Fig. 7.3 The overall framework of our CenterTube model (This figure is reproduced from [30])

The overall framework of our CenterTube is shown in Fig. 7.3. Inspired by center-based detector, our CenterTube decomposes the 4D tubelet detection task into three parallel sub-tasks: center point detection, object size regression and offset prediction. Specifically, given a 3D video sequence to be tracked, we divide it into multiple overlapping segments and take one segment at a time as input. We use a 3D encoder to extract features for each input frame and then flatten the learned features onto the BEV plane. Three parallel branches are used to detect center points, regress box size and predict offset values, respectively, to predict 4D object tubelets within input segment. Finally, we propose a Tubelet BEV-IoU to match object tubelets across segments to form the final object trajectory in 3D video sequence.

7.3.1.2 From 3D Box to 4D Tubelet

In static point clouds, a 3D oriented box is typically used to represent the spatial position of an object in 3D space. However, the 3D MOT task requires the algorithm to track objects over time, i.e., predict the spatio-temporal positions of objects. Here, we propose a simplified 4D tubelet by extending the 3D box along the temporal dimension, thus representing the spatio-temporal positions of objects within point cloud video segment.

4D Tubelet Definition: Stacking 3D bounding boxes of the target at each specific time along the temporal dimension is the crudest extension method. Albeit simple and straightforward, it is obviously not feasible to regress this parameterized tubelet due to the large collection of tubelet parameters. Consequently, we propose a simplified

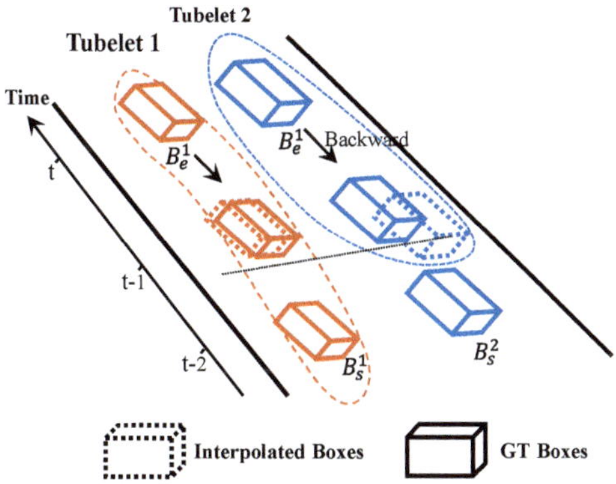

Fig. 7.4 An illustration of the 4D tubelet definition and its generation process within our framework (This figure is reproduced from [30])

version of 4D object tubelet by introducing the linear spline interpolation method. In our definition, an object tubelet is determined by its start box B_s and end box B_e. The remaining boxes in the tubelet, i.e., $\{B_{s+1}, B_{s+2}, \ldots, B_{e-1}\}$ are approximated by applying linear spline interpolation between B_s and B_e. As shown in Fig. 7.4, the proposed 4D object tubelet can effectively encode the spatio-temporal position of the object in space, based on the assumption that the object follows linear motion. Considering that the linear motion assumption of objects in video sequence may not hold in practice, we instead divide the entire point cloud sequence into several short and overlapping segments, within which the object motion can be approximately treated as linear.

4D Tubelet Generation: For a point cloud sequence of K frames with associated 3D box annotations, the ground-truth 4D object tubelet is generated by determining its start box B_s and end box B_e, as shown in Fig. 7.4. Notice that, the length of the generated ground-truth tubelet is not fixed. Specifically, we treat a 3D bounding box at timestamp t as the end box B_e of a specific object tubelet, and then look backward to find its start box. The remaining boxes of the object tubelet are obtained by interpolating B_s and B_e. According to our 4D tubelet definition, the backward search will be terminated when the linear motion assumption no longer holds. That is, the start box B_e is determined when the average 3D intersection-of-union (IoU) between the interpolated boxes and the ground-truth boxes is less than a predefined threshold η_1, i.e., $\text{mean}\{\text{3D\_IoU}(\hat{B}_i, B_i)\} < \eta_1$, $i \in \{s+1, s+2, \ldots, e-1\}$. By traversing each bounding box across various timestamps, we can ultimately obtain a set of 4D object tubelets of varying lengths for training.

Although our object tubelet is defined by its start box and end box, it remains highly challenging to use a neural network to directly regress these parameters (i.e., 14 of freedom). Inspired by center-based detectors, we treat each object tubelet as a trajectory of moving points. In addition, considering our linear motion assumption and the fact that object size keeps consistent in the point cloud sequence, our object tubelet is further simplified as its center point and object size for the end box, and offset of the start box's center with respect to the end box's center. In this way, we use a center-based network to regress 10° of freedom to obtain the object tubelet. Therefore, we decompose the object tubelet detection task into three tasks: center detection, object size regression, and offset estimation.

7.3.1.3 Network Architecture

With 4D tubelets that encode the spatio-temporal position of objects in dynamic point clouds, we can handle the 3D MOT task by detecting and associating predicted 4D tubelets, without a carefully designed frame-level detector. Inspired by center-based detectors [77], we further decompose the 4D tubelet detection task into three sub-tasks: center point detection and box size regression for the end box, as well as offset prediction from the start box's center to the end box's center. These three sub-tasks are implemented by our proposed parallel branches, as shown in Fig. 7.3.

Center Branch: This branch is designed to predict the centers of the end boxes of the object tubelets and recognize their semantic categories. Notably, temporal contextual information is beneficial for localizing objects and reducing false positives. Consequently, we combine the BEV features extracted from each input frame to form a BEV feature volume $\mathbf{f_v} \in \mathbb{R}^{W\times H\times(K\times D)}$, where K is the number of input point cloud frames, W, H, and D are the width, height, and feature dimensions of the BEV features, respectively. The BEV feature volume $\mathbf{f_v}$ is input into our center branch to produce a C-channel center heatmap $Y \in [0, 1]^{W\times H\times C}$, where C is the number of object categories. The centers are determined by finding the local peak of each category in the output heatmap Y. The ground truth heatmap $\hat{Y}$ is obtained by a Gaussian function $\hat{Y}_{x,y,c_i} = exp(-\frac{(x-x_{c_i})^2+(y-y_{c_i})^2}{2\sigma^2})$, where x_{c_i} and y_{c_i} are the horizontal and vertical coordinates of the i-th object target with class c_i, respectively. Following previous center-based detectors, we use the focal loss [27] to train our center branch:

$$l_c = -\frac{1}{N}\sum_{i,j}\begin{cases}(1-Y_{i,j})^{\alpha}\log(Y_{i,j}) & if\ \hat{Y}_{i,j}=1\\ (1-\hat{Y}_{i,j})^{\beta}(Y_{i,j})^{\alpha}\log(1-Y_{i,j}) & otherwise\end{cases} \tag{7.1}$$

where α and β are the hyperparameters in focal loss. N is the number of objects. $\hat{Y}_{i,j}$ represents the presence of an object target at the position (i, j) in the heatmap $\hat{Y}$. Furthermore, we also predict a center offset map $O \in \mathbb{R}^{W\times H\times 2}$ to minimize errors of center prediction introduced by input quantization and the backbone network stride. We use the L1 loss to supervise the center offset prediction.

$$l_{\text{center\_offset}} = \frac{1}{N}\sum_{p}|O_{\widetilde{p}} - (\frac{p}{R} - \widetilde{p})| \tag{7.2}$$

where p represents the ground truth quantized coordinates of the center of the i-th object target, $\widetilde{p} = \lfloor\frac{p}{R}\rfloor$ is its low-resolution equivalent. R denotes the feature stride.

Notice that center offset supervision is applied only at the center points, with all other locations ignored.

Regression Branch: This branch aims to regress the shape attributes of each object tubelet, including 3D size, height-above-ground, and orientation. This can be achieved by estimating the shape attributes for the end box of each object tubelet, based on two key observations: (1) Object size generally remains consistent across frames; and (2) objects within our defined tubelets follow linear motions, resulting in minimal changes in height-above-ground and orientation. Thus, the height-above-ground and orientation remain approximately constant throughout the entire tubelet. Consequently, we take the BEV feature map $\mathbf{f_e} \in \mathbb{R}^{W \times H \times D}$ of the end frame as input, and then predict a shape attribute map $S \in R^{W \times H \times 6}$. The shape attributes of predicted object tubelets can be obtained by indexing the position corresponding to the predicted centers. This branch is trained using L1 loss:

$$l_{\text{shape}} = \frac{1}{N} \sum_{(x_i, y_i)} |S_{x_i, y_i} - \hat{s}_i| \tag{7.3}$$

$$\hat{s}_i = (h, w, l, h_g, \sin(\alpha), \cos(\alpha)) \tag{7.4}$$

where $\hat{s}_i$ denotes the ground truth shape attributes of the i-th object tubelet. (h, w, l), h_g and $(\sin(\alpha), \cos(\alpha))$ denote the 3D size, height-above-ground, and orientation, respectively.

Offset Branch: This branch is designed to predict the offsets from the start boxes' centers to the end boxes' centers. However, due to the varying lengths of object tubelets, the range of offset values becomes too large, making direct prediction of these offsets highly challenging. Therefore, we decompose the offset into the frame interval (i.e., tubelets' length) and the normalized offset. Similar to center branch, we take the BEV feature volume $\mathbf{f_v}$ as its input, and predict an offset map $M \in \mathbb{R}^{W \times H \times 3}$. We also use L1 loss to supervise this branch.

$$l_{\text{offset}} = \frac{1}{N} \sum_{(x_i, y_i)} |M_{x_i, y_i} - \hat{m}_i| \tag{7.5}$$

where $\hat{m}_i$ is the ground truth offset value of the i-th object tubelet.

Training Objectives. The overall training losses are a weighted combination of center loss l_c, center offset loss $l_{\text{center\_offset}}$, shape loss l_{shape}, and offset loss l_{offset}:

$$l = l_c + a \cdot l_{\text{center\_offset}} + b \cdot l_{\text{shape}} + c \cdot l_{\text{offset}} \tag{7.6}$$

where a, b, and c are the hyperparameters.

7.3.1.4 Tubelet Linking

Once the object tubelet detection results for each segment are obtained, the next step is to link these tubelets across overlapping segments to produce the final object trajectories. We propose a novel Tubelet BEV-IoU (TB-IoU), based on the fact that only one target can exist at the same location in outdoor scenes, for tubelet matching. Compared with traditional association metric, our TB-IoU can obtain more robust object tracks.

Tubelet BEV-IoU Definition: Considering the temporal overlap of 4D object tubelets, it is natural to link the predicted tubelets by measuring the similarity of object tubelets within overlapping segments. Therefore, we propose a tubelet-based IoU metric without any trainable parameters for tubelet matching. Since all objects are located on the ground (i.e., BEV plane) in outdoor scenes, we propose a Tubelet BEV-IoU to eliminate height-above-ground prediction errors of object tubelets, which is considered as an extended version of BEV-IoU along the temporal dimension. Specifically, given a 4D object tubelet $\mathcal{T}_{(s_1,e_1)}$ from frame s_1 to frame e_1 and a object trajectory $\mathcal{K}_{(s_2,e_2)}$ from frame s_2 to frame e_2, we first find the overlapping frames between $\mathcal{T}_{(s_1,e_1)}$ and $\mathcal{K}_{(s_2,e_2)}$. If overlapping frames $\mathcal{O}$ exist (i.e., $e_1 >= s_2$ and $e_2 >= s_1$, the range of overlapping frames $\mathcal{O}$ is $[\max(s_1, s_2), \min(e_1, e_2)]$), we first calculate the BEV-IoU between the 3D box $\mathcal{T}_o$ of the object tubelet $\mathcal{T}$ and the 3D box $\mathcal{K}_o$ of the object trajectory $\mathcal{K}$ at the overlapping frames. The Tubelet BEV-IoU is obtained by averaging the BEV-IoU of overlapping frames $\mathcal{O}$:

$$\text{TB\_IoU}(\mathcal{T}_{(s_1,e_1)}, \mathcal{K}_{(s_2,e_2)}) = \frac{\sum_{o\in O} \text{BEV\_IoU}(\mathcal{T}_o, \mathcal{K}_o)}{|\mathcal{O}|} \tag{7.7}$$

where $|\mathcal{O}|$ is the number of overlapping frames. If no overlapping frame $\mathcal{O}$ can be found, the Tubelet BEV-IoU is 0.

Linking Tublets with TB-IoU: After obtaining the output of our model at timestamp t, we have (1) a group of detected 4D object tubelets at timestamp t, i.e., $\mathcal{T}_t = \{\mathcal{T}_t^1, \mathcal{T}_t^2, \ldots, \mathcal{T}_t^m\}$, where m is the number of object tubelets; and (2) a set of object trajectories from timestamp $t-1$, i.e., $\mathcal{K}_{t-1} = \{\mathcal{K}_{t-1}^1, \mathcal{K}_{t-1}^2, \ldots, \mathcal{K}_{t-1}^n\}$, where n is the number of object trajectories. Then, we need to match $\mathcal{K}_{t-1}$ and $\mathcal{T}_t$ to obtain new object trajectories $\mathcal{K}_t$ at timestamp t. Specifically, we sort the object tubelets $\mathcal{T}_t$ in descending order of their object scores (i.e., their corresponding center heatmap values) and select them sequentially. In this way, we can ensure that the object tubelets most likely to be true positives are matched with existing object trajectories. The selected tubelet calculates TB-IoU with each remaining trajectory to obtain an affinity matrix with shape $1 times n_r$, where n_r is the number of unmatched trajectories in $\mathcal{K}_{t-1}$. Then, we find the object trajectory with the highest affinity score to match with the selected tubelet. Notice that the matching is discarded if their TB-IoU values fall below the pre-set linking threshold η_2.

Let us take an example to illustrate the process of trajectory updating. Assume that $\mathcal{T}_{(s1,e1)}$ and $\mathcal{K}_{(s2,e2)}$ are the matched object tubelet and trajectory, respectively, where $s_2 \leq s_1 \leq e_2 \leq e_1$. $O_{(s_3,e_3)}$ is their overlapped part, where $s_3 \leq e_3$. The new trajectory K^{new} is updated as follows:

$$\begin{aligned}\mathcal{K}^{new} &= Link(\mathcal{T}_{(s_1,e_1)}, \mathcal{K}_{(s_2,e_2)}) \\ &= \mathcal{K}_{(s_2,s_3)} + \text{Adap\_Avg}(\mathcal{K}_{(s_3,e_3)}, \mathcal{T}_{(s_3,e_3)}) + \mathcal{T}_{(e_3,e_1)}\end{aligned} \tag{7.8}$$

where s_n and e_n represent the start and end frames of the object tubelet or trajectory, respectively. Symbol + denotes the linking operation, and Adap_Avg$(\cdot,\cdot)$ represents the adaptive average fusion operation for overlapping parts of object tubelet and trajectory. For overlapped part **O**, we use a probability-based adaptive averaging method to minimize deviations introduced by linear interpolation. The 3D box in overlapping frame of new trajectory $\mathcal{K}^{new}$ is calculated as follows:

$$B_n = \lambda_1 * B_{\mathcal{K}} + \lambda_2 * B_{\mathcal{T}} \tag{7.9}$$

where $B_{\mathcal{K}}$ and $B_{\mathcal{T}}$ are the 3D boxes of trajectory $\mathcal{K}_{(s2,e2)}$ and tubelet $\mathcal{T}_{(s1,e1)}$ in overlapping frame, respectively. $\lambda_1 = p_{\mathcal{K}}/(p_{\mathcal{K}} + p_{\mathcal{T}}), \lambda_2 = p_{\mathcal{T}}/(p_{\mathcal{K}} + p_{\mathcal{T}})$, where $p_{\mathcal{K}}$ and $p_{\mathcal{T}}$ are their object scores, respectively.

7.3.2 Experiments

Next, we introduce the tracking results of our proposed CenterTube framework on the KITTI-MOT and nuScenes datasets. To explore the influence of different 3D encoders, we implement two variants of CenterTube: CenterTube-P, based on the PointPillar encoder, and CenterTube-V, built upon VoxelNet.

7.3.2.1 Datasets and Evaluation Metrics

KITTI-MOT [14] is the first large-scale public benchmark for autonomous driving. It contains 21 training sequences and 29 testing sequences, each of which provides point cloud data and 3D box annotation for each frame. Considering that the official evaluation protocol only supports 2D MOT performance testing, we use the evaluation protocol and metrics proposed by [66] for 3D MOT evaluation. The major metrics include average multiple object tracking accuracy (AMOTA), average multiple objects tracking precision (AMOTP), and scaled AMOTA (sAMOTA). We split the training sequences into training and validation sets as in previous methods [66] to facilitate the comparison of 3D MOT performance. In addition, we also use the official 2D MOT evaluation protocol to more comprehensively evaluate our model. The 2D evaluation metrics include most of the CLEAR MOT metrics, e.g., multiple object tracking accuracy (MOTA), multiple objects tracking precision (MOTP), number of mostly tracked trajectories (MT), number of mostly lost trajectories (ML), and number of identity switches (IDS).

nuScenes [5], released by the autonomous driving company Motional, is a large-scale multimodal benchmark focusing on 3D scene perception and understanding tasks in complex urban environments. It has a total of 1,000 sequences, each lasting 20 s and captured from different outdoor scenes. In addition, considering the limitation of computing resources, it also provides a mini-version for evaluation, which contains 10 sequences with accurate 3D tracking box annotations. There are 10 classes in total for detection, and among them, 7 moving classes are used for the evaluation of tracking. For 3D MOT evaluation, we present the overall AMOTA and individual AMOTA of each class.

7.3.2.2 Implementation Details

Our model is implemented using the open-source 3D object detection framework *OpenPCDet*.[1] For data augmentation, we apply random flipping along the X and Y axes, as well as a random global rotation within the range of $[-\pi/4, \pi/4]$. Additionally, we adopt a global scaling with a scaling factor of $[0.95, 1.05]$ for KITTI-MOT and $[0.9, 1.1]$ for nuScenes. To obtain more diverse training samples, we use the *cut-and-paste* method that copies the points within a ground-truth tubelet from one segment and pastes them into another segment, thus achieving diverse combinations of object tubelet instances and point cloud video segments.

Following [77], we train our model using the Adam optimizer [25] with a one-cycle learning rate policy. For the KITTI-MOT dataset, the initial learning rate is set to 3e-3, with weight decay and momentum values of 0.01 and 0.9, respectively. The model is trained for 120 epochs with a batch size of 4. For the nuScenes dataset, we use an initial learning rate of 1e-3, keeping the weight decay and momentum at 0.01 and 0.9, respectively, and train the model for 20 epochs with a batch size of 4.

During training, we take K consecutive point cloud frames as an input video segment, and use the ground-truth boxes of objects of the last frame as the end boxes to generate trainable tubelets. This process avoids the need to pad or drop frames for batch processing. During inference, we create a short video segment of length K for each frame, starting from the K-th frame of a given sequence. For our experiments, K is set to 5, allowing us to split the entire sequence into multiple overlapping segments. We only detect the tubelets where the object appears in the "current frame" (i.e., the end frame of the video segment). For the KITTI-MOT dataset, the tracking range is set to $[0, 70.4\,\text{m}]$ along the X axis, $[-40, 40\,\text{m}]$ along the Y axis, and $[-3, 1\,\text{m}]$ along the Z axis. CenterTube-P uses an XY grid size of $[0.12, 0.12\,\text{m}]$, while CenterTube-V employs a voxel size of $[0.05, 0.05, 0.1\,\text{m}]$. Following [66], we filter out object trajectories with an average confidence below 0.4. For nuScenes evaluation, the point

[1] https://github.com/open-mmlab/OpenPCDet.

cloud range is clipped to [−51.2, 51.2 m] for the X and Y axes and [−5, 3 m] for the Z axis, with an input voxel size of [0.1, 0.1, 0.2 m].

7.3.2.3 Evaluation on KITTI-MOT Dataset

3D MOT evaluation: Table 7.1 summarizes the 3D MOT results of our CenterTube method and different trackers. We observe that our CenterTube-V achieves competitive performance with an AMOTA of 45.65% and an AMOTP of 78.74%, which outperforms the classical TBD method AB3DMOT [66] by 1.39% and 1.33% in terms of AMOTA and AMOTP, respectively. We also notice that our IDS value, for both CenterTube-V and CenterTube-P, is significantly higher than existing methods such as AB3DMOT and GNN3DMOT. We speculate that this may be due to the following two reasons. First, the association method based on the Kalman filter is better suited for the KITTI-MOT dataset, as most of car instances are either stationary or follow simple motion patterns, such as moving in a straight line. Second, the metric penalizes ID recovery [65], meaning that correcting ID identification errors results in lower scores than leaving them uncorrected. The other variant CenterTube-P also achieves promising performance with an AMOTA of 44.47% and an AMOTP of 76.23%.

2D MOT evaluation: We also provide the 2D MOT results among our CenterTube method and several competitive trackers, as shown in Table 7.2. To ensure the comprehensiveness of our experiments, we select representative trackers utilizing different types of input data. We observe that CenterTube-P delivers strong performance, achieving a 2D MOTA of 80.30% and a 2D MOTP of 83.74%. It also attains a high MT rate of 70.31%, surpassing the previous 3D method AB3DMOT [66] by

Table 7.1 3D MOT performance on the KITTI-MOT Car validation set using the 3D MOT evaluation tool proposed in [66]

Methods	Input data	sAMOTA (%)↑	AMOTA (%)↑	AMOTP (%)↑	IDS↓	FPS↑
mmMOT [80]	2D+3D	70.61	33.08	72.45	10	4.8
FANTrack [2]	2D+3D	82.97	40.03	75.01	35	25.0
AB3DMOT [66]	3D	93.28	44.26	77.41	**0**	**214.7**
GNN3DMOT [67]	2D+3D	93.68	45.27	78.10	**0**	5.2
PC-TCNN [69]	3D	**95.44**	**46.47**	–	–	3.2
EagerMOT [24]	2D+3D	94.94	–	80.00	2	–
PolarMOT [23]	3D	94.32	–	–	31	–
CenterTube-P (Ours)	3D	92.00	44.47	76.23	104	11.0
CenterTube-V (Ours)	3D	94.54	45.65	78.74	74	8.1

Table 7.2 2D MOT performance on the KITTI-MOT car test set

Method	Input data	HOTA (%)↑	MOTA (%)↑	MOTP (%)↑	MT (%)↑	ML (%)↓	IDS↓	FRAG↓
CIWT [41]	2D	54.90	74.44	79.32	50.46	11.23	491	552
BeyondPixels [46]	2D	63.75	82.68	85.50	72.61	2.92	934	581
mono3DT [18]	2D	73.16	84.28	85.45	73.08	2.92	379	573
CenterTrack [86]	2D	73.02	88.83	84.97	82.15	2.46	254	227
mmMOT [80]	2D + 3D	62.05	83.23	85.03	72.92	2.92	733	570
FANTrack [2]	2D + 3D	64.36	75.84	82.46	62.77	8.77	743	701
JRMOT [50]	2D + 3D	69.61	85.10	85.28	70.92	4.62	271	273
GNN3DMOT [67]	2D + 3D	–	80.40	85.05	70.77	11.08	113	265
EagerMOT [24]	2D + 3D	74.39	87.82	85.69	80.92	2.46	462	599
PointTrackNet [62]	3D	57.20	67.56	76.83	60.46	12.77	294	756
ComplexerYOLO [56]	3D	–	75.70	78.46	58.00	5.08	1186	2092
AB3DMOT [66]	3D	68.81	83.49	85.17	67.08	11.38	126	254
PolarMOT [23]	3D	75.16	85.08	85.63	80.92	2.46	462	599
CenterTube-P (Ours)	3D	67.92	80.30	83.74	70.31	9.54	607	591
CenterTube-V (Ours)	3D	67.76	81.56	83.86	69.85	8.61	737	589

3.23%. The CenterTube-V variant similarly performs well, obtaining a 2D MOTA of 81.56% and a 2D MOTP of 83.86%.

Despite their strong performance, both CenterTube-P and CenterTube-V fall behind other leading trackers, such as the 2D tracker CenterTrack [86] and the 3D tracker PolarMOT [23]. This performance gap could be attributed to the following three factors. First, the projection of 3D bounding boxes onto the 2D image plane generally results in lower precision and recall compared to the high-performance 2D detectors employed in previous work such as [67]. Second, 2D MOT models often benefit from large-scale training data. For instance, CenterTrack leverages transfer learning by fine-tuning its KITTI-MOT model from one pre-trained on the nuScenes dataset. In contrast, transferring 3D models across datasets is more challenging due to significant differences in object scales [63]. Third, recent 3D trackers like EagerMOT [24] and PolarMOT [23] employ trained state-of-the-art detectors to obtain high-quality 3D detections, focusing on object association. In contrast, our approach is trained end-to-end using only the KITTI-MOT dataset.

Qualitative results: We provide visualizations of tracking results produced by our CenterTube-P tracker on sequence 12 from the KITTI-MOT Car test set. As illustrated in Fig. 7.5, CenterTube effectively tracks objects within 3D space, even in cases of severe occlusion, such as object ID 196. These results highlight the robustness of the proposed 4D tubelet-based MOT framework.

Runtime. Our CenterTube-P tracker achieves near real-time performance, running at approximately 11 frames per second (FPS), while CenterTube-V operates at nearly 8

Fig. 7.5 Visualization results from our CenterTube tracker on sequence 12 of the KITTI-MOT test set (This figure is reproduced from [30])

Table 7.3 3D MOT performance on the nuScenes validation set

Methods	Overall	Car	Bus	Trailer	Truck	Motorcycle
AB3DMOT [66]	17.9	36.0	48.9	11.1	14.2	5.1
AB3DMOT* [66]	50.9	69.4	74.3	35.3	58.1	39.0
Chiu et al. [9]	56.1	73.5	74.1	33.7	58.0	50.6
CenterPoint [77]	63.4	82.7	78.6	51.4	64.9	**55.6**
SimTrack [35]	63.7	82.9	79.9	48.8	**65.2**	54.6
CenterTube-V	**65.8**	**84.1**	**82.5**	**52.7**	63.5	52.4

Table 7.4 3D MOT performance on the mini-version of the nuScenes set

Methods	Overall	Car	Bus	Trailer	Truck	Motorcycle
CenterPoint [77]	64.1	81.9	**70.2**	65.3	59.5	59.1
CenterTube-V	**66.9**	**83.1**	69.5	**66.7**	**60.3**	**59.9**

FPS. This efficiency stands in contrast to existing multi-frame MOT approaches such as PC-TCNN [69] and SimTrack [35], which typically require a computationally intensive pre-processing step involving point cloud registration. As a result, their feature extraction pipeline tends to be significantly more expensive.

7.3.2.4 Evaluation on nuScenes Dataset

Table 7.3 lists the quantitative results among our CenterTube-V method and several competitive trackers such as SimTrack [35] on the nuScenes validation set. It is worth noting that SimTrack is also built as a multi-object tracking extension of the center-based detector *CenterPoint*. From the results, we observe that our CenterTube-V tracker achieves an overall AMOTA of 65.8%, surpassing previous trackers by a margin of 2.1%. In addition, it attains the best AMOTA scores in 3 out of 5 evaluated categories, namely, *Car*, *Bus*, and *Trailer*—highlighting its strong performance across multiple object types.

Table 7.4 presents the 3D MOT results on the mini-version of the nuScenes dataset. Similarly, the proposed CenterTube-V method demonstrates strong performance and substantially outperforms CenterPoint [77] in terms of overall AMOTA.

Table 7.5 Quantitative performance of our tubelet-based model, CenterTube, and the two-stage AB3DMOT [66] using the same detectors on the validation set of the KITTI-MOT dataset

Method	sAMOTA	AMOTA	AMOTP
CenterPoint-P + Kalman	90.47	42.68	73.56
CenterTube-P	**92.00**	**44.47**	**76.23**
CenterPoint-V + Kalman	91.10	43.42	75.41
CenterTube-V	**94.54**	**45.65**	**78.74**

7.3.2.5 Ablation Studies

In this section, a comprehensive group of ablation experiments is conducted to validate the contributions of individual components and to justify the selected hyperparameters.

Effectiveness of Our Tubelet-Based JDT Framework. To further demonstrate the advantages of our tubelet-based JDT framework, we conduct an ablation study by using the same detector in both the two-stage TBD framework and our JDT framework. Specifically, we replace the original PointRCNN [52] in AB3DMOT [66] with the same center-based detector used in our CenterTube, thus establishing it as the TBD baseline for comparison. Table 7.5 presents the quantitative results for cars on the KITTI-MOT validation set. It is evident that our CenterTube framework consistently surpasses the two-stage TBD variant (i.e., CenterPoint + Kalman) across all evaluation metrics, regardless of the underlying detection backbone (VoxelNet or PointPillars). These findings further highlight the effectiveness of our tubelet-based detection approach for 3D MOT task.

Effectiveness of Tubelet BEV-IoU. As introduced in Sect. 7.3.1.4, we propose a simple yet effective tubelet-based IoU strategy, referred to as Tubelet BEV-IoU (TB-IoU), for tubelet association. To further validate its effectiveness, we compare TB-IoU with several alternative tubelet-based metrics that build upon widely used frame-based association metrics (including 3D-IoU [66], and Mahalanobis distance [9]). The comparative results for CenterTube-V are shown in Table 7.6. Our CenterTube-V with TB-IoU achieves a 4.85% gain in sAMOTA and a 2.66% increase in AMOTA over 3D-IoU. These results indicate that TB-IoU effectively mitigates performance drops due to height-above-ground estimation errors.

Tubelet Design. As described in Sect. 7.3.1.2, we design a simplified 4D object tubelet based on the assumption of linear motion for objects within a short segment. Specifically, a 4D tubelet is defined by its start box and end box, which greatly reduces the complexity of regression parameters. To evaluate the effectiveness of this design, we implement a variant of CenterTube-V that predicts three bounding boxes

Table 7.6 Quantitative car-tracking performance of the proposed CenterTube-V with different tubelet-based association metrics on the KITTI-MOT validation set

Method	sAMOTA	AMOTA
3D-IoU [66]	89.70	42.99
Mahalanobis distance [9]	90.81	43.37
BEV-IoU	**94.54**	**45.65**

Table 7.7 Ablation study on our tubelet design

Method	Start box	mid. box	End box	sAMOTA	AMOTA	AMOTP
CenterTube-V	✓	✓	✓	94.39	**45.91**	**79.15**
	✓		✓	**94.54**	45.65	78.79

Table 7.8 Ablation study on orientation change

Method	Orien. change	sAMOTA	AMOTA	AMOTP
CenterTube-V		94.54	45.65	78.74
	✓	**94.71**	**45.68**	**78.79**

per tubelet, corresponding to the start, middle, and end timestamps, thus allowing the model to better approximate mild non-linear motion. As shown in Table 7.7, our CenterTube-V achieves comparable performance to the multi-box regression variant, demonstrating the rationality of our tubelet design.

Orientation Change. We perform an ablation study to assess the influence of incorporating orientation change prediction into the CenterTube framework. As shown in Table 7.8, introducing this design results in marginal improvements across all evaluation metrics. This can be attributed to two main factors: (1) most car instances are either stationary or follow simple motion patterns, such as straight-line movement, and (2) the motion within each segment is largely linear, with minimal variation in orientation.

Voxel Size. In this ablation experiment, we study the impact of input voxel size on tracking performance. Table 7.9 presents the quantitative results of our CenterTube-V with different voxel sizes. It is evident that CenterTube-V delivers the best performance with a voxel size of $[0.05, 0.05, 0.1\,\text{m}]$, whereas CenterTube-P performs optimally at a voxel size of $[0.12, 0.12, 4\,\text{m}]$. As the voxel size decreases (i.e., spatial resolution increases), tracking performance improves.

Number of Input Frames. We present the 3D MOT performance with different numbers of input frames in Table 7.10. The highest scores for sAMOTA, AMOTA,

Table 7.9 3D MOT performance of our CenterTube tracker with varying voxel sizes for input point clouds on the KITTI-MOT validation set

Method	Voxel size	sAMOTA	AMOTA	AMOTP
CenterTube-V	[0.1, 0.1, 0.1]	93.88	45.05	78.22
	[0.05, 0.05, 0.1]	**94.54**	**45.65**	**78.74**
CenterTube-P	[0.2, 0.2, 4]	88.24	42.58	75.43
	[0.16, 0.16, 4]	90.74	42.83	76.16
	[0.12, 0.12, 4]	**92.00**	**44.47**	**76.23**

Table 7.10 3D MOT performance of our CenterTube-V tracker with different numbers of input frames on the KITTI-MOT validation set

#Frames	sAMOTA	AMOTA	AMOTP
4	89.19	43.10	76.59
5	**94.54**	**45.65**	**78.74**
6	91.04	42.89	74.82
7	92.13	44.60	78.13
8	88.85	43.98	75.29

and AMOTP are achieved when using 5 input frames. This result is intuitive: shorter clips (e.g., 4 frames) lack sufficient temporal context, resulting in suboptimal tracking accuracy, while longer clips tend to violate the linear motion assumption underlying our tubelet representation, thus degrading performance.

7.4 3D Multiple Object Tracking with Transformer: AnchorPoint

The success of Transformers in natural language processing has spurred interest in their application to object detection, exemplified by DETR. In previous Transformer-based 2D detectors and trackers, object queries are typically implemented as a set of learned embeddings. However, extending this paradigm to 3D detection and tracking poses challenges due to the absence of explicit physical interpretations and position priors in the learned queries. To address this issue, we introduce the concept of anchors and propose a novel anchor point-based query design. In our design, foreground points extracted from input point clouds serve as anchor points, which are subsequently encoded into object queries. This design ensures that each query has a clear physical meaning and focuses on its surrounding object. In addition, we introduce an instance-aware sampling strategy to select a concise yet representative set of foreground points from the scene. Furthermore, we extend the AnchorPoint framework to 3D multi-object tracking by incorporating a tracking head and modeling each object through its associated anchor point. Extensive experiments on the KITTI-MOT and Waymo datasets demonstrate that our method achieves competitive performance compared to state-of-the-art approaches.

7.4.1 Methodology

7.4.1.1 Overview

In 2D object detectors, anchor points are typically defined as grid points on dense feature maps. In contrast, our query design leverages foreground points from the 3D point cloud as anchor points. However, it also presents a key challenge: *given the presence of thousands of foreground points in a scene, how can we efficiently select a compact yet representative subset to reduce computational and memory overhead?* Existing solutions often adopt task-agnostic sampling techniques such as farthest point sampling (FPS) [44]. Although simple and widely used, these methods may discard most foreground points during progressive downsampling process, thus potential losing valuable information. To address this limitation, we propose an instance-aware sampling strategy that prioritizes the retention of more informative foreground points.

The overall architecture of our proposed detection model, *AnchorPoint*, is illustrated in Fig. 7.6. AnchorPoint adopts a standard encoder-decoder structure. The input LiDAR point clouds are first processed by an encoder composed of four set abstraction layers, following PointNet++ [44], to extract rich point-wise features. During feature extraction, our instance-aware sampling strategy is integrated to progressively reduce the point set while preserving critical foreground information relevant for detection and tracking. The remaining foreground points serve as anchor points and are subsequently encoded into object queries. These queries are then fed into a Transformer-based decoder, which outputs class probabilities and regresses the corresponding 3D bounding boxes. To extend this detection framework for multi-object tracking (MOT), we draw inspiration from point-based tracking paradigms such as FairMOT [82] and introduce a lightweight tracking head. Each object is represented by its associated anchor point, and the tracking head predicts the displacement of these anchor points across frames to model object motion. The full pipeline of our extended MOT framework is depicted in Fig. 7.7.

7.4.1.2 Instance-Aware Downsampling Strategy

For point-based 3D object detection and tracking, it is necessary to sample a compact yet informative subset of foreground points from large-scale input point clouds. Consequently, it is critical that the progressive downsampling process retains as many high-quality foreground points as possible. The retained foreground points should meet two requirements: (1) They should be as close to the object centers

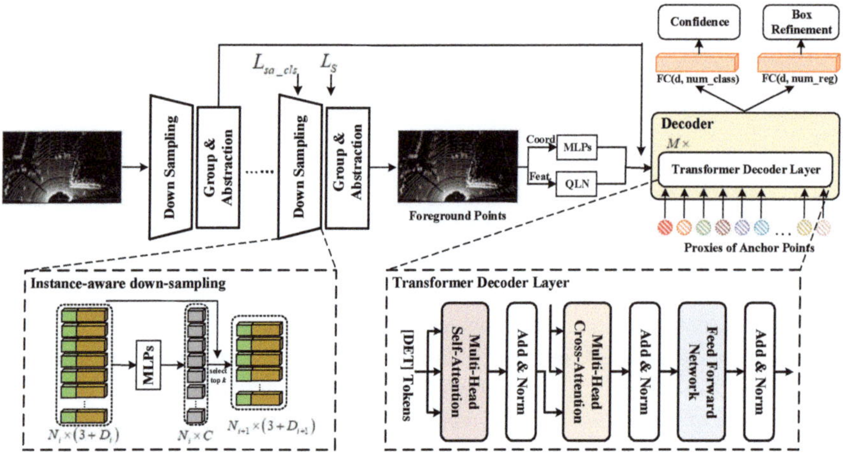

Fig. 7.6 The overall framework of our detection model *AnchorPoint* (This figure is reproduced from [31])

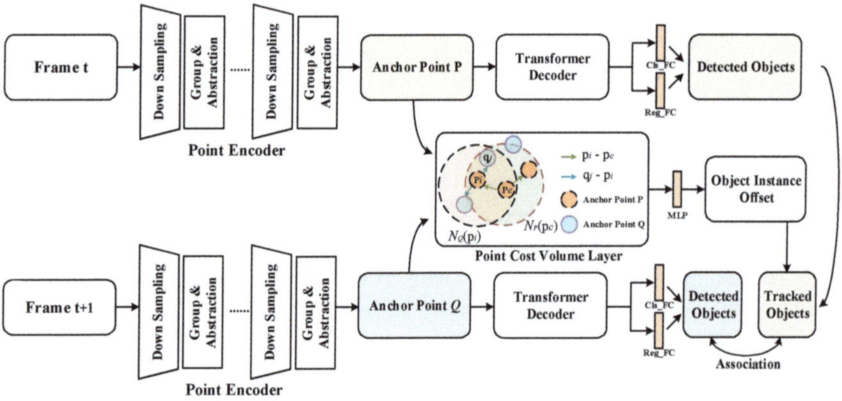

Fig. 7.7 The overall framework of our AnchorPoint-MOT model (This figure is reproduced from [31])

as possible; (2) They should cover all objects in the scene. This ensures that these foreground points not only facilitate the regression of object bounding boxes but also reduce false negatives in the detector.

How to sample foreground points closer to the object centers from input point clouds? We decompose this process into two steps: (1) The first step is to segment the point clouds by leveraging the latent semantics of each point, and then select the points with the top k segmentation (or foreground) scores as downsampling points. To this end, a segmentation head (comprising two MLP layers) is attached to each encoding layer to predict segmentation scores. The vanilla cross-entropy loss is used to train as follows:

$$L_{sa\_cls} = -\sum_{c=1}^{C}(p_i \log(\hat{p}_i) + (1 - p_i)\log(1 - \hat{p}_i)) \tag{7.10}$$

where $\hat{p}_i$ and p_i represent the predicted logits and the one-hot label, respectively. C is the number of segmentation categories.

The second step is to introduce a 3D Centerness metric as a soft mask into L_{sa_cls}, so that the downsampled foreground points are as close as possible to the object centers. The 3D Centerness is a metric to evaluate how close a point is to the center of its corresponding object instance. The 3D Centerness is calculated as follows:

$$3D\_Centerness = \sqrt[3]{\frac{\min(f, b)}{\max(f, b)} \times \frac{\min(l, r)}{\max(l, r)} \times \frac{\min(t, d)}{\max(t, d)}} \tag{7.11}$$

where (f, b, l, r, t, d) represent the distance from the point to the front, back, left, right, top and bottom surfaces of its corresponding object instance, respectively. When a point gradually approaches the center of its corresponding object instance, the value of 3D Centerness becomes larger, and vice versa. The cross entropy loss with the introduced 3D Centerness is defined as follows:

$$L_{sa\_ctr} = -\sum_{c=1}^{C}(Mask_i \cdot p_i \log(\hat{p}_i) + (1 - p_i)\log(1 - \hat{p}_i)). \tag{7.12}$$

Since the soft point mask is multiplied by the loss term of the foreground point, the loss value for foreground points closer to the object center is smaller.

How to ensure that foreground points cover all objects in the scene? To reduce false negatives, we introduce a sampling loss to ensure that the downsampling points S are distributed across all object instances. The sampling loss is calculated as follows:

$$L_s = \frac{1}{|F|}\sum_{f \in F} \min_{s \in S} ||f - s||_2^2 \tag{7.13}$$

where F represents the input points and $|F|$ denote the number of input points. $|| \cdot ||_2$ denotes 2-norm, which is used to calculate the Euclidean distance between two points.

7.4.1.3 Anchor Points to Object Queries

After obtaining the downsampling foreground points, we propose an anchor point-based query design to generate new object queries. Specifically, we use the foreground points as anchor points and encode them into object queries. To enhance the interpretability and discriminability of the queries, we encode the 3D coordinates and features of the anchor points separately. This separation ensures that the spatial and semantic information is explicitly preserved, making the queries more effective for downstream object detection and tracking tasks.

For anchor point feature encoding, we design a Query Learning Network (QLN) that generates query features from anchor points. The QLN consists of a single fully connected (FC) layer with ReLU activation, followed by a skip connection to preserve input information and facilitate gradient flow. To encode the 3D spatial coordinates of anchor points into the query representations, we adopt a learning-based approach that transforms continuous 3D coordinates into high-dimensional positional embeddings using a series of multilayer perceptrons (MLPs). In addition to this learned representation, we also incorporate sine-cosine positional encodings as a handcrafted alternative for encoding spatial positions, ensuring richer geometric awareness in the object queries.

7.4.1.4 Attentions for Decoding Object Queries

The Transformer decoder receives two distinct types of inputs: (1) object queries, denoted as [DET] tokens, and (2) multi-scale feature tokens, denoted as [FEAT], which are extracted by the feature encoder. The decoder employs an attention mechanism to capture the interactions between [DET] tokens (representing target objects) and [FEAT] tokens (encoding the surrounding scene context). Through this attention-driven process, the decoder generates the final set of predictions.

Multi-head Attention. Each Transformer encoder (or decoder) layer is built upon the multi-head attention mechanism, which processes three input sequences of 1D vectors: the query $\mathbf{Q} \in \mathbb{R}^{L \times d}$, the key $\mathbf{K} \in \mathbb{R}^{L \times d}$, and the value $\mathbf{V} \in \mathbb{R}^{L \times d}$, where L denotes the length of the input sequence and d represents the feature dimensions. These inputs are further divided along the feature dimension into multiple heads: $\mathbf{Q} = [\mathbf{Q}_1, \ldots, \mathbf{Q}_H]$, $\mathbf{K} = [\mathbf{K}_1, \ldots, \mathbf{K}_H]$, and $\mathbf{V} = [\mathbf{V}_1, \ldots, \mathbf{V}_H]$, where H is the number of attention heads. We can calculate the output of multi-head attention operation as follows:

$$\mathbf{SA}_i = \text{Softmax}(\mathbf{Q}_i \mathbf{K}_i^T / \sqrt{d/H} + \gamma) \cdot \mathbf{V}_i \tag{7.14}$$

$$\mathbf{MSA} = \text{Concat}([\mathbf{SA}_1, \mathbf{SA}_2, \ldots, \mathbf{SA}_H]) \tag{7.15}$$

where $\mathbf{A} = \text{Softmax}(\mathbf{Q}_i \mathbf{K}_i^T / \sqrt{d/H} + \gamma)$ is the weight matrix, which records the similarity between the query q and key k. γ represents a positional vector.

Transformer Decoder. Our decoder adopts the standard Transformer decoder architecture. Each Transformer decoder layer consists of two main attention operations: [DET] × [DET] self-attention and [DET] × [FEAT] cross-attention:

- [DET]×[DET] Self-Attention: The number of [DET] tokens specifies the maximum number of objects to be detected. Self-attention is applied among these [DET] tokens to enable them to capture relationships and distinguish between different objects.

- [DET]×[FEAT] Cross-Attention: [DET] tokens serve as queries, while [FEAT] tokens act as keys and values. Cross-attention is performed to allow each [DET] token to integrate multi-scale scene features, facilitating precise object localization.

After the attention operations, a feed-forward network (FFN) is incorporated to refine the outputs. The structure of the Transformer decoder layer is illustrated in Fig. 7.6.

Granularity Consistent Attention. We employ granularity consistent attention to enhance the integration of multi-scale features into our [DET] tokens. The input point clouds are processed through encoder layers based on set abstraction to extract point features. Notably, the outputs of the first encoder layer are used as the values for the last Transformer decoder layer, while the outputs of the last encoder layer are used as the values for the first Transformer decoder layer. This design allows the [DET] tokens to simultaneously leverage fine-grained features from the shallow layers and abstract semantic features from the deeper layers.

Auxiliary Decoding Loss. The detection head is appended to each Transformer decoder layer. Each detection head comprises two feed-forward branches: one for box classification and another for box regression. The training losses from all detection heads across different scales are aggregated into the final loss. This multi-scale supervision strategy enables the model to progressively refine its predictions and achieve higher accuracy as the decoder depth increases.

Notice that our transformer differs from the refinement module in [84] in at least two significant aspects. First, The transformer-based vote refinement module in [84] leverages coarse vote clusters to generate refined vote clusters. In contrast, our Transformer decoder takes a set of anchor points as input, integrating multi-scale features to directly produce object prediction sets. Second, each layer in the vote refinement module outputs two components: refined vote cluster centers and corresponding features. On the other hand, our Transformer decoder layers output only the features of anchor points (or object queries), making the module inherently more efficient.

7.4.1.5 Training Objectives

The overall loss L_{total} is composed of four components: the downsampling loss L_{sample}, the classification loss L_{cls}, the box regression loss L_{box}, and the auxiliary decoding loss L_{aux}. It is defined as

$$L_{total} = L_{sample} + L_{cls} + L_{box} + 0.2 * L_{aux}. \tag{7.16}$$

Here, $L_{sample} = L_{sa\_ctr} + L_s$. The box regression loss L_{box} is further decomposed into four sub-losses: a distance regression loss L_{dist}, a size regression loss L_{size}, an angle regression loss L_{angle}, and a corner loss L_{corner}. It is expressed as

$$L_{box} = L_{dist} + L_{size} + L_{angle} + L_{corner}. \tag{7.17}$$

Both distance regression loss L_{dist} and size regression loss L_{size} use the smooth L1 loss to measure differences. Angle regression loss L_{angle} is performed using a bin-based approach. Consequently, L_{angle} includes two components: an orientation classification loss and a residual prediction loss. Corner loss L_{corner} minimizes the discrepancy between the 8 predicted corners and the ground truth corners using an L1 loss. This ensures precise alignment of the bounding boxes.

7.4.1.6 AnchorPoint for Multi-object Tracking

The goal of 3D MOT is to generate a complete and correctly ordered set of object trajectories in a point cloud video. AnchorPoint, as a 3D object detector, already provides most of required information for object tracking, such as object positions, sizes, and orientations. However, it is unable to predict instance movements between consecutive frames, which are essential for object association. Inspired by point-based tracking methods [82, 86], we represent each object using its corresponding anchor point and introduce a lightweight tracking head to predict the inter-frame offset of the anchor point as the instance movement. The overall framework of our AnchorPoint-MOT model is shown in Fig. 7.7.

Tracking head. The tracking head takes as input the anchor points from two consecutive frames, denoted as $P = \{p_j \in \mathbb{R}^3\}_{j=1}^n$ and $Q = \{q_k \in \mathbb{R}^3\}_{k=1}^n$, where n is the number of anchor points. To encodes the 3D motion of anchor points ($P \rightarrow Q$), we utilize a cost volume layer [71] to aggregate feature similarities and spatial relationships. This cost volume layer is computed in a patch-to-patch manner. Specifically, for an anchor point $p_a \in P$, we first determine its neighborhood $N_P(p_a)$ within P. For each $p_i \in N_P(p_a)$, we then locate a neighborhood $N_Q(p_i)$ in Q. The cost volume for p_a is computed as follows:

$$CV(p_a) = \sum_{p_i \in N_P(p_a)} \text{MLP}(p_i - p_a) \sum_{q_j \in N_Q(p_i)} \text{MLP}(q_j - p_i) cost(q_j, p_i) \tag{7.18}$$

where the cost function is defined as

$$cost(q_j, p_i) = \text{MLP}(\text{Concat}(f_i, g_j, q_j - p_i)). \tag{7.19}$$

f_i and g_j represent the features of the anchor points p_i and q_j, respectively. The resulting cost volume is concatenated with the features of anchor points P, followed by three MLP layers to predict 3D displacements of anchor points P. The displacements of these anchor points are regarded as the inter-frame movements of the target instances for association.

Association. After obtaining the 3D instance movements between consecutive frames, the tracked boxes are produced based on the detected boxes from the previous frame. The Hungarian algorithm is then employed to associate the detected boxes with the tracked boxes in the current frame, using 3D IoU as the association cost.

Matched boxes are used to update the existing trajectories, while unmatched boxes are treated as new instances to initialize new trajectories.

Training objectives. The AnchorPoint-MOT model is trained in two stages: first, the AnchorPoint detector is trained to predict 3D oriented boxes, and then its weights are frozen while the tracking head is trained separately. The tracking head is trained with the L1 loss:

$$L_{mot} = \frac{1}{n}\sum_{i=1}^{n}\mathbb{1}(c_i > 0)||IM(p_i) - \widehat{IM}(p_i)||_2 \tag{7.20}$$

where $IM(p_i)$ and $\widehat{IM}(p_i)$ denote the ground-truth and predicted movements of anchor point p_i, respectively. c_i is the classification label, and $\mathbb{1}(c_i > 0)$ ensures that the instance movement loss is computed only for foreground anchor points.

7.4.2 Experiments

7.4.2.1 Experimental Settings

Datasets. The KITTI [14] benchmark is one of the earliest and most widely used datasets for 3D object detection and tracking. The KITTI-DET dataset consists of 7,481 training samples and 7,518 test samples. The training samples are further split into 3,712 samples for training and 3,769 samples for validation. Each sample includes LiDAR point cloud data, camera RGB image data, and a calibration file. For MOT, the KITTI-MOT dataset provides 21 training sequences and 29 test sequences. Following the train-validation split proposed in [66], the training sequences are divided into train and validation sets. The point clouds range is restricted to $[0, 70.4\,\text{m}]$ along the X axis, $[-40, 40\,\text{m}]$ along the Y axis and $[-3, 1\,\text{m}]$ along the Z axis.

The Waymo Open [59] dataset contains 1150 driving sequences, with 798, 202, and 150 sequences for training, validation, and test, respectively. In total, these sequences provide approximately 200,000 LiDAR frames with over 12 million annotated objects. The detection range is set to $[-75.2, 75.2\,\text{m}]$ for both the X and Y axes, and $[-2, 4\,\text{m}]$ for the Z axis.

Evaluation metrics. For KITTI-DET dataset, mean average prevision (mAP) is adopted as main evaluation metric to evaluate our detection model. mAP is calculated over 40 recall positions, with rotated IoU threshold set to 0.7 for *Car* and 0.5 for *Cyclists* and *Pedestrians*. KITTI-DET categorizes object instances into *easy*, *moderate*, and **hard** levels according to their sizes, occlusion levels, and truncated rates. Notice that, we use the results of *moderate* level for comparison. For Waymo Open dataset, we use the mean average precision weighted by heading (mAPH) and standard mAP to jointly evaluate our model. mAPH is considered as an extension of mAP, which further accounts for the orientation information of the detected boxes. Similar to KITTI-DET, Waymo Open divides the objects into LEVEL_1 and LEVEL_2. For MOT task, we use the 3D evaluation metrics proposed in AB3DMOT [66] for model evaluation. The 3D MOT metrics include AMOTA, AMOTP and sAMOTA. Furthermore, we use the 2D MOT metrics such as HOTA [34] and CLEAR MOT [3] as a supplement to comprehensively evaluate the tracking performance of the model.

Network architecture. As illustrated in Fig. 7.6, the network begins with four set-abstraction (SA) layers with multi-scale grouping to extract point features and progressively downsample the input points into size 4096, 1024, 512, 128. For the Waymo dataset, which has a large sensing range and a higher number of potential instances, the downsampled sizes are increased to 16384, 4096, 2048, 1024. The neighboring radii for the SA layers are set to (0.2, 0.8 m), (0.8, 1.6 m), (1.6, 4.8 m) and (4.8, 6.4 m), respectively. The output points of the final SA layer are used as anchor points and encoded into object queries through our query design. These queries are then processed by four Transformer-based decoder layers, which reason about the relations between object queries and their context to generate the final object set. In the MOT framework, anchor points from two consecutive frames are taken as input, and their cost volume [71] is computed with a feature dimension of 128. The neighboring radius for cost volume calculation is set to $10m$. Finally, the cost volume is passed through three MLP layers ($128 \rightarrow 128 \rightarrow 64 \rightarrow 3$) to predict the instance movements.

Training and inference details. For the KITTI dataset, the model is trained for 80 epochs with a batch size of 32 and an initial learning rate of 0.002. For the Waymo Open dataset, the model training is conducted over 30 epochs with a batch size of 16, while maintaining the same initial learning rate of 0.002. When training AnchorPoint-MOT, the weights of the part of the AnchorPoint detector are frozen, and only the tracking module is optimized. This training process of the MOT model spans 80 epochs with a batch size of 16 and a learning rate of 0.001. During the training of AnchorPoint, we employ three widely-used scene-level augmentations: random flipping along the X and Y axes, random rotation with angles sampled from $[-\pi/4, \pi/4]$, and random scaling with scaling factors sampled from [0.95, 1.05]. Additionally, we introduce an object-level augmentation known as *cut and paste*, which extracts ground-truth boxes and their internal points from other scenes and places them at the corresponding locations in the current scene. For training AnchorPoint-MOT, these augmentations are extended to the temporal domain.

In the detection inference stage, AnchorPoint generates potential object positions in a single forward pass. To refine the results, non-maximum suppression (NMS) is applied with a 3D IoU threshold of 0.01 for KITTI and 0.1 for Waymo to eliminate redundant predictions. For MOT inference, detection and tracking boxes are obtained after the NMS step, and the Hungarian algorithm is used to associate these boxes based on a 3D IoU threshold of 0.1. For submissions on the KITTI-MOT test set, we follow AB3DMOT [66] to filter out object trajectories with an average confidence score below 0.4.

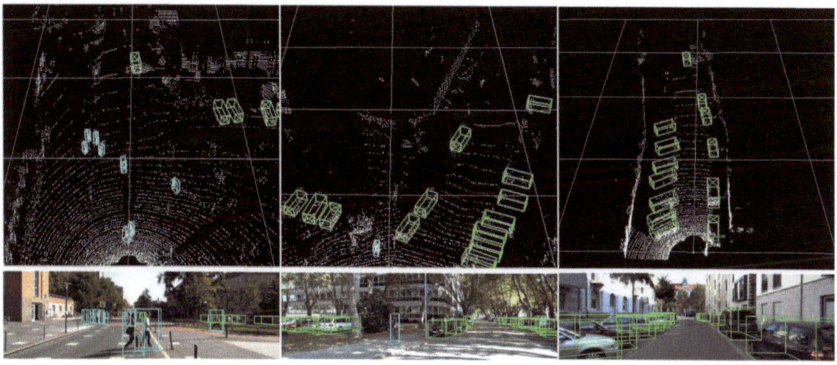

Fig. 7.8 Qualitative results of our AnchorPoint model on the KITTI-DET dataset (This figure is reproduced from [31])

7.4.2.2 Experiments on KITTI-DET Dataset

In Table 7.11, we present the quantitative results of our AnchorPoint and 17 state-of-the-art methods, classified into *voxel-based*, *point-voxel*, and *point-based*, on the KITTI validation set. We can observe that: (1) For 3D detection of the *Car* class, our AnchorPoint demonstrates competitive performance, achieving an AP of 83.21 at the *moderate* difficulty level. This result is on par with the point-voxel detector PV-RCNN [51] and surpasses the performance of the point-based IA-SSD [81] by a margin of 3.81%. (2) For 3D detection of the *Cyclist* class, AnchorPoint achieves the highest AP values across the *easy*/*moderate*/*hard* levels, with scores of 87.23, 71.25, and 66.41, respectively. These results even outperform some strong point-voxel detectors. This improvement can be attributed to the instance-aware downsampling strategy that effectively retains critical foreground points, and the granularity-consistent attention mechanism that leverages fine-grained features for more accurate detection of challenging objects. (3) Beyond its robust detection capabilities, AnchorPoint is remarkably efficient, running at nearly 61 FPS on a single NVIDIA GTX TITAN GPU. However, some results of our AnchorPoint are lower than the best results (e.g., PV-RCNN, Part-A^2). This is likely due to the progressive downsampling in the feature encoder, which causes some informative points to be lost in the point-based detector. By contrast, voxel-based and point-voxel detectors are better at capturing comprehensive structural information from the input point cloud scene.

Figure 7.8 shows visualization results of our AnchorPoint detector on several samples from the KITTI-DET dataset. The visualizations highlight the model's ability to accurately predict the 3D spatial locations of object instances, even in challenging traffic scenarios such as crowded streets, small or distant objects, and instances that are partially occluded.

Table 7.11 Comparative results for the *Car* and *Cyclist* classes on the KITTI-DET [14] validation set

	Method	Car - 3D Detection			Car - BEV Detection			Cyclist - 3D Detection			Cyclist - BEV Detection			Speed
		Easy	Mod.	Hard	Easy	Mod.	Hard	Easy	Mod.	Hard	Easy	Mod.	Hard	
Voxel-based	VoxelNet [87]	81.97	65.46	62.85	89.60	84.81	78.57	67.17	47.65	45.11	74.41	52.18	50.49	4.5
	SECOND [72]	84.94	76.30	75.98	87.91	86.09	85.33	80.41	64.29	60.19	84.63	66.85	63.43	20
	PointPillars [26]	86.46	77.28	74.65	89.65	87.17	84.37	80.05	62.68	59.70	82.27	66.25	62.64	42.4
	Associate-3Ddet [11]	89.29	79.17	77.76	90.50	88.98	87.71	–	–	–	–	–	–	20
	SA-SSD [16]	90.15	79.91	78.78	90.50	88.43	87.49	–	–	–	–	–	–	25
	CIA-SSD [85]	90.04	79.81	78.80	90.51	88.86	87.95	–	–	–	–	–	–	32
	Part-A^2 [53]	89.55	79.40	77.84	90.22	87.95	87.54	85.50	69.90	65.48	86.92	73.35	69.77	12.5
	Voxel-RCNN [10]	89.36	82.77	78.74	90.46	88.53	87.95	86.12	70.94	66.19	87.57	73.29	69.84	32.4
Point-Voxel	Fast Point RCNN [7]	89.12	79.00	77.48	90.12	88.10	86.24	–	–	–	–	–	–	16.7
	STD [75]	89.70	79.80	79.30	90.50	88.50	88.10	–	–	–	–	–	–	12.5
	PV-RCNN [51]	89.35	83.69	78.70	90.09	87.90	87.41	86.06	69.48	64.50	88.53	73.32	70.37	12.5
	VIC-Net [19]	89.60	79.25	78.02	–	–	–	–	–	–	–	–	–	17
	HVPR [40]	90.24	82.05	79.49	–	–	–	–	–	–	–	–	–	36.1
Point-based	PointRCNN [52]	88.86	78.68	77.68	90.07	87.68	86.53	86.32	70.31	65.59	87.17	72.48	67.62	10
	Point-GNN [54]	87.89	78.34	77.38	89.82	88.31	87.16	–	–	–	–	–	–	1.6
	3DSSD [74]	**89.71**	79.45	78.67	90.34	88.07	86.06	–	–	–	–	–	–	28
	IA-SSD [81]	88.90	79.40	78.41	90.05	**88.47**	86.50	86.93	70.90	66.06	**90.49**	72.25	69.58	**83**
	AnchorPoint (Ours)	89.70	**83.21**	**78.79**	**90.51**	88.34	**87.41**	**87.23**	**71.25**	**66.41**	89.95	**72.53**	**69.71**	61

7.4.2.3 Experiments on Waymo Open Dataset

Table 7.12 presents the 3D object detection results for the *Vehicle*, *Pedestrian*, and *Cyclist* classes on the Waymo validation set. It is observed that: (1) For *Vehicle* detection, AnchorPoint delivers comparable performance compared to PV-RCNN [51], while outperforming IA-SSD [81] by 3.38% in mAP and 3.73% in mAPH on LEVEL_1, and by 3.55% in mAP and 3.84% in mAPH on LEVEL_2. (2) For *Pedestrian* detection, AnchorPoint achieves the best results on both LEVEL_1 and LEVEL_2, surpassing several strong voxel-based and point-voxel-based detectors. (3) For *Cyclist* detection, AnchorPoint also sets a new benchmark, outperforming IA-SSD [81] by 2.51% in mAP and 3.35% in mAPH on LEVEL_1, and by 2.78% in mAP and 3.57% in mAPH on LEVEL_2. These results highlight AnchorPoint's superior performance across all three classes, particularly in challenging scenarios represented by LEVEL_2.

7.4.2.4 Experiments on KITTI-MOT Dataset

To thoroughly evaluate the tracking performance of our AnchorPoint-MOT, we conduct two sets of experiments: (1) **3D MOT evaluation**: The model is trained on the training set and evaluated on the validation set using the evaluation protocol proposed in AB3DMOT [66]. This setup provides a detailed assessment of the model's 3D tracking capabilities. (2) **2D MOT evaluation**: The model is trained on the train+val set, and the results for the test set are submitted to the official KITTI-MOT test server for evaluation. This experiment evaluates the performance of AnchorPoint-MOT in 2D tracking scenarios.

3D MOT. Table 7.13 lists the quantitative results of our AnchorPoint-MOT and several competitive trackers on the KITTI-MOT validation set. Our observations include (1) Our extended MOT model achieves comparable performance to the state-of-the-art PC-TCNN [69] and surpasses the classic AB3DMOT in several metrics, boosting sAMOTA, AMOTA, and AMOTP by 1.97, 2.53, and 4.57%, respectively. These gains are primarily due to the strong detection capabilities of AnchorPoint model and the robust object association enabled by our point-based tracking head. (2) Thanks to the superior efficiency of our AnchorPoint detector and the feature reuse approach, AnchorPoint-MOT achieves a tracking speed of 49 FPS on a single NVIDIA GTX TITAN GPU, demonstrating its suitability for real-time applications.

2D MOT. We compare the 2D MOT performance of our AnchorPoint-MOT with several promising trackers, including image-based, LiDAR-based, and joint image-and-LiDAR-based, on the KITTI-MOT test set, as shown in Table 7.14. To conduct 2D MOT comparison, we need to project the predicted 3D trajectories onto the 2D image plane. We observe that AnchorPoint-MOT achieves strong 2D MOT performance, with a HOTA of 71.30%, a 2D MOTA of 86.96%, and a 2D MOTP of 85.63%. Compared to the multi-modality tracker JRMOT [50], HOTA, 2D MOTA, and 2D

Table 7.12 Comparative 3D detection results on the Waymo Open [59] validation set

Method	Type	Vehicle-L1		Vehicle-L2		Pedestrian-L1		Pedestrian-L2		Cyclist-L1		Cyclist-L2	
		mAP	mAPH	mAP	mAPH	mAP	mAPH	mAP	mAPH	mAP	mAPH	mAP	mAPH
PointPillars [26]	Voxel-based	60.67	59.79	52.78	52.01	43.49	23.51	37.32	20.17	35.94	28.34	34.60	27.29
SECOND [72]	Voxel-based	68.03	67.44	59.57	59.04	61.14	50.33	53.00	43.56	54.66	53.31	52.67	51.37
Part-A^2 [53]	Voxel-based	71.82	71.29	64.33	63.82	63.15	54.96	54.24	47.11	65.23	63.92	62.61	61.35
PV-RCNN [51]	Point-Voxel	<u>74.06</u>	73.38	64.99	64.38	62.66	52.68	53.80	45.14	63.32	61.71	60.72	59.18
IA-SSD [81]	Point-based	70.53	69.67	61.55	60.80	69.38	58.47	60.30	50.73	67.67	65.30	64.98	62.71
AnchorPoint	Point-based	73.91	<u>73.40</u>	<u>65.10</u>	<u>64.64</u>	<u>70.37</u>	<u>61.76</u>	<u>61.77</u>	<u>54.08</u>	<u>70.18</u>	<u>68.65</u>	<u>67.76</u>	<u>66.28</u>

Table 7.13 Comparative 3D multi-object tracking results on the KITTI-MOT [14] validation set

Method	Input data	sAMOTA (%)↑	AMOTA (%)↑	AMOTP (%)↑	MOTA (%)↑	MOTP (%)↑	IDS↓	FPS↑
mmMOT [80]	2D+3D	70.61	33.08	72.45	74.07	78.16	10	4.8
FANTrack [2]	2D+3D	82.97	40.03	75.01	74.30	75.24	35	25.0
AB3DMOT [66]	3D	93.28	45.43	77.41	86.24	78.43	0	214.7
GNN3DMOT [67]	2D+3D	93.68	45.27	78.10	84.70	79.03	0	5.2
PC-TCNN [69]	3D	95.44	47.64	–	–	–	–	3.2
EagerMOT [24]	2D+3D	94.94	–	–	–	80.00	2	–
PolarMOT [23]	3D	94.32	–	–	–	–	31	–
AnchorPoint-MOT	3D	95.25	47.96	81.98	91.14	81.71	3	49.0

Table 7.14 Comparative 2D multi-object tracking results on the KITTI-MOT [14] test set

Method	Input data	HOTA (%)↑	MOTA (%)↑	MOTP (%)↑	MT (%)↑	ML (%)↓	IDS↓	FRAG↓
CIWT [41]	2D	54.90	74.44	79.32	50.46	11.23	491	552
BeyondPixels [46]	2D	63.75	82.68	85.50	72.61	2.92	934	581
mono3DT [18]	2D	73.16	84.28	85.45	73.08	2.92	379	573
CenterTrack [86]	2D	73.02	88.83	84.97	82.15	2.46	254	227
mmMOT [80]	2D+3D	62.05	83.23	85.03	72.92	2.92	733	570
FANTrack [2]	2D+3D	64.36	75.84	82.46	62.77	8.77	743	701
JRMOT [50]	2D+3D	69.61	85.10	85.28	70.92	4.62	271	273
GNN3DMOT [67]	2D+3D	–	80.40	85.05	70.77	11.08	113	265
EagerMOT [24]	2D+3D	74.39	87.82	85.69	76.15	2.47	239	390
PointTrackNet [62]	3D	57.20	67.56	76.83	60.46	12.77	294	756
ComplexerYOLO [56]	3D	–	75.70	78.46	58.00	5.08	1186	2092
AB3DMOT [66]	3D	68.81	83.49	85.17	67.08	11.38	**126**	**254**
PolarMOT [23]	3D	75.16	85.08	**85.63**	**80.92**	**2.47**	462	599
AnchorPoint-MOT	3D	71.30	**86.96**	**85.63**	79.54	7.69	183	255

MOTP are increased by 1.69%, 1.86%, and 0.35%, respectively. Similarly, our model outperforms the LiDAR-based tracker AB3DMOT [66] by 2.49%, 3.47%, and 0.46% in the same metrics. However, our AnchorPoint-MOT trails behind the 3D tracker PolarMOT [23]. This is likely because recent 3D trackers such as PolarMOT [23] use a state-of-the-art detector trained on external datasets to produce high-quality 3D detections and thus focus primarily on the association stage. In contrast, our model is trained end-to-end exclusively on the KITTI-MOT dataset.

Figure 7.9 illustrates the 3D MOT results obtained by our AnchorPoint-MOT tracker on the KITTI-MOT test set, specifically on Sequence 03. The visualizations demonstrate the tracker's capability to handle challenging scenarios, such as (1) Heavy occlusion: our tracker effectively maintains accurate tracking even when objects are heavily occluded, as shown by the object with ID 650. These visualizations highlight the robustness of our AnchorPoint-MOT in complex tracking scenarios.

Fig. 7.9 Qualitative results on sequence 03 of the KITTI-MOT [14] test set (This figure is reproduced from [31])

Table 7.15 Ablation study on different downsampling strategies

	Random	D-FPS	F-FPS	Ctr-aware	Ins-aware	Recall (%)	Easy	Moderate	Hard
(1)	✓					69.6	83.75	68.22	65.70
(2)		✓				87.7	86.64	77.88	77.18
(3)		✓	✓			92.4	88.03	78.69	77.89
(4)		✓		✓		95.0	88.23	80.37	77.78
(5)		✓			✓	97.7	89.70	83.21	78.79

7.4.2.5 Ablation Studies

In this section, we present a group of ablation studies to evaluate the effectiveness of the proposed AnchorPoint framework and its extension to multi-object tracking (MOT). For evaluating the detection performance of AnchorPoint, we report results on the *Car* category from the KITTI-Det validation set. For the tracking extension (AnchorPoint-MOT), we provide 3D MOT performance on the KITTI-MOT validation set.

Downsampling strategy. In this ablation study, we evaluate the effectiveness of our proposed instance-aware downsampling strategy. Table 7.15 reports both the instance recall rates and 3D detection results of AnchorPoint under different downsampling strategies. We can obtain the following observations: (1) Detection performance correlates positively with instance recall rate. Preserving more informative foreground points tends to enhance final detection performance. (2) The instance-aware downsampling strategy achieves the highest instance recall rate and detection performance across all three levels. This reflects that our strategy effectively retains more informative foreground points, thus leading to superior detection results.

Positional embedding: We investigate the impact of different types of positional embeddings (PE) on our model, including handcrafted PE and learnable PE. As shown in Table 7.16, the model equipped with learnable PE outperforms the one using handcrafted PE. This improvement can be attributed to the flexibility and robustness of learnable PE.

Cross attention: We investigate the impact of different cross-attention mechanisms within the AnchorPoint framework, including conventional attention, granularity

Table 7.16 Ablation study of AnchorPoint with different types of positional embedding

Type	Easy	Moderate	Hard
Handcrafted	88.95	81.51	78.18
Learnable (Ours)	89.70	83.21	78.79

Table 7.17 Ablation study on cross-attention mechanism

Mechanism	Easy	Moderate	Hard
Conventional	88.49	81.27	78.17
GPA	87.78	80.20	77.90
GCA(Ours)	89.70	83.21	78.79

Table 7.18 Ablation study on auxiliary decoding loss

Aux. loss	Easy	Moderate	Hard
	88.51	81.80	78.16
✓	89.70	83.21	78.79

parallel attention (GPA), and granularity consistent attention (GCA). As shown in Table 7.17, the model equipped with GCA achieves notably superior performance compared to the other two variants. These results highlight the effectiveness of GCA in enhancing feature interactions between object queries and multi-scale scene context.

Auxiliary decoding loss: In Table 7.18, we analyze the effect of the auxiliary decoding loss on detection performance. The results demonstrate that incorporating the auxiliary decoding loss leads to a notable performance boost, achieving improvements of 1.21/1.41/0.63% on the easy, moderate, and hard levels of the *Car* subset, respectively.

Tracking head: Table 7.19 presents the 3D tracking performance of our AnchorPoint-MOT using different tracking heads. Notice that the variants of our AnchorPoint-MOT are implemented by replacing the point cost volume layer [71] with other tracking layers such as the flow embedding layer [33]. We can observe that our tracking model equipped with the point cost volume layer surpasses its variant with the flow embedding layer by 2.49, 2.39, and 2.16% in terms of sAMOTA, AMOTA, and AMOTP, respectively. This is mainly attributed to the point cost volume layer's ability to effectively aggregate geometric similarities and spatial relationships among points in consecutive frames, enabling more accurate and robust object tracking.

Table 7.19 Ablation study on tracking head

Tracking head	sAMOTA↑	AMOTA↑	AMOTP↑	IDS↓
Flow embedding [33]	92.76	45.59	79.82	5
Cost volume (ours)	95.25	47.96	81.98	3

7.5 Conclusion and Future Work

In this chapter, we propose two novel methods for joint 3D object detection and tracking. The first approach, termed CenterTube, introduces a 4D object tubelet representation to better model the spatio-temporal locations of objects within video sequences. Based on this representation, we develop a tubelet-based framework that performs 3D multi-object tracking by directly detecting and associating 4D tubelets in dynamic point cloud sequences. Unlike traditional tracking-by-detection pipelines that separate detection and temporal association, CenterTube performs both tasks simultaneously in a single forward pass. The model is trained in an end-to-end manner, allowing for joint optimization of detection and tracking objectives, which leads to improved robustness and computational efficiency. However, for long-lost objects, it remains challenging for the proposed CenterTube to recover the tubelets. We leave this issue for future exploration.

The second proposed method, named AnchorPoint, introduces a novel query design for Transformer-based 3D object detection and tracking. Instead of relying on previous learnable object query, AnchorPoint grounds each query on a representative foreground point (which is encoded as anchor point), explicitly sampled from the input point cloud. To this end, we design an instance-aware downsampling strategy that selects informative foreground points as anchor points, thus making our query physically grounded and focused on its associated nearby object. Furthermore, we represent each object with its corresponding anchor point and extend the detection model to 3D multi-object tracking by introducing a dedicated tracking head. However, our AnchorPoint still has several limitations. First, since foreground points constitute only a small portion of the scene point cloud, the proposed downsampling strategy is sensitive to class imbalance. Second, our method heavily relies on the selection of anchor points, meaning that the detection and tracking performance is closely tied to, and potentially dominated by, the quality of the anchor points.

In addition to the limitations discussed above, we also outline several promising directions for future research. First, incorporating multi-modal information such as RGB images can enhance the accuracy and robustness of 3D object tracking, particularly in scenarios with sparse or noisy point clouds. Second, developing robust association mechanisms is critical for improving long-term tracking stability, especially under challenging conditions such as occlusion, fast motion, or crowded scenes.

References

1. Bai H, Cheng W, Chu P, Liu J, Zhang K, Ling H (2021) GMOT-40: a benchmark for generic multiple object tracking. In: Proceedings of the IEEE conference on computer vision and pattern recognition (CVPR), pp 6719–6728
2. Baser E, Balasubramanian V, Bhattacharyya P, Czarnecki K (2019) Fantrack: 3D multi-object tracking with feature association network. In: Proceedings of the IEEE intelligent vehicles symposium (IV). IEEE, pp 1426–1433
3. Bernardin K, Stiefelhagen R (2008) Evaluating multiple object tracking performance: the clear mot metrics. EURASIP J Image Video Process 1–10
4. Bewley A, Ge Z, Ott L, Ramos F, Upcroft B (2016) Simple online and realtime tracking. In: Proceedings of the IEEE international conference on image processing (ICIP). IEEE, pp 3464–3468
5. Caesar H, Bankiti V, Lang AH, Vora S, Liong VE, Xu Q, Krishnan A, Pan Y, Baldan, G., Beijbom, O.: nuScenes: a multimodal dataset for autonomous driving. In: Proceedings of the IEEE conference on computer vision and pattern recognition (CVPR), pp 11621–11631
6. Carion N, Massa F, Synnaeve G, Usunier N, Kirillov A, Zagoruyko S (2020) End-to-end object detection with transformers. In: Proceedings of the European conference on computer vision (ECCV). Springer, Berlin, pp 213–229
7. Chen Y, Liu S, Shen X, Jia J (2019) Fast point R-CNN. In: Proceedings of the IEEE international conference on computer vision (ICCV)
8. Chiu HK, Li J, Ambruş R, Bohg J (2021) Probabilistic 3D multi-modal, multi-object tracking for autonomous driving. In: Proceedings of the IEEE international conference on robotics and automation (ICRA). IEEE, pp 14227–14233
9. Chiu HK, Prioletti A, Li J, Bohg J (2020) Probabilistic 3D multi-object tracking for autonomous driving. arXiv:2001.05673
10. Deng J, Shi S, Li P, Zhou W, Zhang Y, Li H (2020) Voxel R-CNN: towards high performance voxel-based 3D object detection. arXiv:2012.15712
11. Du L, Ye X, Tan X, Feng J, Xu Z, Ding E, Wen S (2020) Associate-3Ddet: perceptual-to-conceptual association for 3D point cloud object detection. In: Proceedings of the IEEE Conference on Computer Vision and Pattern Recognition (CVPR), pp 13329–13338
12. Fang Y, Liao B, Wang X, Fang J, Qi J, Wu R, Niu J, Liu W (2021) You only look at one sequence: rethinking Transformer in vision through object detection. In: Proceedings of the advances in neural information processing systems (NeurIPS)
13. Feichtenhofer C, Pinz A, Zisserman A (2017) Detect to track and track to detect. In: Proceedings of the IEEE international conference on computer vision (ICCV), pp 3038–3046
14. Geiger A, Lenz P, Urtasun R (2012) Are we ready for autonomous driving? the kitti vision benchmark suite. In: Proceedings of the IEEE conference on computer vision and pattern recognition (CVPR). IEEE, pp 3354–3361
15. Guan T, Wang J, Lan S, Chandra R, Wu Z, Davis L, Manocha D (2022) M3DETR: multi-representation, multi-scale, mutual-relation 3D object detection with transformers. In: Proceedings of the IEEE winter conference on applications of computer vision (WACV), pp 772–782
16. He C, Zeng H, Huang J, Hua XS, Zhang L (2020) Structure aware single-stage 3D object detection from point cloud. In: Proceedings of the IEEE conference on computer vision and pattern recognition (CVPR), pp 11873–11882
17. Hou R, Chen C, Shah M (2017) Tube convolutional neural network (T-CNN) for action detection in videos. In: Proceedings of the IEEE international conference on computer vision (ICCV), pp 5822–5831
18. Hu HN, Cai QZ, Wang D, Lin J, Sun M, Krahenbuhl P, Darrell T, Yu F (2019) Joint monocular 3D vehicle detection and tracking. In: Proceedings of the IEEE international conference on computer vision (ICCV), pp 5390–5399
19. Jiang T, Song N, Liu H, Yin R, Gong Y, Yao J (2021) VIC-Net: voxelization information compensation network for point cloud 3D object detection. In: Proceedings of the IEEE international conference on robotics and automation (ICRA). IEEE, pp 13408–13414

20. Kalogeiton V, Weinzaepfel P, Ferrari V, Schmid C (2017) Action Tubelet detector for Spatio-temporal action localization. In: Proceedings of the IEEE international conference on computer vision (ICCV), pp 4405–4413
21. Kang K, Li H, Yan J, Zeng X, Yang B, Xiao T, Zhang C, Wang Z, Wang R, Wang X et al (2017) T-CNN: Tubelets with convolutional neural networks for object detection from videos. In: IEEE transactions on circuits and systems for video technology (TCSVT), pp 2896–2907
22. Kang K, Ouyang W, Li H, Wang X (2016) Object detection from video Tubelets with convolutional neural networks. In: Proceedings of the IEEE conference on computer vision and pattern recognition (CVPR), pp 817–825
23. Kim A, Bras'o G, Ošep A, Leal-Taix'e L (2022) PolarMOT: how far can geometric relations take us in 3D multi-object tracking? In: Proceedings of the European conference on computer vision (ECCV)
24. Kim A, Ošep A, Leal-Taixé L (2021) EagerMOT: 3D multi-object tracking via sensor fusion. In: Proceedings of the IEEE international conference on robotics and automation (ICRA)
25. Kingma DP, Ba J (2014) Adam: a method for stochastic optimization. Comput. Sci.
26. Lang AH, Vora S, Caesar H, Zhou L, Yang J, Beijbom O (2019) PointPillars: fast encoders for object detection from point clouds. In: Proceedings of the IEEE conference on computer vision and pattern recognition (CVPR), pp 12697–12705
27. Lin TY, Goyal P, Girshick R, He K, Dollár P (2017) Focal loss for dense object detection. In: Proceedings of the IEEE international conference on computer vision (ICCV), pp 2980–2988
28. Liu C, Yao R, Rezatofighi SH, Reid I, Shi Q (2019) Model-free tracker for multiple objects using joint appearance and motion inference. IEEE Trans Image Process (TIP) 29:277–288
29. Liu H, Guo Y, Ma Y, Lei Y, Wen G (2021) Semantic context encoding for accurate 3D point cloud segmentation. IEEE Trans Multimed 23:2045–2055
30. Liu H, Ma Y, Hu Q, Guo Y (2023) CenterTube: tracking multiple 3D objects with 4D Tubelets in dynamic point clouds. IEEE Trans Multimed (TMM) 25:8793–8804
31. Liu H, Ma Y, Wang H, Zhang C, Guo Y (2023) AnchorPoint: query design for transformer-based 3D object detection and tracking. IEEE Trans Intell Transp Syst (TITS) 24(10):10988–11000
32. Liu W, Anguelov D, Erhan D, Szegedy C, Reed S, Fu CY, Berg AC (2016) SSD: single shot multibox detector. In: Proceedings of the European conference on computer vision (ECCV). Springer, Berlin, pp 21–37
33. Liu X, Qi CR, Guibas LJ (2019) FlowNet3D: learning scene flow in 3D point clouds. In: Proceedings of the IEEE conference on computer vision and pattern recognition (CVPR), pp 529–537
34. Luiten J, Osep A, Dendorfer P, Torr P, Geiger A, Leal-Taixé L, Leibe B (2021) HOTA: a higher order metric for evaluating multi-object tracking. Int J Comput Vis (IJCV) 129(2):548–578
35. Luo C, Yang X, Yuille A (2021) Exploring simple 3D multi-object tracking for autonomous driving. In: Proceedings of the IEEE international conference on computer vision (ICCV), pp 10488–10497
36. Ma Y, Guo Y, Liu H, Lei Y, Wen G (2020) Global context reasoning for semantic segmentation of 3D point clouds. In: Proceedings of the IEEE/CVF winter conference on applications of computer vision (WACV), pp 2931–2940
37. Ma Y, Liu H, Pei Y, Guo Y (2025) Heterogeneous graph learning for scene graph prediction in 3D point clouds. In: Proceedings of the European conference on computer vision (ECCV). Springer, Berlin, pp 274–291
38. Mao J, Xue Y, Niu M, Bai H, Feng J, Liang X, Xu H, Xu C (2021) Voxel transformer for 3D object detection. In: Proceedings of the IEEE international conference on computer vision (ICCV), pp 3164–3173
39. Meinhardt T, Kirillov A, Leal-Taixe L, Feichtenhofer C (2022) TrackFormer: multi-object tracking with transformers. In: Proceedings of the IEEE conference on computer vision and pattern recognition (CVPR), pp 8844–8854
40. Noh J, Lee S, Ham B (2021) HVPR: hybrid voxel-point representation for single-stage 3D object detection. In: Proceedings of the IEEE conference on computer vision and pattern recognition (CVPR), pp 14605–14614

41. Osep A, Mehner W, Mathias M, Leibe B (2017) Combined image-and world-space tracking in traffic scenes. In: Proceedings of the IEEE international conference on robotics and automation (ICRA). IEEE, pp 1988–1995
42. Pang B, Li Y, Zhang Y, Li M, Lu C (2020) TubeTK: adopting tubes to track multi-object in a one-step training model. In: Proceedings of the IEEE conference on computer vision and pattern recognition (CVPR), pp 6308–6318
43. Pang J, Qiu L, Li X, Chen H, Li Q, Darrell T, Yu F (2021) Quasi-dense similarity learning for multiple object tracking. In: Proceedings of the IEEE conference on computer vision and pattern recognition (CVPR), pp 164–173
44. Qi CR, Yi L, Su H, Guibas LJ (2017) PointNet++: deep hierarchical feature learning on point sets in a metric space. In: Proceedings of the advances in neural information processing systems (NeurIPS) (2017)
45. Redmon J, Divvala S, Girshick R, Farhadi A (2016) You only look once: unified, real-time object detection. In: Proceedings of the IEEE conference on computer vision and pattern recognition (CVPR), pp 779–788
46. Sharma S, Ansari JA, Murthy JK, Krishna KM (2018) Beyond pixels: leveraging geometry and shape cues for online multi-object tracking. In: Proceedings of the IEEE international conference on robotics and automation (ICRA). IEEE, pp 3508–3515
47. Shen J, Liang Z, Liu J, Sun H, Shao L, Tao D (2018) Multiobject tracking by submodular optimization. IEEE Trans Cybern 49(6):1990–2001
48. Shen J, Yu D, Deng L, Dong X (2017) Fast online tracking with detection refinement. IEEE Trans Intell Transp Syst 19(1):162–173
49. Sheng H, Cai S, Liu Y, Deng B, Huang J, Hua XS, Zhao MJ (2021) Improving 3D object detection with channel-wise transformer. In: Proceedings of the IEEE international conference on computer vision (ICCV), pp 2743–2752
50. Shenoi A, Patel M, Gwak J, Goebel P, Sadeghian A, Rezatofighi H, Martín-Martín R, Savarese S (2020) JRMOT: a real-time 3D multi-object tracker and a new large-scale dataset. In: Proceedings of the IEEE international conference on intelligent robots and systems (IROS). IEEE, pp 10335–10342
51. Shi S, Guo C, Jiang L, Wang Z, Shi J, Wang X, Li H (2020) PV-RCNN: point-voxel feature set abstraction for 3D object detection. In: Proceedings of the IEEE conference on computer vision and pattern recognition (CVPR), pp 10529–10538
52. Shi S, Wang X, Li H (2019) PointRCNN: 3D object proposal generation and detection from point cloud. In: Proceedings of the IEEE conference on computer vision and pattern recognition, pp 770–779
53. Shi S, Wang Z, Shi J, Wang X, Li H (2020) From points to parts: 3D object detection from point cloud with part-aware and part-aggregation network. IEEE Trans Pattern Anal Mach Intell (TPAMI) 43(8):2647–2664
54. Shi W, Rajkumar R (2020) Point-GNN: graph neural network for 3D object detection in a point cloud. In: Proceedings of the IEEE conference on computer vision and pattern recognition (CVPR), pp 1711–1719
55. Shuai B, Berneshawi A, Li X, Modolo D, Tighe J (2021) SiamMOT: Siamese multi-object tracking. In: Proceedings of the IEEE conference on computer vision and pattern recognition (CVPR), pp 12372–12382
56. Simon M, Amende K, Kraus A, Honer J, Samann T, Kaulbersch H, Milz S, Michael Gross H (2019) Complexer-yolo: real-time 3D object detection and tracking on semantic point clouds. In: Proceedings of the IEEE conference on computer vision and pattern recognition workshops (CVPRW)
57. Song H, Sun D, Chun S, Jampani V, Han D, Heo B, Kim W, Yang MH (2021) ViDT: an efficient and effective fully Transformer-based object detector. In: Proceedings of the international conference on learning representation (ICLR)
58. Sun P, Cao J, Jiang Y, Zhang R, Xie E, Yuan Z, Wang C, Luo P (2020) TransTrack: multiple object tracking with Transformer (2020). arXiv:2012.15460

59. Sun P, Kretzschmar H, Dotiwalla X, Chouard A, Patnaik V, Tsui P, Guo J, Zhou Y, Chai Y, Caine B et al (2020) Scalability in perception for autonomous driving: Waymo open dataset. In: Proceedings of the IEEE conference on computer vision and pattern recognition (CVPR), pp 2446–2454
60. Vaswani A, Shazeer N, Parmar N, Uszkoreit J, Jones L, Gomez AN, Kaiser Ł, Polosukhin I (2017) Attention is all you need. In: Proceeding of the advances in neural information processing systems (NeurIPS)
61. Wang L, Zhang X, Qin W, Li X, Gao J, Yang L, Li Z, Li J, Zhu L, Wang H et al (2023) Camo-mot: combined appearance-motion optimization for 3D multi-object tracking with camera-lidar fusion. IEEE Trans Intell Transp Syst (TITS)
62. Wang S, Sun Y, Liu C, Liu M (2020) PointTrackNet: an end-to-end network for 3D object detection and tracking from point clouds. IEEE Robot Autom Lett (RAL) 5(2):3206–3212
63. Wang Y, Chen X, You Y, Li LE, Hariharan B, Campbell M, Weinberger KQ, Chao WL (2020) Train in Germany, test in the USA: making 3D object detectors generalize. In: Proceedings of the IEEE conference on computer vision and pattern recognition (CVPR), pp 11713–11723
64. Wang Y, Zhang X, Yang T, Sun J (2021) Anchor DETR: query design for Transformer-based object detection (2021). arXiv:2109.07107
65. Weber M, Xie J, Collins M, Zhu Y, Voigtlaender P, Adam H, Green B, Geiger A, Leibe B, Cremers D et al (2021) Step: Segmenting and tracking every pixel (2021). arXiv:2102.11859
66. Weng X, Wang J, Held D, Kitani K (2020) AB3DMOT: a baseline for 3D multi-object tracking and new evaluation metrics. In: Proceedings of the European conference on computer vision workshop (ECCVW)
67. Weng X, Wang Y, Man Y, Kitani KM (2020) GNN3DMOT: graph neural network for 3D multi-object tracking with 2D–3D multi-feature learning. In: Proceedings of the IEEE conference on computer vision and pattern recognition (CVPR), pp 6499–6508
68. Wojke N, Bewley A, Paulus D (2017) Simple online and realtime tracking with a deep association metric. In: Proceedings of the IEEE international conference on image processing (ICIP). IEEE, pp 3645–3649
69. Wu H, Li Q, Wen C, Li X, Fan X, Wang C (2021) Tracklet proposal network for multi-object tracking on point clouds. In: Proceedings of the international joint conference on artificial intelligence (IJCAI)
70. Wu J, Cao J, Song L, Wang Y, Yang M, Yuan J (2021) Track to detect and segment: an online multi-object tracker. In: Proceedings of the IEEE conference on computer vision and pattern recognition (CVPR), pp 12352–12361
71. Wu W, Wang ZY, Li Z, Liu W, Fuxin L (2020) PointPWC-Net: cost volume on point clouds for (self-) supervised scene flow estimation. In: Proceedings of the European conference on computer vision (ECCV). Springer, Berlin, pp 88–107
72. Yan Y, Mao Y, Li B (2018) Second: sparsely embedded convolutional detection. Sensors 18(10):3337
73. Yang J, Yu E, Li Z, Li X, Tao W (2022) Quality matters: embracing quality clues for robust 3D multi-object tracking (2022). arXiv:2208.10976
74. Yang Z, Sun Y, Liu S, Jia J (2020) 3DSSD: point-based 3D single stage object detector. In: Proceedings of the IEEE conference on computer vision and pattern recognition (CVPR), pp 11040–11048
75. Yang Z, Sun Y, Liu S, Shen X, Jia J (2019) STD: sparse-to-dense 3D object detector for point cloud. In: Proceedings of the IEEE international conference on computer vision (ICCV), pp 1951–1960
76. Yin J, Wang W, Meng Q, Yang R, Shen J (2020) A unified object motion and affinity model for online multi-object tracking. In: Proceedings of the IEEE conference on computer vision and pattern recognition (CVPR), pp 6768–6777
77. Yin T, Zhou X, Krahenbuhl P (2021) Center-based 3D object detection and tracking. In: Proceedings of the IEEE conference on computer vision and pattern recognition (CVPR), pp 11784–11793

78. Zeng F, Dong B, Zhang Y, Wang T, Zhang X, Wei Y (2022) MOTR: end-to-end multiple-object tracking with transformer. In: Proceedings of the European conference on computer vision (ECCV). Springer, Berlin, pp 659–675
79. Zhai G, Kong X, Cui J, Liu Y, Yang Z (2020) FlowMOT: 3D multi-object tracking by scene flow association (2020). arXiv:2012.07541
80. Zhang W, Zhou H, Sun S, Wang Z, Shi J, Loy CC (2019) Robust multi-modality multi-object tracking. In: Proceedings of the IEEE international conference on computer vision (ICCV), pp 2365–2374
81. Zhang Y, Hu Q, Xu G, Ma Y, Wan J, Guo Y (2022) Not all points are equal: learning highly efficient point-based detectors for 3D lidar point clouds. In: Proceedings of the IEEE/CVF conference on computer vision and pattern recognition (CVPR), pp 18953–18962
82. Zhang Y, Wang C, Wang X, Zeng W, Liu W (2020) A simple baseline for multi-object tracking. In: Proceedings of the European conference on computer vision (ECCV)
83. Zhang Y, Wang X, Ye X, Zhang W, Lu J, Tan X, Ding E, Sun P, Wang J (2023) Bytetrackv2: 2D and 3D multi-object tracking by associating every detection box. arXiv:2303.15334
84. Zhao L, Guo J, Xu D, Sheng L (2021) Transformer3D-det: improving 3D object detection by vote refinement. IEEE Trans Circuits Syst Video Technol 31(12):4735–4746
85. Zheng W, Tang W, Chen S, Jiang L, Fu CW (2020) CIA-SSD: confident IoU-aware single-stage object detector from point cloud (2020). arXiv:2012.03015
86. Zhou X, Koltun V, Krähenbühl P (2020) Tracking objects as points. In: Proceedings of the European conference on computer vision (ECCV). Springer, Berlin, pp 474–490 (2020)
87. Zhou Y, Tuzel O (2018) VoxelNet: end-to-end learning for point cloud based 3D object detection. In: Proceedings of the IEEE conference on computer vision and pattern recognition (CVPR), pp 4490–4499
88. Zhu G, Porikli F, Li H (2016) Model-free multiple object tracking with shared proposals. In: Proceedings of the Asian conference on computer vision (ACCV). Springer, Berlin, pp 288–304
89. Zhu X, Su W, Lu L, Li B, Wang X, Dai J (2020) Deformable DETR: deformable transformers for end-to-end object detection. arXiv:2010.04159

Chapter 8
Object Completion from Point Clouds

Point cloud completion addresses the challenging task of reconstructing complete 3D geometries from partial scans. Existing methods normally ignore the effectiveness of viewpoint information and adopt task-independent Farthest Point Sampling (FPS) to down-sample point clouds, leading to performance sacrifice. This chapter presents two novel approaches in this domain: Sect. 8.3.1 introduces the Viewpoint-Aware Point Cloud Completion Network (VAPCNet), which explores the potential of unsupervised viewpoint learning for enhanced shape recovery. Section 8.4.1 details the Adaptive Embedding-Disentanglement Network (AEDNet), featuring a dual-path architecture with adaptive embedding-disentanglement modules that simultaneously capture global structural patterns and refine local geometric details. Extensive evaluations on benchmark datasets demonstrate that both methods significantly enhance completion accuracy while achieving state-of-the-art performance.

8.1 Introduction

Occlusion (both self-occlusion and occlusion by other objects) and low sensor resolution often lead to incomplete shapes in 3D scans, making them unsuitable for direct application in tasks like object grasping and Virtual Reality (VR) [11, 12, 21, 35]. To address this issue, shape completion seeks to reconstruct complete 3D shapes from these partial scans.

Current learning-based shape completion methods fall into two categories: volumetric representation-based and point cloud-based approaches. The first category converts a point cloud into 3D occupancy grids and employs 3D convolution operations to predict complete object shapes. However, these volumetric representations typically incur high memory costs and limited shape accuracy. The second category, in contrast, operates directly on point clouds, offering a more memory-efficient approach to represent 3D data. Nonetheless, these point cloud-based methods strug-

Y. Guo et al., *Point Cloud Intelligence*, Advances in Computer Vision and Pattern Recognition, https://doi.org/10.1007/978-981-95-0648-4_8

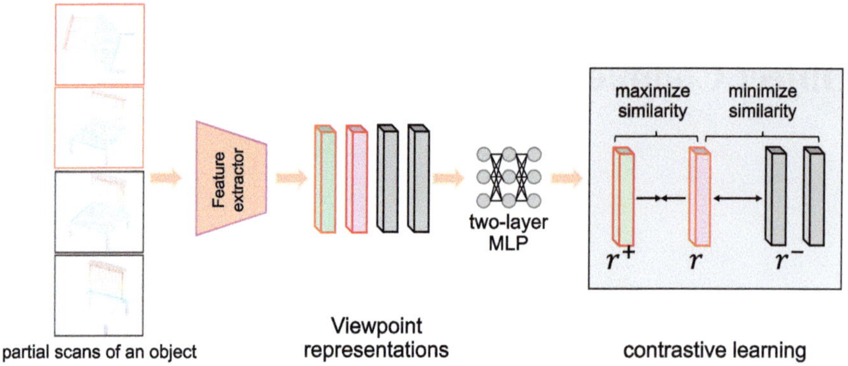

Fig. 8.1 An example of unsupervised viewpoint representation learning (This figure is reproduced from [13])

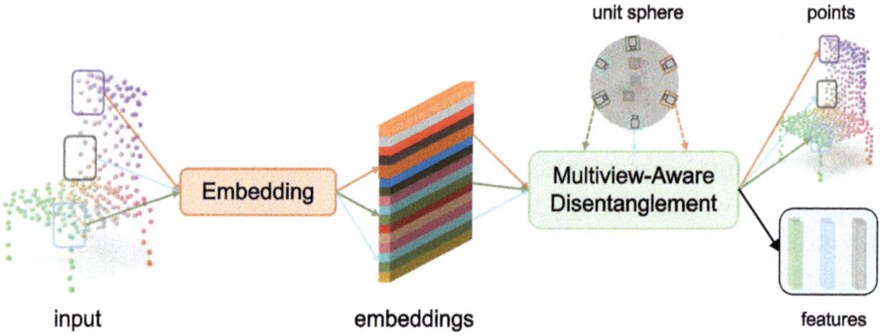

Fig. 8.2 Illustration of the AED Module in AEDNet (This figure is reproduced from [14])

gle to recover fine object details due to the irregular and unordered nature of point clouds.

To address these limitations, we present two synergistic innovations. (1) we propose **Viewpoint-Aware 3D Point Cloud completion Network (VAPCNet)** to first introduce unsupervised viewpoint representation into point cloud completion task (Fig. 8.1). (2) we introduce the **Adaptive Embedding and Multiview-Aware Disentanglement Network (AEDNet)** for point cloud completion (Fig. 8.2), which hierarchically compresses point clouds into global embeddings while disentangling local geometries through multi-view constraints. The details of these two networks are shown in Figs. 8.1 and 8.2, respectively.

8.1.1 VAPCNet

Complete objects are typically composed of visible and missing parts. The visible parts of an object are closely tied to specific viewpoints and can vary significantly when observed from different angles. This implies that the viewpoint information of an incomplete object offers valuable cues for 3D point cloud completion. However, explicitly estimating viewpoints is often computationally expensive and requires extensive annotation, posing a significant challenge. Inspired by recent advancements in contrastive learning [2, 9, 22, 25, 45], we propose an approach that leverages **unsupervised viewpoint representation learning**. By contrasting positive and negative pairs within the latent space (as illustrated in Fig. 8.1), our method generates distinctive latent representations for each incomplete object. Specifically, in the MVP dataset [40], all objects are aligned, with missing parts indicating different incomplete objects scanned from various viewpoints. In Fig. 8.1, incomplete objects in orange and red boxes are scanned from the same viewpoint, while those in black boxes are scanned from different viewpoints. This approach offers two key advantages: **(1) efficiency and discriminative power:** instead of estimating complete viewpoint information, our method learns abstract representations that effectively differentiate between viewpoints. This enables the generation of discriminative viewpoint representations for incomplete objects, providing auxiliary information for completion. **(2) no reliance on ground-truth supervision:** as an unsupervised method, our approach does not require annotated ground-truth viewpoints, making it well-suited for real-world scenarios where viewpoint information is unknown.

We present a viewpoint-guided completion framework for partial 3D geometry reconstruction. Our methodology employs contrastive learning to encode viewpoint representations from incomplete point clouds. The developed Viewpoint-Aware Point Cloud Completion Network (VAPCNet) dynamically adapts its completion strategy based on these learned viewpoint representations through two core components: (1) Adaptive convolutional kernels predicted from viewpoint features for localized geometric synthesis, and (2) Modulated cross-attention mechanisms that selectively aggregate contextual information aligned with viewpoint characteristics.

8.1.2 AEDNet

Existing point cloud completion netwroks normally follows Encoder-Decoder structure. Conventional FPS-based encoding faces dual limitations: (1) noise sensitivity in anchor point selection [52], and (2) excessive focus on local geometries through attention-refined sampling [75], which neglects global structural correlations. This oversight can result in suboptimal sampling for point cloud completion. In the decoding phase, while transformer-driven queries [46] improve coarse shape prediction via anchor correlations, refinement strategies exhibit critical flaws: FoldingNet's linear concatenation restricts complex shape synthesis [60], and deconvolutions lack global contextual awareness [73]. The fundamental tension lies in balancing single global feature constraints [67] with localized pattern recovery [4], necessitating hybrid global-local perception mechanisms.

We address this gap by introducing a global perception and local attention network. We present the Adaptive point cloud Embedding and Disentanglement (AED) module, which includes a global embedding operator and a multiview-aware disentanglement operator (see Fig. 8.2). We treat embedding learning as a form of set learning and propose a slot attention mechanism that groups input point clouds into distinct embeddings. For the multiview-aware disentanglement operator, we use the Fibonacci point sequence generation algorithm [47] to evenly distribute 3D viewpoints ("cameras" in Fig. 8.2) on a unit sphere. We then encode the relationships between these viewpoints and the input point cloud into viewpoint encodings. Geometric details from these embeddings are locally disentangled onto points on a 3D object's surface and the point-wise features within these viewpoints. In the encoder, we integrate the proposed AED module with the point transformer [72] to hierarchically extract point-wise features and sample anchor points from the input partial point clouds. Our AED module establishes long-range dependencies between input points. This leads to improved representation quality. Additionally, the anchor points are sampled with a global understanding of the input point clouds, making the process less sensitive to noisy inputs compared to FPS. In the decoder, we employ a coarse-to-fine completion strategy. We utilize the proposed module in a hierarchical manner. After generating the coarse prediction, the AED module aggregates its geometric patterns into embeddings. It then disentangles additional points by adjusting the number of 3D viewpoints sampled from a unit sphere. Therefore, the AED module functions as both a down-sampler in the encoder and an up-sampler in the decoder.

Comprehensive evaluations on MVP [40] and PCN [67] datasets demonstrate our frameworks' state-of-the-art performances. The key innovations of our approaches include:

- We propose a novel geometric completion framework integrating unsupervised viewpoint representation learning, establishing the first technical solution that bridges viewpoint semantics with 3D reconstruction accuracy through contrastive feature encoding.
- We propose a viewpoint-adaptive architecture combining dynamic convolutional kernel prediction and multi-scale modulated attention mechanisms, where viewpoint-specific operators are generated through contrastive learning while contextual geometric correlations are captured via self-attention weight adaptation.
- We present AEDNet, an innovative network tailored for point cloud completion. It is designed to improve global geometry embedding and local disentanglement.
- We introduce a specially designed slot attention mechanism to enhance the embedding of complex structures within point clouds.
- We propose a multiview-aware disentanglement method to improve local geometry reconstruction for point cloud completion.
- State-of-the-art completion results on both the MVP and PCN datasets.

8.2 Related Work

This section provides an overview of key strategies for learning-based point cloud completion. We focus on volumetric representation and point cloud-based shape completion (Sect. 8.2.1). We also discuss recent advancements in contrastive learning (Sect. 8.2.2).

8.2.1 Learning-Based Point Cloud Completion

Volumetric Representation-based Shape Completion. Structured volumetric representations combined with advanced 3D convolution techniques have improved 3D reconstruction [6, 16] and shape completion [7, 23, 56]. However, these methods are computationally intensive and require significant memory. Sparse representations [17, 43, 50] can help reduce memory usage. Yet, the quantization process often results in a loss of intricate details.

Point Cloud-based Shape Completion. Recent advancements have shifted towards using unstructured point clouds for 3D object representation. This approach reduces memory usage and better preserves fine details. However, standard convolution operations struggle with the unordered nature of point clouds. Innovations like PointNet and its variants [41, 42] enable direct processing of 3D points across various tasks. The PCN network [67] employs a global feature extraction method inspired by PointNet [41] and incorporates a folding technique [63] for point generation. Efforts to capture local structures have led to multi-scale feature extraction methods [70]. Lyu et al. [34] approached point cloud completion as a conditional generation task using Denoising Diffusion Probabilistic Models (DDPM) [27, 33, 74]. While their method achieves fine-grained completion, it is computationally intensive, limiting its use to preliminary stages of coarse point cloud generation. More recently, Chen et al. [5] applied conditional DDPM in the 3D latent space for shape reconstruction. Fu et al. [13] found that incorporating viewpoint information improves completion quality and performance, although it requires an additional trained model for viewpoint representation learning. Advanced architectures like SnowflakeNet [58] and PointTr [65] focus on decoder structures with Transformer-like designs [46]. Additionally, PointAttN [48] and CompleteDT [30] introduce Transformer-based models for point cloud completion. Seedformer [73] and Anchorformer [4] explore local pattern propagation in seed generation and point up-sampling, emphasizing the importance of local geometry for detailed point cloud completion. In contrast, this section proposes a multiview-aware disentanglement approach to recover 3D shape details.

Slot Attention. Slot Attention Networks (SANs) infer a set of latent variables corresponding to objects in an image. Approaches focused on "Object-centric learning" [10, 18, 19, 29, 32] aim to identify generative factors related to parts or objects in a scene. SANs utilize a feed-forward pass with an attention mechanism [46] to assign latent variables to permutation-invariant slots. This technique is well-suited for point cloud processing in deep learning models. In this chapter, slot attention serves as a dynamic clustering tool. It automatically divides the input point cloud into distinct local regions and encodes their geometric features into slots. Unlike the grouping layer in PointNet++ [42], our aggregation occurs in a high-dimensional space without relying on Farthest Point Sampling (FPS). This reduces the impact of noisy input data.

However, current slot attention-based segmentation methods [18, 29, 32] have limitations. They perform well only on synthetic images with uniform colors and layouts or on clearly separated objects. Their performance declines in complex, real-world settings. Challenges include the random initialization of slots, which may fail to capture meaningful context in intricate scenes, and weak semantic connections between different slots.

To address these challenges, we propose modifying the initial slot attention approach. We will use dictionary mapping for initialization and establish inter-slot relationships. Additionally, we introduce an adaptive embedding and disentanglement technique. This combines the proposed slot attention with a novel local geometry disentanglement module to improve accuracy and structural consistency.

8.2.2 Contrastive Learning

Contrastive learning has proven effective in unsupervised representation learning. Earlier methods [8, 15, 37, 69] used auto-encoders for representation learning through input reconstruction. In contrast, contrastive learning aims to maximize mutual information within a representation space. It ensures that the representation of a query sample is more similar to its positive counterparts and less similar to its negative counterparts. Positive counterparts may include transformed versions of the input [2, 25, 57], multiple views of the input [45], and neighboring patches within the same image [26, 38].

Building on the success of contrastive learning in 2D applications, several studies [49, 59, 62, 66, 71] have explored its potential for 3D point cloud understanding. PointContrast [62] implements point-level invariant mapping across two transformed views of a point cloud. Zhang et al. [71] introduced DepthContrast to derive representations from depth scans. Wang et al. [49] developed an encoder-decoder framework for reconstructing occluded point clouds. Inspired by the MAE strategy [24] in image representation learning, Yu et al. [66] proposed Point-BERT. This method recovers original point tokens at masked locations under the guidance of point tokens. In this chapter, we propose to learn viewpoint representations of incomplete point clouds using contrastive learning. Specifically, the partial point cloud generated from the same viewpoint (highlighted with a red box in Fig. 8.1) serves as the positive counterpart. Meanwhile, partial point clouds from other viewpoints (highlighted with black boxes in Fig. 8.1) are treated as negative counterparts.

8.3 Viewpoint-Aware 3D Point Cloud Completion: VAPCNet

8.3.1 *Methodology*

8.3.1.1 An Overview

The proposed point cloud completion framework includes a viewpoint representation encoder and a viewpoint-aware completion network, as shown in Fig. 8.3. First, the partial scan is input into the viewpoint representation encoder (Fig. 8.3 (a)). This encoder generates a viewpoint representation. Next, this representation is used in the viewpoint-aware completion network (Fig. 8.3 (b)) to reconstruct the complete object.

8.3.1.2 Viewpoint Representation Learning

The aim of viewpoint representation learning is to derive a discriminative representation from partial point cloud objects in an unsupervised manner, as illustrated in Fig. 8.1. We assume that the viewpoint representation r of a partial scan is similar to its rotated version r^+ but differs for other viewpoints r^-.

In this context, a partial object is scanned from a specific viewpoint (highlighted by an orange box), serving as the query sample. Its rotated version (marked with a red box) is treated as a positive sample. Partial objects scanned from different viewpoints (shown with black boxes) are considered negative samples. A feature extractor encodes the query, positive, and negative samples to extract viewpoint representations. Inspired by SimCLR [2] and MoCo v2 [3], the resulting representations pass through a two-layer multi-layer perceptron (MLP) projection head to produce r, r^+, and r^-. We employ an InfoNCE loss to encourage similarity between r and r^+ while ensuring dissimilarity with r^-:

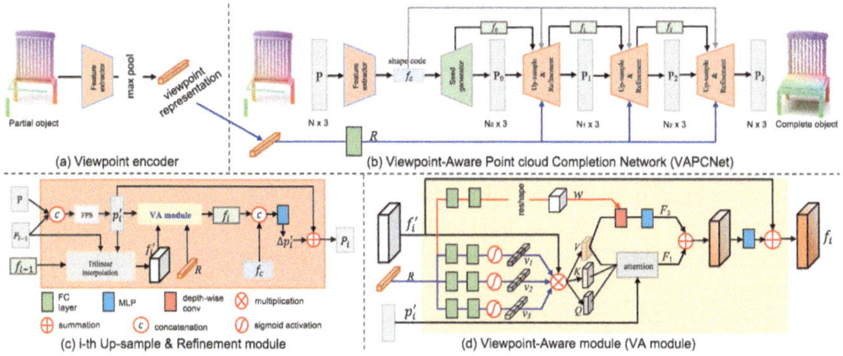

Fig. 8.3 An overview of the proposed VAPCNet (This figure is reproduced from [13])

$$\mathcal{L}_r = -\log \frac{\exp(r \cdot r^+/\tau)}{\sum_{m=1}^{M} \exp(r \cdot r_m^-/\tau) + \exp(r \cdot r^+/\tau)}, \tag{8.1}$$

where M is the number of negative samples, τ is the temperature hyperparameter, and $\cdot$ denotes the dot product between two vectors.

Each object is scanned from B viewpoints, resulting in B partial point cloud objects. During unsupervised training, one partial point cloud is randomly selected as the query sample, while the remaining $B - 1$ objects serve as negative samples. The positive sample is generated by randomly rotating the query sample. The query sample and these B samples are encoded into $p_q \in \mathbb{R}^{1\times512}$ and $p_k \in \mathbb{R}^{B\times512}$ using the feature extractor. For p_q, $p_k^1 \in \mathbb{R}^{1\times512}$ represents the latent representation of the positive sample, while the remaining $B - 1$ latent representations serve as negative samples. The overall loss is defined as:

$$\mathcal{L}_{\text{view}} = -\log \frac{\exp(p_q \cdot p_k^1/\tau)}{\sum_{j=2}^{B} \exp(p_q \cdot p_k^j/\tau) + \exp(p_q \cdot p_k^1/\tau)}, \tag{8.2}$$

where p_k^j represents the jth negative sample.

Discussion. Many existing point cloud completion methods overlook the influence of viewpoints on shape completion. This chapter focuses on learning an effective abstract representation to differentiate a specific viewpoint from others, rather than estimating the viewpoint explicitly. In Sect. 8.3.2.4, we demonstrate that our viewpoint representation learning approach generates discriminative representations. Additionally, our unsupervised method does not require supervision through ground-truth viewpoints.

8.3.1.3 Viewpoint-Aware Point Cloud Completion

We propose a Viewpoint-Aware Point Cloud Completion Network (VAPCNet) to complete the incomplete object using the learned viewpoint representation. Our VAPCNet follows an encoder-decoder structure, as shown in Fig. 8.3 (b).

Encoder-Decoder Architecture. The encoder consists of a feature extractor and a seed generator. The decoder comprises three up-sampling and refinement modules.

Given the incomplete input point cloud $P \in \mathbb{R}^{N\times3}$, the feature extractor uses three layers of set abstraction from [42] to aggregate point features from local to global. A point transformer [72] incorporates local shape context. Max-pooling extracts a shape code f_c of size $1 \times C$ from the point features $p_{fe} \in \mathbb{R}^{32\times C}$ generated by the feature extractor. The seed generator produces a coarse yet complete point cloud P_0 of size $N_0 \times 3$ that captures the geometry and structure of the target shape. The extracted shape code f_c is combined with the point features p_{fe} through an MLP. A transposed convolution splits these aggregated features into N_0 point features f_0, which are passed through an MLP to generate the coarse point cloud P_0.

The decoder reconstructs high-resolution complete point clouds hierarchically. In the up-sampling and refinement module (Fig. 8.3 (c)), we first concatenate the previous low-resolution complete point cloud P_{i-1} with the input point cloud P. We then apply FPS to select N_i points $P_i^{'}$ from the concatenated point cloud $P_c \in \mathbb{R}^{(N+N_{i-1})\times 3}$. Using the previous complete point cloud P_{i-1}, the up-sampled point cloud $P_i^{'}$, and the previous point features f_{i-1}, we apply trilinear interpolation [42] to obtain N_i point features $f_i^{'}$ for the up-sampled point cloud $P_i^{'}$. The features $f_i^{'}$ are then processed by the Viewpoint-Aware module (VA module) to generate refined point features f_i. Finally, the refined point features f_i, concatenated with the shape code f_c, are fed into an MLP to predict the corresponding residual coordinates $\Delta P_i^{'}$. These are added to $P_i^{'}$, resulting in the refined point cloud $P_i = P_i^{'} + \Delta P_i^{'}$.

VA Module. Inspired by [49, 72], our VA module predicts the kernel of a depth-wise convolution and modulated self-attention conditioned on the viewpoint representation $V_R \in \mathbb{R}^{1\times C}$, as shown in Fig. 8.3 (d). The inputs to the VA module include the point features $f_i^{'}$, the viewpoint representation R, and the up-sampled point cloud $P_i^{'}$. The viewpoint representation R is processed in two parts. In the first part, R passes through three branches (indicated by blue lines), each containing two Fully Connected (FC) layers followed by a sigmoid activation. This generates channel-wise modulation coefficients υ_1, υ_2, and υ_3. These coefficients rescale different channel components of $f_i^{'}$, resulting in V, Q, and K. Next, a nearest neighbor search selects a set of points and corresponding point features in the local neighborhood for each point in $P_i^{'}$ and for each point feature in K. Self-attention [72] aggregates local information for each point feature, generating point features F_1. In the second part (indicated by the red line), the viewpoint representation R passes through another two FC layers and a reshape layer to produce a convolutional kernel $w \in \mathbb{R}^{M\times N_i\times n}$. The point feature V undergoes a 1×1 depth-wise convolution (using w) and is processed through an MLP to produce F_2. Finally, F_1 is added to F_2 and passed through subsequent layers to produce the refined point features f_i.

Discussion. Directly concatenating viewpoint representation with point cloud features may not fully utilize the viewpoint information due to the domain gap. To better integrate viewpoint information for 3D completion, we design a depth-wise convolutional kernel and predict channel-wise modulation coefficients within the self-attention unit for feature adaptation. The VA module effectively incorporates the viewpoint representation, enhancing shape completion (as discussed in Sect. 8.3.2.4).

8.3.1.4 Loss Functions

Chamfer Distance (CD) and Earth Mover's Distance (EMD) are used to quantify differences between two point clouds P and Q. We choose Chamfer Distance for its efficiency compared to EMD:

$$\mathcal{L}_{CD}(P, Q) = \frac{1}{|P|}\sum_{x\in P}\min_{y\in Q}\|x-y\|_2 + \frac{1}{|Q|}\sum_{y\in Q}\min_{x\in P}\|y-x\|_2, \tag{8.3}$$

where P and Q represent the predicted complete point clouds and the corresponding ground truth, respectively.

To constrain the point clouds generated by the seed generator and the up-sampling process, we downsample the ground truth point clouds to match the sampling density of P_0, P_1, P_2, P_3. The sum of the four CD losses defines the completion loss, denoted by $\mathcal{L}_{\text{completion}}$:

$$\begin{aligned}\mathcal{L}_{\text{completion}} &= \mathcal{L}_{CD}(P_0, gt_0) + \mathcal{L}_{CD}(P_1, gt_1) \\ &+ \mathcal{L}_{CD}(P_2, gt_2) + \mathcal{L}_{CD}(P_3, gt_3),\end{aligned} \tag{8.4}$$

where gt_0, gt_1, gt_2, gt_3 are the downsampled ground truth point clouds corresponding to P_0, P_1, P_2, P_3.

We also utilize the partial matching loss from [53] to maintain the shape structure of the input point cloud. This unidirectional constraint aligns one shape with another without imposing constraints on the reverse direction. The partial matching loss ensures that the output point cloud partially matches the input, referred to as the preservation loss $\mathcal{L}_{\text{preservation}}$. The total training loss is expressed as:

$$\mathcal{L} = \mathcal{L}_{\text{completion}} + \lambda \mathcal{L}_{\text{preservation}}, \tag{8.5}$$

where λ is set to 0 for the MVP dataset and 1 for the PCN dataset. This ensures a fair comparison with other methods.

8.3.2 *Experiments*

8.3.2.1 Datasets and Implementation Details

We evaluated the proposed VAPCNet on the MVP and PCN datasets.

MVP Dataset [40]. The MVP dataset contains 16 categories of 4000 CAD models. Each model has 26 camera viewpoints sampled to simulate partial scans. In our experiments, complete point clouds consist of 2048, 4096, 8192, and 16384 points. Each incomplete point cloud contains 2048 points. Following [40], we used 62,400 partial-complete point cloud pairs for training and 41,600 pairs for testing. For evaluation, we employed the L_2 version of Chamfer distance.

PCN Dataset [67]. The PCN dataset is based on a subset of the ShapeNet dataset [1]. Each complete point cloud has 16,384 points, while each incomplete point cloud contains 2048 points. The training set includes 28,974 unique models from 8 categories. Each model has a complete point cloud and 8 partial point clouds from different viewpoints for data augmentation. The validation set includes 100 models, and the testing set contains 1200 models, with 150 models per category. We used the L_1 version of Chamfer distance for evaluation, as in [67].

Implementation Details. For the viewpoint representation encoder, we used three layers of set abstraction from [42] to aggregate point features from local to global. A point transformer [72] was included to incorporate local shape context. During pre-training, we optimized using the Adam method [28] with $\beta_1 = 0.9$ and $\beta_2 = 0.999$. We first trained the viewpoint representation encoder by optimizing L_{view} for 40 epochs. The learning rate started at 1×10^{-3} and reduced to 1×10^{-4} after 20 epochs. Afterward, we froze the pre-trained viewpoint representation encoder and trained the entire network for 80 epochs on the MVP dataset and 400 epochs on the PCN dataset. To generate high-resolution complete point clouds, we combined VAPCNet with the Snowflake Point Deconvolution (SPD) module from [58]. The learning rate was initially set to 1×10^{-4} and halved every 40 epochs. All experiments were conducted on 2 NVIDIA 2080Ti GPUs.

8.3.2.2 Completion on the MVP Dataset

For a fair comparison, we trained all methods using the same training strategy on the MVP dataset.

Quantitative comparison. The CD loss and F-score for all evaluated methods are reported in Table 8.1 and Table 8.2, respectively. The proposed VAPCNet outperforms all existing competitive methods in terms of CD and F-score@1%. We also compare our method with existing approaches that support multi-resolution completion in Table 8.3. Our VAPCNet outperforms all the other methods. Specifically, our method using unsupervised viewpoint representation learning outperforms [68] which uses the ground-truth viewpoint as input. This demonstrates the effectiveness of our viewpoint representation learning in terms of extracting accurate viewpoint information.

Qualitative Comparison. The qualitative results are shown in Fig. 8.4. The proposed VAPCNet generates more complete shapes with finer details than other methods. The effectiveness of the proposed VA module is evident in our reconstructed shapes. For example, the missing legs of the chairs (second row in Fig. 8.4) are reconstructed based on the visible legs, considering the scanned viewpoint. In the third row, the lamp base is reconstructed with a better shape for the lampstand compared to other methods. By incorporating additional viewpoint information through the viewpoint representation, VAPCNet effectively reconstructs complete shapes by learning structural relationships from the incomplete point cloud.

8.3.2.3 Completion on the PCN Dataset

We also evaluated our network on the PCN dataset against several state-of-the-art baseline methods. The L_1 Chamfer Distance was used as the evaluation metric. For the baseline methods, results from [39, 70] were obtained using their official codes and pre-trained models. Results from other methods were taken from [54, 58, 61] and their original papers [52, 65].

Quantitative Comparison. The quantitative results are presented in Table 8.4. Our network achieves the lowest average L_1 CD. In the cabinet and car categories, our

Table 8.1 Shape completion results (CD loss multiplied by 10^4) on the multi-view partial (MVP) point cloud dataset (16,384 points)

Method	Airplane	Cabinet	Car	Chair	Lamp	Sofa	Table	Watercraft	Bed	Bench	Bookshelf	Bus	Guitar	Motorbike	Pistol	Skateboard	Avg.
PCN [67]	2.95	4.13	3.04	7.07	14.93	5.56	7.06	6.08	12.72	5.73	6.91	2.46	1.02	3.53	3.28	2.99	6.02
TopNet [44]	2.72	4.25	3.40	7.95	17.01	6.04	7.42	6.04	11.56	5.62	8.22	2.37	1.37	3.90	3.97	2.09	6.36
MSN [31]	2.07	3.82	2.76	6.21	12.72	4.74	5.32	4.80	9.93	3.89	5.85	2.12	0.69	2.48	2.91	1.58	4.90
Wang et al. [51]	1.59	3.64	2.60	5.24	9.02	4.42	5.45	4.26	9.56	3.67	5.34	2.23	0.79	2.23	2.86	2.13	4.30
ECG [39]	1.41	3.44	2.36	4.58	6.95	3.81	4.27	3.38	7.46	3.10	4.82	1.99	0.59	2.05	2.31	1.66	3.58
GRNet [61]	1.61	4.66	3.10	4.72	5.66	4.61	4.85	3.53	7.82	2.96	4.58	2.97	1.28	2.24	2.11	1.61	3.87
NSFA [70]	1.51	4.24	2.75	4.68	6.04	4.29	4.84	3.02	7.93	3.87	5.99	2.21	0.78	1.73	2.04	2.14	3.77
VRCNet [40]	1.15	3.20	2.14	3.58	5.57	3.58	4.17	2.47	6.90	2.76	3.45	1.78	0.59	1.52	1.83	1.57	3.12
Our VAPCNet	**0.78**	**3.19**	**2.10**	**3.05**	**3.16**	**3.14**	**3.26**	**2.15**	**5.36**	**1.92**	**3.08**	**1.68**	**0.33**	**1.39**	**1.34**	**0.95**	**2.40**

Table 8.2 Shape completion results (F-Score@1%) on the multi-view partial (MVP) point cloud dataset (16,384 points)

Method	Airplane	Cabinet	Car	Chair	Lamp	Sofa	Table	Watercraft	Bed	Bench	Bookshelf	Bus	Guitar	Motorbike	Pistol	Skateboard	F1
PCN [67]	0.861	0.641	0.686	0.517	0.455	0.552	0.646	0.628	0.452	0.694	0.546	0.779	0.906	0.665	0.774	0.861	0.638
TopNet [44]	0.798	0.621	0.612	0.443	0.387	0.506	0.639	0.609	0.405	0.680	0.524	0.766	0.868	0.619	0.726	0.837	0.601
MSN [31]	0.879	0.692	0.693	0.599	0.604	0.627	0.730	0.696	0.569	0.797	0.637	0.806	0.935	0.728	0.809	0.885	0.710
Wang et al. [51]	0.898	0.688	0.725	0.670	0.681	0.641	0.748	0.742	0.600	0.797	0.659	0.802	0.931	0.772	0.843	0.902	0.740
ECG [39]	0.906	0.680	0.716	0.683	0.734	0.651	0.766	0.753	0.640	0.822	0.706	0.804	0.945	0.780	0.835	0.897	0.753
GRNet [61]	0.861	0.641	0.686	0.517	0.455	0.552	0.646	0.628	0.452	0.694	0.546	0.779	0.906	0.665	0.774	0.861	0.638
NSFA [70]	0.903	0.694	0.721	0.737	0.783	0.705	0.817	0.799	0.687	0.845	0.747	0.815	0.932	0.815	0.858	0.894	0.783
VRCNet [40]	0.928	0.721	0.756	0.743	0.789	0.696	0.813	0.800	0.674	0.863	0.755	0.832	0.960	0.834	0.887	0.930	0.796
Our VAPCNet	**0.942**	**0.762**	**0.758**	**0.786**	**0.844**	**0.759**	**0.845**	**0.824**	**0.736**	**0.892**	**0.808**	**0.854**	**0.978**	**0.845**	**0.902**	**0.944**	**0.829**

Table 8.3 Shape completion results (CD loss multiplied by 10^4) on multi-view partial point cloud (MVP) dataset with various point cloud resolutions

#Points	2048		4096		8192		16384	
	CD↓	F1↑	CD↓	F1↑	CD↓	F1↑	CD↓	F1↑
PCN [67]	9.77	0.320	7.96	0.458	6.99	0.563	6.02	0.638
TopNet [44]	10.11	0.308	8.20	0.440	7.00	0.533	6.36	0.601
MSN [31]	7.90	0.432	6.17	0.585	5.42	0.659	4.90	0.710
Wang et al. [51]	7.25	0.434	5.83	0.569	4.90	0.680	4.30	0.740
ECG [39]	6.64	0.476	5.41	0.585	4.18	0.690	3.58	0.753
GRNet [61]	7.61	0.353	5.73	0.493	4.51	0.616	3.54	0.700
VRCNet [40]	5.96	0.499	4.70	0.636	3.64	0.727	3.12	0.791
PoinTr [65]	5.79	0.499	4.29	0.638	3.52	0.725	2.95	0.783
PMP-Net++ [55]	–	–	–	–	–	–	3.38	0.687
Zhang et al.[68]	–	–	–	–	–	–	2.42	0.800
Wang et al. [52]	–	–	–	–	–	–	–	0.816
SnowflakeNet [58]	5.71	0.503	4.45	0.648	3.48	0.743	2.69	0.796
Our VAPCNet	**5.40**	**0.521**	**3.96**	**0.658**	**3.02**	**0.763**	**2.40**	**0.829**

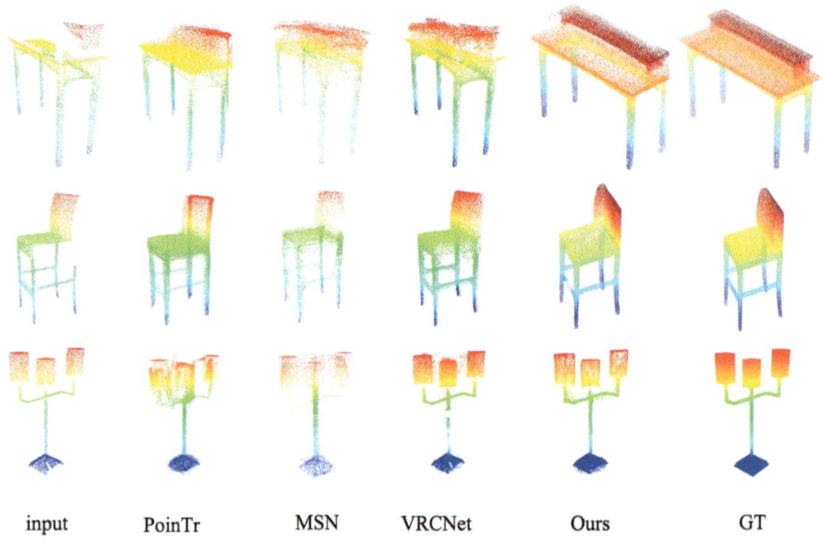

Fig. 8.4 Visual comparisons on MVP dataset (This figure is reproduced from [13])

Table 8.4 Quantitative comparison on PCN dataset with state-of-the-art methods in terms of L1 Chamfer Distance $\times 10^3$

Models	Avg.	Airplane	Cabinet	Car	Chair	Lamp	Couch	Table	Watercraft
AtlasNet [20]	10.58	6.37	11.94	10.10	12.06	12.37	12.99	10.33	10.61
FoldingNet [63]	14.31	9.49	15.80	12.61	15.55	16.41	15.97	13.65	14.99
PCN [67]	9.64	5.50	22.70	10.63	8.70	11.00	11.34	11.68	8.59
TopNet [44]	12.15	7.61	13.31	10.90	13.82	14.44	14.78	11.22	11.12
GRNet [61]	8.83	6.45	10.37	9.45	9.41	7.96	10.51	8.44	8.04
Wang et al. [51]	8.51	4.79	9.97	8.31	9.49	8.94	10.69	7.81	8.05
PMP-Net [54]	8.73	5.65	11.24	9.64	9.51	6.95	10.83	8.72	7.25
ECG [39]	8.63	5.23	10.12	8.36	9.43	8.53	10.94	7.98	8.16
NSFA [70]	8.32	5.03	10.51	9.11	9.16	7.45	10.46	7.56	7.28
SK-PCN [36]	8.49	5.09	9.98	8.22	9.29	8.39	10.80	7.84	8.02
PoinTr [65]	8.38	4.75	10.47	8.68	9.39	7.75	10.93	7.78	7.29
SnowflakeNet [40]	7.21	4.29	**9.16**	**8.08**	7.89	6.07	9.23	6.55	6.40
Wang et al. [52]	7.96	–	–	–	–	–	–	–	–
Our VAPCNet	**7.02**	**4.10**	9.28	8.15	**7.51**	**5.55**	**9.18**	**6.28**	**6.10**

method performs similarly to SnowFlakeNet [58]. In all other categories, our method outperforms others. Specifically, our approach shows an improvement of 8.6% in the lamp category compared to SnowFlakeNet. While [52] outperforms SnowFlakeNet on the MVP dataset, it performs worse on the PCN dataset. In contrast, our method consistently delivers superior performance across both datasets.

Qualitative Comparison. Figure 8.5 presents the qualitative comparison results. Our method predicts more accurate shapes with finer details. For example, in the second and third rows of Fig. 8.5, our approach better recovers the intricate details of the chair's back and the couch. In contrast, results from other methods are noisier. This highlights our network's capability to enhance shapes with local details.

8.3.2.4 Ablation Study

In this section, we evaluate the effectiveness of the viewpoint representation and the proposed VA module.

Viewpoint Representation Learning. Our viewpoint representation focuses on extracting viewpoint information from incomplete objects. To evaluate its effectiveness, we conducted experiments to investigate how different viewpoints of each CAD model impact our viewpoint representations. For each CAD model in the training set, 26 camera poses are uniformly distributed on a unit sphere. During testing, two random rotation angles are applied to rotate the incomplete objects, resulting in three incomplete objects for each viewpoint (78 incomplete objects per CAD model). We pre-trained the viewpoint representation architecture on the training set and tested it on the testing set. In Fig. 8.6, (1) and (2) represent three different CAD models.

Fig. 8.5 Visual comparisons on PCN dataset (This figure is reproduced from [13])

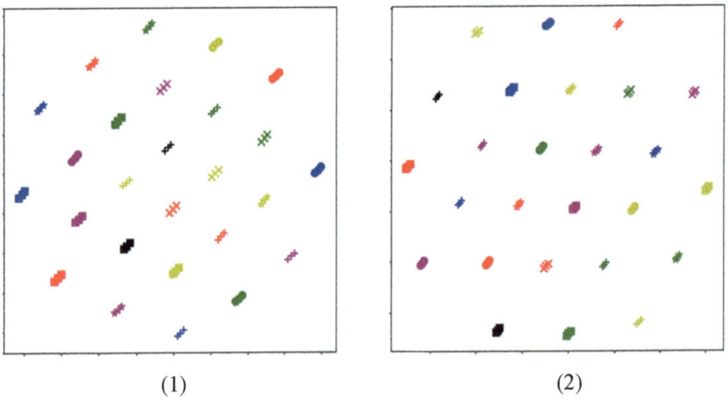

Fig. 8.6 Examples of unsupervised viewpoint representation learning (This figure is reproduced from [13])

Each symbol represents a viewpoint representation. Figure 8.6 illustrates that these 26 latent representations (three per viewpoint) are well-separated. This indicates that the model successfully learns distinct latent representations for each viewpoint. This demonstrates that the pre-trained viewpoint representation architecture can capture discriminative viewpoint information, enhancing the performance of VAPCNet.

Effectiveness of the VA Module. To assess the effectiveness of the proposed VA module, which incorporates convolutional kernels and modulated self-attention, we performed ablation studies on the MVP dataset (with 2048 points), as shown in Table 8.5. In Model 1, viewpoint representation learning is omitted, and MLPs replace the VA module in the up-sample and refinement module. As a result, this model shows limited accuracy. However, introducing the convolutional kernel and modulated self-

Table 8.5 Ablation studies for the proposed VA module

Model	VA module		CD	F1
	Kernel	Modulated self-attention		
1	✗	✗	7.12	0.493
2	✓	✗	5.53	0.513
3	✗	✓	5.54	0.514
4	✓	✓	**5.40**	**0.521**

attention improves performance, reducing the error from 7.12 to 5.53 and 5.54, respectively. With both modules included, Model 4 achieves the best performance, confirming the effectiveness of our viewpoint representation learning and VA module.

8.4 Adaptive Embedding and Multiview-Aware Disentanglement Network: AEDNet

8.4.1 Methodology

8.4.1.1 Overview

Our point cloud completion framework is illustrated in Fig. 8.7 (a). It operates in two main phases: encoding and decoding. The encoder extracts features, while the decoder uses a coarse-to-fine strategy for completion.

Initially, the encoder processes a partial scan using our proposed AED module combined with a point transformer (PT), as shown in Fig. 8.7 (b). This combination enables hierarchical extraction of point-wise features. These features are then passed to the coarse completion stage, depicted in Fig. 8.7 (c). Here, we predict the preliminary shape of the complete 3D object and its global features. Finally, in the refinement phase, the initial shape undergoes systematic point cloud up-sampling using our GAED module, as illustrated in Fig. 8.7 (d).

8.4.1.2 Feature Extraction

Many existing point cloud completion approaches [4, 54, 58, 73] rely on FPS and K-Nearest Neighbors (KNN) to define local neighborhoods for feature extraction. This reliance makes them susceptible to noise. In this work, we leverage the proposed AED and PT techniques to extract features without using FPS.

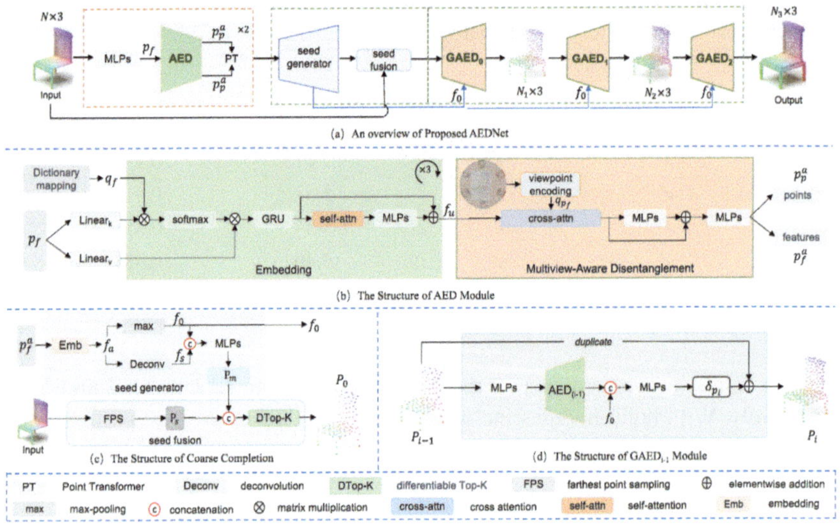

Fig. 8.7 Overview of AEDNet (This figure is reproduced from [14])

For an incomplete point cloud $P_{in} \in \mathbb{R}^{N\times 3}$, our AED module (shown in Fig. 8.7 (b)) performs embedding and disentanglement. It produces M points (where $M < N$) along with their corresponding features, which are then refined using PT.

AED: Embedding (Fig. 8.7 **(b)).** "Object-centric learning" methods [10, 18, 19, 29, 32] use slot attention to identify generative factors associated with components or objects within a scene. However, traditional slot attention techniques excel mainly on synthetic images with uniform colors and layouts. They struggle with the complexities of real-world scenes. The varying shapes of different objects and the recurrence of similar structures within a single object pose significant challenges for conventional slot attention in point cloud completion tasks.

To address these issues, we refine slot attention by improving slot initialization and enhancing the semantic interactions between slots. We first use MLPs to generate point-wise features p_f. These features are then passed through two linear layers to derive key and value features. Building on the standard slot attention mechanism [32], we replace Gaussian-initialized slots with a learnable dictionary mapping. This produces a set of slot features $q_{f_0} \in \mathbb{R}^{M\times C}$. These slot features, along with the key and value features, are input into the attention mechanism and a Gated Recurrent Unit (GRU) for slot feature updates. Additionally, self-attention combined with MLPs establishes semantic connections among slot features, yielding the final slot feature q_{f_i}. This embedding process is iteratively executed three times (i.e., i ranges from 1 to 3), culminating in the final embedding feature $f_u = q_{f_3}$.

AED: Multiview-aware Disentanglement (Fig. 8.7 **(b)).** After embedding point features, we introduce a viewpoint-aware method to disentangle local geometry from these embeddings. We use the Fibonacci point sequence generation algorithm [47] to evenly distribute n 3D viewpoints on a unit sphere. These viewpoints enable external observation of objects, providing a deeper understanding of their geometry and structure.

Next, we compute the relative position encoding between the viewpoints and the sparse input point clouds using MLPs. The resulting viewpoint encodings q_{p_f}, along with f_u, are fed into a cross-attention module. This module effectively isolates geometric details and associates them with the viewpoint encodings q_{p_f}. We then apply MLPs to regress the coordinates and features of the sampled points, p_p^a and p_f^a, respectively. A point transformer module [72] further refines the sampled features by considering positional relationships among the sampled points. Throughout this feature extraction process, our AED module is pivotal in down-sampling the point cloud and learning accurate features.

8.4.1.3 Coarse Completion

Seed Generator (Fig. 8.7 **(b)).** Prior studies [4, 58, 65, 73] emphasize the importance of local geometry diffusion for achieving effective point cloud completion. In our approach, we utilize an embedding and disentanglement strategy to predict the foundational structure of complete objects. After obtaining the extracted features f_e from the feature extraction phase, we proceed with our coarse completion technique (illustrated in Fig. 8.7 (c)) to predict the initial complete point cloud, denoted as $P_0 \in \mathbb{R}^{N_0 \times 3}$. Specifically, we leverage our newly designed embedding module to compile f_e into f_a. Subsequently, f_a is processed through two separate pathways: the first employs max-pooling to extract a global feature f_0, while the second uses deconvolution to expand f_a into f_s, diverging from SnowflakeNet's [58] method of directly generating point-wise features by enhancing the use of geometric information through the up-sampling of f_a. Following this, we merge f_0 with the up-sampled f_s and apply MLPs to generate N_0 points, represented by P_m.

Seed Fusion (Fig. 8.7 **(c)).** Acknowledging the presence of detailed structures within the incomplete inputs, we aim to integrate the predicted $P_m \in \mathbb{R}^{N_0 \times 3}$ with the original incomplete point cloud. This integration begins by combining P_m with P_s, which is derived from the incomplete point cloud P_{in} through FPS. Following this, we employ a differentiable Top-K selection method to isolate N_0 points from this combined set, establishing the initial shape of the complete point cloud as $P_0 \in \mathbb{R}^{N_0 \times 3}$. To refine the accuracy of this initial shape selection, we have formulated a specialized loss function, which is detailed further in Sect. 8.4.1.5.

8.4.1.4 Fine Completion

To achieve detailed object reconstruction, we utilize the proposed GAED method for hierarchically up-sampling the initial complete point cloud shape P_0, as illustrated in Fig. 8.7 (d). In each iteration, GAED uses the previous point cloud prediction P_{i-1} and the global feature f_0 to compute higher-resolution point-wise features p_{w_i}. This process differs from the feature extraction phase. GAED generates more points from a unit sphere than the input points N_{i-1} during the up-sampling stage. Additionally, we focus exclusively on predicting point-wise features at this stage, rather than predicting both points and point-wise features as done in the encoder. Finally, the point-wise features are concatenated with the global feature f_0 to estimate the residuals of the duplicated P_{i-1}.

8.4.1.5 Loss Functions

To measure the difference between two point clouds, we utilize the Chamfer Distance (CD) (Eq. 8.3) due to its computational efficiency compared to Earth Mover's Distance (EMD).

To explicitly constrain the point clouds sampled from the input, we consider the input point cloud as the ground truth and apply a modified CD loss.

$$\mathcal{L}_{\text{sampling}}(P_{in}, P_s) = \lambda \frac{1}{\|P_s\|_1} \sum_{x \in P_s} \min_{y \in P_{in}} \|x - y\|_2 + \frac{1}{\|P_{in}\|_1} \sum_{y \in P_{in}} \min_{x \in P_s} \|y - x\|_2. \tag{8.6}$$

In this scenario, $\lambda = \|P_{in}\|_1 / \|P_s\|_1$, where P_{in} represents the input points, and P_s denotes the sampled points.

To enforce specific constraints on point clouds generated during coarse and fine completion, we down-sample the ground truth point clouds to align with the sampling density of P_0, P_1, P_2, P_3. In the coarse completion stage, the Chamfer Distance (CD) loss is combined with the repulsion loss [64] ($\mathcal{L}_{\text{rep}}$) to define the seed loss, denoted as $\mathcal{L}_{\text{seed}}$. During the fine completion stage, the total of the three CD losses constitutes the completion loss, represented as $\mathcal{L}_{\text{completion}}$.

$$\mathcal{L}_{\text{seed}} = \mathcal{L}_{CD}(P_0, gt_0) + \lambda_s \mathcal{L}_{\text{rep}}(P_0), \tag{8.7}$$

$$\mathcal{L}_{\text{generation}} = \mathcal{L}_{CD}(P_1, gt_1) + \mathcal{L}_{CD}(P_2, gt_2) + \mathcal{L}_{CD}(P_3, gt_3). \tag{8.8}$$

Here, gt_0, gt_1, gt_2, gt_3 denote the down-sampled ground truth point clouds corresponding to P_0, P_1, P_2, P_3, respectively, and λ_s is assigned a value of 0.05.

To maintain the structural integrity of the input point cloud, we utilize the partial matching loss from [53]. This unidirectional constraint aligns one shape to another. It ensures the output point cloud partially aligns with the input, referred to as the preservation loss, $\mathcal{L}_{\text{preservation}}$. The overall training loss is expressed as:

$$\mathcal{L} = \mathcal{L}_{\text{sampling}} + \mathcal{L}_{\text{seed}} + \mathcal{L}_{\text{generation}} + \mathcal{L}_{\text{preservation}}. \tag{8.9}$$

8.4.2 Experiments

In this section, we first describe the datasets and provide implementation details (Sect. 8.4.2.1), followed by presenting our completion results on the MVP (Sect. 8.4.2.2) and PCN datasets (Sect. 8.4.2.3).

8.4.2.1 Datasets and Implementation Details

In AEDNet, we follow previous VAPCNet to test the proposed modules on MVP and PCN datasets [40, 67].
Implementation Details: For feature extraction, we applied two down-sampling operations in AEDNet. This process resulted in 512 points and then 64 points. For coarse completion, we predicted an initial complete shape with 512 points. In the fine completion phase, we performed three up-sampling operations using our GAED module. This generated 512, 1024, and 2048 points, respectively. Specifically, we uniformly sampled these points from the unit sphere during the three consecutive GAED module operations. For training, we used the Adam optimizer [28]. We set $\beta_1 = 0.9$ and $\beta_2 = 0.999$. The training ran for 50 epochs on the MVP dataset and 400 epochs on the PCN dataset. The learning rate was set to 10^{-4}, with a 30% reduction every 20 epochs. All experiments were conducted on an NVIDIA 3090Ti GPU.

8.4.2.2 Completion on the MVP Dataset

We evaluated the MVP dataset using the $\mathcal{L}_2$ Chamfer Distance and F-Score@1% as performance metrics. We compared our results against various state-of-the-art baseline methods. The results for the baseline methods [4, 34, 40, 52, 58] were obtained from the codes and pre-trained models available in their official GitHub repositories. Results for other methods were directly taken from [34, 40] and the original publication [13].
Quantitative Comparison. The performance of all methods is measured by CD loss and F-score@1%. The results are reported in Tables 8.6 and 8.7. Our proposed AEDNet outperforms all competitors in both CD and F-score@1%. Notably, our approach achieves nearly 50% better performance in the lamp category compared to VRCNet. We also evaluated our method against others that support multi-resolution completion, as shown in Table 8.8. This comparison is significant because our AED module can perform various levels of down-sampling and up-sampling on point clouds. In this evaluation, AEDNet demonstrated superior performance over all compared methods.
Qualitative Comparison. The visual comparison in Fig. 8.8 shows that AEDNet produces more accurate complete shapes than competing methods. The effectiveness of our AED module is evident in the completed shapes. For example, the missing legs of the chair (first row of Fig. 8.8) are recovered by referencing the visible legs. This takes into account the perspective from which they were scanned. In the second

Table 8.6 Shape completion results (CD loss scaled by 10^4) on the multi-view partial (MVP) point cloud dataset (16,384 points)

Method	Airplane	Cabinet	Car	Chair	Lamp	Sofa	Table	Watercraft	Bed	Bench	Bookshelf	Bus	Guitar	Motorbike	Pistol	Skateboard	Avg.
PCN [67]	2.95	4.13	3.04	7.07	14.93	5.56	7.06	6.08	12.72	5.73	6.91	2.46	1.02	3.53	3.28	2.99	6.02
TopNet [44]	2.72	4.25	3.40	7.95	17.01	6.04	7.42	6.04	11.56	5.62	8.22	2.37	1.37	3.90	3.97	2.09	6.36
MSN [31]	2.07	3.82	2.76	6.21	12.72	4.74	5.32	4.80	9.93	3.89	5.85	2.12	0.69	2.48	2.91	1.58	4.90
Wang et al. [51]	1.59	3.64	2.60	5.24	9.02	4.42	5.45	4.26	9.56	3.67	5.34	2.23	0.79	2.23	2.86	2.13	4.30
ECG [39]	1.41	3.44	2.36	4.58	6.95	3.81	4.27	3.38	7.46	3.10	4.82	1.99	0.59	2.05	2.31	1.66	3.58
GRNet [61]	1.61	4.66	3.10	4.72	5.66	4.61	4.85	3.53	7.82	2.96	4.58	2.97	1.28	2.24	2.11	1.61	3.87
NSFA [70]	1.51	4.24	2.75	4.68	6.04	4.29	4.84	3.02	7.93	3.87	5.99	2.21	0.78	1.73	2.04	2.14	3.77
VRCNet [40]	1.15	3.20	2.14	3.58	5.57	3.58	4.17	2.47	6.90	2.76	3.45	1.78	0.59	1.52	1.83	1.57	3.12
Our AEDNet	**0.74**	**2.99**	**2.27**	**2.75**	**2.79**	**2.96**	**2.64**	**1.98**	**4.73**	**1.96**	**3.01**	**1.71**	**0.38**	**1.50**	**1.55**	**0.81**	**2.24**

Table 8.7 Shape completion results (F-Score@1%) on the multi-view partial (MVP) point cloud dataset (16,384 points)

Method	Airplane	Cabinet	Car	Chair	Lamp	Sofa	Table	Watercraft	Bed	Bench	Bookshelf	Bus	Guitar	Motorbike	Pistol	Skateboard	F1
PCN [67]	0.861	0.641	0.686	0.517	0.455	0.552	0.646	0.628	0.452	0.694	0.546	0.779	0.906	0.665	0.774	0.861	0.638
TopNet [44]	0.798	0.621	0.612	0.443	0.387	0.506	0.639	0.609	0.405	0.680	0.524	0.766	0.868	0.619	0.726	0.837	0.601
MSN [31]	0.879	0.692	0.693	0.599	0.604	0.627	0.730	0.696	0.569	0.797	0.637	0.806	0.935	0.728	0.809	0.885	0.710
Wang et al. [51]	0.898	0.688	0.725	0.670	0.681	0.641	0.748	0.742	0.600	0.797	0.659	0.802	0.931	0.772	0.843	0.902	0.740
ECG [39]	0.906	0.680	0.716	0.683	0.734	0.651	0.766	0.753	0.640	0.822	0.706	0.804	0.945	0.780	0.835	0.897	0.753
GRNet [61]	0.861	0.641	0.686	0.517	0.455	0.552	0.646	0.628	0.452	0.694	0.546	0.779	0.906	0.665	0.774	0.861	0.638
NSFA [70]	0.903	0.694	0.721	0.737	0.783	0.705	0.817	0.799	0.687	0.845	0.747	0.815	0.932	0.815	0.858	0.894	0.783
VRCNet [40]	0.928	0.721	0.756	0.743	0.789	0.696	0.813	0.800	0.674	0.863	0.755	0.832	0.960	0.834	0.887	0.930	0.796
Our AEDNet	**0.947**	**0.766**	**0.757**	**0.794**	**0.850**	**0.754**	**0.856**	**0.828**	**0.735**	**0.893**	**0.807**	**0.848**	**0.974**	**0.843**	**0.899**	**0.956**	**0.832**

Table 8.8 Shape completion results (CD loss multiplied by 10^4) on the multi-view partial (MVP) point cloud dataset with different point cloud resolutions

#Points	2048		4096		8192		16384	
	CD↓	F1↑	CD↓	F1↑	CD↓	F1↑	CD↓	F1↑
PCN [67]	9.77	0.320	7.96	0.458	6.99	0.563	6.02	0.638
TopNet [44]	10.11	0.308	8.20	0.440	7.00	0.533	6.36	0.601
MSN [31]	7.90	0.432	6.17	0.585	5.42	0.659	4.90	0.710
Wang et al. [51]	7.25	0.434	5.83	0.569	4.90	0.680	4.30	0.740
ECG [39]	6.64	0.476	5.41	0.585	4.18	0.690	3.58	0.753
GRNet [61]	7.61	0.353	5.73	0.493	4.51	0.616	3.54	0.700
VRCNet [40]	5.96	0.499	4.70	0.636	3.64	0.727	3.12	0.791
PoinTr [65]	5.79	0.499	4.29	0.638	3.52	0.725	2.95	0.783
PMP-Net++ [55]	–	–	–	–	–	–	3.38	0.687
Wang et al. [52]	–	–	–	–	–	–	–	0.816
SnowflakeNet [58]	5.71	0.503	4.45	0.648	3.48	0.743	2.69	0.796
PDR [34]	5.66	0.499	4.26	0.649	3.35	0.754	2.61	0.817
VAPCNet [13]	5.40	0.521	3.96	0.658	3.02	0.763	2.40	0.829
AnchorFormer [4]	5.89	0.482	4.35	0.655	3.21	0.763	2.60	0.819
Our AEDNet	**5.12**	**0.522**	**3.75**	**0.675**	**2.90**	**0.770**	**2.24**	**0.832**

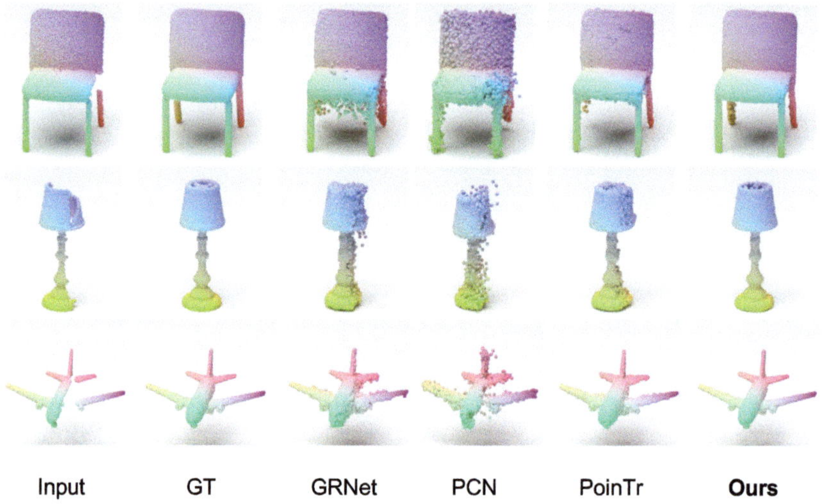

Fig. 8.8 Visual comparisons on MVP dataset (This figure is reproduced from [14])

row of Fig. 8.8, the lamp base is reconstructed more accurately. This results in a better-shaped lampstand compared to other methods. This achievement is due to the embedding-and-disentangling strategy used by AEDNet. It efficiently reconstructs complete shapes by learning structural relations at each up-sampling stage through the AED module.

Table 8.9 Quantitative comparison of SOTA methods on the PCN dataset

Models	Avg.	Airplane	Cabinet	Car	Chair	Lamp	Couch	Table	Watercraft
AtlasNet [20]	10.58	6.37	11.94	10.10	12.06	12.37	12.99	10.33	10.61
FoldingNet [63]	14.31	9.49	15.80	12.61	15.55	16.41	15.97	13.65	14.99
PCN [67]	9.64	5.50	22.70	10.63	8.70	11.00	11.34	11.68	8.59
TopNet [44]	12.15	7.61	13.31	10.90	13.82	14.44	14.78	11.22	11.12
GRNet [61]	8.83	6.45	10.37	9.45	9.41	7.96	10.51	8.44	8.04
Wang et al. [51]	8.51	4.79	9.97	8.31	9.49	8.94	10.69	7.81	8.05
PMP-Net [54]	8.73	5.65	11.24	9.64	9.51	6.95	10.83	8.72	7.25
ECG [39]	8.63	5.23	10.12	8.36	9.43	8.53	10.94	7.98	8.16
NSFA [70]	8.32	5.03	10.51	9.11	9.16	7.45	10.46	7.56	7.28
SK-PCN [36]	8.49	5.09	9.98	8.22	9.29	8.39	10.80	7.84	8.02
PoinTr [65]	8.38	4.75	10.47	8.68	9.39	7.75	10.93	7.78	7.29
SnowflakeNet [40]	7.21	4.29	9.16	8.08	7.89	6.07	9.23	6.55	6.40
VAPCNet [13]	7.02	4.10	9.28	8.15	7.51	5.55	9.18	6.28	6.10
Anchorformer [4]	6.59	3.70	8.94	7.57	**7.05**	5.21	8.40	6.03	5.81
Our AEDNet	**6.52**	**3.61**	**8.90**	**7.51**	**7.05**	**5.15**	**8.32**	**5.82**	**5.74**

8.4.2.3 Completion on the PCN Dataset

In the PCN dataset, we benchmarked our network against SOTA methods. We used the $\mathcal{L}_1$ Chamfer Distance as our evaluation metric. The results for the baseline methods from [39, 70] were obtained using the codes and pre-trained models available in their official GitHub repositories. We collected results for other methods from [54, 58, 61, 73] and their respective original publications [52, 65].

Quantitative Comparison. The data presented in Table 8.9 show that our network achieves the lowest average $\mathcal{L}_1$ Chamfer Distance (CD). In the chair category, AEDNet performs comparably to Anchorformer [4]. However, in other categories, our approach outperforms Anchorformer. Unlike Anchorformer, which reconstructs the 3D shape from a set of key points, our method disentangles the embedding to reconstruct the shape. Key points from incomplete point clouds typically relate only to their immediate local neighborhoods. In contrast, our embedding strategy connects with all input points. This facilitates a comprehensive understanding of the input partial objects.

Qualitative Comparison. Fig. 8.9 presents the qualitative comparison results. Our method excels in predicting shapes with greater accuracy and finer details. For example, in the second and third rows of Fig. 8.9, our approach effectively restores the complex structures of the airplane's wings and the lampshade. In contrast, reconstructions from other methods appear considerably noisier. This highlights our network's ability to refine shapes with localized details.

Fig. 8.9 Visual comparisons on the PCN dataset (This figure is reproduced from [14])

Table 8.10 Ablation studies for our AEDNet

Model	Description	CD ↓	F1 ↑
1	Backbone [58] +CC+ FC	5.38	0.510
2	FE + CC [58] + FC	5.43	0.506
3	FE + CC + SPD [58]	5.54	0.501
4	Emb + Deconv [73]	5.44	0.504
5	**Our AEDNet**	**5.12**	**0.522**

8.4.2.4 Ablation Study

This section evaluates the performance of our model's components. We focus on feature extraction, coarse completion, fine completion, and multi-view-aware disentanglement modules. The evaluation uses the MVP dataset, which contains point clouds with 2048 points. We also assess the effectiveness of the modified slot attention mechanism in enhancing point cloud completion tasks. To quantify performance, we use the Chamfer Distance (CD) and F-Score@1% as our evaluation metrics (Fig. 8.9).
Feature Extraction (FE): During the encoding phase, our AED module downsamples the point cloud and extracts features. We assess the efficiency of our feature extraction method by comparing it to the feature extractor from SnowFlakeNet [58], referred to as $Model1$. As shown in Table 8.10, AEDNet outperforms $Model1$ in both Chamfer Distance (CD) and F-Score@1%. This demonstrates the superiority of our feature extraction process for point cloud completion tasks. Our model automatically identifies and selects the most crucial keypoints for completion. This is a significant advantage over the points chosen by FPS, as depicted in Fig. 8.10.
Coarse Completion (CC): Previous methods [58, 65, 67] typically reconstructed 3D shapes using either global features alone or anchor points for shape querying.

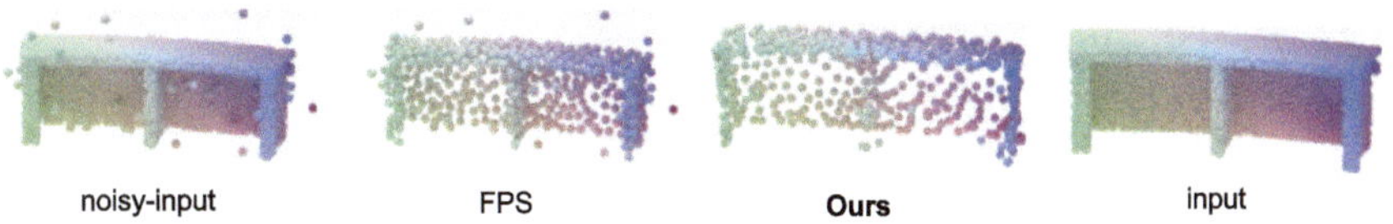

Fig. 8.10 Visualization of Point Cloud Down-sampling Techniques (This figure is reproduced from [14])

In contrast, our approach first reconstructs a coarse 3D object by combining global features with learned embeddings. We then employ a differentiable Top-K method to automatically select informative points for the up-sampling phase. When comparing our coarse completion with that of SnowFlakeNet, referred to as $Model2$, our method shows a significant performance improvement.

Fine Completion (FC): Traditional point cloud up-sampling methods [20, 40, 58, 63, 65, 73] generate points using various techniques. To evaluate our GAED module, we replace it with the Snowflake Point Deconvolution (SPD) [58], referred to as $Model3$. The results in Table 8.10 show that AEDNet outperforms $Model3$. This highlights the effectiveness of our GAED module in enhancing point cloud generation.

Multiview-aware Disentanglement: We assess the effectiveness of our multiview-aware disentanglement operator in the GAED module. We replace it with a deconvolution method [73], referred to as the embedding and deconvolution module (denoted as $Model4$). The results in Table 8.10 indicate that our multiview-aware disentanglement operator outperforms the deconvolution-based network ($Model4$). This demonstrates the effectiveness of our operator in improving detailed point cloud upsampling.

Slot Attention Modifications: We investigate the impact of modifying slot initialization and promoting slot interactions. We shift from Gaussian noise initialization to dictionary mapping initialization. Additionally, we introduce self-attention mechanisms within each iteration to encourage slot interactions. The results in Table 8.11 show that these changes lead to significant improvements in model performance. This indicates that our adjustments to slot attention effectively capture the detailed structures of 3D objects. These modifications enhance the model's ability to understand complex spatial relationships.

Table 8.11 Ablation studies investigating the impact of slot initialization and slot interaction

Model	Modifications	CD ↓	F1 ↑
i	Original slot attention	5.45	0.488
ii	Only DMI	5.34	0.502
iii	Only slot interaction	5.38	0.510
iv	**Ours**	**5.12**	**0.522**

8.5 Conclusion and Future Work

In this chapter, we present the VAPCNet and AEDNet for point cloud completion. In **VAPCNet**, we proposed an unsupervised viewpoint representation learning approach for detailed 3D point cloud completion. Rather than explicitly estimating the viewpoints of incomplete scanned objects, we leverage contrastive learning to extract discriminative representations that differentiate various viewpoints. We then utilized these learned representations to handle partial objects scanned from different viewpoints. Our results demonstrate that the viewpoint representation learning scheme effectively extracts discriminative features for accurate viewpoint information, while the proposed VAPCNet is capable of recovering detailed and precise complete point clouds. In **AEDNet**, the key innovation is the emphasis on global perception and local attention. These factors are critical for effective point cloud completion. We enhanced the original slot attention mechanism. This improvement allows for more adaptive embedding of complex 3D structures. We focused on refining slot initialization and interaction. Additionally, we integrated multi-view information into the disentanglement process. This integration provides an external perspective of objects, leading to a more comprehensive geometric understanding. The number of 3D points sampled from a unit sphere can be adjusted for flexible sampling. Experimental results show that our VAPCNet and AEDNet achieve state-of-the-art performance on both MVP and PCN datasets.

Future work will focus on generating more discriminative shape codes to further enhance point cloud completion performance across a wider range of object categories. Additionally, we will aim to reduce the computational cost of the sampling method. We also plan to extend this approach to related tasks, such as point cloud up-sampling and denoising.

References

1. Chang AX, Funkhouser T, Guibas L, Hanrahan P, Huang Q, Li Z, Savarese S, Savva M, Song S, Su H, et al (2015) Shapenet: an information-rich 3D model repository. arXiv preprint arXiv:1512.03012
2. Chen T, Kornblith S, Norouzi M, Hinton G (2020) A simple framework for contrastive learning of visual representations. In: International conference on machine learning, pp 1597–1607. PMLR
3. Chen X, Fan H, Girshick R, He K (2020) Improved baselines with momentum contrastive learning. arXiv preprint arXiv:2003.04297
4. Chen Z, Long F, Qiu Z, Yao T, Zhou W, Luo J, Mei T (2023) Anchorformer: point cloud completion from discriminative nodes. In: IEEE conference on computer vision and pattern recognition (CVPR), pp 13581–13590
5. Chen Z, Long F, Qiu Z, Yao T, Zhou W, Luo J, Mei T (2024) Learning 3D shape latent for point cloud completion. IEEE Trans Multimed (TMM)
6. Choy CB, Xu D, Gwak J, Chen K, Savarese S (2016) 3D-r2n2: a unified approach for single and multi-view 3D object reconstruction. In: European conference on computer vision (ECCV), pp 628–644. Springer

7. Dai A, Ruizhongtai Qi C, Nießner M (2017) Shape completion using 3D-encoder-predictor cnns and shape synthesis. In: IEEE conference on computer vision and pattern recognition (CVPR), pp 5868–5877
8. Doersch C, Gupta A, Efros AA (2015) Unsupervised visual representation learning by context prediction. In: Proceedings of the IEEE international conference on computer vision, pp 1422–1430
9. Dosovitskiy A, Springenberg JT, Riedmiller M, Brox T (2014) Discriminative unsupervised feature learning with convolutional neural networks. Adv Neural Inf Process Syst 27
10. Eslami S, Heess N, Weber T, Tassa Y, Szepesvari D, Hinton GE, et al (2016) Attend, infer, repeat: fast scene understanding with generative models. Adv Neural Inf Process Syst (NeurIPS) 29
11. Feng M, Hou H, Zhang L, Guo Y, Yu H, Wang Y, Mian A (2023) Exploring hierarchical spatial layout cues for 3D point cloud based scene graph prediction. IEEE Trans Multimed
12. Fu Z, Hong S, Liu M, Laga H, Bennamoun M, Boussaid F, Guo Y (2023) Multi-stage information diffusion for joint depth and surface normal estimation. Pattern Recogn 141:109660
13. Fu Z, Wang L, Xu L, Wang Z, Laga H, Guo Y, Boussaid F, Bennamoun M (2023) Vapcnet: viewpoint-aware 3D point cloud completion. In: IEEE international conference on computer vision (ICCV), pp 12108–12118
14. Fu Z, Wang L, Xu L, Wang Z, Laga H, Guo Y, Boussaid F, Bennamoun M (2024) Aednet: adaptive embedding and multiview-aware disentanglement for point cloud completion. In: European conference on computer vision, pp 127–143. Springer
15. Gidaris S, Singh P, Komodakis N (2018) Unsupervised representation learning by predicting image rotations. arXiv preprint arXiv:1803.07728
16. Girdhar R, Fouhey DF, Rodriguez M, Gupta A (2016) Learning a predictable and generative vector representation for objects. In: European conference on computer vision (ECCV), pp 484–499. Springer
17. Graham B, Engelcke M, Van Der Maaten L (2018) 3D semantic segmentation with submanifold sparse convolutional networks. In: Proceedings of the IEEE conference on computer vision and pattern recognition, pp 9224–9232
18. Greff K, Kaufman RL, Kabra R, Watters N, Burgess C, Zoran D, Matthey L, Botvinick M, Lerchner A (2019) Multi-object representation learning with iterative variational inference. In: International conference on machine learning (ICML), pp 2424–2433. PMLR
19. Greff K, Van Steenkiste S, Schmidhuber J (2017) Neural expectation maximization. Adv Neural Inf Process Syst (NeurIPS) 30
20. Groueix T, Fisher M, Kim VG, Russell BC, Aubry M (2018) A papier-mâché approach to learning 3D surface generation. In: Proceedings of the IEEE conference on computer vision and pattern recognition, pp 216–224
21. Guo Y, Wang H, Hu Q, Liu H, Liu L, Bennamoun M (2020) Deep learning for 3D point clouds: a survey. IEEE Trans Pattern Anal Mach Intell (TPAMI) 43(12):4338–4364
22. Hadsell R, Chopra S, LeCun Y (2006) Dimensionality reduction by learning an invariant mapping. In: 2006 IEEE computer society conference on computer vision and pattern recognition (CVPR'06), vol 2, pp 1735–1742. IEEE
23. Han X, Li Z, Huang H, Kalogerakis E, Yu Y (2017) High-resolution shape completion using deep neural networks for global structure and local geometry inference. In: ICCV, pp 85–93
24. He K, Chen X, Xie S, Li Y, Dollár P, Girshick R (2022) Masked autoencoders are scalable vision learners. In: Proceedings of the IEEE/CVF conference on computer vision and pattern recognition, pp 16000–16009
25. He K, Fan H, Wu Y, Xie S, Girshick R (2020) Momentum contrast for unsupervised visual representation learning. In: Proceedings of the IEEE/CVF conference on computer vision and pattern recognition, pp 9729–9738
26. Henaff O (2020) Data-efficient image recognition with contrastive predictive coding. In: International conference on machine learning, pp 4182–4192. PMLR
27. Ho J, Jain A, Abbeel P (2020) Denoising diffusion probabilistic models. Adv Neural Inf Process Syst (NeurIPS) 33:6840–6851

28. Kingma DP, Ba J (2014) Adam: a method for stochastic optimization. arXiv preprint arXiv:1412.6980
29. Kosiorek A, Kim H, Teh YW, Posner I (2018) Sequential attend, infer, repeat: generative modelling of moving objects. Adv Neural Inf Process Syst (NeurIPS) 31
30. Li J, Guo S, Wang L, Han S (2024) Completedt: point cloud completion with information-perception transformers. Neurocomputing 592:127790
31. Liu M, Sheng L, Yang S, Shao J, Hu SM (2020) Morphing and sampling network for dense point cloud completion. In: AAAI conference on Artificial Intelligence (AAAI), vol 34, pp 11596–11603
32. Locatello F, Weissenborn D, Unterthiner T, Mahendran A, Heigold G, Uszkoreit J, Dosovitskiy A, Kipf T (2020) Object-centric learning with slot attention. Adv Neural Inf Process Syst 33:11525–11538
33. Luo S, Hu W (2021) Diffusion probabilistic models for 3D point cloud generation. In: IEEE conference on computer vision and pattern recognition (CVPR), pp 2837–2845
34. Lyu Z, Kong Z, Xu X, Pan L, Lin D (2021) A conditional point diffusion-refinement paradigm for 3D point cloud completion. arXiv preprint arXiv:2112.03530
35. Miao B, Bennamoun M, Gao Y, Mian A (2023) Spectrum-guided multi-granularity referring video object segmentation. arXiv preprint arXiv:2307.13537
36. Nie Y, Lin Y, Han X, Guo S, Chang J, Cui S, Zhang J et al (2020) Skeleton-bridged point completion: from global inference to local adjustment. Adv Neural Inf Process Syst (NeurIPS) 33:16119–16130
37. Noroozi M, Pirsiavash H, Favaro P (2017) Representation learning by learning to count. In: Proceedings of the IEEE international conference on computer vision, pp 5898–5906
38. Oord AVD, Li Y, Vinyals O (2018) Representation learning with contrastive predictive coding. arXiv preprint arXiv:1807.03748
39. Pan L (2020) Ecg: edge-aware point cloud completion with graph convolution. IEEE Robot Autom Lett 5(3):4392–4398
40. Pan L, Chen X, Cai Z, Zhang J, Zhao H, Yi S, Liu Z (2021) Variational relational point completion network. In: Proceedings of the IEEE/CVF conference on computer vision and pattern recognition, pp 8524–8533
41. Qi CR, Su H, Mo K, Guibas LJ (2017) PointNet: deep learning on point sets for 3d classification and segmentation. In: IEEE conference on computer vision and pattern recognition, pp 652–660
42. Qi CR, Yi L, Su H, Guibas LJ (2017) PointNet++: deep hierarchical feature learning on point sets in a metric space. Adv Neural Inf Process Syst 30
43. Su H, Jampani V, Sun D, Maji S, Kalogerakis E, Yang MH, Kautz J (2018) Splatnet: sparse lattice networks for point cloud processing. In: CVPR, pp 2530–2539
44. Tchapmi LP, Kosaraju V, Rezatofighi H, Reid I, Savarese S (2019) Topnet: structural point cloud decoder. In: IEEE conference on computer vision and pattern recognition (CVPR), pp 383–392
45. Tian Y, Krishnan D, Isola P (2020) Contrastive multiview coding. In: European conference on computer vision, pp 776–794. Springer
46. Vaswani A (2017) Attention is all you need. arXiv preprint arXiv:1706.03762
47. Viswanath D (2000) Random Fibonacci sequences and the number 1.13198824.... Math Comput 69(231):1131–1155
48. Wang J, Cui Y, Guo D, Li J, Liu Q, Shen C (2022) Pointattn: you only need attention for point cloud completion. arXiv preprint arXiv:2203.08485
49. Wang L, Wang Y, Dong X, Xu Q, Yang J, An W, Guo Y (2021) Unsupervised degradation representation learning for blind super-resolution. In: Proceedings of the IEEE/CVF conference on computer vision and pattern recognition, pp 10581–10590
50. Wang PS, Liu Y, Guo YX, Sun CY, Tong X (2017) O-cnn: octree-based convolutional neural networks for 3D shape analysis. ACM Trans Graph (TOG) 36(4):1–11
51. Wang X, Ang Jr, MH, Lee GH (2020) Cascaded refinement network for point cloud completion. In: IEEE conference on computer vision and pattern recognition (CVPR), pp 790–799

52. Wang Y, Tan DJ, Navab N, Tombari F (2022) Learning local displacements for point cloud completion. In: IEEE conference on computer vision and pattern recognition (CVPR), pp 1568–1577
53. Wen X, Han Z, Cao YP, Wan P, Zheng W, Liu YS (2021) Cycle4completion: unpaired point cloud completion using cycle transformation with missing region coding. In: IEEE conference on computer vision and pattern recognition (CVPR), pp 13080–13089
54. Wen X, Xiang P, Han Z, Cao YP, Wan P, Zheng W, Liu YS (2021) Pmp-net: point cloud completion by learning multi-step point moving paths. In: CVPR, pp 7443–7452
55. Wen X, Xiang P, Han Z, Cao YP, Wan P, Zheng W, Liu YS (2022) Pmp-net++: point cloud completion by transformer-enhanced multi-step point moving paths. IEEE Trans Pattern Anal Mach Intell (TPAMI) 45(1):852–867
56. Wu Z, Song S, Khosla A, Yu F, Zhang L, Tang X, Xiao J (2015) 3D shapenets: a deep representation for volumetric shapes. In: IEEE conference on computer vision and pattern recognition (CVPR), pp 1912–1920
57. Wu Z, Xiong Y, Yu SX, Lin D (2018) Unsupervised feature learning via non-parametric instance discrimination. In: Proceedings of the IEEE conference on computer vision and pattern recognition, pp 3733–3742
58. Xiang P, Wen X, Liu YS, Cao YP, Wan P, Zheng W, Han Z (2021) Snowflakenet: point cloud completion by snowflake point deconvolution with skip-transformer. In: Proceedings of the IEEE/CVF international conference on computer vision, pp 5499–5509
59. Xiao A, Huang J, Guan D, Lu S (2022) Unsupervised representation learning for point clouds: a survey. arXiv preprint arXiv:2202.13589
60. Xie C, Wang C, Zhang B, Yang H, Chen D, Wen F (2021) Style-based point generator with adversarial rendering for point cloud completion. In: IEEE conference on computer vision and pattern recognition (CVPR), pp 4619–4628
61. Xie H, Yao H, Zhou S, Mao J, Zhang S, Sun W (2020) Grnet: gridding residual network for dense point cloud completion. In: European conference on computer vision (ECCV), pp 365–381. Springer
62. Xie S, Gu J, Guo D, Qi CR, Guibas L, Litany O (2020) Pointcontrast: unsupervised pre-training for 3D point cloud understanding. In: Computer vision–ECCV 2020: 16th European conference, Glasgow, UK, August 23–28, 2020, Proceedings, Part III 16, pp 574–591. Springer
63. Yang Y, Feng C, Shen Y, Tian D (2018) Foldingnet: point cloud auto-encoder via deep grid deformation. In: IEEE conference on computer vision and pattern recognition, pp 206–215
64. Yu L, Li X, Fu CW, Cohen-Or D, Heng PA (2018) Pu-net: point cloud upsampling network. In: IEEE conference on computer vision and pattern recognition (CVPR), pp 2790–2799
65. Yu X, Rao Y, Wang Z, Liu Z, Lu J, Zhou J (2021) Pointr: diverse point cloud completion with geometry-aware transformers. In: IEEE international conference on computer vision (ICCV), pp 12498–12507
66. Yu X, Tang L, Rao Y, Huang T, Zhou J, Lu J (2022) Point-bert: pre-training 3D point cloud transformers with masked point modeling. In: Proceedings of the IEEE/CVF conference on computer vision and pattern recognition, pp 19313–19322
67. Yuan W, Khot T, Held D, Mertz C, Hebert M (2018) Pcn: point completion network. In: International conference on 3D vision (3DV), pp 728–737. IEEE
68. Zhang B, Zhao X, Wang H, Hu R (2022) Shape completion with points in the shadow. In: SIGGRAPH Asia 2022 conference papers, pp 1–9
69. Zhang R, Isola P, Efros AA (2016) Colorful image colorization. In: Computer vision–ECCV 2016: 14th European conference, Amsterdam, The Netherlands, Oct 11–14, 2016, Proceedings, Part III 14, pp 649–666. Springer
70. Zhang W, Yan Q, Xiao C (2020) Detail preserved point cloud completion via separated feature aggregation. In: European conference on computer vision (ECCV), pp 512–528. Springer
71. Zhang Z, Girdhar R, Joulin A, Misra I (2021) Self-supervised pretraining of 3D features on any point-cloud. In: Proceedings of the IEEE/CVF international conference on computer vision, pp 10252–10263

72. Zhao H, Jiang L, Jia J, Torr PH, Koltun V (2021) Point transformer. In: Proceedings of the IEEE/CVF international conference on computer vision, pp 16259–16268
73. Zhou H, Cao Y, Chu W, Zhu J, Lu T, Tai Y, Wang C (2022) Seedformer: patch seeds based point cloud completion with upsample transformer. In: European conference on computer vision (ECCV), pp 416–432. Springer
74. Zhou L, Du Y, Wu J (2021) 3D shape generation and completion through point-voxel diffusion. In: IEEE international conference on computer vision (ICCV), pp 5826–5835
75. Zong D, Sun S, Zhao J (2021) Ashf-net: adaptive sampling and hierarchical folding network for robust point cloud completion. In: Proceedings of the AAAI conference on artificial intelligence (AAAI), vol 35, pp 3625–3632

Chapter 9
Semantic Instance Completion of 3D Point Cloud Scenes

This chapter introduces WSSIC-Net, a weakly-supervised approach for semantic instance completion. It reconstructs complete 3D objects from partial 2.5D scans without requiring full 3D supervision. This method addresses a significant limitation in current 3D scene understanding. Fully-supervised techniques often rely on expensive complete 3D annotations, which hinders practical deployment. The research makes three key contributions. First, it shows that semantic instance completion can be achieved using only bounding box annotations and unpaired synthetic data. Second, it presents a novel dual-branch architecture. This architecture combines supervised detection with weakly-supervised completion. Third, it demonstrates that competitive performance can be attained with significantly reduced annotation requirements. The framework consists of two synergistic components. The first is a fully-supervised 3D detection branch for proposal generation. The second is a weakly-supervised completion branch that uses adversarial learning with synthetic references. This design enables effective knowledge transfer from synthetic complete shapes to real-world partial scans while maintaining semantic consistency. Validation on ScanNet v2 shows that our method matches or exceeds fully-supervised approaches. This proves that weakly-supervised learning can be equally effective while being more practical. This chapter represents a significant step toward scalable 3D scene reconstruction by reducing dependency on costly annotations.

9.1 Introduction

3D scene understanding from partial scans is challenging. Factors such as occlusions, viewpoint constraints, and poor lighting conditions complicate the task [10, 20, 28, 77, 87]. Semantic instance completion aims to reconstruct semantic labels of voxels or points. It also focuses on the poses and 3D geometries of objects from partial scene observations, such as depth images or point clouds

Y. Guo et al., *Point Cloud Intelligence*, Advances in Computer Vision and Pattern Recognition, https://doi.org/10.1007/978-981-95-0648-4_9

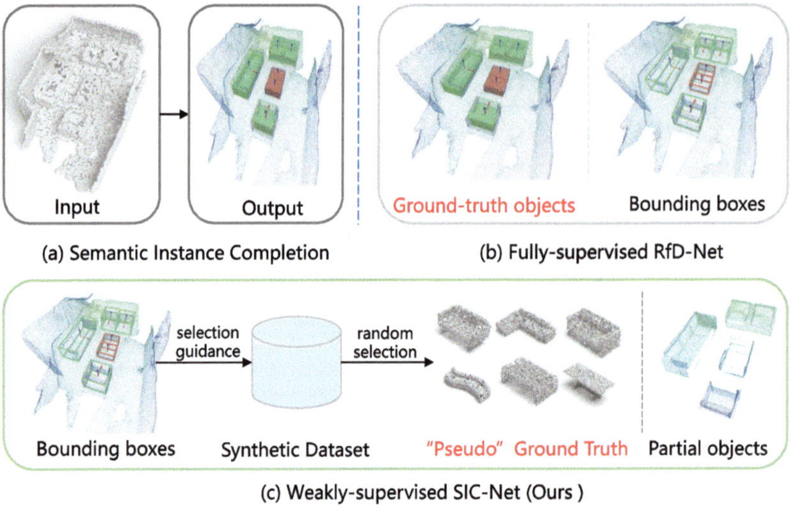

Fig. 9.1 An overview of semantic instance completion and current supervision strategies (This figure is reproduced from [18])

(see Fig. 9.1 (a)). This type of scene completion is critical for various applications. These include robot navigation, human-robot interaction, and object grasping [24, 27, 33, 40, 59].

Various strategies have been explored in the literature to recover missing 3D shapes. **(1) Completion-from-scans:** This method uses a 3D convolutional encoder-decoder architecture. It predicts voxel occupancy and object categories based on 2.5D partially scanned surfaces. However, these methods rely on 3D convolutions at the scene level. As a result, they can only recover 3D scenes at low resolution [12, 23, 29, 35, 39, 57]. **(2) Completion-from-retrieval:** This approach searches for CAD models that match incomplete objects [1–3, 32, 55]. The efficiency and accuracy of these methods depend on the size of the model dataset. However, retrieved CAD models have fixed shapes. **(3) Completion-from-objects:** This method views the scene as a collection of multiple objects. It employs a reconstruction-from-detection strategy, which includes 3D object detection and instance completion [26, 46]. By leveraging 3D object detection, these methods complete partial scans and reconstruct object details. Unlike completion-from-scans, completion-from-objects requires ground truth for bounding boxes. Most existing methods are fully supervised, limiting their applicability in real-world scenarios.

Rendering synthetic yet realistic 3D structures is much easier than capturing them in real-world environments. 3D objects within the same category often share similar geometric shapes. The labeling process for these objects is also simpler. It typically involves creating 3D bounding boxes and assigning semantic labels. This is less complex than generating a complete 3D point cloud for the scene's ground truth. With this in mind, we propose constructing "pseudo" ground truths for 3D shapes. We use an equal number of complete synthetic objects from the same category as the real-world partial scans. This approach enables semantic scene completion using only partial objects, bounding boxes, and "pseudo" ground truth (Fig. 9.1 (c)). Thus, our method does not require the ground truth of complete 3D objects. In contrast, existing state-of-the-art methods rely on complete RGB-D scans as ground truth (RevealNet [26]) or use watertight meshes as ground truth (RfDNet [46]) (Fig. 9.1 (b)).

In this chapter, we adopt a reconstruction-from-detection strategy. First, we locate object positions using bounding boxes based on a supervised method. Next, we perform weakly-supervised mesh reconstruction of the objects. We use a 3D detector backbone to extract proposal features from partial objects in a raw point cloud. These features are processed through two branches. The first branch employs a dedicated detection module to detect 3D objects in a supervised manner. The second branch uses a weakly-supervised approach for instance completion. In the instance completion branch, proposal features of partial objects are completed using "complete" latent features. These features are learned by a pre-trained encoder on synthetically complete point cloud objects. We utilize a Generative Adversarial Network (GAN) and the unidirectional Hausdorff distance loss (HL) [31] for this purpose. The synthetically complete point cloud objects serve as "pseudo" ground truth. They are randomly selected from a synthetic dataset based on the number and category of ground-truth bounding boxes (e.g., two tables and four sofas in Fig. 9.1 (c)). Partial objects, segmented using ground-truth bounding boxes, are incorporated into the Hausdorff Distance Loss (HL) [31] for 3D shape refinement. Then, the completed proposal features are then passed to a pre-trained decoder to generate full meshes of the objects. Additionally, we introduce an Objectness-aware Chamfer Distance (OCD) loss. This loss jointly optimizes the 3D detection module and the instance completion module. In the OCD loss, objectness scores are predicted in the detection branch. These scores assess the likelihood of an object being present in a proposal. Chamfer distance is commonly used in point cloud completion. Experiments on the ScanNet v2 Dataset [49] demonstrate that our weakly-supervised semantic instance completion method performs similarly to the fully supervised state-of-the-art RfD-Net [46] in both 3D detection and instance reconstruction tasks on raw point clouds.

The main contributions of this chapter are as follows:

- We propose a Weakly-Supervised Semantic Instance Completion Network (WSSIC-Net) for scene-level point cloud completion. To minimize reliance on manually created ground truth, we utilize synthetically completed point clouds of objects as "pseudo" ground truth for real-world partial point clouds of objects.
- We present an OCD loss for the joint optimization of 3D detection and point cloud instance completion tasks. Our results demonstrate that the instance completion task, guided by unpaired complete synthetic point clouds of objects, significantly improves object detection performance in real-world scenarios.

This chapter is organized as follows. Section 9.2 reviews related works briefly. Section 9.3 describes the proposed network in detail. The experimental results are discussed in Sect. 9.4. Finally, Sect. 9.5 summarizes the findings and concludes the paper.

9.2 Related Works

This section provides an overview of the literature on 3D point cloud object detection, shape completion, generative adversarial networks for 3D completion, and semantic 3D scene completion.

9.2.1 3D Point Cloud Object Detection

The goal of 3D point cloud object detection is to identify objects by detecting their bounding boxes and classifying them. Early methods [8, 14, 34, 61, 73, 78, 88] typically project 3D point clouds onto 2D grids and apply established 2D detection pipelines. To enhance accuracy, some methods integrate RGB images [8, 69, 74]. However, many rely on predefined anchors and two-stage region proposal networks, leading to high computational costs [54]. PointRCNN [58] improves detection by using foreground point segmentation without anchors. VoteNet [50] employs point feature grouping, sampling, and voting for detection. Shi et al. [56] combine voxel and point representations to enhance detection. Zhang et al. [86] propose an instance-aware downsampling approach for efficient detection. Yang et al. [75] regress 3D bounding boxes directly from global features in a single pass. Feng et al. [16] introduce a relation graph network for end-to-end trainable point cloud detection.

More recently, Misra et al. [45] present the end-to-end transformer model (3DTR), which uses non-parametric queries and Fourier positional embeddings. Liu et al. [41] propose the Group-free transformer framework, which groups foreground points for detection. Mao et al. [42] develop the Voxel Transformer to capture long-range voxel relationships. Cai et al. [4] introduce the 3D Cascade RCNN, which employs a completeness-aware re-weighting strategy across multiple detectors. Wang et al. [66] propose the Bridged Transformer (BrT), combining RGB images and point clouds for detection. Recent research also explores 3D object detection with limited annotations [17, 44, 79, 80].

In this chapter, 3D object detection is crucial for extracting features from partial point cloud objects. Our main focus is on instance completion. To ensure a fair comparison with the state-of-the-art RfD-Net [46], we utilize VoteNet [50] as our 3D detector.

9.2.2 3D Object Shape Completion

The objective of this task is to recover missing geometries from partial scans. Yuan et al. [82] introduced the end-to-end PCNnet, which processes raw point clouds without assuming a specific shape structure. Current point-based techniques [30, 38, 47, 60, 63] focus on reconstructing high-resolution 3D geometries. Groueix et al. [19]

proposed AtlasNet, which represents 3D shapes as collections of parametric surface elements. This enables the generation of shapes at arbitrary resolutions without memory limitations. ASFM-Net [70] and VRCNet [48] use encoder-decoder architectures to match encoded latent features with shape priors for high-quality completion. To preserve the observed geometry during fine reconstruction, MSN [38] and VRCNet use Minimum Density Sampling (MDS) or Farthest Point Sampling (FPS) along with skip connections. GRNet [71] integrates a volumetric sub-architecture to maintain discretized input geometries. More recent approaches, such as PMP-Net [68], gradually reconstruct the full object from the observed partial object to the nearest occluded regions. PoinTr [81], one of the first transformer-based frameworks for point cloud completion, refines reconstructions by predicting only the occluded geometries. Wang et al. [65] proposed an adaptive downsampling and upsampling method for detailed point cloud completion.

Compared to other methods, AtlasNet [19] can generate a complete 3D shape of arbitrary resolution using a fixed number of ground-truth point clouds. It also allows for mesh reconstruction from point clouds without requiring watertight meshes. Therefore, we selected AtlasNet for instance reconstruction, transforming partial proposal features from a partial point cloud scan into a complete 3D shape at any resolution.

9.2.3 Generative Adversarial Networks for 3D Completion

Yang et al. [76] and Wang et al. [62] integrate 3D-CNNs with generative adversarial networks (GANs) for supervised shape completion. Gurumurthy and Agrawal [22] approach point cloud completion as a denoising Auto-Encoder (AE) problem, using adversarial training to optimize the AE's latent space. Wen et al. [67] propose Cycle4Completion, which employs synchronous cycle transformations between the latent spaces of complete and incomplete 3D shapes. Zhang et al. [83] introduce ShapeInversion, a GAN inversion technique that integrates GANs into shape completion. This method searches for a latent code that reconstructs a partial scan input using a GAN pre-trained on complete shapes. Li et al. [37] present HSGAN, which transforms a random code into a representation graph via Graph Convolution Networks (GCN) and self-attention. Li et al. [36] introduce PU-GAN, an up-sampling network based on GANs that learns point distributions in latent space. PC-GAN combines hierarchical Bayesian networks with implicit generative architectures for interpretable sampling. Cheng et al. [9] propose DPCG-Net, an end-to-end GAN-based dense point cloud completion architecture that maps global feature distributions from partial point clouds to ground truth.

In this work, inspired by ShapeInversion [83], we use an auto-encoder pre-trained on synthetically complete shapes combined with a GAN. This approach searches for a latent code that accurately identifies the complete shape for a given real-world 3D partial scan input. Unlike ShapeInversion, our method is tailored for completing real-world point cloud scenes, which present significant challenges, as discussed in Sect. 9.3.3.

9.2.4 *Semantic 3D Scene Completion*

This task aims to reconstruct a complete 3D representation of volumetric occupancy or point clouds with semantic labels for the objects in the scene. SSCNet [57] is the first to integrate these tasks in an end-to-end framework. ESSCNet [84] introduce Spatial Group Convolution (SGC), which partitions the input volume into groups before applying 3D sparse convolution. VVNet [21], combining 2D and 3D CNNs with a differentiable projection layer, provides an efficient solution for reducing computational costs and extracting features from multi-channel input. ForkNet [64] uses a multi-branch generative architecture to create new training data pairs, addressing the challenge of limited real-world scene samples. Zhang et al. [85] propose CCPNet, a self-cascaded context aggregation network that bridges semantic gaps in multi-scale 3D contexts while maintaining local geometric details. Chen et al. [7] introduce a depth-based geometric embedding mechanism in their SketchSSC framework to predict 3D sketches and efficiently estimate invariant feature resolutions. Hou et al. [26] develop RevealNet, a 3D network that combines joint color and geometry feature learning to detect object instances and infer full geometries from incomplete RGB-D scans. Moving away from volumetric approaches, RfD-Net [46] integrates VoteNet [50] for 3D object detection and employs implicit functions for per-instance reconstruction from incomplete scene point clouds.

Our work shares the goal of achieving semantic instance completion from raw point cloud scenes. However, unlike RfD-Net [46], our proposed method is **weakly-supervised**, requiring only bounding boxes to complete point cloud scenes.

9.3 Label Efficient Instance Completion: WSSIC-Net

9.3.1 *Overview*

We propose a weakly-supervised instance completion framework for raw point clouds (see Fig. 9.2). This framework reduces the dependence on ground truth for partial scans. Given a partial point cloud scan $\mathbf{P}_{in} \in \mathbb{R}^{N\times 3}$ as input, a 3D detector backbone encodes each scene into proposal features. These features are processed by two modules: a fully supervised 3D detection module (Detector) and a weakly-supervised instance completion module (Completor). **(1) For 3D detection**, we use multi-layer perceptrons (MLPs) to regress bounding box parameters in a fully supervised manner. Further details are provided in Sect. 9.3.2. **(2) The point cloud completion**

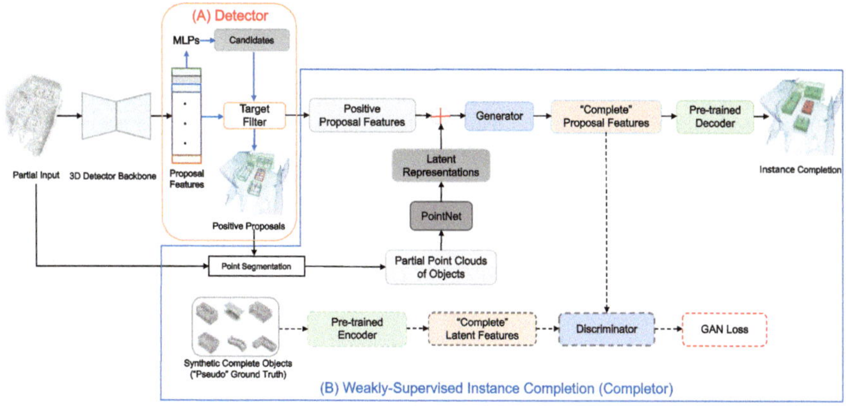

Fig. 9.2 The framework for weakly-supervised point cloud instance completion (This figure is reproduced from [18])

of objects is performed using our proposed weakly-supervised method. An auto-encoder is pre-trained on synthetically complete point clouds of objects. We utilize predicted objectness scores for target filtering. This helps mitigate the impact of negative proposal features. To reduce the influence of background points, we concatenate positive features with latent representations of segmented points from positive proposals. These concatenated features are transformed into "complete" proposal features via a Generative Adversarial Network (GAN). This transformation is supervised by GAN loss and the unidirectional Hausdorff distance loss (HL) [31]. The complete proposal features are then passed through a pre-trained decoder to generate complete point clouds of objects. **(3) For joint training of 3D detection and instance completion**, we propose an Objectness-aware Chamfer Distance (OCD) loss. This loss jointly optimizes both the 3D detection and instance completion modules. The pre-trained encoder and discriminator modules are only used during the training phase.

9.3.2 Fully Supervised Object Detection in 3D Point Clouds

We start by training a 3D detector to identify objects from partial 3D point clouds, denoted as $\mathbf{P} \in \mathbb{R}^{N\times 3}$. Our framework uses raw point cloud scans to generate N proposal features, represented as $\mathbf{F} \in \mathbb{R}^{N\times D}$. Next, we estimate the parameters of bounding box candidates. These parameters include the center $\mathbf{c} \in \mathbb{R}^3$, scale $\mathbf{s} \in \mathbb{R}^3$, orientation angle $\theta \in \mathbb{R}$, class label l, and objectness score O_s. All these parameters are derived from the proposal features $\mathbf{F}$. A target filter is then applied to remove redundant candidates. This filter selects positive proposals during both training and inference. The features $\mathbf{F}$ are learned by aggregating local geometry around partial objects. This aggregation captures both semantic and geometric information from the local region. The detector head, composed of multi-layer perceptrons (MLPs), regresses these parameters. The objectness score helps determine if an object is present in the predicted box. This determination is based on the $\mathcal{L}_1$ distance between the predicted box and any ground truth center. Importantly, we use the ground-truth bounding boxes as supervision signals for this module.

9.3.3 Proposed Weakly-Supervised Instance Completion

The proposal features, which are partial representations of incomplete objects, are denoted as $\mathbf{F} \in \mathbb{R}^{N \times D}$. These features are input into our weakly-supervised coarse-to-fine instance completion module. This module transforms them into "complete" proposal features, as illustrated in Fig. 9.2. To achieve this, we first pre-train an auto-encoder in a self-supervised manner using a complete synthetic dataset. We utilize AtlasNet [19] as the auto-encoder framework. AtlasNet can reconstruct full 3D mesh models without requiring watertight 3D inputs. The pre-training occurs on the ShapeNetCore dataset [13]. The encoder outputs "complete" latent features $\mathbf{C}_f \in \mathbb{R}^{M \times 1024}$, while the decoder generates full-shape point clouds $\mathbf{P}_c \in \mathbb{R}^{2500 \times 3}$. The encoder and decoder are then utilized at different stages throughout the pipeline.

(1) General Shape Generation: To enhance geometric information in the proposal features, we segment point clouds of partial objects $\mathbf{P}_p \in \mathbb{R}^{2048 \times 3}$ from the predicted positive proposals. We encode these point clouds into latent features $\mathbf{Obj}_f \in \mathbb{R}^{M \times 1024}$ using PointNet [51]. Next, we concatenate the latent features $\mathbf{Obj}_f$ with the positive proposal features. This forms the refined proposal features. These refined features are passed to a generator, which produces the "complete" proposal features. This process is supervised by the "pseudo" ground truth and the GAN loss. Finally, the generated "complete" proposal features $\mathbf{C}_g \in \mathbb{R}^{M \times 1024}$ are fed into a pre-trained decoder. This decoder generates the complete point clouds of objects $\mathbf{P}_{re} \in \mathbb{R}^{M \times 2500 \times 3}$ for the corresponding categories.

(2) Synthetic-to-Real-World Point Cloud Completion: The GAN loss ensures that the generated complete point clouds correspond to the general 3D structures of each category (see Fig. 9.3 in Sect. 9.4.5). These general structures are then adapted to the unique shapes of the corresponding objects in the partial scene. This adaptation is achieved by applying the unidirectional Hausdorff distance loss (HL) [31] between the partial input and its completion. The GAN loss and the unidirectional Hausdorff distance loss are used to generate general and specific latent representations, respectively.

Although this framework significantly reduces reliance on the ground truth of complete 3D objects, several challenges still remain.

- **Geometrical Alignment.** Synthetic objects typically have fixed orientations and sizes, while real-world objects exhibit significant variability in orientation and scale, as illustrated in Fig. 9.2.

- **Negative Proposals.** Instance completion relies on object detection outputs. When training a 3D object detector end-to-end, it is often beneficial to estimate a fixed, larger number of objects from a partial point cloud scene. However, this leads to negative proposals, which can adversely affect instance completion.
- **Synthetic-to-Real Domain Alignment.** The synthetic point clouds of objects may have significant differences from real-world point clouds in terms of data distribution, posing challenges for direct application.
- **Semantic Alignment.** In the absence of ground truth for complete point cloud scenes, establishing correspondences between the partial objects in input scenes and synthetic objects is both a crucial and challenging task.

In the subsequent part of this section, we outline the detailed strategies implemented to address the aforementioned challenges. The effectiveness of these strategies will be demonstrated in the experimental section (see Sect. 9.4).

- **Geometrical Alignment.** To address misalignment between partial point clouds and complete synthetic point clouds, we propose two data augmentation strategies for training the auto-encoder.
  (1) The first strategy is tailored for each category. It considers the orientation and size of objects in partial scenes, using ground-truth bounding boxes.
  (2) The second strategy randomly selects synthetically complete point clouds. These point clouds match the number of points and categories of the input to the 3D detector. When partial point cloud scenes and their corresponding "pseudo" ground truth are fed into the network, the pre-trained encoder can better capture the orientation and size information of objects. Consequently, the pre-trained decoder reconstructs complete objects that align with the orientations and sizes of the partial objects. To further achieve geometric alignment, we apply the unidirectional Hausdorff distance loss (HL) [31]. This loss measures the distance from the partial input to its completion. It helps transform general 3D structures within the bounding boxes into the unique shapes of the corresponding objects in the partial scene.
- **Negative Proposals.** To mitigate the impact of negative proposals, we leverage both the training and inference phases. During training, we filter negative proposal features $\mathbf{F} \in \mathbb{R}^{N \times D}$ based on predicted objectness scores. We introduce the Objectness-aware Chamfer Distance (OCD) loss function. This function incorporates the predicted objectness scores of each box proposal into the Chamfer Distance (CD) [15]. It globally regularizes the distance between the predicted complete scene and the partial input (see Sect. 9.3.5). During inference, we apply 3D Non-Maximum Suppression (NMS) [50] to eliminate redundant box proposals and the points within these boxes.
- **Synthetic-to-Real Domain Alignment.** To tackle the synthetic-to-real domain alignment challenge, we propose a GAN-based approach. First, we learn latent representations $\mathbf{Obj}_f \in \mathbb{R}^{M \times 1024}$ of point clouds from objects segmented from positive proposals. We use PointNet [51], which shares the same structure as the pre-trained encoder. Next, we combine these latent representations $\mathbf{Obj}_f$ with

the positive proposal features $\mathbf{F}_p \in \mathbb{R}^{M \times D}$. This forms refined proposal features $\mathbf{R}_p \in \mathbb{R}^{M \times (D+1024)}$. This integration incorporates object-level geometric information into the positive proposal features. We then pass the refined proposal features to the generator. It produces the "complete" proposal features $\mathbf{C}_g \in \mathbb{R}^{M \times 1024}$. Both $\mathbf{C}_g$ and the "complete" latent features $\mathbf{C}_f \in \mathbb{R}^{M \times 1024}$ are fed into the discriminator. The discriminator predicts "false" and "true" for the "complete" features, respectively. This process narrows the domain gap between the positive proposal features of partial point clouds and the "complete" latent features of the "pseudo" ground truth.

- **Semantic Alignment.** We establish semantic alignment between the partial point clouds of objects and their ground truth of complete 3D objects. However, aligning partial point clouds with synthetic complete objects requires careful design. To address this, we construct "pseudo" ground truth from the synthetic dataset for each partial point cloud scan. We randomly select complete point clouds that match the number and category of the detection ground truth for each partial scan. This approach enables the pre-trained decoder to decode complete objects that maintain semantic correspondence with the partial objects.

9.3.4 *Joint Task Learning*

The dedicated 3D detector identifies the positions of partial objects. Meanwhile, the instance completer reconstructs the full shapes of these objects. A more complete partial object can enhance the performance of 3D object detection. Additionally, the estimated orientations and sizes of the bounding boxes from the 3D detection algorithm significantly impact the point cloud completion branch's performance. In this chapter, we introduce an Objectness-aware Chamfer Distance (OCD) loss. This loss jointly optimizes both 3D detection and point cloud completion. Details of the proposed OCD loss are provided in Sect. 9.3.5.

9.3.5 *Loss Functions*

In this section, we summarize the learning objectives and their corresponding loss functions.

Detection Loss. The 3D detector predicts several parameters: the center $\mathbf{c} \in \mathbb{R}^3$, scale $\mathbf{s} \in \mathbb{R}^3$, orientation angle $\theta \in \mathbb{R}^1$, class label l, and objectness score O_s. Following RfD-Net [46], the objectness scores O_s are supervised based on their proximity to ground truth object centers. Votes located within 0.3 m of a center are considered positive. Votes more than 0.6 m away are treated as negative. Objectness predictions for other proposals are not penalized.

We supervise objectness using a cross-entropy loss, normalized by the number of non-ignored proposals in the batch. For positive proposals, we also supervise bounding box estimation and class prediction based on the nearest ground truth bounding box. The box center loss $\mathcal{L}_c$ is calculated using Smooth-L1 loss. The scale loss $\mathcal{L}_s$ and heading angle loss $\mathcal{L}_\theta$ combine classification (cross-entropy) and regression (Smooth-L1) losses, as described in [50, 53]. We use standard cross-entropy loss for semantic classification. Additionally, we include an extra vote loss for using VoteNet as the backbone [50]. For the weights of the 3D detection loss function, we set $\lambda_{\text{cls}} = 0.1$. This represents the hybrid ratio of classification and regression losses, i.e., $\lambda_{\text{cls}}\mathcal{L}_{\text{cls}} + \mathcal{L}_{\text{reg}}$. The overall box loss $\mathcal{L}_{\text{det}}$ is defined as

$$\mathcal{L}_{\text{det}} = \mathcal{L}_v + \mathcal{L}_c + \mathcal{L}_s + \mathcal{L}_\theta + \lambda_l \mathcal{L}_l + \lambda_{\text{obj}} \mathcal{L}_{\text{obj}}. \tag{9.1}$$

Here, $\lambda_{\text{obj}} = 0.5$ and $\lambda_l = 0.1$. The terms $\mathcal{L}_v$, $\mathcal{L}_c$, $\mathcal{L}_l$, and $\mathcal{L}_{\text{obj}}$ represent the vote loss, box center loss, classification loss, and objectness loss, respectively.

Completion Loss. We employ a GAN to train our weakly-supervised instance completion model. The input to the GAN includes the "complete" latent features $\mathbf{C}_f \in \mathbb{R}^{M\times 1024}$ and the generated "complete" proposal features $\mathbf{C}_g \in \mathbb{R}^{M\times 1024}$. Our goal is to optimize the following completion loss $\mathcal{L}_{\text{com}}$ with respect to the generator G_θ and the discriminator D_χ.

$$\mathcal{L}_{\text{com}} = \min_{\theta} \max_{\chi} \mathbb{E}[log(D_\chi(\mathbf{C}_f))] + \mathbb{E}[log(1 - D_\chi(G_\theta(\mathbf{C}_g)))]. \tag{9.2}$$

In our experiments, we design a GAN based on the least square GAN [43]. This design is more stable and easier to train. We minimize both the discriminator and generator losses, defined as follows:

$$\mathcal{L}_{D_\chi} = \mathbb{E}[D_\chi(\mathbf{C}_f) - 1]^2 + \mathbb{E}[D_\chi(G_\theta(\mathbf{C}_g))]^2. \tag{9.3}$$

$$\mathcal{L}_{G_\theta} = \mathbb{E}[D_\chi(G_\theta(\mathbf{C}_g)) - 1]^2. \tag{9.4}$$

The loss $\mathcal{L}_{G_\theta}$ ensures that the point cloud predicted by the pre-trained decoder corresponds to a complete object of a specific category. However, it does not guarantee that the complete prediction aligns with the shape of the partial input. To address this, we introduce the unidirectional Hausdorff distance loss (HL) $\mathcal{L}_{\text{rec}}^{HL}$, which measures the distance from the partial input to its corresponding complete object. This loss adjusts the complete prediction to closely match the input shape. Consequently, the generator loss can be rewritten as

$$\mathcal{L}_{G_\theta} = \alpha\mathbb{E}[D_\chi(G_\theta(\mathbf{C}_g)) - 1]^2 + \beta\mathcal{L}_{\text{rec}}^{HL}(S_{p_i}, D_{ec}(\mathbf{C}_{g_i})). \tag{9.5}$$

Here, S_{p_i} denotes the i-th partial point cloud of an object, $\mathbf{C}_{g_i}$ represents the i-th refined latent feature, and D_{ec} is the pre-trained decoder. We set the parameters α and β to 0.25 and 0.75, respectively, following [6].

Objectness-aware Chamfer Distance Loss. The bidirectional distance treats all points equally, assigning the same weight to each point [15]. In contrast, we assign different weights based on the predicted objectness scores. This approach allows for simultaneous optimization of both object detection and instance completion, as described in Eq. 9.6.

$$\mathcal{L}_{\text{OCD}} = \mathbf{S}_{\text{obj}}\mathbf{CD}(\mathbf{P}_{re}, \mathbf{P}_{in_{\text{obj}}}). \tag{9.6}$$

In this equation, $\mathbf{S}_{\text{obj}}$ represents the objectness score of points, $\mathbf{P}_{re}$ denotes the predicted point clouds of objects, and $\mathbf{P}_{in_{\text{obj}}}$ refers to the input partial point clouds of objects. The term $\mathbf{CD}(\mathbf{P}_{re}, \mathbf{P}_{in_{\text{obj}}})$ represents the bidirectional Chamfer Distance (CD) loss. This loss enables joint optimization of the network.
Total Loss. Finally, the total loss $\mathcal{L}_{\text{total}}$ combines the detection loss $\mathcal{L}_{\text{det}}$, the completion loss $\mathcal{L}_{\text{com}}$, and the OCD loss $\mathcal{L}_{\text{OCD}}$:

$$\mathcal{L}_{\text{total}} = \mathcal{L}_{\text{det}} + \mathcal{L}_{\text{com}} + \mathcal{L}_{\text{OCD}}. \tag{9.7}$$

9.4 Experiments

9.4.1 Datasets

The ScanNet v2 Dataset [11]. ScanNet v2 includes 1,513 real-world scans. The point clouds are labeled at the instance level. Similar to RevealNet [26] and RfD-Net [46], we perform scene completion on this dataset. In our experiments, we only use the ground-truth bounding boxes during training.
The ShapeNetCore Dataset [13]. The ShapeNetCore dataset serves as the synthetic dataset in our experiments. It is a subset of the full ShapeNet dataset. This subset consists of single, clean 3D models with verified category and alignment annotations. It includes 55 common object categories and approximately 51,300 unique 3D models. For pre-training the auto-encoder, we selected 8 categories: display, bathtub, trash bin, sofa, chair, table, cabinet, and bookshelf. These categories match those in the ScanNet v2 dataset [11].
The Scan2CAD Dataset [1]. Scan2CAD aligns ShapeNet [5] models with object instances in ScanNet. In our experiments, we use the Scan2CAD dataset exclusively during the testing phase. This helps assess the performance of the proposed method.

9.4.2 Evaluation Metrics

We evaluate our method, which includes both 3D object detection and instance completion, using several standard metrics. Similar to RfDNet [46] and RevealNet

[26], we use the mean average precision at a 3D IoU threshold of 0.5 (mAP@0.5) to evaluate both tasks.

9.4.3 Implementation Details

We implement our approaches using PyTorch and train them on NVIDIA GeForce GTX 1080 Ti GPUs. In this chapter, we utilize AtlasNet [19] as the auto-encoder framework. AtlasNet can reconstruct complete 3D meshes without requiring watertight data. Initially, we pre-train AtlasNet on the ShapeNetCore dataset [13] for 200 epochs. We optimize the model using the Adam optimizer with a learning rate of 0.001. The input to AtlasNet consists of 2500 points. During pre-training, we apply two types of data augmentation. The first type varied the orientations and sizes of objects. The second type randomly selected synthetically complete point clouds that matched the number and category of ground-truth bounding boxes in each batch. For instance, if a batch contains two partial chairs and three tables, we randomly select two complete chairs and three complete tables from the synthetic dataset to create a "pseudo" ground truth. After pre-training the auto-encoder, we use the encoder and decoder components of AtlasNet in the weakly-supervised instance completion process. To segment the point clouds from the positive proposals, we group points within a radius r of the box centers using a group layer, as described in [52].

For training the 3D detection and instance completion, we randomly sample 80K points from a partial scene in the ScanNet v2 dataset. We follow four steps to train the proposed WSSIC-Net. **First**, we ensure a fair comparison with RfD-Net [46] by adopting the same 3D object detection architecture and training strategy. The pre-trained 3D detection model provides object positions for our weakly-supervised instance completion model. **Second**, we froze the weights of the detection module. We then use the pre-trained encoder and decoder of AtlasNet to train both the generator and the discriminator, which are 3-layer perceptrons. **Third**, we jointly train the entire network without the proposed OCD loss. **Fourth**, we improve performance by jointly training the entire network with the proposed OCD loss.

9.4.4 Comparison to the State-of-the-Art

Quantitative Evaluation of 3D Detection. In this section, we compare our 3D object detection results with those from 3D-SIS [25], MLCVNet [72], RevealNet [26], and RfD-Net [46] (see Table 9.1). 3D-SIS [25] integrates multi-view RGB images into TSDF grids. MLCVNet [72] extends VoteNet [50] by incorporating contextual information between objects. RevealNet [26] converts input scans into a volumetric grid, preprocessing them as a TSDF. In contrast, we leverage the sparsity of point clouds, similar to RfD-Net [46]. This approach allows us to ignore empty regions, reducing computational load and improving reconstruction efficiency. Our

Table 9.1 3D detection comparisons

Models	Input	mAP
3D-SIS [25]	Geo+Image	25.70
MLCVNet [72]	Geo Only	33.40
RevealNet [26]	Geo Only	29.29
RfD-Net [46]	Geo Only	38.71
Ours (w/o joint)	Geo Only	34.78
Ours (w/ joint)	Geo Only	**39.44**

method surpasses RfD-Net [46] because the Objectness-aware Chamfer Distance loss integrates additional geometric constraints from the completion module into the detection module. Note that the 3D detection performance for RfD-Net [46] was obtained by directly testing the pre-trained module available at https://github.com/yinyunie/RfDNet.

Quantitative Evaluation of Semantic Instance Completion. We evaluated our semantic instance completion by measuring how well the predicted object meshes align with the ground truth from the Scan2CAD dataset [1]. We compared our results to RevealNet [26] and RfD-Net [46]. For the instance-level scene completion task, we followed the experimental protocols of RevealNet [26]. This involved combining prior work on instance segmentation [25] with shape completion [13], or combining scan completion [12] with instance segmentation [25]. Our results show that our joint approach significantly outperforms the decoupled method. It is comparable to, or even better than, RfD-Net [46] and RevealNet [26]. While our method achieves slightly lower performance than RfD-Net [46], it is important to note that RfD-Net benefits from fully supervised learning. This enables it to capture more specific latent representations (Table 9.2).

Qualitative Comparisons. We compare our semantic instance completion method with the fully supervised RfD-Net [46]. As shown in Fig. 9.4, our method achieves superior detection accuracy compared to RfD-Net. This is evident in both the number and scale of the bounding boxes. Additionally, our method demonstrates comparable or even better instance completion performance than RfD-Net, as illustrated in Fig. 9.4. This improvement is due to the effective constraints used in training our weakly supervised model. Our approach also leverages a larger amount of synthetic

Table 9.2 Semantic instance completion comparison

Models	Display	Bathtub	Trashbin	Sofa	Chair	Table	Cabinet	Bookshelf	mAP
Inst Seg [25]+Shape Comp [13]	2.27	1.14	1.68	14.86	9.93	3.90	7.11	3.03	5.49
Scan Comp [12]+Inst Seg [25]	1.65	4.55	11.25	9.09	9.09	0.64	0.18	5.45	5.24
RevealNet [26]	13.16	13.64	18.19	24.79	15.87	11.28	8.60	10.60	14.52
RfD-Net [46]	26.67	27.57	23.34	15.17	12.23	1.92	14.48	13.39	16.90
Our WSSIC-Net	22.33	26.54	22.48	16.27	12.44	1.98	13.52	12.75	16.56

training data generated by the GAN. As seen in the first, third, and fifth rows of Fig. 9.4, our method reconstructs more detailed tables and chairs than RfD-Net [46]. This is because we generate complete meshes from full point clouds, unlike RfD-Net, which relies on incomplete point sampling.

9.4.5 Ablation Studies

We perform our ablation study using the ScanNet v2 dataset [11]. We evaluate the impact of various components on semantic instance completion performance. Specifically, we test different data augmentations. This includes varying orientation and size (w/o Aug1) and mimicking the distribution of real-world 3D scans (w/o Aug2). We also examine the PointNet module (w/o $\mathbf{Obj}_f$), the Hausdorff Loss (w/o HL), and the Objectness-aware Chamfer Distance (w/o OCD) in the unpaired structure. These experiments aim to assess the effects of geometrical alignment, domain alignment, semantic alignment, and negative proposals on semantic instance completion. Additionally, we explore the relationship between 3D detection and instance completion. This study involves three models: the detection-only (det-only) model, the detection with completion model (det-com-joint), and the detection with completion model including OCD loss (det-com-OCD).
Semantic Instance Completion Ablation. Table 9.3 shows the performance drop when specific parts of the pipeline are omitted. **(1)** The Hausdorff Loss (HL) has the greatest impact, causing a performance drop of approximately 26%. Without the HL term in the generator loss, our method produces only general 3D structures. This leads to misalignment with the Scan2CAD dataset (see Fig. 9.3). The GAN loss alone generates a general "complete" proposal feature. However, the HL loss adjusts the generated feature to better match the partial object. **(2)** The data augmentation with varying orientations and sizes (w/o Aug1) also results in a performance drop of about 20%. This occurs because HL loss requires accurate orientation and size predictions for the objects. **(3)** Comparing the *com-only* and *w/o OCD* modules highlights the benefits of joint training for detection and completion tasks. **(4)** A

Fig. 9.3 Illustration of the Impact of the HL Loss (This figure is reproduced from [18])

Fig. 9.4 Qualitative comparison to RfD-Net in 3D detection and instance completion (This figure is reproduced from [18])

comparison between the *w/o OCD* module and our full WSSIC-Net demonstrates the effectiveness of the proposed OCD loss. This loss adds geometric constraints to 3D detection. It improves the accuracy of object orientations and scales, leading to fewer negative proposals. More accurate box proposals enhance point cloud matching and, consequently, the performance of semantic instance completion. **(5)** Data augmentation that mimics the distribution of real-world 3D scans for auto-encoder pretraining (w/o Aug2) is beneficial. This strategy helps bridge the domain gap between synthetic and real-world datasets. **(6)** The latent representations $\mathbf{Obj}_f \in \mathbb{R}^{M\times 1024}$ of

Table 9.3 Ablation study on semantic instance completion

Models	Display	Bathtub	Trashbin	Sofa	Chair	Table	Cabinet	Bookshelf	mAP
w/o HL	21.03	21.70	17.66	13.18	9.16	1.82	11.33	10.08	12.25
w/o Aug1	21.66	22.68	18.18	13.98	9.82	1.86	11.86	10.88	13.18
com-only	21.78	22.86	18.35	14.26	10.14	2.48	11.78	11.75	13.66
w/o Aug2	22.08	25.87	21.96	15.58	11.28	1.86	12.02	11.48	14.81
w/o OCD	22.12	26.16	22.10	15.72	11.36	1.94	12.25	12.24	15.68
w/o Obj	22.68	26.34	22.17	15.88	11.48	1.93	12.68	12.56	16.06
Our WSSIC-Net	**23.33**	**26.54**	**22.48**	**16.27**	**12.44**	**1.98**	**13.52**	**12.75**	**16.56**

Table 9.4 Ablation study on 3D detection

Models	Display	Bathtub	Trashbin	Sofa	Chair	Table	Cabinet	Bookshelf	mAP
det-only	10.83	27.87	16.48	49.72	75.99	48.51	32.95	15.86	34.78
det-com-joint	18.04	26.98	22.51	54.49	76.28	50.89	33.29	26.37	38.58
det-com-OCD	18.46	28.28	32.93	56.22	74.78	42.24	33.66	27.43	**39.32**

point clouds, combined with filtered proposal features, have the least impact on performance. However, they still provide more geometric information, resulting in better performance.

Detection Ablation. We also investigate the effect of combining 3D detection and scene completion, as shown in Table 9.4. The *det-only* model represents a 3D detection model trained on the ScanNet v2 dataset [11]. The *det-com-joint* and *det-com-OCD* models represent the complete pipeline of 3D detection and instance completion. These models are jointly trained on the ScanNet v2 dataset, with and without the proposed OCD loss. The *det-only* model is supervised by ground-truth 3D bounding boxes from the ScanNet v2 dataset. In contrast, both *det-com-joint* and *det-com-OCD* are supervised by ground-truth 3D bounding boxes and unpaired complete objects from the ShapeNetCore dataset. Compared to the *det-only* model, the results indicate that high-performance scene completion improves 3D detection performance. Moreover, the proposed OCD loss further enhances the performance of both 3D detection and instance completion. This ablation study demonstrates that 3D detection and instance completion tasks benefit from each other, even when using unpaired complete objects. A comparison between the performance of RfD-Net [46] in Table 9.1 and the *det-com-joint* module in Table 9.4 shows that ground-truth complete objects yield better 3D detection performance than synthetic complete point clouds. This is because the ground-truth objects provide more accurate 3D geometric information than their synthetic counterparts.

9.5 Conclusion and Future Work

In this chapter, we introduce a Weakly-Supervised Semantic Instance Completion Network (WSSIC-Net) for point clouds. The WSSIC-Net transforms each partial point cloud object into a proposal feature using a specialized 3D detection model. Next, we filter positive proposal features from the set of all proposals. These features are then concatenated with the latent features of partial objects, which are segmented from the positive proposals. The concatenated features are fed into a GAN that learns from "complete" latent features. These features are represented by a pre-trained encoder using "pseudo" ground truth. A pre-trained decoder generates complete point clouds for the objects from the "complete" proposal features. We also introduce two data augmentations, along with the use of "pseudo" ground truth, HL loss, and OCD loss. These elements address challenges related to geometrical alignment, semantic alignment, domain alignment, and negative proposals. Experiments on the ScanNet v2 dataset show that our weakly-supervised approach achieves performance comparable to or better than state-of-the-art supervised methods. The results indicate that the 3D detection task benefits from the instance completion task, even when supervised by unpaired synthetic complete point clouds. One limitation of our approach is the requirement for the "pseudo" ground truth dataset to include all object categories found in real-world scenes. In future work, we aim to explore the benefits of incorporating additional modalities, such as normals and colors. We will also leverage large-scale generative models for zero-shot large-scale scene completion.

References

1. Avetisyan A, Dahnert M, Dai A, Savva M, Chang AX, Nießner M (2019) Scan2CAD: learning cad model alignment in rgb-d scans. In: IEEE conference on computer vision and pattern recognition (CVPR), pp 2614–2623
2. Avetisyan A, Dai A, Nießner M (2019) End-to-end CAD model retrieval and 9dof alignment in 3D scans. In: ICCV, pp 2551–2560
3. Avetisyan A, Khanova T, Choy C, Dash D, Dai A, Nießner M (2020) SceneCAD: predicting object alignments and layouts in rgb-d scans. In: ECCV, pp 596–612. Springer
4. Cai Q, Pan Y, Yao T, Mei T (2022) 3D cascade rcnn: high quality object detection in point clouds. arXiv preprint arXiv:2211.08248
5. Chang AX, Funkhouser T, Guibas L, Hanrahan P, Huang Q, Li Z, Savarese S, Savva M, Song S, Su H, et al (2015) Shapenet: an information-rich 3D model repository. arXiv preprint arXiv:1512.03012
6. Chen X, Chen B, Mitra NJ (2019) Unpaired point cloud completion on real scans using adversarial training. arXiv preprint arXiv:1904.00069
7. Chen X, Lin KY, Qian C, Zeng G, Li H (2020) 3D sketch-aware semantic scene completion via semi-supervised structure prior. In: CVPR, pp 4193–4202
8. Chen X, Ma H, Wan J, Li B, Xia T (2017) Multi-view 3D object detection network for autonomous driving. In: CVPR, pp 1907–1915
9. Cheng M, Li G, Chen Y, Chen J, Wang C, Li J (2021) Dense point cloud completion based on generative adversarial network. IEEE Trans Geosci Remote Sens 60:1–10

10. Cheng S, Chen X, He X, Liu Z, Bai X (2021) Pra-net: point relation-aware network for 3D point cloud analysis. IEEE Trans Image Process 30:4436–4448
11. Dai A, Chang AX, Savva M, Halber M, Funkhouser T, Nießner M (2017) Scannet: Richly-annotated 3D reconstructions of indoor scenes. In: CVPR, pp 5828–5839
12. Dai A, Ritchie D, Bokeloh M, Reed S, Sturm J, Nießner M (2018) Scancomplete: large-scale scene completion and semantic segmentation for 3D scans. In: CVPR, pp 4578–4587
13. Dai A, Ruizhongtai Qi C, Nießner M (2017) Shape completion using 3D-encoder-predictor cnns and shape synthesis. In: IEEE conference on computer vision and pattern recognition (CVPR), pp 5868–5877
14. Ding X, Lin W, Chen Z, Zhang X (2019) Point cloud saliency detection by local and global feature fusion. IEEE Trans Image Process 28(11):5379–5393
15. Fan H, Su H, Guibas LJ (2017) A point set generation network for 3D object reconstruction from a single image. In: Proceedings of the IEEE conference on computer vision and pattern recognition, pp 605–613
16. Feng M, Gilani SZ, Wang Y, Zhang L, Mian A (2020) Relation graph network for 3D object detection in point clouds. IEEE Trans Image Process 30:92–107
17. Feng T, Wang W, Wang X, Yang Y, Zheng Q (2023) Clustering based point cloud representation learning for 3D analysis. In: Proceedings of the IEEE/CVF international conference on computer vision, pp 8283–8294
18. Fu Z, Guo Y, Chen M, Hu Q, Laga H, Boussaid F, Bennamoun M (2025) Wssic-net: weakly-supervised semantic instance completion of 3D point cloud scenes. IEEE Trans Image Process
19. Groueix T, Fisher M, Kim VG, Russell BC, Aubry M (2018) A papier-mâché approach to learning 3D surface generation. In: Proceedings of the IEEE conference on computer vision and pattern recognition, pp 216–224
20. Guo Y, Wang H, Hu Q, Liu H, Liu L, Bennamoun M (2020) Deep learning for 3D point clouds: a survey. IEEE Trans Pattern Anal Mach Intell (TPAMI) 43(12):4338–4364
21. Guo YX, Tong X (2018) View-volume network for semantic scene completion from a single depth image. arXiv preprint arXiv:1806.05361
22. Gurumurthy S, Agrawal S (2019) High fidelity semantic shape completion for point clouds using latent optimization. In: WACV, pp 1099–1108. IEEE
23. Han X, Zhang Z, Du D, Yang M, Yu J, Pan P, Yang X, Liu L, Xiong Z, Cui S (2019) Deep reinforcement learning of volume-guided progressive view inpainting for 3D point scene completion from a single depth image. In: IEEE conference on computer vision and pattern recognition (CVPR), pp 234–243
24. Han XF, Laga H, Bennamoun M (2019) Image-based 3D object reconstruction: state-of-the-art and trends in the deep learning era. IEEE Trans Pattern Anal Mach Intell 43(5):1578–1604
25. Hou J, Dai A, Nießner M (2019) 3D-sis: 3D semantic instance segmentation of rgb-d scans. In: CVPR, pp 4421–4430
26. Hou J, Dai A, Nießner M (2020) Revealnet: seeing behind objects in rgb-d scans. In: CVPR, pp 2098–2107
27. Hu Q, Yang B, Khalid S, Xiao W, Trigoni N, Markham A (2022) Sensaturban: learning semantics from urban-scale photogrammetric point clouds. Int J Comput Vision 130(2):316–343
28. Hu Q, Yang B, Xie L, Rosa S, Guo Y, Wang Z, Trigoni N, Markham A (2021) Learning semantic segmentation of large-scale point clouds with random sampling. IEEE Trans Pattern Anal Mach Intell 44(11):8338–8354
29. Hu W, Fu Z, Guo Z (2019) Local frequency interpretation and non-local self-similarity on graph for point cloud inpainting. IEEE Trans Image Process 28(8):4087–4100
30. Huang Z, Yu Y, Xu J, Ni F, Le X (2020) Pf-net: point fractal network for 3D point cloud completion. In: IEEE conference on computer vision and pattern recognition (CVPR), pp 7662–7670
31. Huttenlocher DP, Klanderman GA, Rucklidge WJ (1993) Comparing images using the hausdorff distance. IEEE Trans Pattern Anal Mach Intell 15(9):850–863
32. Ishimtsev V, Bokhovkin A, Artemov A, Ignatyev S, Niessner M, Zorin D, Burnaev E (2020) Cad-deform: deformable fitting of CAD models to 3D scans. In: ECCV, pp 599–628. Springer

33. Laga H, Jospin LV, Boussaid F, Bennamoun M (2020) A survey on deep learning techniques for stereo-based depth estimation. IEEE Trans Pattern Anal Mach Intell 44(4):1738–1764
34. Li J, Chen BM, Lee GH (2018) So-net: self-organizing network for point cloud analysis. In: CVPR, pp 9397–9406
35. Li J, Han K, Wang P, Liu Y, Yuan X (2020) Anisotropic convolutional networks for 3D semantic scene completion. In: CVPR, pp 3351–3359
36. Li R, Li X, Fu CW, Cohen-Or D, Heng PA (2019) Pu-gan: a point cloud upsampling adversarial network. In: ICCV, pp 7203–7212
37. Li Y, Baciu G (2021) Hsgan: hierarchical graph learning for point cloud generation. IEEE Trans Image Process 30:4540–4554
38. Liu M, Sheng L, Yang S, Shao J, Hu SM (2020) Morphing and sampling network for dense point cloud completion. In: AAAI conference on Artificial Intelligence (AAAI), vol 34, pp 11596–11603
39. Liu S, Hu Y, Zeng Y, Tang Q, Jin B, Han Y, Li X (2018) See and think: disentangling semantic scene completion. NeurIPS 31
40. Liu X, Liu X, Liu YS, Han Z (2022) Spu-net: self-supervised point cloud upsampling by coarse-to-fine reconstruction with self-projection optimization. IEEE Trans Image Process 31:4213–4226
41. Liu Z, Zhang Z, Cao Y, Hu H, Tong X (2021) Group-free 3D object detection via transformers. In: ICCV, pp 2949–2958
42. Mao J, Xue Y, Niu M, Bai H, Feng J, Liang X, Xu H, Xu C (2021) Voxel transformer for 3D object detection. In: ICCV, pp 3164–3173
43. Mao X, Li Q, Xie H, Lau RY, Wang Z, Paul Smolley S (2017) Least squares generative adversarial networks. In: ICCV, pp 2794–2802
44. Meng Q, Wang W, Zhou T, Shen J, Jia Y, Van Gool L (2021) Towards a weakly supervised framework for 3D point cloud object detection and annotation. IEEE Trans Pattern Anal Mach Intell 44(8):4454–4468
45. Misra I, Girdhar R, Joulin A (2021) An end-to-end transformer model for 3D object detection. In: ICCV, pp 2906–2917
46. Nie Y, Hou J, Han X, Nießner M (2021) Rfd-net: point scene understanding by semantic instance reconstruction. In: CVPR, pp 4608–4618
47. Nie Y, Lin Y, Han X, Guo S, Chang J, Cui S, Zhang J et al (2020) Skeleton-bridged point completion: from global inference to local adjustment. Adv Neural Inf Process Syst (NeurIPS) 33:16119–16130
48. Pan L, Chen X, Cai Z, Zhang J, Zhao H, Yi S, Liu Z (2021) Variational relational point completion network. In: Proceedings of the IEEE/CVF conference on computer vision and pattern recognition, pp 8524–8533
49. Peng S, Niemeyer M, Mescheder L, Pollefeys M, Geiger A (2020) Convolutional occupancy networks. In: European conference on computer vision (ECCV), pp 523–540. Springer
50. Qi CR, Litany O, He K, Guibas LJ (2019) Deep hough voting for 3D object detection in point clouds. In: ICCV, pp 9277–9286
51. Qi CR, Su H, Mo K, Guibas LJ (2017) PointNet: deep learning on point sets for 3d classification and segmentation. In: IEEE conference on computer vision and pattern recognition, pp 652–660
52. Qi CR, Yi L, Su H, Guibas LJ (2017) PointNet++: deep hierarchical feature learning on point sets in a metric space. Adv Neural Inf Process Syst 30
53. Ren S, He K, Girshick R, Sun J (2015) Faster r-cnn: towards real-time object detection with region proposal networks. NeurIPS 28
54. Rethage D, Wald J, Sturm J, Navab N, Tombari F (2018) Fully-convolutional point networks for large-scale point clouds. In: ECCV, pp 596–611
55. Rouhani M, Sappa AD, Boyer E (2014) Implicit b-spline surface reconstruction. IEEE Trans Image Process 24(1):22–32
56. Shi S, Guo C, Jiang L, Wang Z, Shi J, Wang X, Li H (2020) Pv-rcnn: point-voxel feature set abstraction for 3D object detection. In: CVPR, pp 10529–10538

57. Song S, Yu F, Zeng A, Chang AX, Savva M, Funkhouser T (2017) Semantic scene completion from a single depth image. In: CVPR, pp 1746–1754
58. Su H, Jampani V, Sun D, Maji S, Kalogerakis E, Yang MH, Kautz J (2018) Splatnet: sparse lattice networks for point cloud processing. In: CVPR, pp 2530–2539
59. Tao A, Duan Y, Wei Y, Lu J, Zhou J (2022) Seggroup: seg-level supervision for 3D instance and semantic segmentation. IEEE Trans Image Process 31:4952–4965
60. Tchapmi LP, Kosaraju V, Rezatofighi H, Reid I, Savarese S (2019) Topnet: structural point cloud decoder. In: IEEE conference on computer vision and pattern recognition (CVPR), pp 383–392
61. Wang C, Samari B, Siddiqi K (2018) Local spectral graph convolution for point set feature learning. In: ECCV, pp 52–66
62. Wang W, Huang Q, You S, Yang C, Neumann U (2017) Shape inpainting using 3D generative adversarial network and recurrent convolutional networks. In: ICCV, pp 2298–2306
63. Wang X, Ang Jr, MH, Lee GH (2020) Cascaded refinement network for point cloud completion. In: IEEE conference on computer vision and pattern recognition (CVPR), pp 790–799
64. Wang Y, Tan DJ, Navab N, Tombari F (2019) Forknet: multi-branch volumetric semantic completion from a single depth image. In: ICCV, pp 8608–8617
65. Wang Y, Tan DJ, Navab N, Tombari F (2022) Learning local displacements for point cloud completion. In: IEEE conference on computer vision and pattern recognition (CVPR), pp 1568–1577
66. Wang Y, Ye T, Cao L, Huang W, Sun F, He F, Tao D (2022) Bridged transformer for vision and point cloud 3D object detection. In: CVPR, pp 12114–12123
67. Wen X, Han Z, Cao YP, Wan P, Zheng W, Liu YS (2021) Cycle4completion: Unpaired point cloud completion using cycle transformation with missing region coding. In: IEEE conference on computer vision and pattern recognition (CVPR), pp 13080–13089
68. Wen X, Xiang P, Han Z, Cao YP, Wan P, Zheng W, Liu YS (2021) Pmp-net: point cloud completion by learning multi-step point moving paths. In: CVPR, pp 7443–7452
69. Wu B, Wan A, Yue X, Keutzer K (2018) Squeezeseg: convolutional neural nets with recurrent crf for real-time road-object segmentation from 3D lidar point cloud. In: ICRA, pp 1887–1893. IEEE
70. Xia Y, Xia Y, Li W, Song R, Cao K, Stilla U (2021) Asfm-net: asymmetrical siamese feature matching network for point completion. In: ACM MM, pp 1938–1947
71. Xie H, Yao H, Zhou S, Mao J, Zhang S, Sun W (2020) Grnet: gridding residual network for dense point cloud completion. In: European conference on computer vision (ECCV), pp 365–381. Springer
72. Xie Q, Lai YK, Wu J, Wang Z, Zhang Y, Xu K, Wang J (2020) Mlcvnet: multi-level context votenet for 3D object detection. In: CVPR, pp 10447–10456
73. Xu D, Anguelov D, Jain A (2018) Pointfusion: deep sensor fusion for 3D bounding box estimation. In: CVPR, pp 244–253
74. Xu Y, Fan T, Xu M, Zeng L, Qiao Y (2018) Spidercnn: deep learning on point sets with parameterized convolutional filters. In: ECCV, pp 87–102
75. Yang B, Wang J, Clark R, Hu Q, Wang S, Markham A, Trigoni N (2019) Learning object bounding boxes for 3D instance segmentation on point clouds. NeurIPS 32
76. Yang B, Wen H, Wang S, Clark R, Markham A, Trigoni N (2017) 3D object reconstruction from a single depth view with adversarial learning. In: ICCVW, pp 679–688
77. Yang J, Xu J, Li K, Lai YK, Yue H, Lu J, Wu H, Liu Y (2020) Learning to reconstruct and understand indoor scenes from sparse views. IEEE Trans Image Process 29:5753–5766
78. Ye X, Li J, Huang H, Du L, Zhang X (2018) 3D recurrent neural networks with context fusion for point cloud semantic segmentation. In: ECCV, pp 403–417
79. Yin J, Fang J, Zhou D, Zhang L, Xu CZ, Shen J, Wang W (2022) Semi-supervised 3D object detection with proficient teachers. In: ECCV, pp 727–743. Springer
80. Yin J, Zhou D, Zhang L, Fang J, Xu CZ, Shen J, Wang W (2022) Proposalcontrast: unsupervised pre-training for lidar-based 3D object detection. In: ECCV, pp 17–33. Springer

81. Yu X, Rao Y, Wang Z, Liu Z, Lu J, Zhou J (2021) Pointr: diverse point cloud completion with geometry-aware transformers. In: IEEE international conference on computer vision (ICCV), pp 12498–12507
82. Yuan W, Khot T, Held D, Mertz C, Hebert M (2018) Pcn: point completion network. In: International conference on 3D vision (3DV), pp 728–737. IEEE
83. Zhang J, Chen X, Cai Z, Pan L, Zhao H, Yi S, Yeo CK, Dai B, Loy CC (2021) Unsupervised 3D shape completion through gan inversion. In: CVPR, pp 1768–1777
84. Zhang J, Zhao H, Yao A, Chen Y, Zhang L, Liao H (2018) Efficient semantic scene completion network with spatial group convolution. In: ECCV, pp 733–749
85. Zhang P, Liu W, Lei Y, Lu H, Yang X (2019) Cascaded context pyramid for full-resolution 3D semantic scene completion. In: ICCV, pp 7801–7810
86. Zhang Y, Hu Q, Xu G, Ma Y, Wan J, Guo Y (2022) Not all points are equal: learning highly efficient point-based detectors for 3D lidar point clouds. In: CVPR, pp 18953–18962
87. Zheng Y, Xu X, Zhou J, Lu J (2022) Pointras: uncertainty-aware multi-resolution learning for point cloud segmentation. IEEE Trans Image Process 31:6002–6016
88. Zhou Y, Tuzel O (2018) Voxelnet: end-to-end learning for point cloud based 3D object detection. In: CVPR, pp 4490–4499

Chapter 10
Conclusions and Perspectives

In this book, we have systematically explored a wide array of deep learning techniques for point cloud processing, encompassing fundamental principles, advanced methodologies, and real-world applications. Beginning with the basics of point cloud representation and acquisition, we have progressively introduced sophisticated approaches for local feature learning, registration, object detection, segmentation, and completion. Each chapter has been structured to build upon the previous one, ensuring a coherent and comprehensive understanding of the challenges and complexities involved in 3D point cloud processing.

Looking ahead, several emerging trends and future directions are expected to shape the field of deep learning-based point cloud processing. One notable development is the growing availability of large-scale 3D datasets, facilitating the training of more robust and generalizable models. Additionally, the integration of multimodal data—combining point clouds with RGB images, depth maps, and semantic information—holds great potential for enhancing scene understanding. This fusion of data modalities can lead to significant improvements in tasks such as object detection, segmentation, and tracking, ultimately advancing the capabilities of 3D perception systems.

Y. Guo et al., *Point Cloud Intelligence*, Advances in Computer Vision and Pattern Recognition, https://doi.org/10.1007/978-981-95-0648-4_10

Index

Y. Guo et al., *Point Cloud Intelligence*, Advances in Computer Vision and Pattern Recognition, https://doi.org/10.1007/978-981-95-0648-4

U

V

W

Z

MIX
Papier aus verantwortungsvollen Quellen
Paper from responsible sources
FSC® C105338

If you have any concerns about our products,
you can contact us on
ProductSafety@springernature.com

In case Publisher is established outside the EU,
the EU authorized representative is:
Springer Nature Customer Service Center GmbH
Europaplatz 3, 69115 Heidelberg, Germany

Printed by Libri Plureos GmbH
in Hamburg, Germany